BARRON'S
Legal-Ease

Corporations
STEP·BY·STEP

David Minars, M.B.A., J.D., CPA

BARRON'S

This book is dedicated to my wife, Iris Elaine Minars, for her *joir de vivre*. My thanks to Anna Damaskos for her inspiration, support, and wise counsel.

This publication is designed to provide accurate and authoritative information in regard to the subject matter covered. It is sold with the understanding that the publisher is not engaged in rendering legal, accounting, or other professional services. If legal advice or other expert assistance is required, the services of a competent professional person should be sought.

All inquiries should be addressed to:
Barron's Educational Series, Inc.
250 Wireless Boulevard
Hauppauge, New York 11788

International Standard Book No. 0-8120-9635-5

Library of Congress Catalog Card No. 96-17901

Library of Congress Cataloging-in-Publication Data
Minars, David.
      Corporations step-by-step / by David Minars.
          p.   cm. — (Barron's Legal-ease series)
      Includes index.
      ISBN 0-8120-9635-5
      1. Corporation law—United States—popular works. I. Title.
   II. Series.
   KF1414.6.M56   1996
   346.73'066—dc20
   [347-30666]   96-17901
                                                    CIP

PRINTED IN THE UNITED STATES OF AMERICA

987654321

Contents

9 CORPORATE MANAGEMENT STRUCTURE: THE ROLE OF DIRECTORS

10 CORPORATE MANAGEMENT STRUCTURE: THE ROLE OF THE OFFICERS

11 THE CORPORATE OWNERSHIP: THE ROLE OF THE SHAREHOLDERS

12 DIVIDENDS, DISTRIBUTIONS, STOCK SPLITS, AND STOCK REPURCHASES

13 TERMINATING THE CORPORATION: DISSOLUTION, MERGERS AND CONSOLIDATIONS, AND BANKRUPTCY

14 ESTABLISHING THE ACCOUNTING RECORDS

15 TAXATION OF CORPORATIONS

16 HOW TO BUY AND/OR SELL AN ONGOING BUSINESS

CHAPTER 1

Introduction

WHAT THIS BOOK IS ALL ABOUT

The objective of this book is not to make you into a CPA or an attorney. It was, however, written for those individuals who wish to start out in their own business, with minimum capital and risk, and with the knowledge that in case their efforts are not successful, there are legal escape hatches for ending the enterprise at minimum personal cost (see Chap. 13). This book will also help you avoid fundamental and costly tax pitfalls.

There are many reasons why people go into business today. Many individuals feel that they have the expertise and ability to "make a go of it," or they want the personal freedom to achieve certain economic and personal goals, or they simply want their name on the door. This book will assist you in forming your own business, with minimal capital and legal requirements, and with the best legal protection available to any new business—the corporation. Note that there are a variety of legal forms through which you can conduct a business. The corporation is but one of these vehicles, the others being sole proprietorships, partnerships, joint ventures, and some other useful organizations. The corporate form of doing business may be in the mode of a small enterprise owned by a single person, as well as in the form of a multinational enterprise owned by thousands of individuals dispersed throughout the world. While the advantages of and the reasons for forming the corporate form will be explained throughout this book, it is important to note that the corporation is treated as a separate legal body with its own rights, privileges, duties, and liabilities. In addition, the corporation is subject to greater governmental regulation, taxation, and report filing than any other type of business enterprise. Regardless of these handicaps, the corporation remains the most viable and safest form of doing business. One of the greatest advantages of doing business as a corporation is that it permits individuals who are stockholders to carry on business for profit without subjecting their personal fortunes to unlimited personal liability due to the hazards of business failure.

STARTING OUT: LAWS AND REGULATIONS AFFECTING YOUR CORPORATION

Corporations are usually formed under state law, but federal laws also impose a heavy financial and regulatory burden on the emerging enterprise. For example, the corporate statutes of the state in which the corporation is formed are binding on the corporation no matter where it conducts its actual business. This means that the corporation is subject to regulation and taxation both in the home state of its incorporation, as well as in all other states where the corporation does business. Secondly, not only is the corporation itself subject to intense regulation, but also those individuals who are an integral part of the corporation's operations, such as its officers, directors and shareholders. Thirdly, the Internal Revenue Code permits the federal government to share in the corporation's profits.

Besides the federal and state laws that regulate corporations, there are laws and administrative regulations that govern the corporation's day-to-day operations, its bylaws, board of director resolutions, shareholder agreements, loan agreements, employment contracts, and payroll tax requirements. However, despite these difficulties, corporate opportunities can be maximized with minimum governmental interference.

Note that the corporation is a fictitious being or artificial entity independent of its owners or investors. However, despite this legal fiction, operating in the corporate mode has many advantages. A corporation is permitted to conduct business, acquire assets, and incur liabilities as if it was a "real person."

This volume will serve as your legal and financial handbook by explaining the expanding body of federal and state corporate regulations and how they apply to your growing corporation. We will show you how to avert potential financial and operating problems, and how to avoid costly tax traps thereby allowing you to harvest your hard earned corporate profits at minimum tax cost. With the knowledge and ideas learned from this book, your corporation will grow and prosper to the point where you may eventually decide "to go public" by selling stock in your successful venture. In short, this book will familiarize you with the complex maze of rules, regulations, and financial and tax procedures that must be followed when creating what is today probably the best way to start and operate a new and profitable business.

SEARCHING FOR CAPITAL IN YOUR GROWING BUSINESS

Most small corporations start up with capital of less than $100,000. However, as the successful corporation grows, it will need additional capital. Capital sources might include friends, relatives, banks, venture capital companies, and public offerings.

Venture capitalists are profit-oriented corporations who seek to purchase shares in young and growing corporations. They generally look for a potential return on their investment of 300 to 500 percent within five to seven years followed by a quick profit from the sale of the shares. Typically, they might invest $2 million to $5 million in a business. Because of the high risk involved, venture capitalists will look very closely at the business, including product line, services to be performed, and market potential. When investing, they may demand more than 50 percent ownership in the outstanding shares. Although they may have a controlling interest, they will usually allow the directors and officers to continue in control of the corporation's daily activities. Basically, the shareholders must weigh the benefits of receiving additional capital against a smaller share of the business. Most venture capitalists prefer to purchase equity (meaning ownership) interests in computer, communications, and biotechnology companies.

Assistance in finding venture capital private investors may be obtained from Venture Capital Networks, P.O. Box 882, Durham, New Hampshire 03824. A list of venture capital companies may be found in *The Guide to Venture Capital Sources* (Illinois: Capital Publishing Corporation, 10 South LaSalle Street, Chicago, Illinois 60603).

A corporation may also seek to go public by selling their shares to other investors in the marketplace. "Going public" is not for every corporation and should only be considered by high-growth companies with proven track records. A successful public offering results in an infusion of capital, imposed corporate image, the retention of key employees, and the possibility of listing on an organized stock exchange or traded in the over-the-counter (OTC) market. Both Apple Computer and MCI are traded OTC. The downside is dilution (meaning reduction) of the shareholder's interest, loss of privacy, and the costly legal and accounting expenses associated with a public offering. Such offering requires an initial filing with the Securities and Exchange Commission (SEC) followed by continuous periodic and annual reports. Most corporate owners never seriously consider selling to the public to finance growth and expansion because it is both time-consuming and very expensive. Instead they may seek a loan from a bank or involve themselves in a Small Company Offering Registration (SCOR). SCOR, also known as the Uniform Limited Offering Registration (ULOR), is now available in a majority of states. The SEC created SCOR to cut the cost of a regular SEC registration and make the process simpler and less costly. SCOR involves the services of a lawyer, an accountant, and a brokerage firm. The capital ceiling on a SCOR issue is $1 million, and the price of each share must be at least $5. Under SCOR regulations, corporations can sell common, preferred, and convertible shares, as well as other types of shares.

Blue sky laws are state statutes that regulate the sale of securities to the public. Most blue sky laws require the registration of new issues of securities with a state agency that reviews selling documents for accuracy and completeness. Where a corporation is required to register with the SEC, such filing usually serves as a substitution for a state filing.

The Small Business Administration (SBA) should also be contacted to determine if the corporation qualifies for a loan. The SBA regulates both Small Business Investment Companies (SBICs) and Minority Enterprise Small Business Investment Companies (MESBECs) who provide long-term capital to small businesses. The major difference between SBICs and MESBECs is that a MESBEC can only invest in small businesses that are at least 51 percent owned by minorities and socially and economically disadvantaged people.

ACTING AS YOUR OWN LAWYER

It is an old maxim of law that a man who acts as his own attorney has a fool for a client. Although the process of corporate formation is essentially very simple, most basic business situations can become complicated and require the guidance of an attorney. Remember that your trusted counsel is aware of both your personal idiosyncracies, business acumen, and most likely, your current financial status. Thus, your lawyer is in an excellent position to do the following: advise you in choosing whether to operate as a sole proprietorship, partnership, or corporation; help

you to establish the corporation; deal with any possible stock and securities laws; register trademarks, patents, and copyrights; file for licenses; purchase real estate for the business; negotiate a lease; deal with customer disputes and potential litigation; assist in estate planning; and handle possible liquidation or bankruptcy proceedings should the need arise.

For a fee, incorporation services are also available to help form your corporation. However, many of these costs, and in some cases virtually all of your start-up costs, can be reduced or eliminated by careful study and application of all the money-saving techniques discussed in this book.

Thus, the individual, before starting a business, should understand all basic issues, determine what legal aspects, if any, can be handled without legal help, and to then decide whether it is worthwhile in terms of time and money to proceed independently.

SELECTING A LAWYER

While wealthy individuals and corporations retain lawyers to handle their legal problems and to monitor unusual or complex transactions, the small business individual generally cannot afford this luxury. Upon analyzing the specific needs of the business, it might be prudent to enlist the services of an attorney whose skills and experience can help solve both common and unforeseen legal problems. The attorney can assist you in setting up the type of enterprise that you need, such as a partnership or corporation, and can negotiate any loans, leases and contracts applicable to your business. She will also advise your accountant as to what transactions must be recorded on your books and records for tax, environmental, health and safety regulations, and minimum wage requirements. If possible, avoid hiring an attorney on a costly monthly retainer basis. Find an attorney who bills by the hour and what services comprise billable hours. Thus, you will only be paying for services that you actually use rather than burdening your business with fixed monthly costs. Determine the attorney's rates in advance. Like any other professional, shop around for any attorney in whom you have trust and whose fees your new business can afford.

Selection is no easy task, but here are some suggestions for finding the right legal professional.

1. Talk to people in your community and ask who they use;
2. Talk to your accountant or banker;
3. Ask friends and relatives;
4. Look in the "yellow pages" for a listing of lawyers who specialize in business matters; and
5. In many states, the bar association will provide a lawyer referral and information service. This service can provide you with the name of a local practitioner in your area who can be contacted. An initial consultation may be obtained at a minimal fee or possibly free of charge if the attorney is seeking new clientele.

In selecting a lawyer, just don't settle on the first lawyer on your list. Set up an interview, ask about her education, area of expertise, and prior experience in business matters. Also determine whether you are comfortable with this person. Are her fees reasonable? Does she return calls quickly? Also determine whether she is practical minded and can fine tune your business, if necessary, without getting involved in complex legal issues that might prove costly.

CHAPTER 2   Why the Corporation Is Best for You

FORMS AND FACTORS IN SELECTION

The selection of the best form of doing business is based on both tax and nontax factors. From a nontax viewpoint, there are at least eight principal forms of doing business. They include the sole proprietorship, general partnership, limited partnership, joint-stock company, business trust, corporation, limited liability company, and professional corporation. Each of these forms can be molded to take into account the particular situation of one or more individuals. For example, if a person wishes to start out with minimum legal restraints and capital, it is best to start off as a sole proprietorship. Later on, as the business grows, the individual can take in a partner and operate as a partnership. If the enterprise continues to grow even further, the partners can choose to incorporate to take advantage of fringe benefits, pension plans, and, perhaps, to raise additional capital. In addition, should later events occur that make it unprofitable to continue operations in the corporate form, a corporate liquidation, with minimal tax consequences, is always available to the unhappy corporate shareholders.

Furthermore, the Internal Revenue Code distinguishes between individuals, partnerships, and corporations (including associations). The sole proprietorship pays taxes at individual rates. A partnership pays no taxes while the partners do. Finally, a corporation is subject to tax rates as high as 35 per-

cent although these rates can be avoided by making an "S corporation election" (see Chap. 15).

Other factors that enter into the selection of the form of doing business include formality of organization, capital and credit requirements, management and control, number of participants, the determination of salaries, how profits and losses are to be shared, the transferability of an ownership interest, and whether there is continuity of existence should an owner die or sell his interest.

Whether a single form of doing business, or a multiple of business organizations should be used requires careful consideration of additional tax and other aspects. For example, the use of multiple organizations might be used to achieve the following:

1. Separation of corporate functions, such as sales from product development to simplify operations and to increase efficiency;
2. Creating a separate enterprise to handle a new untried or competitive product;
3. Limiting the liabilities of each entity;
4. The protection of corporate assets in case of bankruptcy;
5. The protection of owners from lawsuits;
6. Minimizing the exposure of corporate assets to outside claims and lawsuits;

5

7. Simplify estate tax planning;
8. Eventually selling the entities so as to obtain lower capital gains rates; and
9. Flexibility in changing the form in response to business and legal developments.

On the other hand, multiple entities might result in increased legal and accounting costs, duplication of operations, problems when operating in different states and municipalities due to a multiplicity of state and municipal tax laws, and possible antitrust violations. Thus, considerable care should be taken when selecting the form or forms appropriate under the particular circumstances to achieve the best form of doing business in light of all possible contingencies.

EXAMPLE Henderson Tool Manufacturing Company is nationally known for the quality of its high-cost products. It now seeks to manufacture and sell a cheaper line of low-cost tools. However, Henderson's management believes that the image of quality long associated with its current products would be harmed by the introduction of a new and cheaper product line under Henderson's name. Therefore, Henderson sets up a separate corporation called Quality Hand Tools Inc. to manufacture and sell its new and cheaper line. The new company, in the eyes of the consuming public, would be a different company apart from Henderson. Thus, the manufacture and sale of a cheaper line of tools by a different company, separate and unassociated with Henderson, would not reflect negatively on the high quality products manufactured by Henderson.

THE INDIVIDUAL (OR SOLE) PROPRIETORSHIP
Definition
As the name suggests, this is a natural form of doing business at lowest initial cost. A major advantage to this form is that if the venture is successful, it may be converted into a partnership by the admittance of a new partner, or the venture may be converted into a corporation tax-free. The sole proprietor is the "boss." He may employ others, raise capital by borrowing, and enter into contracts that bind him personally. He is also liable for all negligent acts committed by him personally, as well as those committed by his employees within the operation of the business. Credit can be obtained based on the extent of the business assets, as well as the proprietor's personal wealth. His personal liability is, therefore, unlimited. Of course, personal liability can always be reduced by either contractual limitation or insurance. There are no formalities involved in starting a business as a sole proprietor beyond any capital requirements. Thus, this form is very suitable for an individual who is seeking to start a one-person enterprise.

When operating as a sole proprietor, there is, generally, no continuity of existence, and, upon the death of the decedent (or owner), the business will generally terminate. However, the owner may, by will, permit the executor of the will to continue the business so that his heirs may receive a going concern. In effect, this technique permits a beneficiary, as a new owner, to continue what is perhaps a thriving business.

In a sole proprietorship, the owner pays individual taxes on net profits that may run from 15 to 39.6 percent. The sole proprietorship would also be subject to federal self-employment tax. Net losses generated by the business can be used to offset ordinary income. Thus, the choice is whether to incorporate with heavy governmental regulation, or to operate as a sole proprietor with minimal government scrutiny, a large degree of secrecy, and unlimited liability.

Advantages of a Sole Proprietorship
1. Requires minimal start-up capital.
2. Minimum legal and accounting fees upon start-up.
3. Lack of operating formalities, such as meetings of a board of directors. The individual is in complete control of the proprietorship.
4. Free access to trade in all state jurisdictions with minimum legal burdens.
5. A sole proprietor's protection as an individual by the Fifth Amendment's guarantee against self-incrimination.
6. Less governmental regulation than a corporation.

7. Possible availability of credit based not only on the business assets but also on the personal assets of the owner/proprietor.

8. Minimal legal and accounting problems upon termination.

9. Opportunity of a sole proprietorship to generate losses, which the owner can use to offset taxable income. This is particularly advantageous if large operating losses are expected in the initial years of operation.

10. Opportunity to operate under an "assumed" or "trade" name. If the sole proprietorship desires to conduct business under an assumed name, state statutes in many jurisdictions merely require that a certificate be filed in a public office.

11. Availability of certain types of pension plans to offset the effects of federal taxation.

Disadvantages of a Sole Proprietorship

1. Death of the principal automatically terminates the business.

2. The owner is subject to unlimited liability in case of breach of contract or liability due to some negligent action on the part of the owner or his employees. However, this disadvantage can be mitigated somewhat by the use of various forms of liability insurance.

3. The amount of capital available for use in the business is limited to the resources of the owner.

4. Income obtained by the owner from other sources will put the owner of a profitable business into a tax bracket as high as 39.6 percent.

5. The sole proprietorship form limits the number of retirement and profit-sharing plans that may be utilized.

In some cases, the sole proprietorship option is virtually ruled out by circumstances. For example, a high exposure to legal risks may require operation in the corporate form in order to provide greater protection against personal liability, as in the case of a manufacturer of potentially hazardous consumer products.

THE GENERAL PARTNERSHIP
Definition

The Uniform Partnership Act (UPA), which is the law in virtually all states, defines a partnership as "an association of two or more persons to carry on as co-owners a business for profit." Partnerships are either general partnerships or limited partnerships. General partnerships consist of partners who are all general partners, while a limited partnership has both general and limited partners. The limited partnership is discussed in the next section.

Characteristics of a Partnership

A partnership is not a separate entity distinct from its owners, the partners. In a partnership, every partner is an agent of the partnership in dealing with third parties, and each partner is jointly (meaning that each copromisor is liable for the entire debt) and/or severally liable (meaning that each party is liable alone or individually) for the debts of the partnership. Thus, each partner may be sued individually for the entire amount of the alleged debt or for his proportionate share. No person can become a partner without the consent of all the other partners, and the death of a partner dissolves the partnership. A basic fiduciary relationship (meaning one of trust) among the partners imposes upon all of them the highest standards of good faith and loyalty.

Advantages of a Partnership

1. Partnerships are easy to create and generally require no approval from state or local authorities.

2. There are no formal annual meeting requirements, such as those mandated for corporations.

3. Partnerships are generally simple to operate.

4. The partnership is not subject to as many formal reporting requirements as imposed on corporations.

5. A partnership also has a tax advantage because it is not directly subject to federal income tax.

Profits and losses flow through to each individual partner on the personal level. Thus, the partnership acts as a "conduit" for partnership profits and losses.

6. Partnerships can also utilize various qualified pension and profit-sharing plans.

7. Partnerships may dissolve by mutual agreement while other types of entities, such as a corporation, requires statutory compliance when dissolving.

Disadvantages of a Partnership

1. Members are subject to unlimited personal liability for all the liabilities of the business.

2. Death of a partner terminates the partnership, which can cause difficulties in the continued operation of the business. Besides the death of a partner, a dissolution may occur when any partner indicates an intention to disassociate from the partnership. Dissolution can also occur when a change in the law prohibits further operation or by judicial decree, such as where the partnership can only be operated at a loss, or a partner perpetuates a fraud upon the other partners.

3. A partnership, because of its size and minimal assets, may find it difficult to raise any required capital.

4. A partner's interest in the partnership is not readily transferable.

5. Under the Internal Revenue Code, partner's profits are taxable to him whether or not there is an actual distribution of the profits to him. Thus, if the partnership decides to reinvest the partnership's profits, the partners must come up with the necessary cash with which to pay the applicable income taxes on the undistributed profits.

Important Partnership Agreement Provisions

Should individuals contemplating the appropriate form of doing business initially elect to operate as a partnership, they would have to draft an agreement containing the following elements in order to avoid potential disputes.

1. The identity of the partners.

2. The business of the partnership. Given the potential for unlimited personal liability, each partner should have the right to veto an attempt to expand the partnership's business purposes.

3. The nature and amount of each partner's capital contribution to the business, i.e., whether cash or property made available to the partnership is a loan or a capital contribution.

4. The duration of the partnership, including both its start-up date and termination date.

5. The ratio in which both profits and losses will be shared (the ratios need not be the same for both). If there is no provision in the partnership agreement relating to the distribution of profits and losses, profits and losses are shared equally by the partners regardless of differences in the amounts of their capital contributions.

6. The salaries and drawing accounts that will be paid or made available to partners.

7. The duties and responsibilities of each partner. If the partners are to serve in different capacities, then a clear delineation of each partner's job functions should be set out in the agreement.

8. The conditions upon which the partners will be admitted to the venture and the minimum qualifications a person must possess in order to become a partner.

9. The bases for dissolution prior to the agreed-to date of termination.

10. The rights of partners against a partner who wrongfully causes dissolution.

11. The identity of the winding-up partner or partners and whether the winding-up partners must provide a bond.

12. The terms upon which a partnership can be continued by the remaining partners upon the death, resignation, or bankruptcy of a partner (including a buy-out agreement that would be necessary if a continuation is to take place).

Experience among lawyers has shown that without a detailed written agreement governing its operations friction, lawsuits, and breakup will inevitably occur in a general partnership.

Once a partnership begins operations, a new partner cannot be admitted without the consent of all of the partners unless the agreement says otherwise. A partner can, however, assign his interest in the partnership, but the individual receiving the assigned interest, and who is called an assignee, cannot take part in partnership affairs. Finally, upon the death of a general partner, his estate does not become a partner in the firm. Upon the death of a partner, the surviving partners have a right to use of specific partnership property. However, they also have a duty to account to the decedent's estate for the value of the deceased partner's interest in the partnership. Because of these deficiencies, a partnership generally cannot raise large amounts of investment capital for its business through the broad distribution of ownership. It is because of these limitations individuals tend to view the corporation as the preferable mode of operation when contemplating any new business venture.

THE LIMITED PARTNERSHIP
Definition
The limited partnership form of doing business can only be created according to the formalities stated in the Uniform Limited Partnership Act (ULPA), which has been adopted in virtually all states. Furthermore, a majority of states have adopted the Revised Uniform Limited Partnership Act (RULPA).[1] These statutes form the basis for the limited partnership.

Under the ULPA, a limited partnership is defined as a "partnership formed by two or more persons having as members one or more general partners and one or more limited partners." The limited partners, as such, shall not be bound by the obligations of the partnership. In many respects, the principles applicable to a general partnership also apply to a limited partnership.

Operating the Limited Partnership
A limited partnership requires that there be at least one partner who will assume the risks of a general partner and be subject to unlimited liability. Contributions of a limited partner may consist of cash or other property, but not services. A limited partner has no control over the business nor may he participate in the management of partnership affairs.

Because of his lack of participation in management, the personal liability of a limited partner is limited to his capital contribution. Because of the restricted role of a limited partner the death or assignment of her interest in the partnership does not interrupt the continuity of the limited partnership. In effect, the limited partner's right to assign his interest is almost identical to that of a corporate shareholder. If a limited partnership wishes to do business in another state, it must first comply with the statutory provisions of that jurisdiction. Failure to comply with such provisions may result in the limited partner being subject to liability as a general partner.

Formation
Under ULPA, two or more persons desiring to form a limited partnership shall sign and swear to a certificate, which shall state:

1. The name of the partnership;
2. The character of the business;
3. The location of the principal place of business;
4. The name and place of residence of each member; general and limited partners being respectively designated;
5. The term for which the partnership is to exist;
6. The amount of cash and a description of and the agreed value of the other property contributed by each limited partner;

---

[1]States that have enacted RULPA include Alabama, Arizona, Arkansas, California, Colorado, Connecticut, Delaware, Florida, Georgia, Hawaii, Idaho, Illinois, Indiana, Iowa, Kansas, Kentucky, Maryland, Massachusetts, Michigan, Minnesota, Mississippi, Missouri, Montana, Nebraska, Nevada, New Hampshire, New Jersey, New Mexico, New York, North Carolina, North Dakota, Ohio, Oklahoma, Oregon, Pennsylvania, Rhode Island, South carolina, South Dakota, Tennessee, Texas, Virginia, Washington, West Virginia, Wisconsin, and Wyoming. Louisiana has not enacted either the ULPA or RULPA.

7. The additional contributions, if any, agreed to be made by each limited partner and the times at which or events on the happening of which they shall be made;

8. The time, if agreed upon, when the contribution of each limited partner is to be returned;

9. The share of the profits or the other compensation by way of income, which each limited partner shall receive by reason of his contribution;

10. The right, if given, of a limited partner to substitute an assignee as contributor in his place, and the terms and conditions of the substitution;

11. The right, if given, of the partners to admit additional limited partners;

12. The right, if given, of one or more of the limited partners to take priority over other limited partners, as to contributions or as to compensation by way of income, and the nature of such priority;

13. The right, if given, of the remaining general partner or partners to continue the business on the death, retirement, or illness of a general partner; and

14. The right, if given, of a limited partner to demand and receive property other than cash in return for his contribution.

The certificate must then be filed in the appropriate office as determined by state law.

THE LIMITED LIABILITY PARTNERSHIP (LLP)

The limited liability partnership (LLP) is a relatively new form of business entity that has grown rapidly in recent years. It combines the corporate characteristic of limited liability for the owners with the nontaxability applicable to a partnership. The LLP is formed under a separate state statute that generally applies to organizations offering services. Many large law and accounting firms have become LLPs in recent years.

THE CORPORATION
Definition

The corporation is the dominant form of doing business in the United States today. Corporations range in size from one shareholder to millions as in the case of General Motors. Although formed according to state statute, there are innumerable capitalization and operating structures that can be utilized by the corporation.

How A Corporation Differs From Other Types of Doing Business

State corporate statutes set forth requirements that must be met before the corporate entity is deemed to be validly formed. Upon compliance with certain state formalities, such as the preparation of articles of incorporation (sometimes called the certificate of incorporation or corporate charter), the payment of organization taxes and filing fees, the drafting of bylaws, and an initial meeting of incorporators and a board of directors, the corporation comes into existence.

Comparison With a Partnership

Each partner is personally liable for the debts of the partnership. In addition, the death, illness, or bankruptcy of any partner dissolves the partnership. Thus, the partnership is subject to limited duration. In a corporation, the shareholders are generally subject to limited liability, i.e., the amount of capital (cash or property) that they have invested in the corporation. In addition, the death, illness, or bankruptcy of any director, officer, or shareholder does not dissolve the corporation.

Comparison With a Limited Partnership

A limited partnership has one or more general partners and one or more limited partners. The liability of a general partner is unlimited while the liability of a limited partner to partnership creditors shall not exceed the amount of their investment. This liability is similar to that of a corporate shareholder.

Broadly speaking, corporations cannot come into existence until there has been strict compliance with a state's incorporation law. The failure to comply with all prescribed legal formalities can result in the entity being treated as either a partnership, a sole proprietorship, or a debtor-creditor relationship based on the fact that one or more parties are using the capital (i.e., cash and property) belonging to another group (i.e., the shareholders). The result would be unlimited liability for all parties concerned.

Advantages of a Corporation

1. Shareholders enjoy limited liability. For example, if they each invest $5,000 into the corporation and it eventually fails, they have lost no more than the amount invested. Furthermore, under the Internal Revenue Code, they can deduct up to $3,000 per year in stock losses on their personal tax return.

....

WARNING *This limitation is not absolute. In many states, corporate shareholders of a small business corporation are personally liable for unpaid corporate wages. For example, under Section 630 of the Business Corporation Law of New York State, the ten largest shareholders shall be jointly and severally liable for the unpaid wages and salaries of corporate employees. This rule does not apply to publicly listed corporations.*

....

2. It may be formed for a variety of purposes, both profit and nonprofit. Note that the thrust of this book is a detailed discussion of only profit-oriented corporations.
3. Ownership of corporate stock may be freely transferred by sale or gift, subject only to certain corporate restrictions.
4. The corporation has an unlimited life and is not affected by the death of a director, officer, or shareholder, no matter what the size of the shareholder's ownership in the corporation.
5. The corporation may purchase, hold, and sell property in the corporate name.
6. The corporation enjoys great flexibility in selecting the methods it will use in raising capital.
7. The corporation has numerous tax advantages available to it, such as pension and profit-sharing and the election of S corporation status (see Chap. 15).
8. A corporate employee, even if there is only one, can receive workers' compensation, an insurance benefit not available to a self-employed person operating as a sole proprietor. This feature provides a strong incentive for one shareholder to incorporate and operate as a single-shareholder corporation.

Disadvantages of a Corporation

The corporation is an expensive way of doing business. The cost varies based upon the amount and type of stock to be authorized and issued, the size of the planned corporation, the amount of business done, and the type of labor force needed. In addition, initial incorporation costs include filing fees, organization taxes, and attorney's and legal fees. Of course, these fees vary with the size of the corporation to be formed.

1. The corporation is subject to greater governmental regulation and control than any other form of doing business, and there are more formalities and restrictions that must be observed.
2. The corporation is subject to double taxation, once at the corporate level and again at the shareholder level when a distribution of profits, called dividends, is made. However, the Internal Revenue Code offers certain tax elections, such as the S corporation election, that can mitigate and even eliminate taxes at the corporate level.
3. Majority shareholders may be in a position to make business decisions that are not in the best interests of the minority shareholders. This danger is greater in close corporations that have three to five shareholders who may have different operating philosophies.
4. Voting rights enjoyed by shareholders may be diluted where there is a wide-spread or increased ownership of corporate stock.
5. Management and control of the corporation rests with the duly elected directors and officers and are, thus, separate from the shareholders who are the true owners of the corporation.

THE LIMITED LIABILITY COMPANY (LLC)
Definition

The limited liability company (LLC) is a recent form of organization that may offer greater business and tax advantages than a regular corporation, and provide better business and structuring advantages than a general or limited partnership. There has been a rapid increase in states adopting LLC statutes, and a majority of states now have LLC statutes.

While an LLC resembles a partnership, it is actually a legal entity distinct from its members. An LLC must file articles of incorporation similar to the articles of incorporations of a regular corporation. The articles must contain the name, purpose, duration, registered agent, and principal office of the LLC. LLC members own a membership interest rather than a share of stock or a partnership interest. An enterprise wishing to operate as an LLC must meet all Internal Revenue Code rules and regulations. It must also file its operating agreement with its respective state and meet the state's requirements for organization. LLC statutes presently vary from state to state.

....

OBSERVATION *Why should an LLC be used rather than an S corporation or partnership? S corporations cannot have more than 35 shareholders and one class of stock. LLCs have no such restrictions. In a general partnership, the partners are personally liable. Members of LLCs have limited liability.*

....

THE CLOSELY HELD (OR FAMILY) CORPORATION

A "closely held" corporation is one whose shares are owned by one stockholder or a closely knit group of shareholders. There is no definite maximum number, but it is a general thought that a corporation with less than fifteen shareholders is a closely held corporation. Delaware corporate law provides that a close corporation cannot have more than thirty shareholders. If the shareholders are related, the entity is sometimes referred to as a family corporation.

The main purpose of a closely held corporation is to assure the limited liability of all shareholders and to keep ownership and control within a group of shareholders who share the same profit-directed goals. If the business operated as a partnership, the lack of limited liability would be a major problem (although partially solvable by the use of liability insurance). Generally, the traditional corporate "hats" of director and officer, normally separate functions performed by different people (except for corporate presidents),

are simultaneously worn by the shareholders at all times. Thus, the separate identities of directors, officers, and shareholders are missing with the result that a few individuals own and operate the corporation. Unlike publicly held corporations, a closely held corporation's securities are not generally traded on the open market.

Advantages of a Closely Held Corporation

1. Besides limited liability, internal operations of the enterprise can be controlled as if it were a partnership.
2. Admission of new shareholders can also be restricted.
3. Unless agreed to otherwise, all shareholders, acting as directors, may participate equally in the management of the business.
4. Shareholders can settle disagreements with relative ease.
5. The shareholders can always convert the corporation into an S corporation that will enjoy tax-free treatment similar to that of a partnership.

Disadvantages of a Closely Held Corporation

1. Shareholders of a closely held corporation tend to impose strict limitations on the authority of the directors to manage the affairs of the corporation.
2. A closely held corporation must still adhere to the formalities of a larger corporation, such as the filing of a certificate of incorporation, and rules requiring board of directors and mandated annual shareholder meetings.
3. Shareholders might have difficulty selling their stock since outsiders might be reluctant to purchase closely held corporate stock of unknown value, and that may also be subject to certain restrictions.

PROFESSIONAL SERVICE CORPORATIONS (PSCs)

Members of the professions (i.e., those entities engaged in the practice of law, medicine, or accountancy etc.) have found themselves confronted with a substantial tax liability because of their status as either sole proprietorships or partnerships. By forming a professional service corporation (also called a professional association or PA in some states) and incorporating their practice, professionals and their employees become eligible to participate in employee fringe benefit and pension and profit-sharing plans. The corporate contributions to these plans are tax deductible, and the income generated by these retirement plans accumulates tax-free until later distribution to its employee/participants. All states have enacted corporate legislation with similar characteristics allowing professionals to incorporate their practices. For example, statutes generally require that only people who are individually eligible to provide the professional service may do any of the following:

1. Own stock in the corporation;
2. Serve as an officer or director;
3. Perform professional services on behalf of the corporation.

Formation of the professional corporation does not shield the professional shareholder from personal liability to third parties caused by his own negligence. However, the express language of most professional corporate statutes creates liability solely against the doctor who rendered or supervised the negligent service. This prevents other practitioners who are shareholders from being held jointly liable for the negligence of other employees unless the practitioners supervised the wrongful professional acts or participated in the wrongdoing.

EXAMPLE A patient sued a doctor for malpractice. The doctor was a shareholder, along with other doctor/shareholders, in a professional corporation. The patient also sued all of the other doctor/shareholders. The express language of most professional corporate statutes creates liability solely against the doctor who rendered or supervised the negligent service and not against nonparticipating doctors.

Due to the enormous liability exposure of professional practitioners, such as doctors, lawyers, and accountants, it is still essential that all professional shareholders carry liability (malpractice) insurance.

Occasionally, the outlook and demeanor of a particular professional or group of professionals prevents the use of the professional corporation. That is, do they have their own personalized approach or are they too casual in their practices to be burdened with the requirements of corporate life. Each professional's situation must be carefully reviewed so that the decision to incorporate can be prudently made.

WHICH TYPE OF ENTITY IS BEST FOR YOU?

Before starting a new business venture, the prudent individual must determine which form of doing business is best. The three basic forms are the sole proprietorship, the partnership, and the corporation. There are also hybrid operating forms, such as the limited partnership, the professional service corporation (PC or PA), and limited liability company (LLC). If there is a special tax benefit to be gained from a particular form of doing business, then that form should be studied carefully. After the selection of the best-suited type of organization has been made and operation has begun, the business must be reviewed periodically for any potential problems. This process should be undertaken in consultation with the owner's attorneys, accountants, and bankers. For the present, business owners with substantial personal assets to protect will undoubtedly use the corporate form. Partnerships are risky due to the unlimited liability applicable to its owner/partners. At the same time, LLCs are relatively new; and business advisors are much more comfortable with established forms, such as corporations. With the commencement of any new business, entrepreneurs may eventually find that another form of doing may be more suitable than the one they are now using based on the entity's current operating problems. If so, adoption of another form of doing business is usually readily available.

CHAPTER 3   Operating As a Corporation

INTRODUCTION

When properly formed, the corporation is a separate legal (or artificial) entity that has the power to hold property in the corporate name, sue and be sued, enjoys unlimited life, and can be held criminally liable for crimes that it commits. Control of the corporation is centralized in its board of directors who are elected by the shareholders. The actions, purposes, and goals of the corporation, as a distinct and separate entity, are wholly separate from the demands of the shareholders, even if there is only one shareholder. Thus a shareholder has no interest in the corporate property itself, but merely those rights conferred by state law and/or the corporation's articles of incorporation based on ownership of corporate shares.

EXAMPLE The board of directors of Growth Hormone Products Inc. purchased 1,000 shares of Lewmark Ironworks Corporation stock at a bargain price. Lon Thaddeus, the sole shareholder of Growth, sees an opportunity to "make a quick killing in the stock market" by having the shares transferred to him at the original purchase price for eventual sale at an opportune moment. Growth's directors have a valid objection asserting that the shares are the property of the corporation.

In effect, Thaddeus, although the sole shareholder, has no valid claim to the Lewmark shares.

Note that in a closely held corporation the majority shareholders generally elect qualified associates and friends as directors to assure their continued loyalty. The power to remove a director at the next annual shareholders meeting goes a long way in assuring the directors' allegiance to the shareholders.

On occasion, courts will ignore the corporate enterprise in cases where the corporation is used to perpetuate a fraud. For example, the corporate form has in the past been used to defraud creditors, circumvent certain laws, and/or to promote certain fraudulent or criminal acts. In such situations, the courts have disregarded the corporation in order to criminally charge the shareholders who are participants in the illegal schemes.

THE CORPORATION AS A "PERSON"

A corporation is an "artificial being" existing only in accordance with state or federal statutes. It has many of the rights, duties, powers, and liabilities given to natural persons. Thus, the corporation is usually regarded as a person with certain constitutional protections.

The corporation enjoys the right against unreasonable searches and seizures granted by the

United States Constitution.[2] The corporation does not have the privilege afforded individuals against self-incrimination, but it is entitled to due process and equal protection under the law.[3]

Although state statutes give the corporation the right to sue and be sued, it cannot appear in a court of law unless represented by a duly licensed attorney.

THE CORPORATION AS "CITIZEN AND RESIDENT OF A STATE"

A corporation is usually a resident of its state of incorporation. Corporate residence is relevant for various purposes, such as whether it can sue and be sued in a particular state, the type and amount of taxes payable, and the statute of limitations applica-ble to certain lawsuits. A statute of limitations requires the party (called the plaintiff) to file a law-suit within a specified period of time after the legal claim arises. The plaintiff who fails to file suit within the period of limitation loses the right to recover on the claim.

Besides the state of incorporation, the corporation can also be treated as a resident of any place where it is qualified to do business or is actually doing business.

A corporation can only act through its corporate officers (i.e., the president, vice-president, and so on) who are the agents of the corporation. An agent is one who acts on behalf of another, in this case the corporation.

[2]Fourth Amendment.
[3]Fifth and Fourteenth Amendments of the U.S. Constitution.

CHAPTER 4 Selecting a State in Which to Set Up Your Corporation

INTRODUCTION

If you decide to incorporate, the next step is to select a state in which to do business. If the intended corporate operation is primarily localized, or the entity intends to hold property exclusively in one state, then it is usually best to incorporate in that state. However, if the business plans to operate in more than one state, it might be wise to form two or more corporations, or one in each state, to promote flexibility in operation. Judicious selection requires a comparison of whether it is advantageous to have one or more corporations, or just one corporation engaged in multi-state activities. Of course, should the incorporators elect to do business as a single corporation, they can later dissolve, liquidate, and incorporate in another state or several states as the situation dictates. What follows is a discussion for determining which state or jurisdiction has the most favorable business climate for corporate activities.

WHAT FACTORS TO CONSIDER WHEN INCORPORATING

The consequences of incorporating and doing business in one or more states is based on many factors. Before incorporation, the following critical factors should be considered.

1. What are the fees for incorporation?
2. What are the applicable corporate tax rates?
3. Is there a state stamp tax on the issuance of shares?
4. What are the restrictions on the use of a corporate name?
5. Must the books and records be kept within the state?
6. For what purposes can a corporation be incorporated?
7. Can there be only one shareholder?
8. What is the minimum amount of capital required in order to begin operations?
9. Are there any restrictions on what the corporation may own?
10. How broad are the powers given to the corporation (i.e., Can they make loans to third parties or employees, borrow money, issue certain classes of stock, make charitable contributions)?
11. Can different classes of shares be issued, (i.e., preferred and common shares, voting and non-voting)?
12. How may shares be acquired (i.e., besides cash, can they be issued for goods and services)?
13. What are the rules with regard to the payment of cash, stock, and property dividends?

14. Are there limitations on the voting rights of shareholders?
15. Can the stock carry preemptive rights?
16. To what extent do incorporators enjoy limited liability?[4]
17. What are the minimum number of shareholders that must be present in order to hold a valid shareholder meeting?
18. Must shareholder meetings be held in the state of incorporation?
19. What are the rules applicable to proxies?
20. Can shareholders create voting agreements?
21. Can the corporation issue convertible shares?
22. Can the board of directors hold meetings outside the state of incorporation?
23. What are the procedures for removing a director?
24. What are the rules for corporate dissolution?
25. Are court decisions and administrative regulations supportive of corporations?

DELAWARE: THE BEST STATE FOR INCORPORATING

Delaware remains the most popular state for incorporation. The advantages offered by Delaware far outweigh the benefits available in other states, and no other jurisdiction offers the accommodations available to a corporation's formation and management. At least forty percent of the corporations listed on the New York Stock Exchange are incorporated in Delaware.

Incorporating in Delaware offers the following advantages.

1. Perpetual or limited existence;
2. Lenient rules for reserving a corporate name;
3. Broad operating powers, including the incorporation for any lawful business purpose;

4. Reasonable filing and incorporation fees;
5. The issuance of a broad class of stocks, such as common and preferred;
6. Minimal restrictions on the payment of dividends;
7. Vote by a majority of the shareholders on such matters as corporate merger and dissolution;
8. The election of only one or more directors.
9. Liberal provision for the indemnification of officers and directors for litigation expenses; and
10. Simple annual reports that permit the corporation a high degree of privacy.

Note that the freedom to operate a corporation with minimal legal and regulatory standards is of little value for those individuals wishing to operate as a closely held corporation. Unless a corporation plans to have a large number of directors, officers, and/or shareholders, and/or seeks to operate in more than one state, there is little advantage in incorporating in Delaware. In fact, the advantages of Delaware as the state of incorporation have been mitigated as other states have modernized their corporate statutes.

THE MODEL BUSINESS CORPORATION ACT (MBCA) AND THE LATER REVISED MODEL BUSINESS CORPORATION ACT (RMBCA)

Although Delaware has distinct advantages for incorporating large publicly held and private corporations, many businesses, including those closely held, choose to incorporate where their principal place of business is to be located. This is due to the fact that in many states, corporation law is influenced by the Model Business Corporation Act (MBCA) and the later Revised Model Business Corporation Act (RMBCA).[5] This act is designed to

---

[4]For example, under Section 630 of the Business Corporation Law (BCL) of New York State, the ten largest shareholders are jointly and severally liable personally for all wages and salaries due to its employees and laborers for services that were performed for the corporation. This rule is applicable to nonpublic corporations only.

[5]States that have statutes based in whole or in part upon the MBCA and its later revisions include Alabama, Alaska, Arizona, Arkansas, Colorado, Connecticut, Florida, Georgia, Hawaii, Idaho, Illinois, Indiana, Iowa, Kentucky, Louisiana, Maine, Maryland, Massachusetts, Michigan, Mississippi, Montana, Nebraska, New Jersey, New Mexico, New York, North Carolina, North Dakota, Oregon, Pennsylvania, Rhode Island, South Carolina, South Dakota, Tennessee, Texas, Utah, Vermont, Virginia, Washington, West Virginia, Wisconsin, and Wyoming.

balance the interests of management, shareholders, and the public. Although competition for business and the adoption of the MBCA and RMBCA has tended to promote uniformity in most states' corporate law, there are still major differences remaining among the various states that have adopted either the MBCA or RMBCA. Some states do not follow either act. For example, New York State uses the Business Corporation Law (BCL).

The RMBCA, which is discussed throughout this book, has been adopted at least in whole or in part by a majority of the states in the nation. Thus, the rules and regulations creating and governing the corporation vary from state to state and the specific statutes must be consulted for details. For incorporators planning only single purpose local operations with minimal capital and a small number of directors and stockholders, incorporation in the state where they plan to principally do business is probably preferable.

CHAPTER 5

Promoters and Preincorporation Transactions

WHAT IS A PROMOTER?

A promoter is an individual who provides the organizational initiative for forming the corporation for a specific purpose or purposes. Promoters are often called "insider," as opposed to the "outsiders" or ultimate investors because their initial efforts and resources help establish the corporation. Prior to incorporation, promoters usually have the status of joint venturers subject to unlimited liability. Once the corporation is formed, promoters sometimes continue in control. Promoters can be but need not be shareholders.

If there is more than one promoter, the law imposes fiduciaries duties (meaning a trust relationship) towards one another and towards the future corporation. Note that since the corporation is not yet in existence, any self-dealing is not improper. However, once the corporation is formed, promoters must make full disclosure to the board of directors and/or to any shareholders regarding any transactions involving secret and regular profits so that the newly formed corporation has an opportunity to consent or reject the transactions. Failure to make disclosure may make the promoter personally liable for any profits earned from these transactions.

Technically, the promoter lacks any power to bind a corporation not yet formed. In addition, the corporation, upon its formation, does not become automatically bound by the promoter's contracts. Instead, the corporation's board of directors weighs the advantages of the contract prior to its approval. Therefore, contracts made by the promoter usually bind the promoter personally unless the agreement stipulates that only the corporation shall be held liable. If such a provision exists, there is usually also a clause stating that if the corporation is never formed, or the board of directors do not accept the promoter's contracts, the promoter will not be held liable.

A promoter's compensation may take the form of cash, stock, stock options, or a salaried position.

CORPORATE LIABILITY FOR A PROMOTER'S CONTRACTS

As a general rule, promoters are personally liable for the contracts they make, even though made on behalf of a corporation to be formed. The imposition of personal liability is based on the principle that one who acts as an agent for a nonexistent principal (the corporation) is himself liable on the contract in the absence of an agreement to the contrary. Note that a contract signed by a promoter before the corporation is formed is not binding on the corporation. Not until the board of directors' approval of the contract does the corporation become liable.

DRAFTING THE PREINCORPORATION AGREEMENT TO AVOID PROBLEMS

Promotional activities made in anticipation of the formation of a corporation consist of developing a business opportunity, investigating whether the proposed business can be economically viable, hiring an attorney to draw up articles of incorporation, assembling the necessary corporate personnel, and acquiring property to set the corporation in motion. Agreements also include those made among the promoters themselves, agreements among prospective shareholders, stock subscriptions agreements whereby individuals agree to take and pay for unissued shares of the future corporation, and in the case of a large corporation, underwriting agreements (the act of investigating the marketplace prior to selling corporate shares).

OBSERVATION *To avoid litigation, all preincorporation agreements must explicitly clarify the rights, duties, and intentions of all parties. The written contracts should stipulate the rights and duties of all parties, whether the promoter is initially bound, whether her liability is to continue upon the formation of the corporation, and the legal consequences to all parties if the corporation refuses to ratify or adopt any or all parts of a contract. These agreements must be also be written in conformity with the statutory requirements of the state of incorporation.*

CHAPTER 6

Incorporation

STEPS IN THE FORMATION OF THE CORPORATE ENTITY

The power to grant a certificate or articles of incorporation is vested in the individual states. The federal government has no power to grant corporate charters except as to territories under its jurisdiction, such as the District of Columbia, and except as incident to the conduct of its own business. Incorporation procedures vary from state to state, and corporate existence may begin at different times, depending on the statutes and court decisions applicable to corporations in the state of incorporation. A private corporation, which is the focus of this book, is one organized by private individuals with a profit motive, with governmental consent.

DOMESTIC VERSUS FOREIGN CORPORATIONS

A corporation doing business in the state where it is incorporated is known as a domestic corporation. All other corporations doing business in that state are foreign corporations. For example, a Delaware corporation incorporated in Delaware and doing business in both New York State and Delaware is a domestic corporation for Delaware purposes but a foreign corporation while doing business in New York State.

A corporation wishing to do business in a state other than its state of incorporation must meet the licensing requirements of the state where it intends to do business. The usual procedure is to file an application with the secretary of state in the state where it intends to operate certifying to the corporation's name, date and state of incorporation, the nature of its business, the location of its principal place of business, and enclosing a copy of its certificate of incorporation and other significant data. This information is usually accompanied by a registration fee payable to the intended state. Once operation commences, the corporation is then also subject to all rules applicable to domestic corporations within the state, such as use of a corporate name and the payment of corporate income and franchise taxes.

A DE JURE CORPORATION VERSUS A DE FACTO CORPORATION

As stated in Chap. 2, a corporation cannot come into existence except upon compliance with the statutory laws of the state of incorporation. Once the details regarding the new corporation are settled, the promoters, now known as the "incorporators," must draw up and sign the articles of incorporation, or as it is sometimes called, the corporate charter, and file it with the secretary of state. The signatures of the incorporators are generally notarized and must be accompanied by the proper fees. A properly filed corporation is referred to as a *de jure* corporation. A *de facto* corporation arises when there has been a good faith attempt to comply fully with the state's statutory corporate laws and an exercise of corporate powers. A de facto corporation's existence cannot be attacked by anyone except the state of incorporation. Thus a de facto corporation enjoys the benefits of a properly formed corporation which means that the shareholders have the same limited liability as those enjoyed by a properly formed corporation.

What the applicable RMBCA section says *Section 2.03 of the RMBCA states that unless a delayed effective date is specified, the corporate existence begins when the articles of incorporation are filed. The secretary of state's filing of the articles of incorporation is conclusive proof that the incorporators satisfied all conditions precedent to incorporation except in a proceeding by the state to cancel or revoke the incorporation or involuntarily dissolve the corporation.*

THE ROLE OF THE INCORPORATOR

The person or persons who execute the articles of incorporation, or certificate, are known as the incorporators. In most states, they must be at least eighteen years of age. The steps taken by one or more incorporators for incorporation purposes, in varying combinations or in different chronological order, usually begin as follows:

1. Select a state of incorporation;
2. Select and obtain clearance for use of a corporate name, reserve name if deemed advisable;
3. Have the first meeting of incorporators to adopt bylaws. Minutes of this first meeting, and all subsequent meetings, must be kept;
4. Draw up any required preincorporation agreements;
5. Publish the notice of intention to incorporate, if required by state law;
6. Draft and have signed (and in most states have signatures notarized) the articles of incorporation;
7. File the properly signed articles of incorporation with the proper state authorities, usually the secretary of state;
8. Secure the necessary governmental approval, whether it be federal or state, to issue the appropriate number of shares;

9. Obtain subscriptions from investors for a given number of shares;
10. Secure payment by subscribers of minimum capital;
11. Order the corporate stationery, such as the corporate seal, share ledger, minute book, and shares of stock, usually from a law stationer;
12. Adopt a system of accounting and select either a calendar or fiscal year end pursuant to the Internal Revenue Code;
13. Apply for an employer identification number;
14. Establish one or more corporate bank accounts;
15. Make all advantageous tax elections, if deemed beneficial, such as S corporation status and Section 1244 small business stock election;
16. Obtain payments for additional shares of stock;
17. Issue shares after payment of appropriate transfer taxes;
18. Subsequently file with the state listing the shareholders, directors, number of officers, location of main office, and designation of agent to receive any legal notices or claims;
19. Investigate and if deemed beneficial, establish employee benefit and stock option plans;
20. If the corporation is to take over a going business, a target date should be set at some time in the future, so that all steps can be taken, such as the acquisition of assets and the assumption of liabilities, without unnecessary haste.

What the applicable RMBCA section says *Section 2.01 states that one or more persons may act as the incorporator or incorporators of a corporation by delivering articles of incorporation to the secretary of state for filing.*

THE ARTICLES OR CERTIFICATE OF INCORPORATION

Except for minor variations, the required contents of an articles of incorporation, or certificate, are fairly uniform among the states. Generally, the articles must set forth the following standard information.

The Name of the Corporation

The name of the corporation must include the word "corporation," "incorporated," "company," or "limited." Abbreviations such as "Corp.," "Inc.," "Co.," and "Ltd." are also permitted. The secretary of each state usually maintains a list of pre-existing corporate names that cannot be used for the new corporation. The proposed name should not be allowed to deceive the public as to the corporation's purposes, nor may it be the same as that of another existing domestic or foreign corporation authorized to do business in the state. The thrust of this rule is to make sure that each corporation has a unique name, that is not deceptively misleading, and to prevent fraud. As a practical matter, to avoid costly and time-consuming litigation, the incorporators should select at least two other corporate names, in order of preference, should the first name selected be unobtainable. If the intended corporation plans to do business in other states, check with those states to see that the name is also available. In determining the actual corporate name, the correct spelling, punctuation, and inclusion of the word "The," if desired, should be precisely set forth.

Words that are generally prohibited in a corporate name include "bank," "bank and trust," and "insurance," since these words imply corporate powers that the newly formed entity may not have. When selecting a name, keep in mind the cost of reproducing the name on corporate stationery and other property. A name should also be chosen that is easily recognizable so that any future goodwill generated will be quickly identified with the name.

Because corporate names are granted to corporations on a first-come, first-served basis, many states permit the reservation of a corporate name. This technique permits the still-to-be-formed corporation, for a nominal fee, to hold the corporate name for a limited period of time, usually sixty days, with the power to request an additional sixty-day extension until the corporate papers can be prepared and filed.

What the applicable RMBCA section says *Section 4.02 (a) allows the reservation of a corporate name for a non-renewable 120-day period.*

If the name is similar to that of another affiliated company doing business within the state, the incorporators must obtain written permission (sometimes called a letter of consent) from the existing corporation to use the name.

What the applicable RMBCA section says *Section 4.01, governing the use of a corporate name, states that a corporate name must contain the word "corporation," "incorporated," "company," or "limited," or the abbreviation "corp." "inc.," "co.," or "ltd.," or words or abbreviations of like import in another language. In addition, the name may not contain language stating or implying that the corporation is organized for a purpose other than that permitted by the RMBCA and its articles of incorporation.*

A corporation may use the name (including the fictitious name) of another domestic or foreign corporation that is used in this state if the other corporation is incorporated or authorized to transact business in this state and the proposed user corporation has merged with the other corporation.

The Purposes of the Corporation
The usual practice is to define the principal business actually contemplated by the corporation. In most jurisdictions, the purposes clause states that the corporation may engage in "any lawful purpose." The purposes clause should be drafted so as to prevent ventures into unauthorized areas that may be deemed risky. On the other hand, the purposes clause should be general enough to permit current operations and to allow for expansion and growth without having to amend the articles of incorporation should new corporate opportunities arise. Thus, the drafting of the purposes clause should be done in the most general of terms without going into specific terminology or circumstances.

The Powers of the Corporation
Corporate purposes should not be confused with corporate powers although there is a tendency in many jurisdictions to define the principal purpose of the business without differentiating between its purposes and powers. The articles of incorporation must include the scope and powers of the operation. The extent of the authority of a corporation to con-

duct its business is limited by the laws of the state under which it is incorporated. Every state corporation act contains a list of corporate powers that every corporation organized within its jurisdiction automatically possesses. Thus, the express powers of the corporation need not be specifically enumerated, but except for those powers restricted by law, a corporation may engage in any act in furtherance of its lawful purposes, i.e., dealing in real estate. Implied powers are those that are inferred from the express powers and are incident to the furtherance of the corporation's business.

An *ultra vires* act is one which is beyond the powers of the corporation. As will be discussed in Chap. 9, *ultra vires* acts result in certain legal consequences.

Thus, the safest procedure when forming a corporation is to express its purposes in the most general terms pursuant to the prevailing philosophy of the catchall "lawful purpose" clause and to avoid enumerating any express powers that may be implied under law.

Duration of Life

A corporation generally enjoys perpetual or unlimited life. Some state statutes mandate that if the life is not "perpetual," it must be so stated in the articles of incorporation. Virtually all corporations elect perpetual life since termination of corporate existence after a stated period will result in a legally questionable status.

Authorized Shares That May Be Issued and Their Description

All jurisdictions require that the articles of incorporation set forth the kinds and amounts of capital stock (or shares) the corporation is authorized to issue. This requirement defines the number of shares (or certificates) in each class, such as common and preferred, and whether they are par value or no par value shares. In every corporation, one class of stock must represent the basic ownership interest. Where a corporation issues only one class of stock, the shares are generally referred to as "common shares." Common shares generally vote for directors. They are also entitled to profits in the form of dividends declared by the directors, and the right to receive corporate assets in case of liquidation after all creditors have been paid.

In an effort to appeal to all types of investors, corporations may issue two or more classes of stock with different rights or privileges or in a series at specific dates. Thus, special classes, called preferred stock, with certain rights and/or privileges may be created. A common type of preference is to give the preferred shareholders a prior claim to earnings. Because they are to receive certain special preferences, preferred shareholders are usually called upon to sacrifice certain inherent rights of capital stock, such as the right to vote for directors.

Par Value Stock

Shares that are given a fixed, arbitrary, and not necessarily, realistic market value are called par value shares. At present, the par value associated with most capital stock issuances is very low (i.e., $1, $5, $10). As will be discussed later in this book, the purpose of these low amounts per share is to encourage the sale of stock and to avoid the contingent liability associated with stock sold below its par value. Stock with a low par value is rarely, if ever, sold below its par.

In some states, organization and transfer taxes are based on either authorized number of shares, the total par value of all of the shares authorized, on the issuance of the shares, or on the transfer of shares. In states that charge a transfer tax based on par value, a low par value may result in lower taxes.

No Par Value Stock

Stock that has no fixed value is called no par value stock. The rights and privileges of the no par value holders are the same as those who hold par value. The issuance of no par value stock avoids the issue of contingent liability for stock that was issued for less than par value (called a discount). It also avoids the question of determining the true value of the stock because presumably, the stock will be issued at its fair market value. Thus, the distinction between the two is not a distinction of rights and privileges, but of the form of issuance and the shareholder's liability in connection with the price paid for the stock.

OBSERVATION *Many states have statutes that require that before a corporation commences to do business, it must receive for its stock a minimum amount of compensation. In many states the minimum amount specified is $1,000.*

What the applicable RMBCA section says *Section 2.02(a)(3), governing the articles of incorporation, states that:*

> *a. The articles of incorporation must set forth:*
>
> > *1. a corporate name for the corporation that satisfies the requirements as to a proper designation, such as "Corporation" or "corp.";*
> >
> > *2. the number of shares the corporation is authorized to issue;*
> >
> > *3. the street address of the corporation's initial registered office and the name of its initial registered agent at the office; and*
> >
> > *4. the name and address of each incorporator.*
>
> *b. The articles of incorporation may set forth:*
>
> > *1. the names and addresses of the individuals who are to serve as the initial directors;*
> >
> > *2. the purpose or purposes for which the corporation is organized;*
> >
> > *3. any provision that under the RMBCA is required or permitted to be set forth in the bylaws; and*
> >
> > *4. a provision eliminating or limiting the liability of a director to the corporation or its shareholders for money damages for any action taken, or any failure to take any action, as a director, except liability for (A) the amount of a financial benefit received by a director to which he is not entitled; (B) an intentional infliction of harm on the corporation or the shareholders; (C) unlawful distributions; or (D) an intentional violation of criminal law.*

Designation of Secretary of State or Registered Agent

In most jurisdictions, the secretary of state and/or a registered office with a registered agent must be designated for service of process. In some states, the corporation must have designated *both* the secretary of state and registered agent, while in other states it is optional. Even without designating the secretary of state as an agent, most jurisdictions have statutory provisions that automatically make the secretary of state the agent for service of process, other notices and demands, and official communications with the state. Later changes in the registered office and/or agent must be filed with the secretary of state. The purpose of having a registered office and an agent is that a third party may have difficulty finding a corporation and therefore, should have, at all times, a place or person on which to serve notice of process.

Limitations on Directors

The certificate of incorporation designates the number of directors, their terms of service and duties, and their liability to the shareholders. When the membership of the first board of directors has been decided upon prior to the filing of the articles of incorporation, the articles may list their names. Naming the directors in advance may assist in the completion of the incorporation process. However, there is no requirement that they be selected in advance because they can be subsequently chosen at the first meeting of the incorporators or at the first shareholders meeting. To a limited extent, a corporation may indemnify its directors and officers for the reasonable expenses of a lawsuit by or on behalf of a corporation. The corporation may also indemnify directors and officers for judgments, settlements, and fines levied against them for actions committed by them, which they deemed to be in the best interests of the corporation. The corporation may also indemnify a director or officer in criminal cases where it is shown that the individuals believed that they acted in good faith, without knowing that they were in violation of the law, and that they did not personally profit from the transactions that they are charged with. Many states require that the directors be shareholders unless the articles or bylaws state otherwise.

The maximum and minimum number of directors is purely discretionary and may be increased or decreased from time to time as circumstances dictate.

Other Provisions

Incorporators may insert other provisions, mainly for the regulation of the internal affairs of the corporation. These directives cannot contravene existing corporate statutes and/or existing public policy. Examples of these provisions include the following:

1. the requirement, if not stated in the jurisdiction's statutory law, that the directors and officers be shareholders;
2. that certain procedures involving a vote of shareholders be higher than the percentage required by state law;
3. limitations on the power of corporate officers to enter into contracts (i.e., contracts for more than $100,000 require approval of the board of directors);
4. that certain matters, while solely within the discretion of the board of directors to act upon, also be submitted to the shareholders for their approval, (i.e., that the corporation purchase the stock of another corporation);
5. the time and place of shareholders meetings;
6. corporate transactions involving directors;
7. the procedure for terminating directors with and without cause;
8. filling director vacancies;
9. management's compensation;
10. restrictions on the transfer of shares.

The articles of incorporation in all jurisdictions must be signed by the incorporator or incorporators. Some states also require acknowledgement. The purpose of requiring acknowledgment by the incorporators is to prevent the employment of fictitious signatures. Approval of other state agencies, such as for example the state education department in case the new corporation intends to operate as a school, is sometimes required. Publication in a newspaper may also be mandated. Upon filing, the state issues a certificate of incorporation, which is either conclusive or presumptive evidence that the new corporation is in full compliance with the law and can commence operations. The articles of incorporation can always be amended at a future date, usually with shareholder consent.

COMPLETING THE ORGANIZATION OF THE NEW CORPORATION

Once the formalities discussed above have been completed, certain procedures must be undertaken to insure the smooth transition from an intangible concept into an actual operating entity. Steps that must be taken to complete the incorporation process include the calling of an initial meeting by the incorporators. At this meeting the incorporators will, among other things, appoint the requisite individuals who will prepare and adopt the corporate bylaws, set up the requisite books and records, obtain a corporate seal, and open a company bank account.

Accounting systems, payroll records, and other employee fringe benefits must also be established. These vital record keeping procedures will be discussed in detail in Chap. 12. All corporate books and records are normally kept at the corporation's principal place of business.

FUNCTIONS AND PURPOSES OF THE INITIAL CORPORATE MEETING

The launching of the new corporation is usually initiated at the first meeting of the new corporation. The first meeting, assuming the presence of a quorum (a simple majority), is generally called by the incorporators who take the following actions.

1. The election of permanent directors if the incorporators have elected to act as "dummy" or "temporary" directors.
2. The adoption of stock subscription agreements by the new board of directors. An individual may become a shareholder in a new corporation by subscribing to shares either before or after incorporation. This subscription contract is then adopted by the newly appointed board of directors.
2. The election of corporate officers.
3. The approval of business related matters, such as any employment agreements, leases, and the transfer of property to the corporation.
4. The adoption and approval of the bylaws and corporate seal.
5. The approval of legal and other expenses incurred in the formation of the corporation.
6. An application may be submitted for approval allowing the corporation to request authorization to operate in jurisdictions other than the state of incorporation.

7. The election of S corporation status pursuant to the provisions of the Internal Revenue Code allowing the corporation tax treatment similar to that accorded a partnership.

8. The election of Section 1244 of the Internal Revenue Code applicable to the corporate stock so that ordinary losses of up to $50,000 on a single tax return or $100,000 on a joint tax return can be taken in case the business fails.

9. The selection of the corporation's general counsel and independent accountant.

10. The approval of the setting up of the corporate records and the accounting system.

DRAFTING AND ADOPTING BYLAWS

Bylaws govern the internal conduct of the corporation. The initial bylaws may be formulated by the incorporators, shareholders, or board of directors. They must be reasonable and not arbitrary, and must be consistent with both the state statutory laws and the articles of incorporation. For example, they must apply equally to all persons within the same class (i.e., the common or preferred shareholders). Bylaws cannot restrict the fundamental rights of shareholders. For example, they cannot obstruct the right of a shareholder to examine the corporation's books and records for legitimate purposes such as possible mismanagement of the corporation. They are usually adopted by the directors at their first corporate meeting and are binding on the corporation, its officers, and its directors. Standard bylaws include the following:

1. The qualifications for being a corporate officer;
2. The duties and powers of the corporate officers;
3. The date of the annual stockholders meeting;
4. Quorum requirements for shareholders meetings;
5. The qualifications for serving as a director;
6. Compensation to be paid to officers and directors;
7. The rules for conducting shareholders and directors meetings;
8. Creating committees of directors;
9. Fixing the method of declaring dividends;
10. The rules regulating voting and proxies;
11. Indemnification of officers, directors, and other corporate employees;
12. The year-end accounting period to be used by the corporation;
13. The method of accounting to be adopted, i.e., cash or accrual, and other accounting practices;
14. Who is responsible for certain records, reports, and audits;
15. How important documents must be executed; and
16. Establishing a method for amending the bylaws.

Generally, the power to alter or repeal any bylaws are vested in the board of directors unless the power to do so is reserved to the shareholders in the articles of incorporation. In addition, the shareholders usually have the power to amend or repeal any board-adopted bylaw. Generally, the procedures for amending bylaws are easier than those applicable to the amending of the articles of incorporation, because unlike the articles of incorporation, the bylaws are not required to be filed with the secretary of state.

What the applicable RMBCA section says *Section 10.20, governing the amending of bylaws, states that a corporation's board of directors may amend or repeal the corporation's bylaws unless either the articles of incorporation reserve this act exclusively to the shareholders; or the shareholders, in amending or repealing a particular bylaw provide expressly that the board of directors may not amend or repeal that bylaw. In addition, a corporation's shareholders may amend or repeal the corporation's bylaws even though the bylaws may also be amended or repealed by the board of directors.*

THE MECHANICS OF ISSUING STOCK CERTIFICATES

Generally, corporate books and records are sold in complete packages through legal stationers or corporate service companies, such as Julius Blumberg, Inc. located in New York City. These records come in the form of a three-ring looseleaf binder consisting of a copy of the articles of incorporation, the corporate seal, a section for keeping the corporate minutes of each directors and shareholders meeting, a stock ledger containing the authorized number of shares upon which the corporation's name is printed, and all other documents required by law pertaining to the operation of the corporation. Although in most jurisdictions a corporate seal is no longer necessary, it is sometimes used to affix the corporation's mark on stock certificates, bonds, and other important documents to indicate that this is a corporate transaction rather than that of an individual director or shareholder.

A stock certificate represents ownership in a corporation. Statutes permit the issuance of stock certificates only after they have been fully paid for. The usual stock certificate is hand-engraved, is generally eight inches by eleven inches in size, and is usually purchased from a legal stationer. If there is more than one class of stock, each class is printed in a different color. The certificates are bound in a stock transfer ledger that is part of the corporate package, but they are easily separated from a ledger stub by tearing along a perforated line. Each certificate is prenumbered and contains an empty box, usually in the upper right hand corner of the certificate, permitting the appropriate corporate officer to designate the number of shares purchased so long as the amount does not exceed the number of shares authorized in the articles of incorporation. The certificate usually states that the corporation is organized under the laws of a specific state, the name of the stockholder purchasing the certificates, whether they are common or preferred, and whether the shares are par or no par value. An example of a typical share of stock appears on page 189. When issued, the stockholder's name and address is entered in the corporation's stock ledger account and on a stub in the stock book, with the number of shares issued, the amount paid for the shares, and the amount of stock transfer taxes paid. The certificates are usually signed by two or more corporate officers, such as the corporate secretary and president and may be imprinted with the corporate seal. If the shares were bought from another shareholder, the seller's name will also appear in the records. If there is more than

one class of stock issued (i.e., common and preferred), then another stock ledger account containing the same information must be maintained for this other class. The corporation relies upon the stock register to ascertain who is to receive corporate notices and dividends, and who is entitled to vote in corporate matters. Thus, it is important that the purchasing stockholder make sure that his name is entered in the corporate stock records. Shares that are previously owned and that are sold to a new shareholder are indorsed on the back of the certificate by the seller. The stock purchaser then has the right to have the shares registered in his name merely by displaying the properly indorsed stock certificate to the appropriate corporate officer.

OBSERVATION *The prudent shareholder who purchases shares should keep them in his own personal possession (a vault is suggested) rather than leave them with the corporation. Allowing the corporation to retain the shares is unadvisable and may lead to accounting errors and possible fraud.*

Unless there is notice of a possible forgery of the indorser's name, or fraud, the corporation is legally required to enter the new stockholder's name in the corporate records.

OBSERVATION *Prior to commencing operations, it would be wise to have the independent CPA who is hired by the corporation to audit the books and records also audit the stock transfer book to determine that all stock certificates, whether issued to stockholders or unissued, tie into the number of certificates printed by the printer. Missing or unaccounted for certificates may result in potential lawsuits by rightful shareholders who may claim that they were not apprised of certain corporate actions that required shareholder approval.*

Appropriate printed declarations on the certificates may also indicate the relative rights and restrictions governing a particular class of stock, such as a prior shareholder voting agreement to vote the shares a certain way.

CHAPTER 7

Recognition or Disregard of the Corporate Entity

INTRODUCTION

One of the principal purposes of forming a corporation is that shareholders escape unlimited liability by recognizing that the corporation is an entity separate, distinct, and apart from its shareholders. However, under certain circumstances, courts will sweep aside this dual personality concept by concluding that the corporation and its shareholders are really one entity thereby making the shareholders personally liable for all corporate debts. Lawyers call this concept "piercing the corporate veil." Remember that while the corporate form will shield its shareholders against liability for breach of contracts and corporate negligence (called torts), a corporation cannot be formed to defeat existing creditors.

EXAMPLE George owed his creditors $100,000. He, therefore, incorporates the X Corporation and has the board of directors call a meeting authorizing the corporation to assume all of George's debts. Thus, the sole purpose of this entire arrangement is to defeat the claims of George's creditors for pre-existing personal debts. Nevertheless, the newly formed corporation cannot be used as a shield to defeat the rights of the creditors, and George remains personally liable. Had the corporation initially incurred the debts, George, as its sole shareholder, would enjoy complete protection from the claims of the corporate creditors.

Even if a corporation is a de jure corporation (see Chap. 6) or one that is validly formed, a shareholder may still be liable for a corporation's debts and illegal acts if the corporation is being used as a vehicle to perpetrate a fraud or for criminal activities. Thus, in cases involving such activities, courts will pierce the corporate veil and hold the shareholders personally liable under the rule that the corporation is a sham, "alter ego" or "instrumentality" of the shareholders. On the other hand, where corporate formalities are substantially observed, and the corporation was not formed to cheat or defraud third parties or to engage in unlawful activities, even a sole controlling shareholder will enjoy limited liability.

What the applicable RMBCA section says *Section 2.04, governing liability for preincorporation transactions, states that all persons purporting to act as or on behalf of a corporation, knowing there was no incorporation under the RMBCA, are jointly and severally liable for all liabilities created while so acting.*

PERSONAL LIABILITY DUE TO DEFECTIVE INCORPORATION

In Chap. 6, it was stated that a de facto corporation arises when there has been a good faith attempt to comply fully with the state's statutory corporate laws and an exercise of corporate powers.

Furthermore, a de facto corporation enjoys the same benefits that a properly formed corporation possesses, such as perpetual existence, the right to operate as a corporation, and the power to elect S corporation status. At the same time, the shareholders have limited liability.

However, this rule does not mean that the shareholders can completely ignore the legal requirements of forming a corporation and still avoid personal liability.

To avoid problems after incorporation you should observe these steps:

1. Follow all corporate formalities listed in this book;
2. Issue stock only after it is fully paid for;
3. Make sure you call director(s) and shareholder(s) meetings;
4. Keep accurate books and records;
5. Open up a corporate checking account;
6. Do not use the corporate funds to pay your own personal expenses; and
7. Hire an independent accountant to review the corporate books and records.

EXAMPLE Three shareholders attempted to form a corporation. However, they did not have a final meeting with their attorney so they could sign the articles of incorporation, there was no issuance of corporate stock, and no directors or shareholders meetings were ever held. In addition, the shareholders failed to distinguish between the property owned by them personally and the property to be owned by the corporation. These facts indicate a defective incorporation, thereby preventing the shareholders from enjoying the protection against personal liability afforded by a properly formed corporation.

There are several other factors that will also cause the courts to ignore the legitimate existence of the corporation thereby making the shareholders personally liable. They include domination of the corporation by one shareholder, thus permitting operation as a "dummy" corporation, incorporation to evade legal restrictions, lack of minimal initial capital, and shareholder-employees of a professional corporation who are involved in negligent or wrongful conduct.

OPERATING AS A PROFESSIONAL SERVICE CORPORATION

The use of the professional corporation does not significantly alter the personal relationship that exists between the individual practitioner and his client. The professional corporation must, however, still maintain the formalities of a regular corporation. For example, most state laws provide that each shareholder-employee of a professional corporation shall be personally and fully liable for any negligent or wrongful act or misconduct committed by her or by any person under her direct supervision and control while rendering professional services on behalf of such corporation.

Note, however, that the shareholders of a professional corporation do enjoy freedom from personal liability when it involves the contractual debts and obligations of the corporation. Thus, all business contracts executed by the corporation will not subject the shareholder of the professional service corporation to personal liability.

EXAMPLE Shareholder-employees of a professional corporation will not be held liable for a rental lease executed on behalf of the corporation and naming the corporation as tenant.

WARNING *This chapter was devoted to the principle that so long as the legal corporate fiction is properly maintained and that all corporate formalities are observed, shareholder liability will be avoided in virtually all instances. However, if a shareholder, seeking to help the corporation, makes a personal guarantee of payment to a creditor, should the corporation fail to pay, then the advantage of unlimited liability vanishes. The ultimate result is the personal liability of the shareholder for this particular transaction should the corporation eventually default.*

CHAPTER 8

Financing the Corporation

INTRODUCTION

A corporation raises or obtains capital, i.e., cash, land, buildings, and operating equipment, through the issuance of shares of stock, sometimes called equity securities or capital stock. These shares represent the collective ownership in the corporation and may consist of one class of stock, called common shares, or several classes of stock, called common, common class A, common class B, etc., or preferred shares.

What the applicable RMBCA sections says *Section 1.40(21) states that "shares" mean the unit into which the proprietary interests in a corporation are divided.*

Because the capital stock is supposed to reflect the total value of the corporation's assets, the law insists that the shares be issued for equivalent value. The consideration paid by the shareholder or shareholders is recorded or credited to the corporation's capital stock or stated capital account. Thus, if $100,000 has been paid into the corporate treasury in return for stock issued, the capital of the corporation is $100,000. The corporation's balance sheet, which is a listing of a corporation's assets, liabilities, and capital (also called owners' or shareholders' equity) at a particular date (let's assume January 1, 19XX), after receipt of $100,000 in return for its common stock, would appear as follows:

THE THROCKMORTON CORPORATION
Corporate Balance Sheet
January 1, 19XX

Assets	
Cash	$100,000

Capital	
Common Stock (or Stated Capital)	$100,000

Note that while the total value of the stock issued is fixed, a corporation's net assets (assets less liabilities) will grow or shrink once business commences. If net assets grow and exceed the corporation's capital there will be a *surplus* or earned surplus. CPAs call it retained earnings. If the net assets fall below capital, the corporation is said to have a *deficit* in retained earnings.

Using the above balance sheet data, assume that Throckmorton made $50,000 in profits for the month of January, 19XX. This $50,000 resulted in additional cash of $25,000 and accounts receivable (monies owed to the corporation from sales) of $25,000. The balance sheet at the end of January would appear as follows:

THE THROCKMORTON CORPORATION
Corporate Balance Sheet
January 1, 19XX

Assets		
Cash	$125,000	
Accounts Receivable	25,000	$150,000
Capital		
Common Stock (or Stated Capital)	$100,000	
Retained Earnings (or Surplus)	50,000	$150,000

Note that corporate profits don't always automatically translate into immediate cash.

The authorized number, classes of shares that may be issued, and their rights and limitations, is found in the articles of incorporation.

What the applicable RMBCA section says *Section 6.03 states that a corporation may issue the number of shares of each class or series authorized by the articles of incorporation. Shares that are issued are outstanding shares until they are reacquired, redeemed, converted, or cancelled. Secondly, the reacquisition, redemption, or conversion of outstanding shares is subject to the limitations set forth in the RMBCA. Third, at all times that shares of the corporation are outstanding, one or more shares that together have unlimited voting rights and one or more shares that together are entitled to receive the net assets of the corporation upon dissolution must be outstanding.*

Sufficient shares should be authorized to meet both the corporation's present and future operating requirements. If the corporation issues more shares than are legally permissible, the excess number of shares issued are void.

What the applicable RMBCA section says *Section 6.01 (a) states that the articles of incorporation must prescribe the classes of shares and the number of shares of each class that the corporation is authorized to issue. If more than one class of shares is authorized, the articles of incorporation must prescribe a distinguishing designation for each class, and prior to the issuance of shares of a class, the preferences, limitations, and relative rights of that class must be described in the articles of incorpora-*

tion. All shares of a class must have preferences, limitations, and relative rights identical with those of other shares of the same class except to the extent otherwise designated in the articles of incorporation.

Secondly, the articles of incorporation must authorize (1) one or more classes of shares that together have unlimited voting rights, and (2) one or more classes of shares (which may be the same class or classes as those with voting rights) that together are entitled to receive the net assets of the corporation upon dissolution.

Shares sold by a corporation are called *issued and outstanding.* Shares authorized but not yet issued are called *unissued* shares. Ownership of the shares does not mean that the shareholders or stockholders directly owns the assets of the corporation. For example, assume that a corporation owns a delivery truck. Corporate records will list the corporation as the true owner of the truck and not the name of any particular shareholder. On the other hand, the ownership of shares entitles the shareholders to share proportionally in profits and losses, to corporate assets if there is a partial or complete liquidation, indirect control over the affairs and operations of the corporation by allowing shareholders to vote for directors, and perhaps, the right to purchase new issues of stock of the same class (called the preemptive right). As we shall see, there may also be restrictions and limitations. Thus, a share of stock is viewed as a collection of rights and restrictions in the hands of the shareholder.

Debt securities represent legal obligations that must be repaid and create a debtor (the corporation) - creditor relationship. Debt securities consist of notes and bonds issued by the corporation that must be repaid ahead of all of the common and, if there are any, the preferred shareholders in the event of liquidation of the corporation. The chief distinction between debt and stock is that the corporation is under no obligation to repay its shareholders the amounts that they have invested in the corporation, whereas, the corporation is obligated to repay all debts by various specified due dates.

If the articles of incorporation so state, the board of directors may be obligated to set up a sinking fund (a redemption fund in the hands of a trustee) to retire (or redeem) large amounts of debt, such as bonds, and to retire certain types of outstanding common and preferred stock at specified future dates.

PAID-IN CAPITAL

When a corporation receives payment for its shares in excess of its par or stated value, the excess is allocated to a capital account called paid-in capital. No such account exists where the corporation issues only no par value stock.

The board of directors can, however, elect to give no par value a definite or stated value. If this is the case, then any proceeds received in excess of the designated stated value is treated as paid-in capital.

EXAMPLE 1 $110,000 has been paid into the treasury of Zen Transit Corporation as compensation for 10,000 shares with a $10 par value stock. The corporation's balance sheet would appear as follows:

Assets		
Cash		$110,000

Capital		
Common Stock	$100,000	
Paid-In Capital	10,000	$110,000

EXAMPLE 2 Using the facts illustrated in **EXAMPLE 1**, suppose that instead the corporation issued 10,000 shares of no par value stock for the same $110,000. The corporation's balance sheet, would appear as follows:

Assets	
Cash	$110,000

Capital	
Common Stock (or Stated Capital)	$110,000

EXAMPLE 3 Using the facts illustrated in **EXAMPLE 1**, suppose that the corporation issued 10,000 shares of no par value stock, but with a stated value of $11 for the same $110,000. The corporation's balance sheet, would appear as follows:

Assets	
Cash	$110,000

Capital		
Common Stock	$100,000	
Paid-In Capital (or Stated Capital)	10,000	$110,000

The result would be the same as if the corporation issued $10 par value stock for $11 per share.

COMMON STOCK

The articles of incorporation authorize a corporation to issue several kinds of stock having varying rights, preferences, privileges, and limitations. Thus, the capital stock of a corporation usually consists of both *common stock* and *preferred stock*. Common stock represents the residual interest of the corporation, which means the common shareholders bear the risk of loss and enjoy the benefits of any profits. If a corporation issues only one class of stock, that issue is by definition common stock.

Each share of common stock represents a right to participate proportionately in the control of the corporation by exercising the right to vote on corporate matters submitted to them, the right to any dividends declared by the board of directors, and the right to distributions of corporate assets upon liquidation. Note that the common shareholder's participation in distributions due to a partial or complete corporate dissolution occurs only after payment of all claims having priority, such as to holders of debt securities (notes and bonds) and/or to preferred shareholders. Thus, all other claims against the corporation must be paid ahead of those of the common shareholders. These types of distributions are sometimes referred to as liquidating dividends, which could, under certain circumstances, be fully or partially taxable under the Internal Revenue Code.

••

OBSERVATION *If a corporation's common stock is owned by one shareholder, the number of shares authorized but unissued is immaterial for ownership purposes.*

••

In an effort to appeal to various groups of investors, a corporation can issue more than one class of stock. While classes of stock having preferential rights are called preferred stock, a corporation can accomplish the same thing by issuing two classes of common stock, Class A and Class B. In this type of situation, Class A usually has the right to vote while Class B does not. In turn, Class B stockholders have priority over the Class A shareholders when it comes to dividend payouts and distributions due to a partial or complete corporate dissolution. There are other novel strategies involving Class A and Class B common stock.

EXAMPLE 1 The Georgetown Oil Corporation was incorporated by five individuals. The articles of incorporation stipulate that the corporation is authorized to issue 10,000 shares of Class A common with the right to vote which will be issued equally to all five shareholders. The corporation is also authorized to issue 1,000,000 shares of Class B nonvoting common stock to be sold to the public in the event that the corporation is successful and wishes "to go public."

EXAMPLE 2 The articles of incorporation of Maximum Manufacturing Inc. stipulates that the corporation is authorized to issue 10,000 shares of Class A common with the exclusive right to vote for directors and will pay $1 in dividends per share annually. The corporation also plans to issue Class B shares that shall have the exclusive right to vote on all other corporate matters and will pay $2.50 annually in dividends.

In a smaller corporation, the issuance of more than one class of common stock can also be done to assure control to a minority shareholder.

EXAMPLE The Polemus Watch Corporation has three shareholders, Allen, Bates, and Charles. The corporation can issue one share of Class A Common Stock to Allen who contributes $100, two shares of Class B Common to Bates for $200, and two shares of Class C Common to Charles for $200. The shares of all three classes can have identical rights, such as the right to receive dividends if declared and the right to assets upon dissolution; the shares will only

be different in that each class will have the right to elect one director and to vote as a class on any matter requiring shareholder approval.

Both common and other classes of shareholders may be given the option to exchange their shares into common stock and vice versa. This is known as the *convertibility* feature applicable to a particular class of shares. For example, the Class A shares could be convertible into Class B shares at the option of the shareholders.

Using the technique whereby there are two classes of common stock, voting and nonvoting, is also an effective shield against takeover by another company should another group of investors attempt to acquire the corporation by purchasing a large block of the Class B common shares.

What the applicable RMBCA section says *Section 6.01 (c) states that the articles of incorporation may authorize one or more classes of shares that have special, conditional, or limited voting rights, or no right to vote, except to the extent prohibited by the RMBCA. The shares may also be redeemable or convertible as specified in the articles of incorporation at the option of the corporation or the shareholder, or another person or upon the occurrence of a designated event; for cash, indebtedness, securities, or other property; and in designated amounts or by formula. Thirdly, the articles of incorporation may also state that the shares may entitle the holders to distributions calculated in any manner, including dividends that may be cumulative, noncumulative, or partially cumulative. Finally, articles can declare that the shares may have preference over any other class of shares with respect to distributions, including dividends and distributions upon the dissolution of the corporation.*

PREFERRED STOCK

In order to permit the corporation to create unique ownership schemes when raising capital, corporate statutory laws permit the issuance of other types of stock, called preferred stock. Holders of this class of stock sacrifice certain rights, such as the right to vote in return for other special rights, such as a high dividend payment, the right to guaranteed annual dividends, and the right to convert into common stock (called convertible preferred). Preferred dividends can be cumulative, cumulative-to-the-extent-there-are-earnings, noncumulative, participating and nonparticipating, issued in a series at different dates, and convertible into common stock at the option of the holder. A corporation may also have other preferred stock classifications, such as Class A and Class B with certain rights.

EXAMPLE The incorporators of Lumen Corporation wish to raise $200,000 in capital. The articles of incorporation stipulate that 10,000 shares of $10 par value common shares are to be authorized and issued while 1,000 shares of $100 par value nonvoting preferred shares will also be issued. While $200,000 ($100,000 in common + $100,000 in preferred) in capital may ultimately be raised by the corporation, only the common shareholders, with the authority to vote, will have control over the corporation.

The rights enjoyed by each class of preferred stock must be spelled out in the articles of incorporation. For example, the annual dividend to be paid on each share of stock can be expressed in terms of specific dollar amounts ($4 per share preferred) or as a percentage of par value (4 percent preferred). Most preferred stock has a par value.

EXAMPLE The Bohemia Pottery Corporation plans to issue 10,000 shares of $100 par value preferred stock paying $5 per share annually. Alternatively, the articles of incorporation could state that each share will pay 5 percent annually meaning $5 per share ($100 × 5 percent).

Dividends on preferred stock are usually paid quarterly. A dividend, in full or in part, can only be paid if declared by the board of directors.

Other types of preferred stock can be issued by a corporation. They are as follows:

Noncumulative Preferred Stock

If a dividend is not declared on this type of stock for any given year, the obligation ceases for that particular year. The board of directors, in their discretion, can pass up the opportunity to declare a dividend for the year for various reasons, such as the reinvest-

ment of corporate funds for growth or a poor earnings record for the year.

EXAMPLE The Peterson Extrusion Corporation earned $1,000,000 in net income after taxes but decided to plow back all of the profits in a program of plant modernization. Thus, it is a reasonable and legitimate business purpose and the board of directors is under no obligation to declare a dividend to the preferred shareholders for that particular year.

Cumulative Preferred Stock

Cumulative preferred stock gives the shareholder the right to receive a dividend, usually each quarter before the payment of any common dividends. If the dividends are not paid for a particular period, they accumulate and are called dividends in arrears. The articles of incorporation can be written to provide that "the holders of preferred stock shall be entitled to cumulative dividends of 6 percent per year to be paid out of net income after federal taxes or out of retained earnings (surplus)."

EXAMPLE 1 In 19XX, the Simpson Quarry Corporation has issued 10,000 shares 5 percent cumulative $100 par value preferred stock for a total of $1,000,000. If in 19XX no dividends were paid, at the end of the year there would be preferred dividends of $50,000 (10,000 shares × $100 × 5 percent) in arrears. If the board seeks to declare dividends in 19X1, they would have to pay the arrears of $50,000 plus the 19X1 dividend before any dividends can be paid in 19X1 to the common shareholders.

EXAMPLE 2 Using the facts given in **EXAMPLE 1**, assume that in 19X1, the board of directors declare a cash dividend of $125,000. $100,000 ($50,000 + $50,000) would be paid for 19XX and 19X1 to the preferred shareholders and the balance of $25,000 would be paid to the common stockholders.

Dividends in arrears do not become an actual corporate liability until declared so by the board of directors. Of course, a corporation cannot guarantee that a dividend will be paid every year, so that the arrearages accumulate every year until paid. Since the

	Preferred Stock	Common Stock	Total
Regular dividend, preferred (5,000 shares × $8)	$40,000		$40,000
Dividend to common shareholders (25,000 shares × 4):		$100,000	100,000
Remaining $60,000 ($200,000 − $140,000):			
Preferred $\dfrac{\text{5,000 shs.}}{\text{30,000 shs.}} \times \$60,000$	10,000		10,000
Common $\dfrac{\text{25,000 shs.}}{\text{30,000 shs.}} \times \$60,000$		50,000	50,000
Total dividends	$50,000	$150,000	$200,000
Number of shares outstanding	5,000	25,000	
Dividend per share	$10.00	$6.00	

amount of arrears may influence potential investors, they should be reported in the financial statements as a footnote.

Participating Preferred Stock

Participating preferred stock allows preferred shareholders to receive additional amounts of dividends after the dividends stipulated in the articles of incorporation are paid to both the preferred and common shareholders on a ratable basis. The formula for payment can be based on either the total outstanding par value for each class of stock or on the number of shares of each class outstanding.

EXAMPLE Zinc Metals Corporation has outstanding stock composed of 5,000 shares of 8 percent, $100 par value participating preferred stock and 25,000 shares of no par common stock. The preferred stock is entitled to participate equally with the common, share for share, in any dividend distributions, which exceed the regular preferred dividend of 8 percent and a $4 per share common dividend. In 19XX, the board of directors declare dividends of $200,000 for the current year. The dividends for both the preferred and common stock will be $10 and $6, respectively, computed as shown above.

Nonparticipating Preferred Stock

Nonparticipating preferred stock is preferred stock that is entitled to its current annual dividend only, regardless of the dividends paid to the common shareholders. There is no unanimous agreement among the states as to whether nonparticipating preferred stock is cumulative or not. If the incorporators want to issue noncumulative preferred stock, it should state so in the articles of incorporation with such wording as "preferred shares issued and outstanding shall be non-participating."

Preferred Shares With a Liquidating Preference

The articles of incorporation may provide that in the event that the corporation is liquidated, the preferred shareholders are to receive assets up to a specified amount, for example, up to their par value. This preference makes the preferred shares more attractive to investors.

"Callable" or Redeemable Preferred Stock

This type of stock is subject to involuntary redemption at the option of the board of directors at a fixed price at specific future dates. The call or redemption price is usually a fixed price containing a premium above the price originally paid for the stock or its par value. The premium sometimes consists of a stated percentage of the price paid or a year's worth of dividends. When preferred stock is cumulative, all dividends in arrears must be paid in addition to any other premiums. A corporation will usually exercise its redemption privilege when it no longer needs the capital generated by the preferred stock and/or when the required dividends attributable to the preferred stock are high in relation to market conditions. The articles of incorporation can be written to include a statement, such as "the holders of any preferred stock shall be subject to a redemption of $110 per share plus any unpaid dividends in arrears."

Preferred stock cannot be redeemed when it will create a situation whereby creditors might not be paid.

EXAMPLE Major Paint Supply Inc. wishes to call in (or redeem) $500,000 of its callable preferred stock because of its high annual dividend requirement. The corporation has $500,000 in its treasury, but also owes its creditors an equal amount. The preferred stock cannot be redeemed because there is the risk that there will not be sufficient funds with which to pay the creditors.

Both the issued and outstanding common and preferred stock are presented on a corporation's balance sheet in the capital stock section.

EXAMPLE At its inception, the Tennessee Line and Tackle Corporation sold 10,000 shares of $10 par value common stock for $115,000. It also sold 1,000 shares of its noncumulative 6 percent $100 par value preferred stock for $100,000. The corporation's balance sheet would appear as follows:

Assets		
Cash		$215,000
Capital		
Preferred Stock		$100,000
Common Stock	$100,000	
Paid-In Capital	15,000	$115,000
		$215,000

Preferred Stock Issued in a Series

This technique permits a corporation to authorize a class of preferred shares that will be issued in installments over a period of time as fixed by the board of directors. This permits the corporation to sell blocks of shares in the marketplace when economic circumstances deem it most advantageous.

TAX ASPECTS REGARDING THE ISSUANCE AND SALE OF CORPORATE STOCK
Capital Gains and Losses

Eventually, a shareholder may want to dispose of his stock in the corporation. Under the Internal Revenue Code, stock held for longer than one year that is sold results in either a long-term gain or loss. This means that if the stock is sold at a gain, it cannot be taxed at a rate of more than 28 percent. Short-term capital gain (stock held for less than a year) is taxed at ordinary rates (i.e., up to a maximum rate of 39.6 percent). If the stock is sold at a loss, both long-term and short-term capital losses offset ordinary income up to $3,000 per year. Under the Internal Revenue Code, a net capital loss in excess of $3,000 can be carried over to offset future capital gains or, subject to the $3,000 annual limitation, offset against other income on a dollar-for-dollar basis until used up.

EXAMPLE For 19XX, John Varney earned $50,000 in ordinary income and sustained a long-term capital loss of $5,000. He may offset $3,000 against his current year's salary and carry forward the remaining $1,000 to be deducted in 19X1 against capital gains and ordinary income.

Section 1244 Stock

Section 1244 permits a special tax treatment for losses due to the sale of certain stock. The stock must be the common stock, voting or nonvoting, of a domestic corporation. This means that other types of stock convertible into common stock cannot qualify as Section 1244 stock. Ordinarily, stock losses are characterized as either long-term or short-term and thus, will have limited use in offsetting ordinary income. However, if the stock is "Section 1244 stock," a large part of the stock loss (up to $100,000 on a joint tax return) can be taken as an ordinary deduction if the owner of the stock is an individual or a partnership. The technique for electing the tax benefits of Section 1244 are discussed in Chap. 15.

Partial 50% Capital Gain Exclusion for Small Business Stock

A noncorporate taxpayer who holds for more than five years qualified small business stock issued after August 10, 1993, can exclude 50 percent of any gain on the investor's sale or exchange of the stock. This tax benefit is discussed in Chap. 15.

TREASURY SHARES

Sometimes the corporation reacquires outstanding shares. Outstanding shares that are reacquired by the corporation are called treasury shares. The corporation may reacquire shares for several reasons; to fund a company pension plan, to reduce the number of shareholders who have an interest in the corporation, to eliminate dissident or unhappy shareholders, to keep outsiders from gaining control of the corporation, to use the stock to acquire other companies, and for later reissuance as circumstances dictate. Treasury shares are essentially the same as unissued capital stock.

The reacquired treasury shares do not have any voting rights, nor do the shares participate in the distribution of dividends or net assets upon dissolution. Under the Internal Revenue Code, as a general rule, the sale of treasury shares by the corporation does not result in a taxable gain or deductible loss to the corporation.

STOCK SUBSCRIPTIONS AND STOCK OPTION PLANS

Corporations may have difficulty finding an individual who is willing to pay for all of the stock at once. Rather than lose a potential purchaser, the corporation may draw up a contract allowing a specified number of shares to be purchased and paid for in full or in installments as determined by the corporation's board of directors. Thus, a subscription contract provides a future corporation of assurance of capital.

Many state incorporation statutes contain provisions authorizing the board of directors to establish stock option plans as a performance incentive. A stock option plan is an agreement to issue stock at terms that are beneficial to either a certain group of employees or to all employees. Stock option plans are used by corporate employers to attract, retain, and motivate key management. A stock option plan is usually based on a company's expected favorable performance, which will usually cause the price of the stock to rise. When this occurs, the employees have the right to purchase the stock at its lower option price and then sell at the higher market price. The price at which the stock may be purchased may be its fair market value at the time of its purchase. In other cases, the stock option plan may give the employee the right to purchase stock at a future date at a fixed price. Shares that are part of an option plan cannot be voted until the option is exercised, and the stock is paid for and issued. Share options are usually evidenced by certificates known as "warrants."

What the applicable RMBCA section says *Section 6.24, governing share options, states that a corporation may issue rights, options, or warrants for the purchase of shares of the corporation. The board of directors shall determine the terms upon which the rights, options, or warrants are issued, the form and content, and the consideration for which the shares are to be issued.*

The taxation of stock option plans are largely governed by the Internal Revenue Code. If the employee exercises his option, the purchase price becomes the cost basis of the stock. If the stock is later sold at a profit, and certain other conditions mandated by the Internal Revenue Code are met, the profits are taxed as long-term capital gain at rates no greater than 28 percent.

PREEMPTIVE RIGHTS

Frequently, the board of directors of an existing corporation will issue additional shares to finance corporate expansion and operations. These new shares might be the result of a new authorization or due to an amendment to the articles of incorporation. In this particular situation, existing shareholders may enjoy "preemptive rights." Preemptive rights allow an existing shareholder to purchase a new issue of shares in proportion to the amount of shares that he currently owns before it is offered to others. Thus, if the shareholder owns 1,000 common shares out of 10,000 common shares outstanding, he is permitted to purchase 10 percent of the new issue.

As a general rule, holders of one class of stock do not have a preemptive right to acquire the shares of another class of stock to be issued. The certificate of incorporation may also specifically deny or limit preemptive rights. Thus, the board of directors may have to amend the articles of incorporation to specifically authorize this type of shareholder option.

What the applicable RMBCA section says *Section 6.30, governing preemptive rights, states that the shareholders of a corporation do not have the preemptive right to acquire the corporation's new issues except to the extent that the articles of incorporation so provide. However, a statement in the articles that "the corporation elects to have preemptive rights" (or words of similar import) means that the shareholders have a preemptive right.*

EXAMPLE 1 During 19XX, the Mason Brick and Mortar Corporation, with an authorization of 10,000 $1 par value common stock, has issued 9,000 of its $1 par value Class A Common shares. Roland Hook, a shareholder owning 15 percent of the outstanding common shares, demands the right to subscribe to the rest of the shares in proportion to his present holdings. Since the remaining 1,000 common shares do not represent a new issue, Roland cannot exercise any preemptive right.

EXAMPLE 2 Using the facts in **EXAMPLE 1**, assume that in December 19XX, the corporation authorizes the issuance of 10,000 shares of Class B Common shares. Since this is a newly authorized issue, Roland may exercise his preemptive rights in proportion to his current percentage of ownership. Thus, Roland has a preemptive right to purchase 15 percent of the newly authorized stock.

Preemptive rights do not apply to treasury stock nor to shares covered by option plans offering stock to directors, officers, and key employees.

OBSERVATION *A closely held corporation owned by a small group of shareholders might find the utilization of preemptive rights useful in maintaining control of the corporation. By exercising their rights to participate in the issuance of any newly authorized shares, they are in a position to maintain their proportional ownership in the existing corporation.*

If shares of the corporation are expected to be widely held or of different classes, it might be wise to prohibit the use of preemptive rights to avoid unforseen problems regarding the exercise of any rights.

CONSIDERATION FOR WHICH CAPITAL STOCK CAN BE ISSUED

For the protection of creditors and any existing stockholders, shares can only be issued for equivalent value. This means that par value stock, or stated value, can only be issued for its full value in cash, tangible and intangible property, or services already performed for the corporation. As previously noted, stock cannot be sold for less than its par value, or at a discount. Generally, neither the promise of rendering future services to the corporation, the issuance of notes payable in the future, nor the rendering of preincorporation services, represents valid consideration.

EXAMPLE 1 An attorney forms a corporation. Her basic legal fee for forming a corporation is $1,500 but she accepts 150 shares of $10 par value common stock in return for her services. The value of her services paid for by the issuance of the corporation's $10 par value common stock is based on the honest judgment of the board of directors. Absent fraud or capriciousness on the part of the board, the value of the consideration received for the stock cannot be challenged by any creditor or other stockholder.

EXAMPLE 2 The Silver Diecast Corporation issued ten shares of its $10 par value common stock to Martin in return for his note promising to pay $100 in one month. Thus, it is a mere promise to pay and is not valid consideration.

Once par value stock has been issued, the purchasing stockholder can eventually resell it for any price the selling shareholder is able to obtain. On the other hand, if the issuing corporation were to repurchase the stock, it can do so and the stock, in the hands of the purchasing corporation, becomes treasury stock. The corporation can then resell the stock again for any discretionary value without regard to any par of stated value.

No par value stock can be issued for any consideration representing the fair market value of the stock as determined by the board of directors or if the articles of incorporation so provided, by the shareholders.

....

What the applicable RMBCA section says *Section 6.21 (b) states that the board of directors may authorize shares to be issued for consideration consisting of any tangible or intangible property for the benefit of the corporation, including cash, promissory notes, services performed, contracts for service to be performed, or other securities of the corporation.*
....

THE SALE OF DEBT INSTRUMENTS TO FINANCE THE NEW CORPORATION

As previously stated, the sale of stock represents ownership and entitles the shareholder to a share of earnings, control of the business, and a proportionate share of assets in case of liquidation. However, in some situations, a corporation may want to resort to debt financing (the issuance of bonds and notes payable) for such matters as financing operations on a short-term basis or as a source of funds for large financial commitments, such as the purchase of land and buildings. The use of debt is also a useful technique for a small corporation in a situation where the shareholders do not wish to dilute their control over the corporation by issuing additional shares of stock. When used by a corporation, debt financing creates a debtor (corporation) and creditor (lender) relationship. Bonds issued by a corporation are generally governed by an indenture or trust agreement. The indenture generally contains the basic terms of the issuance, the face or par value of the bonds (i.e., $1,000, $5,000, $10,000), the rate of interest to be paid (i.e., a "coupon" rate of 6 percent annually or 3

percent every six months), the maturity date of the issuance, whether the bonds are secured, any conversion features, and whether the corporation is required to set up a bond sinking fund to redeem the bonds at their maturity date. Most bond issues also have a call feature. This feature gives the corporation a chance to buy back and retire the bonds at a given price, usually above their face value, before maturity. These callable bonds give the corporation a great deal of financial flexibility. If the market rate of interest on loans drops below the rate being paid on the bonds, the corporation can exercise their call option and buy back the costly bonds. They can later issue new bonds at a lower price.

....

OBSERVATION *Convertible bonds, like all other bonds, carry the benefit of having priority of repayment before all preferred and common shareholders. There is also the additional opportunity to convert to preferred or common stock should the possibility of potential stock appreciation occur thereby causing a conversion from bond to stock ownership. In view of the speculative nature of the bonds, the articles of incorporation must contain an authorized amount sufficient to cover the possible conversion of all bonds in stock.*
....

Notes can also be issued on either a short-term or long-term basis. When issuing notes, the lending contract names the parties involved, a description of the debt, the rate of interest to be paid, and whether the loan is secured by company assets (called a secured loan), by a shareholder's personal guarantee, or both.

One basic distinction between debt and stock, or equity ownership, is that there is no obligation to repay the shareholder at any time in the future, whereas the corporation is legally bound to ultimately repay the debt. Secondly, debt instruments are required to pay interest annually, which is tax deductible by the corporation. Dividend payments are not tax deductible because they represent a distribution of profits and not a cost of financing.

The authority to borrow money is generally not stated in the articles of incorporation but falls within the general authority of the board of directors who manage the affairs of the corporation. However, the articles of incorporation might contain provisions that restrict the power of the board to incur debt. These restrictions might include what percentage of corporate assets may be pledged as security for the loans and the requirement that all borrowings by the corporation above a certain amount, i.e., $500,000, be approved by a majority or all of the shareholders. These restrictions are generally upheld by courts if they are deemed reasonable.

Note that in case of a corporation liquidation, the creditors who own notes and bonds issued by the corporation have priority over all shareholders.

CONVERTIBLE SHARES AND DEBT INSTRUMENTS

A convertible security is a security that can, by its terms, be exchanged for other securities, i.e., bonds convertible into preferred stock or common stock (i.e., $1,000 shares of $1 par value common received by shareholder in exchange for one $1,000 bond), or preferred stock convertible into common stock according to some predetermined ratio. The conversion is generally at the option of the owner of the security. Conversion privileges for holders of both shares of stock and bonds are found in the articles of incorporation. Some states permit bondholders to convert their bonds into either common or preferred shares upon the happening of some specific event, such as the failure to make an interest payment to the bondholders at the specified due date. If an individual converts bonds into additional shares or one class of shares is converted into another class (i.e., preferred shares into common), the securities received by the corporation generally revert to the status of authorized but unissued.

EXECUTING AND ISSUING THE SHARES

Generally, shares are not issued until fully paid for. They may bear the corporate seal but are usually signed by two or more corporate officers, such as the president and vice president or corporate secretary and treasurer. State statutes usually require corporations to maintain records of their shareholders in their stockholder ledger accounts showing names and addresses and the number and classes of stock held. The record book is normally open to reasonable inspection by directors, officers, and shareholders. For legal purposes, the name in the corporate records is conclusive evidence of stock ownership.

THE DUTY OF THE ISSUING CORPORATION TO REGISTER STOCK CERTIFICATES

The Uniform Commercial Code, or UCC, which is the law in virtually all states, contains the rules that govern the registration of stock certificates. The UCC sets forth the conditions that must be satisfied before the issuer is required to register the securities. The conditions that must be met in order to register the securities are as follows:

1. The securities must be properly indorsed,
2. There must be reasonable assurance that the indorsements are genuine,
3. The issuer has no duty to inquire into adverse claims,
4. The applicable tax laws have been complied with and
5. The transfer, pledge, or release is in fact rightful.

Where the above preconditions are satisfied, the issuing corporation must register the transfer of stock or risk being held liable for damages for the wrongful refusal to do so. Conversely, an issuer may refuse to register the securities where any precondition is not met.

CHAPTER 9

Corporate Management Structure: The Role of Directors

INTRODUCTION

Since the corporation is a legal fiction, it can only operate through its agents who are composed of its board of directors, officers, and designated employees. An agent is one who is given the authority to act on behalf of another. While ultimate control of the corporation rests with the shareholders, actual conduct of the corporation's affairs is delegated by the shareholders to duly elected corporate directors.

• •

What the applicable RMBCA sections say *Section 8.01 states that except as provided by a shareholder agreement (discussed in Chap. 11), each corporation must have a board of directors. In addition, all corporate powers shall be exercised by or under the authority of, and the business and affairs of the corporation managed under the direction of, its board of directors, subject to any limitation set forth in the articles of incorporation or in a previously executed shareholder agreement.*

Section 8.03 of the RMBCA states that a board of directors must consist of one or more individuals, with the number specified in or fixed in accordance with the articles of incorporation or bylaws.

If a board of directors has power to fix or change the number of directors, the board may increase or decrease by 30 percent or less the number of directors last approved by the shareholders, but only the shareholders

may increase or decrease by more than 30 percent the number of directors last approved by the shareholders.

The articles of incorporation or bylaws may establish a variable range for the size of the board of directors by fixing a minimum and maximum number of directors. If a variable range is established, the number of directors may be fixed or changed from time to time, within the minimum and maximum, by the shareholders or the board of directors. After shares are issued, only the shareholders may change the range for the size of the board or change from a fixed to a variable-range size board or vice versa.

Finally, directors are to be elected at the first annual shareholders meeting and at each annual meeting thereafter unless their terms are staggered.
• •

The directors, operating *as a board and not as individuals,* have the supreme power of control and broad operating authority over the corporation. Their authority is exercised at a properly convened meeting of the board. As a general rule, the articles of incorporation cannot limit the authority or qualifications of directors to manage the business if it is a publicly listed corporation. However, some state statutes permit the "sterilization" or restriction of the authority of the board of directors of a nonpublic, or closely held corporation. This limitation must be set forth in the articles of incorporation. This provision relieves the directors of liability due to their negligence while in office and instead makes shareholders totally liable. This limitation, in effect nullifying the authority of the directors, must also be noted conspicuously on the face or back of every voting and nonvoting stock certificate issued by the corporation.

EXAMPLE A provision in the certificate of incorporation of Salvo Sales Corporation, a closely held corporation, transfers the board of directors' authority to manage the corporation to all of the shareholders. All of the incorporators and all of the existing shareholders are aware of this provision and have approved. The issued shares also contain notification of the transfer of the directors' authority to the shareholders on the front of every certificate. This arrangement is valid and nullifies the shareholders' benefit of limited liability with respect to any negligent acts or illegal acts authorized by them. Their liability arises from the fact that it is now the shareholders of the closely held corporation, and not the directors, who are initiating and approving corporate actions.

Both the articles of incorporation and/or the bylaws can prescribe qualifications for serving as a board member.

EXAMPLE The articles of incorporation of Freemont Financial Corporation Ltd., a closely held nonpublic corporation, requires that there be at least five directors, that each board member own at least 10 percent of the outstanding shares, and that two board members be officers of the corporation. The remaining three members must not be employees of the corporation. The articles of incorporation also requires that no nonemployee director be an attorney connected with or associated with a banking institution doing business with the corporation.

The basic structure of the corporation appears as follows:

It should be noted that by selecting directors whose views and business philosophy mirror that of the shareholders, the shareholders indirectly control the corporation's affairs. Thus, certain groups of shareholders, who own large blocks of stock, can influence the management of the corporation by electing directors sympathetic to certain stockholder interests, thereby shaping and controlling the composition of the board.

RELATIONSHIP OF DIRECTORS TO CORPORATION

Although the directors are selected by the shareholders, once elected, they serve the corporation, and not the stockholders. The directors guide the general policies of the corporation. The directors' position is one of a fiduciary (or trustee on behalf of the corporation) and owe a duty of loyalty only to the corporation. This means that their business decisions must take into account the best interests of the corporation and must not reflect personal motivation or self-interest.

EXAMPLE The directors of Formica Tops Inc. are seeking land on which to construct their new manufacturing facility. Marsha Collins, a director of Formica, is aware that her brother Norville owns land that would make a suitable plant site. The fair market value of the property is $10,000. Marsha, as director, and without notifying the remaining board members that the seller is her brother, induces the remaining directors to purchase the land for $50,000, thereby benefiting her brother. Marsha has breached her fiduciary duty to Formica. Upon discovering the facts, Formica, through its other directors, may sue Marsha to recover any excess purchase price, in this case, $40,000.

Note that in the above example, the corporate director will most likely be removed from her place on the board due to breach of her fiduciary duty.

Since the directors' responsibilities are fiduciary in nature, they cannot permit another party to attend directors' meetings in their place. Thus, directors cannot vote by proxy. A proxy is a grant of authority given by one individual to another to vote in his place (see Chap. 11).

EXAMPLE Arthur Daniel is elected a director of the Macro Tube Corporation. He cannot attend the first meeting of the directors so he sends his attorney in his place. This act is in violation of his fiduciary responsibilities because he has no authority to delegate his functions as a director to third parties, even though the individual appointed may be equal to or even better qualified than the director to serve in such capacity.

What the applicable RMBCA sections says *Section 8.60, governing conflicting interests, states that a conflicting interest means the interest a director of the corporation has with respect to the proposed transaction involving the corporation. Sections 8.61, 8.62, and 8.63 state any transaction in which a director (and even an officer) has an interest are voidable by the corporation unless the transaction is either fair to the corporation or is approved, ratified, or authorized by a vote of the disinterested directors or shareholders after full disclosure of all the relevant facts.*

NUMBER AND QUALIFICATION OF DIRECTORS

Traditionally, shareholders select board members from their own ranks. Usually, a director must be at least 18 years old. While state statutes do not place a maximum on the number of directors that a corporation may have, most state statutes prescribe a minimum of three. Some state statutes now permit one or two directors where there are only one or two shareholders. In other states, a single incorporator can designate herself as the sole director. A shareholder is sometimes also a director but this is not a necessary

requirement to be a director unless the articles of incorporation or bylaws require such ownership.

OBSERVATION *To lessen the chance of a deadlock in matters brought before the board, it is preferable to have an odd number of directors.*

As previously stated, the authority of the directors to act is vested in the entire board. In most states, the "entire board" means the number of directors in office if there are no vacancies. The number of directors permitted to serve may be fixed by the articles of incorporation, the bylaws, or by action of the shareholders and may be changed by a vote of the "entire board."

What the applicable RMBCA section says *Section 8.02 states that the articles of incorporation or bylaws may prescribe qualifications for directors. A director need not be a resident of this state or a shareholder of the corporation unless the articles of incorporation or bylaws so prescribe.*

OBSERVATION *Many professional ethics pronouncements prevent outside professionals doing business with the corporation from serving on the board. For example, the independent certified public accountant who renders an opinion regarding the financial condition of the corporation cannot serve on the board since her membership would impugn her creditability as an independent evaluator of the financial condition of the corporation.*

DIRECTORS: HOW CHOSEN

While the original directors are named in the articles of incorporation, they usually serve as "dummies" who then resign when the shareholders select their successors at the first meeting of the shareholders. A director whose term has expired generally continues to serve until a successor is chosen at a special meeting called for this purpose or at the next annual meeting of the stockholders. A valid annual shareholder meeting to elect a director requires a *quorum* of shares present. A quorum means the majority of shares entitled to vote. Once the quorum is present, the meeting will not be terminated if one of the shareholders leaves. Usually, each share of voting stock is entitled to one vote.

EXAMPLE 1 The Thompson Asphalt Co. Ltd. has 100 common stock shareholders. Seventy-five shareholders show up at the annual shareholders meeting. One hour later, thirty shareholders leave. This is a valid shareholder meeting since a quorum (majority entitled to vote) was initially present.

EXAMPLE 2 The board of directors of Hancock Fruit Inc. is composed of nine members. Six members show up at the first directors meeting and ratify an important contract. The corporation's articles of incorporation and bylaws contain no provision relating to quorum requirements. A quorum is present and the ratification is valid.

In some states, all directors can be chosen by a plurality (meaning the largest number of votes cast) of the shareholder votes cast providing that there is a quorum present.

EXAMPLE The Ludwig Supply Ltd. has 100 common stock shareholders. Seventy-five shareholders show up at the annual shareholders meeting. Three directors must be chosen out of a list of ten candidates. Candidate A gets 30 votes, Candidate B gets 20 votes, and candidate C gets 15 votes. The remaining shareholders vote for the other available candidates. Since Candidates A, B, and C have received the largest amount of votes, they have been elected directors at the valid shareholder meeting.

The term "plurality" is not to be confused with majority, which means receiving more than half of the votes cast. Some states require a majority of the votes cast in order to elect a director.

The selection of directors may also be staggered. For example, the articles of incorporation may have one third of the directors elected to three-year terms. This allows for greater continuity and less disruption regarding the functioning of the corporation.

In a closely held corporation, it is sometimes mandated in the articles of incorporation that all shareholders be present at a shareholder meeting in order to constitute a quorum so that directors can be elected. The danger here is deadlock, in that the mere absence of a single shareholder can stymie the corporation's ability to elect a viable and functioning board of directors. Thus this technique is dangerous and should be avoided.

Once elected, a director always has the power to resign by tendering his resignation. The resignation will not however, relieve her from liability for any gross negligence or other fraudulent acts committed while serving on the board.

PRINCIPAL DUTIES AND POWERS OF DIRECTORS

A director has one vote, and generally, the majority rules. Corporate directors, acting as a collective board and not as individuals, hire and fire corporate officers, i.e., the president and vice president establish director and officer compensation, set corporate policy regarding product and service pricing, oversee major contract negotiations, make decisions regarding the declaration and payment of dividends, obtain corporate financing, enter into borrowing arrangements, execute the issuance of notes and bonds, authorize the purchase and sale of major corporate assets, and commence lawsuits against third parties.

The board may hire outside consultants to assist in the management of the corporation so long as the board retains ultimate supervisory authority.

A director has an absolute right to inspect the corporate books and records that can be enforced in a court of law. Should a director abuse this right, she is subject to damages for breach of her fiduciary duty. She may also be removed from the board.

EXAMPLE Selena Troy owns 15 percent of the voting common shares of the Down Corporation. She heads up a group of shareholders who are dissatisfied with the performance of the current board and opposes their reelection in 19XX. Selena has asked for a list of the shareholders so she can procure their proxies. Down's board of directors refuses her request. Selena can go to court to force the board to give her the list. The acquisition of the list for the solicitation of proxies is a legitimate business reason.

Directors generally have the authority to designate executive committees composed of at least two directors, to exercise board authority in such matters as executive compensation, employee pension and retirement benefits, and accounting principles to be adopted by the corporation. Executive committees generally do not have the power to approve basic fundamental changes in the operation of the corporation, such as a merger or consolidation with another corporation. Delegation of authority to the executive committee does not, however, relieve the entire board of directors of any liability with respect to any decisions made by the committee.

While directors generally have the authority to designate executive committees, they do not have the power to delegate policy-making and discretionary powers to corporate officers.

What the applicable RMBCA section says *Section 8.25 states that unless the articles of incorporation or bylaws provide otherwise, a board of directors may create one or more committees and appoint members of the board of directors to serve on them. Each committee must have two or more members who serve at the pleasure of the board of directors. The committees may function pursuant to powers granted by the board, but do not have the power to authorize distributions, approve a plan of merger, adopt, amend, or repeal bylaws, or fill vacancies on the board of directors or on any committee.*

TIME AND PLACE OF DIRECTORS MEETINGS

Meetings of the board, whether regular, special, or annual, may be held at any designated place either within or outside the state of incorporation unless otherwise provided for in the articles of incorporation or bylaws.

What the applicable RMBCA section says *Section 8.01, governing directors meetings, states as follows that the board of directors may hold irregular or special meetings in or out of this state. Second, unless the articles of incorporation or bylaws provide otherwise, the board of directors may permit any or all directors to participate in a regular or special meeting by, or conduct the meeting through the use of, any means of communication by which all directors participating may simultaneously hear each other during the meeting. A director participating in a meeting by this means is deemed to be present in person at the meeting.*

HOW A BOARD OF DIRECTORS MEETING FUNCTIONS

In general, the vote of the majority of the directors present if a quorum (the minimum number of directors that must be present before business can be transacted) is present, constitutes an act of the board.

What the applicable RMBCA section says *Section 8.24, governing directors' quorum and voting, states that unless the articles of incorporation or bylaws require a greater number, a quorum of a board of directors shall consist of a majority of the fixed number of directors if the corporation has a fixed board size; or majority of a defined number of directors are present. The articles of incorporation or bylaws may authorize a quorum of directors to consist of no fewer than one third of a fixed or defined number of directors.*

Note that some very small corporations think that these meetings are unnecessary. They are wrong.

The board of directors generally meet once a month. Smaller corporations may find that a meeting every three to six months, or even annually is legally sufficient to take care of any old, current, or new business. Special meetings can be called if demanded by unusual circumstances. Directors may also participate in meetings by means of a conference call or other similar procedure so long as they can hear one another. A corporation may also be bound for the actions taken by the board even if there has been no actual meeting.

EXAMPLE Lawrence Behr, a member of the board of directors of the Premier Fuel Corporation negotiated with the Star Real Estate Ltd. for newer and larger office quarters. No formal board meeting was held regarding the authorization and signing of the contract, but a majority of Premier's other board members were aware of the transaction and knew that larger office space was needed but never voiced their objections to the deal. The facts indicate that there was ratification or acquiescence of the contract by the board.

The date of any regular directors meetings are found in the articles of incorporation or bylaws. Minutes are kept of the meeting by an officer of the corporation, usually the corporate secretary.

OBSERVATION *Some articles of incorporation require a unanimous vote of all of the directors in order to validate any action taken by the board of directors. This type of provision is dangerous in that it can lead to "the tyranny of one" whereby one director will refuse to validate the actions approved by the remaining members of the board unless his demands are met.*

DIRECTORS' COMPENSATION

Directors have the authority to fix their own compensation. With the increased risk of possible shareholders' lawsuits for mismanagement, directors' compensation has shown a noticeable increase. Directors fees are fully taxable for federal tax purposes.

What the applicable RMBCA section says *Section 8.11 states that unless the articles of incorporation or bylaws provide otherwise, the board of directors may fix the compensation of directors.*

LIABILITY OF DIRECTORS FOR INDIVIDUAL AND BOARD ACTIONS

Corporate directors have traditionally been held personally liable for gross negligence only and not for normal errors of business judgment.

What the applicable RMBCA section says *Section 8.30, governing the general standards of conduct applicable to directors, states that a director shall discharge his duties as a director, including his duties as a member of a committee, in good faith, with the care of an ordinarily prudent person in a similar position, and in a manner that he believes to be in the best interests of the corporation. In discharging his duties, the director is entitled to rely on the information, opinions, reports, and statements presented by other corporate officers, other employees, legal counsel, public accountants, and other experts. A director shall not be liable for any action taken as a director, or for any failure to take action if he performs his duties in compliance with this section.*

Thus, under the so-called business judgment rule, a corporate director or officer can usually avoid liability for poor business judgments. Directors can also be held liable if they knowingly, or even unknowingly, authorize the corporation to engage in ultra vires acts (acts beyond the scope of the corporation), and for the corporation's failure to comply with federal and/or state laws and regulations. They may also be subject to criminal penalties. Liability has also been found when the directors declare improper dividends.

EXAMPLE Martin Bonner, a certified public accountant and director of the Worthington Pump Co. Ltd., voted with the corporation's board to declare a dividend that was in fact illegal. The shareholders can remove him for negligence in office and hold him liable for damages. As a CPA, he should have known that the dividend was illegal.

Directors are also held accountable after being put on notice of possible wrongdoing or negligent acts by corporate employees if they fail to investigate.

EXAMPLE The board of directors of Purifoy Carton Corporation authorized Max Samson, its president, to sell one of the corporation's buildings, a major asset. It appeared that the president subsequently entered into a contract whereby the building was sold at half its alleged true value to his father. Several shareholders complained to the board, which, in turn, failed to investigate the allegations. Finally, one of the complaining shareholders hired an independent real estate firm, which verified the fact that the building was sold at a price far below its true market value. The directors will be held liable for failing to investigate the questionable acts of one of its key corporate employees after being put on notice.

Directors who *personally* guarantee the faithful contracts and other obligations in their own capacity as private individuals are personally liable.

EXAMPLE Vera Tow was a director of the India Spice Corp. Ltd. The corporation was in financial difficulties and the corporate treasurer asked Vera to personally guarantee all contracts for the purchase of goods. Fearing that the corporation would go bankrupt if it was unable to purchase its inventory, Vera personally signed all subsequent corporate contracts as guarantor. Unfortunately, the corporation was unable to pay for the goods, and Vera was forced to pay out of her own pocket. Of course, Vera can always seek reimbursement from the corporation, which under the circumstances appears highly unlikely.

Directors may, however, engage in independent business so long as these activities do not compete with the corporation's business.

While corporate directors may be held accountable for gross negligence and other acts of noncompliance with various laws, courts rarely interfere with a decision of the board unless fraud or intentional wrong can be shown. Courts cannot force directors to act wisely, but they can compel them to act honestly.

Thus, as more and more corporations find themselves in financial difficulties due to poor management performance, there is an increasing tendency by shareholders to sue the directors for their mistakes. Many directors are now finding themselves at greater risk if they choose to serve on a corporate board. As a result of their increased legal exposure, most corporations maintain insurance polices that indemnify the directors for damages that may result from adverse judgments. In effect, by paying the insurance premiums, the corporation is indirectly agreeing to reimburse the directors for any liabilities associated with their performance as directors.

Corporate policy regarding indemnification for the costs of defending a lawsuit, as well as repayment for any adverse judgments rendered against a director, is found in the corporation's articles of incorporation and its bylaws.

....
What the applicable RMBCA section says *Section 8.51, which governs corporation indemnification for a director's legal costs, fees, and judgments, states that a corporation may indemnify an individual made a party to a proceeding because he is a director if the director conducted himself in good faith and reasonably believed that he was acting in the best interests of the corporation. He may also be reimbursed in the case of any criminal proceeding if he had no reasonable cause to believe that his conduct was unlawful.*
....

HOW TO AVOID DIRECTORS' DEADLOCK

Dissension and directors' deadlock is very common in a closely held corporation. In a typical closely held corporation, the shareholders elect themselves both directors and officers, and friction and distrust is commonplace. A deadlock usually occurs when there are an equal number of directors who have split their votes equally on a corporate matter thereby preventing the corporation from functioning. The result is potential chaos and possible bankruptcy to a profitable corporation. There are, however, mechanisms that can be utilized to prevent directors' deadlock from permanently harming the corporation.

One such technique is the buy-sell agreement whereby all the parties agree either in advance or at the time the deadlock occurs that one faction should buy out the other at a fair price. Often it is the senior directors who will buy out the junior members. A second possibility is to have one of the shareholders set a price at which he is willing to repurchase the stock of the other shareholders. Buy-sell agreements are discussed in Chaps. 15 and 16.

A third possibility is to simply dissolve the corporation. For dissolution to occur, there must be a directors' deadlock that the shareholders are unable to break that will eventually cause the corporation irreparable damage and possibly force it into bankruptcy. Corporate dissolution is discussed in detail in Chap. 13.

A fourth possibility is to submit the issue causing the deadlock to an arbitrator. The advantages of arbitration are that it is quick, inexpensive, and informal as opposed to a court proceeding.

Finally, the parties can agree in advance that where there is an even number of directors and the split is 50/50, the parties shall petition a court of proper jurisdiction to appoint a provisional director who will determine the facts and render a decision, thereby breaking the deadlock.

UNAUTHORIZED ACTS: THE ULTRA VIRES DOCTRINE

Operating as a director carries not only a duty of loyalty to the corporation, but the concurrent duty to act within the legal confines of the articles of incorporation. Most corporate articles give the corporation broad operating powers that also carry the implied power to undertake any transaction that is incident to the normal operation of the corporation. Unfortunately, a corporation may enter into a transaction that is beyond the legal authority of the corporation. Such acts are termed *ultra vires* acts, meaning beyond the authority of the corporation to act. Ultra vires acts are not necessarily illegal, but an illegal act would automatically be ultra vires.

EXAMPLE Klondike Soda Distributors Inc., purchased 10,000 cases of vodka for resale. State statutes require that a corporation engaged in the wholesale purchase and resale of beer, wine, and spirits have a liquor license. In addition, all corporate officers must be licensed by the state liquor authority to sell such products. Officers receive their licenses after an extensive personal background check. Since the corporation has not met state legal standards, the purchase of the vodka is unauthorized, illegal, and ultra vires.

OBSERVATION *A corporation is prohibited from making political contributions in federal elections by the Federal Elections Campaign Act of 1974 (18 United States Code Section 321). Such contributions are unlawful and carry severe civil penalties for both the board of directors and the corporation.*

What the applicable RMBCA section says *Section 3.04, which governs ultra vires acts, states that:*

a. *Except as provided in section (b) below, the validity of corporate action may not be challenged on the ground that the corporation lacks or lacked power to act.*

b. *A corporation's power to act may be challenged:*

1. *in a proceeding by a shareholder against the corporation to prevent the ultra vires act;*

2. *in a proceeding by the corporation, directly, derivatively, or through a receiver, trustee, or other legal representative, against an incumbent or former director, officer, employee, or agent of the corporation; or*

3. *in a proceeding by the Attorney General for fraudulent or illegal acts.*

c. *In a shareholder's proceeding to prevent an unauthorized corporate act, the court may prevent or set aside the act, if equitable to all the parties to the proceeding, and may award damages for loss (other than anticipated profits) suffered by the corporation or another party because of the prevention of the unauthorized act.*

CHAPTER 10

Corporate Management Structure: The Role of the Officers

INTRODUCTION

Corporate officers are hired by the board of directors. In certain instances, the articles of incorporation may provide that the shareholders and not the directors have the authority to hire corporate officers. (See Chap. 9.) Although in the general sense the board of directors are the definitive administrators of corporation policy, the corporate officers are the true agents of the corporation. Each officer has the authority to bind the corporation for the day-to-day acts within the officer's actual or apparent authority.

EXAMPLE 1 Martha Fray is a major shareholder and director of the Wisconsin Sales Corporation. She hires Johanna Norton as vice president of sales and signs her to a two-year contract. Norton is aware that Fray is not a corporate officer but accepts the employment anyway. Xavier Hollis, president of the corporation, repudiates the agreement, and Norton sues. The corporation will prevail because an individual who is a director has no actual or apparent authority to bind the corporation.

EXAMPLE 2 Suppose that in **EXAMPLE 1**, Norton was unaware that Fray was not a corporate officer and acted in good faith in accepting employment. Since it appeared that Fray acted within her apparent authority as a corporate "officer," Norton will pre-

vail in a subsequent lawsuit for breach of her employment contract.

ELECTION OF OFFICERS: PERIOD OF SERVICE

Officers serve for a period as fixed by the articles of incorporation or bylaws. Unless the articles of incorporation or bylaws state otherwise, corporate officers generally serve for one year. They may also be removed during this period with or without cause by the board of directors.

EXAMPLE Felton Smith is hired as president of Kimble Threads Inc. for a period of one year. After six months, Kimble's board meets and determines that Smith's performance as president is unsatisfactory and removes him. The board has exercised their legal prerogative of removal. Of course, there is always the likelihood that Smith will sue for unlawful breach of his employment contract claiming that he was terminated without just cause.

An officer elected by the shareholders cannot be removed by the board, although the board does have the authority to suspend the officer's powers for cause. On the other hand, an officer elected by the shareholders may be removed with or without cause by a vote of the shareholders.

EXAMPLE William Hyams was president of the Radcliffe Laser Disc Corporation. He held his position by a vote of the shareholders. The corporation was having financial difficulties selling its products due to tough competition from other forms of entertainment. Therefore, Hyams formed the Cleveland Sound Corporation making himself the sole shareholder. Cleveland then used a "front man," and acting as its president negotiated a contract whereby Radcliffe sold laser discs to Cleveland at a 50 percent discount, well below their regular wholesale price. He also kept Radcliffe's board of directors in complete ignorance about the financial terms of the contract. Upon discovery, the board had the authority to suspend him from office for cause and to seek his eventual removal.

If no successor has been appointed, a corporate officer holds over and continues to serve in office until re-election or appointment of a new officer.

QUALIFICATIONS OF A CORPORATE OFFICER

There are no statutory qualifications for being a corporate officer. However, the articles of incorporation or bylaws may require that an officer be either a director or own a stated number of the corporation's shares. Some states permit an officer to hold more than one office but other states may have limitations. For example, New York State statutes permit two or more offices to be held by the same person except for the offices of president and secretary.

DESIGNATION OF CORPORATE OFFICERS

The usual corporate officers appointed by the board are the president, vice president, secretary, treasurer, and general manager. In addition, the nature of the corporation's business may require additional corporate officers, such as assistant treasurers, and auditors. Subordinate officers, pursuant to the corporate bylaws, are usually appointed by senior officers.

The President

The president usually has the authority to manage the business of the corporation. These dealings include the signing of contracts, stock certificates, checks, notes, hiring key personnel, institute corporate litigation, and making all other commitments on behalf of the corporation. However, absent specific authority from the board of directors, the president does not have the authority to make unusual or extraordinary contracts. Some corporations refer to the president as the "CEO" or "chief executive officer" but use of this imprecise title varies from corporation to corporation.

EXAMPLE Francine Whitman, president of the Alluvia Paper and Timber Co. Inc. entered into a contract with Sturdevant Real Estate Corporation to sell all of its timberlands to Sturdevant. Without these valuable lands, Alluvia cannot continue to operate. This extraordinary contract, absent authority from the board of directors, is beyond the authority of the president to execute.

The Vice President

Although the vice president has no authority in his individual capacity, he is empowered to act in place of the president in case of the latter's death, illness, or incapacity. The vice president may also be authorized to perform additional duties and may also be subject to certain restrictions as stated in the corporation's bylaws.

EXAMPLE Calvin Cooler is vice president of Seaforth Towel Co. Ltd. Calvin, although an officer, was not a director. The bylaws of the corporation required that any person holding the office of president must also be a director. Upon the death of the president of the corporation, Calvin would be unable to become president due to the restriction in the bylaws.

OBSERVATION *Where the bylaws require that the president also be a director, removal from the board would automatically disqualify the president from continuing in such capacity.*

The Corporate Secretary

The corporate secretary exercises authority equal to that of a general manager. In her limited role, she usually attends all corporate meetings, keeps minutes, distributes corporate notices, certifies corporate records, and has possession of the corporate seal when the circumstances dictate. Unless specifically given such authority, the corporate secretary has no right to enter into contracts on behalf of the corporation.

The Corporate Treasurer

The corporate treasurer is the chief financial officer of the corporation. As chief custodian of the corporate funds, she is frequently designated to countersign notes, checks, miscellaneous corporate instruments, and stock certificates. She also has the duty to see the corporate records are accurately kept to insure the faithful reporting of the corporation's financial condition. The corporate treasurer, like the corporate secretary, cannot enter into contracts on behalf of the corporation.

The General Manager

The role of the general manager is to administer the ordinary business of the corporation. Her general functions include hiring and firing employees, setting their compensation, purchasing materials and supplies, and paying corporate debts. If the corporation is a small corporation, the directors or shareholders may have narrowed these functions. The office of general manager requires no formal appointment board of directors and is usually appointed by the president of the corporation.

Unauthorized acts committed by corporate officers, unless illegal, may be ratified by the express authority of the board of directors. The board may also impliedly ratify the unofficial acts of the officer by accepting the benefits of the transaction.

EXAMPLE The vice president of a corporation, although authorized to enter into contracts not exceeding $100,000, entered into a $1 million contract. Shortly thereafter, the president of the corporation, who was also a director, authorized payment. The board was duly apprised of the payment but no formal action was taken by them to approve the payment. The board was deemed to have impliedly accepted the benefits of the unauthorized act.

What the applicable RMBCA section says *Under Section 8.41, each officer has the authority to perform the duties set forth in the bylaws or those prescribed by the board of directors.*

RESIGNATION OR REMOVAL OF OFFICERS

An officer can resign at any time by delivering notice to the corporation. The resignation is usually effective when the notice is delivered to the corporation. The board of directors may also remove a director either with or without cause at any time. The resignation or removal of an officer does not absolve him of any liability for negligent, fraudulent, or criminal acts committed while in office.

What the applicable RMBCA section says *Under Section 8.43, an officer can resign at any time by delivering notice to the corporation. The resignation is effective when the notice is delivered to the corporation unless the notice specifies a later effective date. The board of directors may also remove a director either with or without cause at any time.*

COMPENSATION OF THE OFFICERS

Officers' compensation is fixed by the board of directors. In view of the litigious nature of most shareholders, officers who are also board members should avoid voting on a resolution fixing their compensation. Officers' compensation must be reasonable in amount based upon the size and complexity of the corporation's activities. Excessive compensation is considered a waste of corporate assets. Directors who approve excessive compensation to officers can be held liable for negligence in failing to determine the appropriate amount of compensation due an officer.

EXAMPLE Frank Donald is hired as vice president in charge of marketing for the Rya Manufacturing Corporation. Although various amounts of compensation have been discussed between the board and Donald, no specific amount has been agreed upon. Donald starts work and begins receiving a small draw on which to live until his salary is determined. After working three months, the board has still not come to a decision regarding his salary. In disgust, Donald quits the corporation and sues for his unpaid salary. He may recover the reasonable value of his services.

OBSERVATION *Never hire a corporate officer without first determining her rate of compensation, and other* *employee benefits, i.e., group insurance, stock options, medical benefits, etc. in advance.*

TRANSACTIONS WITH THE CORPORATION

Officers, like directors, are fiduciaries who owe complete loyalty to the corporation.

What the applicable RMBCA section says *Section 8.42, which governs the standards of conduct of a corporate officer, states that an officer shall discharge his duties in good faith, with the care of an ordinarily prudent person in a similar position, and in a manner that he believes to be in the best interests of the corporation. In discharging his duties, the officer is entitled to rely on the information, opinions, reports, and statements presented by other corporate officers or employees, legal counsel, public accountants, and other experts. An officer shall not be liable if he performs his duties in compliance with this section.*

Officers may, however, make contracts with the corporation so long as they deal openly and in good faith. If they secretly benefit in their dealings with the corporation, they may be required to disgorge their profits to the corporation because they have breached their fiduciary duty. The corporation may also be entitled to damages. Officers must also refrain from taking personal advantage of corporate opportunities that are presented to the corporation.

EXAMPLE Margaret Johnson was the president of Acme Investments Ltd. The corporation specialized in buying and selling stocks, bonds, and other types of securities. Margaret was personally given the right to purchase 100 acres of valuable shorefront property and exercised this option. Margaret need not account to Acme since the opportunity came to her personally and the corporation was not in the business of acquiring real estate. Of course, if she later negotiates the sale of the land to Acme, and realizes a secret profit, she could be compelled to account to the corporation.

Officers may, however, engage in independent businesses so long as their activities do not compete with the corporation's business.

EXAMPLE Preston Phillips is president of the Jacoby Medical Supply Corporation. The corporation manufactures and sells medical equipment, office furniture for medical offices, personalized stationery, office computers, and medical software. Preston sets up another corporation, making himself the sole shareholder, that will sell furniture to the general public. Preston's new corporation is in direct competition with that of his current employer, and Preston is in breach of his fiduciary duties.

LIABILITY FOR NEGLIGENCE

Officers, like directors, are liable for gross negligence while in office. The corporate officer is also held liable for the negligent acts of subordinates that she could have detected through the exercise of reasonable care and business judgment. Note that as a senior officer of the corporation, she must review the conduct and activities of subordinates. Officers are not, however, liable for ordinary judgmental errors made in the course of exercising their corporate responsibilities.

EXAMPLE Wallace Ford, treasurer of the Totem Woodworking Corporation, was required to obtain the countersignature of either the president or, in his absence, vice president of the corporation where the amount exceeded $10,000. Through a series of ingenious stratagems, he was able to forge the signatures of either corporate officer when required to do so. The corporation usually issued at least ten checks weekly in amounts exceeding $10,000. Such amounts were needed to meet the weekly payroll, as well as inventory purchases. All of the officers met weekly to discuss corporate business. At no time was the absence of the issuance of large check amounts ever discussed. Upon discovery, the corporate treasurer was held criminally liable for fraud and immediately dismissed. The shareholders and directors may also hold the president and vice president for negligence. It appears that they were derelict in failing to question how the corporation could issue checks for large amounts over an extended period of time without being asked to countersign.

OBSERVATION *In the above situation, the outside auditors could also be held liable for failing to detect the fraud perpetrated by the treasurer.*

While corporate officers may be held liable for the acts of subordinates that they could have detected through the exercise of reasonable care and business judgment, directors are only liable *after being put on notice* of possible wrongdoing by corporate employees and fail to investigate.

LIABILITY BASED UPON PERSONAL GUARANTEE OF A CORPORATE OFFICER

Officers who *personally* guarantee the faithful contracts and other obligations in their own capacity as private individuals and not as corporate officers are personally liable.

EXAMPLE Paul Morton was president of Cutie Pie Clothing Co. Inc. The Bell Corporation wished to enter into a contract to sell Cutie Pie $1 million of raw materials for the manufacturing of clothing. Fearing that Cutie Pie would be unable to pay for the goods, Bell asked Morton to personally sign the contract in his own individual capacity, as well as in his capacity as corporate president. Should Cutie Pie prove unable to pay for the goods, Morton will have to pay for the goods out of his own pocket. Of course, Morton can always seek reimbursement from Cutie Pie.

DETERMINING REASONABLE COMPENSATION UNDER THE IRC: PAYMENTS TO SHAREHOLDER-EMPLOYEES

With corporate tax rates as high as 35 percent, the denial of part of an officer's compensation as a deduction can result in a hefty tax bite.

Compensation paid to a shareholder-officer, such as a president or vice president in the form of salary, bonus, or fringe benefits is tax deductible. Compensation payments are deductible by the corporation as long as they are reasonable and necessary in amount. They are also taxable to the officer-employee. If however, the salary is deemed unreasonable, excess compensation may be treated as a nondeductible dividend thereby resulting in an additional tax liability to the corporation.

EXAMPLE The South Gas Corporation is 100% owned by Philip Merritt, who also serves as the corporation's president. For the year 19XX, the income statement of the corporation appeared as follows:

Sales		$900,000
Cost of goods sold		500,000
Gross Profit		400,000
Operating expenses	$150,000	
Merritt's salary as president of South Gas	250,000	400,000
Net income		$ -0-

After the tax return was filed in 19X1 for 19XX, the Internal Revenue Service, on audit, challenged Merritt's salary payment claiming that his salary was not reasonable in amount. After a lengthy battle, the corporation settled for a salary deduction of $200,000, as opposed to $250,000. Assuming a corporate tax rate of 15 percent on the first $50,000 of corporate taxable income, the corporation will owe an additional $7,500 ($50,000 × 15 percent) in taxes. However, Merritt's total income from the corporation remains unchanged since the disallowed $50,000 is now treated as dividend income in Merritt's hands.

Reasonableness of compensation is determined on a case-by-case basis. Such factors as the officer-employee's qualifications, nature and extent of his work, the complexities and size of the business, salary amounts paid to officers in similar positions in other corporations within the same industry, and whether nondeductible dividends were declared and paid are some of the elements that determine reasonableness.

The board of directors and the corporation can avoid the question of unreasonable compensation by setting the officer's salary at the beginning of the year in a written contract so as to be independent of the corporation's final net income for the year. The directors' resolution fixing the officer's salary should also state the reasons for the high salary, such as increased sales and responsibilities and outstanding past performance.

Closely held corporations should also consider payments of tax-free benefits to shareholder employees, such as medical plans and group-term life insurance.

Some owners of closely held corporations elect to be taxed under the rules of Subchapter S in order to avoid double taxation. Other owners of closely held corporations retain regular corporation, or Subchapter C status, to utilize the 15 and 25 percent marginal corporate tax rates and to benefit from tax-free fringe benefits, such as health and accident insurance.

NEGOTIATING A COMPREHENSIVE EMPLOYMENT AGREEMENT

The following is a checklist of points that must be covered in any employment contract.

1. The names of the parties.
2. The title and duties associated with the position.
3. That the officer shall engage in no other outside activities without permission from the board of directors.
4. The period of employment.
5. Compensation and other benefits.
6. Conditions under which employment will be terminated.
7. What the estate of the officer is to receive in case of death.
8. The rights of the parties in case of the officer's sickness or disability.
9. Retirement benefits.
10. The officer cannot disclose any trade secrets or confidential information learned by reason of her association either during or after ceasing to be associated with the corporation.
11. For a certain period of time after the officer ceases to be associated with the corporation, she will not manage, operate, or join any business entity such as a partnership or corporation that competes with her current employer.
12. Any inventions, designs, etc. conceived during the employment of the officer shall belong to the corporation.
13. Should a breach of contract occur, all parties shall agree to submit to personal jurisdiction before a proper court in the state where the principal office of the corporation is located.
14. That the agreement shall be governed by the laws of a particular state.
15. That this agreement supersedes all previous employment agreements (if any) entered into between the parties.
16. The agreement must be signed by both parties.

A comprehensive employment agreement is an excellent method of avoiding potential conflicts and lawsuits.

CHAPTER 11

The Corporate Ownership: The Role of the Shareholders

INTRODUCTION

The stockholder is the true owner of the corporation, whether at law, where the stock is held in the name of the shareholder, or in equity where the stock is held by one person for the benefit of another. Examples would be shares held by guardians for minors or by executors or administrators of an estate.

· ·
What the applicable RMBCA section says *Section 1.40(22) states that a "Shareholder" means the person in whose name shares are registered in the records of the corporation or the beneficial owner of shares to the extent of the rights granted by a nominee certificate on file with the corporation.*
· ·

Shares, which are treated as transferable personal property (meaning that it is movable as opposed to real estate, which cannot be moved) can also be the subject of co-ownership, such as a joint tenancy (with rights of survivorship) or a tenancy in common.

EXAMPLE 1 Barnes and Nobel own 100 shares of the Pennsalt Corporation as joint tenants with the right of survivorship. If Barnes dies, Barnes's ownership in the shares passes automatically to Nobel and not to Barnes's heirs.

EXAMPLE 2 Barnes and Nobel own 100 shares of the Pennsalt Corporation as tenants in common. Barnes stipulates in his will that when he dies, Endicott is to receive his interest in the shares. When Barnes dies, Endicott receives 50 shares. If Barnes sold his interest to Zemoli before he dies, then Zemoli and Nobel would be co-owners as tenants in common.

When a corporation issues shares, the name and address of the purchasing shareholder is recorded in the corporation's stockholders' ledger account together with the number of shares owned. This person is called the "record owner." If a shareholder pays for the share but fails to subsequently receive them, she is still the "equitable or beneficial owner" who may compel the corporation to issue the shares to her together with any applicable dividends.

A QUICK OVERVIEW OF THE RIGHTS AND PRIVILEGES OF A SHAREHOLDER

The more common rights of a shareholder is the right to a stock certificate, the right to transfer the stock, the right to vote, the right to dividends if and when declared, the right to inspect the corporate books, a possible "pre-emptive right" to purchase a percentage of any new issuances, and the right to a proportional share of corporate assets upon a corporate dissolution.

OBSERVATION *As discussed in Chap. 8, where a shareholder claims that the security has been lost, destroyed, or wrongfully taken, the issuing corporation must issue a new security in place of the original security if certain requirements imposed by the issuer are met.*

BASIC RECORDS RELATING TO STOCK: THE STOCK CERTIFICATE AND STOCK TRANSFER BOOK

Stock certificate and stock transfer books are part of the special corporate records involved in accounting for stock. A stock certificate book contains stock certificates that are issued when bought by the shareholder. They are removed from the stock book when issued leaving a stub on which is written the name of the stockholder, the number of shares issued, the serial number applicable to each share (i.e., certificate number 777) and the date the shares were issued. The stock certificate ledger contains the names of the stockholders, their addresses, the number on the certificates, and the number of shares issued. A sample of the stock transfer ledger appears on pages 190 and 191.

OBSERVATION *In many states, the board of directors may provide for uncertified stock under Article 8 of the UCC. This means that the actual stock need not be issued. Instead, the corporation sends the holder of stock a letter or some other form of notice containing the same information found on the face of the stock certificates.*

What the applicable RMBCA section says *Section 6.26, governing shares without certificates, states that unless the articles of incorporation or bylaws provide otherwise, the corporation may authorize the issue of some or all of the shares of any or all classes without certificates. Within a reasonable period of time after the issue, the corporation must send the shareholder a letter or some other form of notice containing the same information found on the face of the stock certificates.*

The corporation must maintain a current list of shareholders so that dividend payments, notices of annual stockholder meetings, and voting proxies may be sent to the proper persons.

THE EXERCISE OF DIRECT AND INDIRECT CONTROL OF THE CORPORATION BY SHAREHOLDERS

Generally, unless they sit on the board of directors, shareholders have no authority to control the day-to-day operations of the corporation. Indirectly, shareholders can exert their influence by electing directors and amending the certificate of incorporation, which requires a vote of the majority of the outstanding shares entitled to vote.

Shareholders may also, by a two-thirds vote of all outstanding shares, approve such organizational changes, such as a merger or sale of all corporate assets.

As discussed in Chap. 9, some state statutes permit the "sterilization" or restriction of the authority of the board of directors of a nonpublic or closely held corporation. This limitation must be set forth in the articles of incorporation. Thus, all management authority is transferred to the shareholders. This arrangement also nullifies the shareholders' benefit of limited liability with respect to any negligent acts or illegal acts authorized by them acting in place of a duly constituted board of directors.

EXAMPLE A provision in the certificate of incorporation of Standard Horse Farms Inc., a closely held corporation, transfers to all of the shareholders the board of directors' authority to manage the corporation. The shareholders' management powers also subject them to personal liability arising from the fact that they, acting in place of the directors, are initiating and approving corporate actions.

What the applicable RMBCA section says *Section 7.32, regarding shareholder agreements, states that an agreement among the shareholders of a corporation that complies with this section is effective among the shareholders and the corporation even though it is inconsistent with one or more other provisions of the RMBCA in that it eliminates the board of directors or restricts the discretion or powers of the board of directors. The existence of an agreement authorized by this section shall be noted conspicuously on the front or back of each certificate for outstanding shares or on the information statement required within a reasonable time after the issuance of the certificates.*

An agreement authorized by this section shall cease to be effective when shares of the corporation are listed on a national securities exchange or regularly traded market.

OBSERVATION *Shareholders' agreements cannot be used to deny the right of shareholders to inspect the corporation's books and records, to bring stockholders' derivative actions, or to seek dissolution alleging corporate waste of assets.*

CONVENING SHAREHOLDERS MEETINGS

Shareholders may convene either "regular" or "special" meetings at a time and place fixed in the bylaws. "Regular" meetings are held at least once a year for the election of directors and to conduct any other required corporate business. "Special" meetings are called when circumstances dictate.

To control the number of special meetings that may be called by troublesome shareholders, the corporate bylaws may state that a minimum percentage of shares, i.e., 10 percent to 50 percent, be owned by the shareholder demanding that a special meeting of shareholders be convened. In addition, many corporate statutes state that a shareholder may only call a special meeting with regard to matters that are the proper subject of shareholder review. Matters regarding the normal activities of the corporation, such as the hiring and firing of officers, setting product prices, and borrowing money, are not subject to shareholder action. However, shareholder action is permitted where the directors contemplate fundamental changes in the corporate structure or the election or removal of a corporate director.

EXAMPLE Brenda Carton, a major shareholder of Solis Paper Goods Corp. Ltd., was unhappy with the performance of the board of directors. She felt that the directors had taken a series of steps that were detrimental to the future growth of the corporation and wanted to have their actions reviewed at a duly called special meeting of the shareholders. The certificate of incorporation stated that any person holding more than five percent of the outstanding common shares of the corporation may request that board of directors (or designated corporate officer) call a special meeting within 30 days after a written request for such meeting. Pursuant to the corporation's bylaws, the meeting must be held at corporate headquarters. Following such guidelines, Brenda sought to have a special meeting of the shareholders convened. Such action cannot be taken by Brenda since her request pertains to the board's activities involving the normal operations of the corporation.

PLACE AND TIME OF MEETINGS

The place designated for shareholders meetings may be within or outside the state of incorporation. If no place is designated, most state laws fix the place of the meeting at the corporate headquarters. All notices must state the place, time, and hour of the meeting. Notice of the meeting must be given to every shareholder entitled to vote, either personally or by mail. Notice of any meetings need not be given to any shareholder who gives the corporation a signed waiver of notice prior to a called meeting of the shareholders.

What the applicable RMBCA section says *Section 7.20, governing shareholders' list of meetings, states that after fixing a record date for a meeting, a corporation shall prepare an alphabetical list of the names of all its shareholders who are entitled to notice of a shareholders meeting. The shareholders' list must be available for inspection by any shareholder, beginning two business days after notice of the meeting is given or which the list was prepared. Refusal or failure to prepare or make available the shareholders' list does not affect the validity of action taken at the meeting.*

WHO IS ELIGIBLE TO VOTE?

Every shareholder who is registered on the books as owning shares is entitled to vote. If the shares are pledged and transferred to a pledgee or nominee, the pledgor, who is still the true owner, is entitled to vote. Shares held by a domestic or foreign corporation can be voted by an officer of the owner shareholder corporation as the owner corporation's bylaws permit. Eligibility of a shareholder to vote is determined by the record date, which is fixed in advance by the board of directors. The record date is generally ten to fifty days before the date of the shareholders' scheduled meeting. Trustees of a voting trust may vote shares only if the shares have been transferred into the trustee's name. Treasury shares owned by the corporation are *not* entitled to vote.

WHAT IS A PROXY?

A proxy is a power of attorney given by a stockholder authorizing a designated person to vote the shareholder's stock. A proxy must be in writing and signed by the shareholder granting the proxy. The person exercising the proxy need not be a shareholder in the corporation although this is usually the case. Proxies are generally valid for a period not exceeding eleven months but can be extended.

Proxies are generally revocable. Proxies can also be revoked due to the death or incompetency of the shareholder. Proxies can be made *irrevocable* by a shareholder, who in a signed authorization (or appointment) granting the proxy, states that it is irrevocable, and the person granted the proxy has either agreed to buy the shares or has loaned the shareholder money and is holding the shares as security against repayment. Irrevocable proxies are also created pursuant to a voting trust agreement (see the next section).

What the applicable RMBCA section says *Section 7.22, governing proxies, states that a shareholder may vote his shares in person or by proxy. An appointment of a proxy is valid for eleven months unless a longer period is expressly provided in the appointment form. A proxy is revocable unless the appointment form states that it is irrevocable and is coupled with an interest (meaning that the proxy holder has an interest in the stock).*

VOTING TRUST AGREEMENTS

The voting trust agreement is a device to concentrate shareholder control in one or more trustees who seek to control corporate affairs by electing specific directors. Voting trustees can also exercise any other ordinary shareholder rights associated with the ownership of the shares. A voting trust arrangement requires that the shareholders transfer their shares to a voting trustee who will in return issue voting trust certificates to the beneficial owners (the

shareholders who are the real owners of the shares). The voting trustee is the legal owner of the shares who can vote the shares as she sees fit. Thus, the voting trustee occupies a fiduciary position in relation to the shareholder members and can be removed by them for violating this trust. Most voting trust agreements are good for ten years and can be renewed for an additional ten year period.

Voting trust agreements are generally irrevocable unless all of the members mutually agree to terminate the arrangement.

What the applicable RMBCA section says *Section 7.30, governing voting trusts, states that one or more shareholders may create a voting trust, conferring on the trustee the right to vote or otherwise act for them. They must sign an agreement setting out the provisions of the trust (which may include anything consistent with its purpose) and transferring their shares to the trustee. A voting trust is valid for not more than ten years after its effective date and may be extended for an additional ten year period.*

VOTING AGREEMENTS

Two or more shareholders may enter into an agreement to vote their shares in a certain way. This "pooling agreement," which must be in writing, requires that the members cast their votes in a certain way, such as which directors to elect. The advantage of a voting agreement over a voting trust agreement is that it is easier to form and that unlike a voting trust agreement, legal title remains with the shareholders. To avoid potential conflicts among the parties, most voting agreements contain an arbitration clause stating that all disputes arising among the parties be settled by binding arbitration. Some agreements contain a provision giving the arbitrator an irrevocable proxy allowing her to vote the shares as she sees fit should the shareholders fail to agree on the way to vote certain matters.

As stated on page 58 in convening shareholders meetings, matters regarding the normal activities of the corporation are not subject to approval by a voting agreement. However, a shareholder agreement to dissolve the corporation is generally held to be valid.

....

What the applicable RMBCA section says *Section 7.31, governing voting agreements, states that two or more shareholders may provide for the manner in which they will vote their shares by signing an agreement for that purpose. This agreement is specifically enforceable.*

....

RESTRICTING THE TRANSFERABILITY OF SHARES: THE RIGHT OF FIRST REFUSAL

A corporation, by its articles of incorporation, bylaws, or by shareholder agreement, typically has the power to reasonably restrict the free transferability of its outstanding shares. This can be done by conspicuously noting the restriction on the front or back of the certificate. For example, the corporation or the other shareholders can be given the *right of first refusal*, meaning the opportunity to purchase the shares at the best price obtained by the shareholder from outside third parties. A variation of this arrangement may require that the selling shareholder first offer the shares to the other shareholders.

....

What the applicable RMBCA section says *Section 6.27, governing the restriction of shares, states that the articles of incorporation, the bylaws, an agreement among shareholders, or an agreement between the shareholders and the corporation may impose restrictions on the transfer or registration of transfer of shares of the corporation. A restriction does not affect shares issued before the restriction was adopted unless the holders of such shares are parties to the restriction agreement. The restriction must be conspicuously noted on the front or back of the certificate.*

....

HOW MANY SHARES DOES IT TAKE TO HOLD A VALID SHAREHOLDERS MEETING?

A quorum is the number of votes necessary to validate a meeting. The certificate of incorporation or bylaws usually fixes the number of shares necessary to constitute a valid meeting of the shareholders. Once a valid shareholders meeting is commenced, no quorum is necessary to adjourn the meeting.

The normal quorum is the majority of shares entitled to vote.

EXAMPLE Label Sticker and Tag Co. Inc. has 1,000 common shares outstanding. The certificate of incorporation provides for a majority of the shares to be present to constitute a valid meeting. At a duly called stockholders meeting, 5 out of 20 shareholders, owning 515 common shares attend the meeting. The normal quorum requirement has been met because the shareholders present own the majority of the outstanding shares and the meeting can proceed.

The certificate of incorporation can provide for a lesser quorum, that is a lesser amount of shares to be present, but in no case, less than one third of the amount of shares entitled to vote.

EXAMPLE Hedon Hydrogen Producers Inc. has 300 common shares outstanding. The certificate of incorporation provides for a lesser quorum of one third of the shares to be present to constitute a valid meeting. At a duly called stockholders meeting, 2 out of 10 shareholders, owning 105 common shares attend the meeting. The lesser quorum requirement has been met because the shareholders present own over one-third (105/300) of the outstanding shares and the meeting can proceed.

In many states, a greater quorum, i.e., more than a majority, can be required for a valid shareholders meeting but only if provided for in the certificate of incorporation and not in the bylaws.

Shareholders present at a meeting where the number of shares necessary to constitute a quorum has not been met have the authority to adjourn the meeting.

EXAMPLE Roxberry Apple Farms Ltd. has 100 common shares outstanding. At a duly called stockholders meeting, 2 out of 10 shareholders, owning 105 common shares attend the meeting. The lesser quorum requirement has been met because the shareholders present own over one-third (105/300) of the outstanding shares and the meeting can proceed.

Shareholders meetings are called annually to elect directors. Directors are elected by a plurality (meaning the largest number of votes cast). All other actions require a majority of the votes cast. One major exception to these voting requirements is that any proposed merger, sale of corporate assets, or dissolution requires a positive vote of two-thirds of the shares entitled to vote.

EXAMPLE Kramer Public Relations, Inc. had 75 common shares outstanding. Since the corporation was not doing well, the directors, at the corporation's annual meeting, proposed that the corporation be dissolved. Thus, all the assets were to be sold, all corporate liabilities paid, and the balance of the proceeds distributed to the shareholders. At least 50 shares (or two-thirds) would have to vote yes to approve the proposed dissolution.

HOW CUMULATIVE VOTING WORKS

Usually, the articles of incorporation provide that shareholders vote for an entire slate in a "straight" vote. Thus, the shareholders with the most shares (called the majority shareholders) will always be able to outvote minority shareholders (those shareholders with minimal votes) relating to either the election of directors or other ordinary corporate matters. Cumulative voting is a technique whereby minority shareholders concentrate all of their voting strength on one or more individual directors with the hope that they are elected. It is an excellent way of helping to preserve minority shareholder representation on the board of directors. The formula is the number of shares held times the number of individual directors to be elected.

EXAMPLE 1 Barton Cain owns 105 shares of Soloway Sugar Refining Corp. Soloway's articles of incorporation stipulate cumulative voting for the election of directors. Barton may cast 420 votes (number of shares held [105] times directors to be elected [4]) for one or more directors of his choice.

EXAMPLE 2 Mary Benis owns 105 shares and Todd Tryon owns the other 300 shares of the Rochester Travel Agency Ltd. Rochester's articles of incorporation stipulate cumulative voting for the election of directors. Mary wants to elect A, B, and C as directors while Todd wants X, Y, and Z. In straight voting, Todd would be able to elect X, Y, and Z, thereby, denying Mary representation on the board. However, under cumulative voting, Mary would have 315 votes (105 shares × 3 directors). If Mary concentrates *all* of her votes on either A, B, or C, she will be able to elect at least one director. Todd has 900 votes (300 shares × 3 directors).

If Todd spreads all of his votes among X, Y, and Z, each will receive 300 votes (900/3). Since Mary's 315 votes will always exceed the votes needed to elect at least one director, she is always assured at least some representation on the board.

Thus, cumulative voting is an excellent device for use in a closely held corporation where minority shareholders always fear that they will be shut out from representation on the board. Note that cumulative voting only applies to the election of directors. All other corporate matters are usually decided by straight voting.

THE RIGHT TO INSPECT THE CORPORATION'S BOOKS AND RECORDS

Shareholders have an unqualified right to inspect the corporation's books and records, including the minutes of shareholders meetings, by making a demand on a corporate officer or director. Such inspection is permitted if done in good faith and its purpose is to protect either the corporation's or shareholders' interests. For example, an inspection of the list of shareholder's names for purposes of instituting a challenge to the current board by soliciting proxies is a proper demand for seeking an inspection. Even a competitor who owns shares can seek inspection although information relating to clients and other business secrets may be withheld.

Generally, inspection is limited to individuals of record for at least six months or to shareholders who own at least 5 percent of any stock or 5 percent in aggregate of all shares outstanding.

EXAMPLE 1 Susan Beckwith, a 20 percent shareholder in the Express Bus Service Corporation, seeks to obtain a list of the shareholders' names so that she can solicit enough proxies to challenge the current board of directors. Her action is deemed to have as its purpose the protection of shareholder rights, and indirectly the corporation, and is, therefore, a proper request.

EXAMPLE 2 Ronald Walters, is a 15 percent shareholder in the Planet Restaurant Inc., a closely held corporation. Ronald seeks to obtain information regarding the value of certain investments held by the corporation. This information will enable him to value his shares in the corporation. His action is deemed to have a valid business purpose and is a proper request.

Generally, prior to inspection, a shareholder is required to furnish an affidavit to the corporation stating that her sole purpose is not contrary to the interests of the corporation, and that for the next five years, she will not sell the shareholders list to an outside third party. Upon written request to inspect the corporation's books and records, most state statutes require that the corporation mail to the shareholder the latest annual balance sheet, income statement, and any applicable interim financial report.

••

What the applicable RMBCA section says *Section 16.01, governing corporate records, states that a corporation shall keep as permanent records minutes of all meetings of its shareholders and board of directors, a record of all actions taken by shareholders or board of directors without a meeting, and all actions taken by committee. The corporation shall maintain a record of its shareholders in a form that permits a list of the names and addresses of all shareholders in alphabetical order by class of shares showing the number and class of shares held by each.*

••

THE RIGHTS OF A MINORITY SHAREHOLDER

Although minority shareholders must abide by the decisions of the majority shareholders, they can object to certain majority actions under one or more conditions. These conditions include when the minority shareholders feel that the vote of the majority is contrary to the best interests of the corporation, when a vote is solely for the benefit of the majority, or when the action of the majority is in contravention of the corporation's articles of incorporation or bylaws. It is said that the majority have a fiduciary duty to the minority shareholders and must do their utmost to act in good faith.

EXAMPLE 1 At a duly called annual meeting of the Doughboy Musical Corporation, the majority shareholders vote to transfer rights to valuable musical

compositions to a competitor, thereby crippling the corporation. The actions of the majority may be restrained by the legal action of the minority.

EXAMPLE 2 Exeter, Fredrico, and Grainger, who constitute all of the shareholders of the Amalfi Pizza Cheese Corporation, unanimously adopt a bylaw stating that no shareholder may dispose of his shares without first offering them to the corporation for purchase at their fair market value. The purpose of the bylaw was to prevent the sale of the shareholders' stock to a stranger who may prove hostile to the best interests of the corporation. Exeter and Fredrico later sought to repeal the bylaw. Such action may be prevented by Grainger, the minority shareholder.

Note that in that last example, the shareholders adopted a bylaw to give the corporation the first opportunity to purchase stock that a shareholder wishes to sell. Frequently, shareholders eventually want to sell, or sometimes die leaving their shares to a next of kin. This of course creates a potential risk to the corporation that an individual may inherit the stock who is less than compatible with the other shareholders or stated goals of the corporation. The problem in case of a proposed sale or death of a shareholder is that the corporation may not have the cash funds required to purchase the shares at their fair market value.

To avoid this potential problem, small closely held corporations usually take out an insurance policy on the life of each shareholder covering the current and potential value of the shares that they own. Should a shareholder die, the proceeds are paid to the corporation who uses them to repurchase the shareholder's outstanding stock. These policies must be reviewed annually to make sure that the insurance coverage is sufficient to repurchase the stock.

MINORITY SHAREHOLDERS' SUITS

Any wrongs committed against the corporation are supposed to be redressed by the board of directors. Sometimes, however, the board acts for the benefit of the majority shareholders to the detriment of the minority owners. In such cases, the obligation of the minority shareholder is to first make a demand upon the directors to correct the alleged wrong. If the directors fail to heed the request of the minority shareholders, or if they investigate and find wrongdoing but fail to take corrective action, the aggrieved minority shareholder may bring a *derivative action* on behalf of the corporation. Although the corporation is named as a defendant, the corporation is the real party in interest, i.e., the party entitled to recover if the plaintiff wins. The lawsuit is brought in the name of and in behalf of the corporation. The relief sought is in the form of compelling abusive directors and officers to account to the corporation for losses caused by their negligence, breach of fiduciary duty, or any other misconduct.

To maintain a derivative suit, the plaintiff must be the actual owner in the shares or have a beneficial interest in the shares of the corporation against whom the derivative action is sought.

EXAMPLE In 19XX, five shareholders of Dalton Dance Schools Inc. entered into a voting trust agreement. The shareholders transferred their shares to the trustee and received in return voting trust certificates. Any one of the shareholders may maintain a derivative action on behalf of Dalton.

Note that any damages recovered usually go to the corporation because it is said that the shareholders who bring such lawsuits are acting as guardians of the corporate entity.

PERSONAL LIABILITIES APPLICABLE TO THE SHAREHOLDERS

While a stockholder's liability is ordinarily limited to the amount of his investment, under certain conditions they may become liable to the corporation, to judgment creditors, and to wage earners.

Liability to the Corporation

The unpaid balance of a stock subscription is an asset of the corporation. A shareholder will, therefore, be liable to the corporation for the unpaid balance of his stock subscription (see Chap. 8). For example, when stock is bought on the installment basis, payment must be made on the due date of the installment. If payment is not made, the corporation may exercise its option to sue for the balance of the price of the shares or declare a forfeiture of the stock.

Second, if par value stock is issued for less than its full value (i.e., discounted stock), the stockholder is liable to the corporation for the difference between the price paid and the par value of the stock. In legal terms, the corporation is said to have issued *watered stock*.

EXAMPLE Lido Photography Studios, Inc. issued $5,000 of common stock to their attorney for legal services involving the formation of the corporation. In fact, the services were worth only $1,000. The attorney has been issued watered stock and is liable to the corporation for the $4,000 ($5,000 – $1,000) difference.

Finally, a shareholder may be liable to the corporation when the corporation is insolvent and, in contravention of state statutes, pays an illegal dividend. If the corporation fails to seek repayment, another stockholder, in the form of a shareholders' derivative suit or as stated below, a judgment creditor, may do so.

Liability to Corporate Creditors

In cases of corporate insolvency, an unpaid creditor, having unsuccessfully sued the corporation, may sue the shareholder for the unpaid balance of the subscription price.

Second, par value stock may have been issued for less than its full value (discounted stock or watered stock). Thus, besides being personally liable to the corporation, the shareholder will also be held liable to an unpaid creditor in case of corporate insolvency for the difference between the price paid and the par value of the stock.

Finally, a shareholder may be liable for unlawful dividends received by her. A corporation may not declare and pay dividends if it causes its liabilities to exceed its assets. Thus, state corporate statutes generally declare illegal any dividends that would cause corporate liabilities to exceed corporate assets.

EXAMPLE The Sunset Steamship Corporation was virtually insolvent. The board of directors declared and paid a cash dividend thereby rendering the corporation insolvent and unable to pay its creditors. To the extent that the dividend payments rendered the corporation insolvent, they were illegal since their payment denied recovery to the creditors. Thus the stockholders are generally liable for any dividends received by them.

Note that in the above case, the recovery of any dividends from the shareholders does not exonerate the directors for their negligence or wrongful intent in declaring and paying the illegal dividend. Directors who vote in favor of an illegal dividend are jointly and severally liable to the corporation for the amount declared. On the other hand, directors who, in good faith, rely on the corporate financial statements prepared by others to declare a dividend will not be held liable.

EXAMPLE The certified public accountants for Budget Tool and Equipment Rental Corporation prepared the company's financial statements without listing a $500,000 judgment levied against the corporation. Thus, the statements showed the corporation to be solvent when in fact it was insolvent due to the judgment. The board of directors, believing the corporation to be in sound financial condition, declared and paid a $100,000 cash dividend, thereby rendering the corporation insolvent. The directors will not be held liable because they relied on the financial statements prepared by their outside independent accountants.

In some states, shareholders are not liable if they received their dividends in good faith and were unaware that the declaration and payment of dividends were illegal.

What the applicable RMBCA section says *Section 6.22 states that a purchaser from a corporation of its own shares is not liable to the corporation or its creditors with respect to the shares except to pay the consideration for which the shares were authorized to be issued.*

Thus, the RMBCA makes the shareholder liable for the difference, or discount, between the price actually paid for the stock and the consideration, i.e., the par or stated value, fixed by the board of directors.

Liability of Shareholders for Unpaid Wages

In some states, the ten largest shareholders of a non-public closely held corporation are personally liable for all unpaid wages owed by the corporation to its employees. This liability does not extend to independent contractors. An independent contractor is one who does not work for the corporation in an employee capacity and has complete charge and supervision over the work she does for another. Examples of independent contractors include outside legal counsel or the corporation's independent certified public accountant.

EXAMPLE Haddon Art Galleries Inc. declared itself bankrupt in Federal Bankruptcy Court. At the time of its bankruptcy, it owed its employees back wages. Haddon was owned by fifteen shareholders. The ten largest shareholders will be held personally liable, if after the bankruptcy proceeding is terminated, the wages remain unpaid.

DIVIDEND DISTRIBUTIONS

Shareholders seek income in the form of stock appreciation and the payment of dividends. Dividends may take the form of cash, stock, or other corporate property and may be paid either out of profits or in liquidation. This complex topic will be discussed in Chaps. 13 and 15.

CHAPTER 12

Dividends, Distributions, Stock Splits, and Stock Repurchases

INTRODUCTION

Dividends represent payments by a corporation of an equal amount to each shareholder of both preferred and common stock outstanding. Each dividend, in the form of either cash, the corporation's stock, or property, is based on the number of shares held by each shareholder. Cash and property dividends are usually taxable to the shareholder. Stock dividends are generally nontaxable. A corporation does not have a legal obligation to pay dividends. While creditors can force a corporation into involuntary bankruptcy if it does not meet its required interest payments on debt, shareholders, even as owners, do not have a similar right if the corporation is unable to pay dividends.

While the most common type of dividend is in the form of cash, a corporation may, at its option, pay dividends in the form of its own stock, called a stock dividend, or in property. Stock and property dividends are usually paid by a corporation that is short of cash.

EXAMPLE The Speedy Fleet Taxi Service, Inc. is owned by 40 shareholders. Since it was in the process of upgrading its fleet of taxis, it sought to conserve its cash. At the same time, the shareholders were demanding a dividend. The board of directors therefore declared and paid a stock dividend of one

share of common stock for every ten common shares outstanding. This means that a shareholder owning ten shares would receive one share.

OBSERVATION *In all states, dividend payments are prohibited if the corporation is insolvent or would be rendered insolvent by the distribution. Insolvency in this sense means that if the corporation made the payments, it would be unable to pay any debts as they become due in the ordinary course of the debtor's business. Insolvency can also occur when a corporation's liabilities exceed its assets.*

EXAMPLE Calhoun Leather Crafts Ltd. has a deficit of $1,000 in its retained earnings account at the end of the year. It seeks to pay a $1,000 cash dividend to its shareholders. Calhoun, because of its deficit, cannot pay the dividend. This rule would also be applicable if the corporation sought to save cash by paying either a stock dividend or distributing property other than cash to the shareholders.

UNDERSTANDING ACCOUNTING PRINCIPLES GOVERNING THE PAYMENT OF DIVIDENDS

The basic accounting equation for any business entity, including a corporation, is as follows:

Assets = Liabilities + Capital (or Shareholder's Equity)

Assets consist of cash, accounts receivable, inventory, equipment, land and buildings, and other miscellaneous holdings. Liabilities consist of accounts payable, wages payable, long-term notes and mortgages payable, and other miscellaneous payables.

Shareholders' equity consists of common stock and preferred stock (if any) issued and outstanding, and earned surplus (simply called surplus). Certified public accountants preparing financial statements refer to surplus as *retained earnings*.

EXAMPLE Ramirez Movie Theaters Corporation issued 1,000 shares of $10 par value preferred stock for $10,000 and 15,000 no par value shares of common stock for $15,000. Assume that the company also had retained earnings of $5,000 at November 1, 19XX. If the corporation earned $13,400 for the month and paid $2,000 in dividends, the ending stockholders' equity section of the balance sheet would show the following:

RAMIREZ MOVIE THEATERS CORPORATION
Stockholders' Equity
For the Period Ended November 30, 19XX

Preferred Shares (Par Value $10: 1,000 Shares Issued and Outstanding)	$10,000
Common Stock	$15,000
Total Value of Shares Outstanding	$25,000
Retained Earnings	$16,400
Total Shareholders' Equity	$41,400

Any dividends paid to stockholders would come out of retained earnings. The payment of dividends is a distribution of corporate profits and *not* an expense of doing business. That is why dividends paid are not tax deductible by the corporation.

A statement of retained earnings for the period would show the following activities for the period.

RAMIREZ MOVIE THEATERS CORPORATION
Statement of Retained Earnings
For the Period Ended November 30, 19XX

Retained Earnings November 1, 19XX	$5,000
Net Income for the Period	$13,400
Subtotal	$18,400
Less: Dividends	$ 2,000
Retained Earnings, November 30, 19XX	$16,400

A corporation that does not have any retained earnings, which is usually the result of continuous operating losses, generally cannot pay dividends. A corporation lacking retained earnings is said to have a *deficit*.

Note that there is no corollary between the balance sheet figures based on costs and estimates and the true value of the business. The reason is that accountants use the cost principle rather than valuing assets at their true fair market value at the date the financial statements are presented. Thus, land bought by the corporation in 1980 for $10,000 might be worth $100,000 in today's market, but is still shown on the books of the corporation at its original cost of $10,000. Therefore, the term "book value" is a misnomer and does not reflect the true value of the stock.

EXAMPLE At year end, Climate Tree Nurseries Ltd. had assets consisting of land with a cost basis of $100,000, total liabilities of $50,000, and 10,000 shares of authorized $5 par value common stock of which 1,000 shares were issued and outstanding. The book value of the common shares outstanding is $50 per share calculated as follows:

Total Assets	$100,000	
Less: Total Liabilities	50,000	
Shareholders' Equity	$ 50,000	
		= $50
Divided by Outstanding Common Shares	1,000	

Now assume that the land, which had a cost basis of $100,000, had a fair market or liquidation value of $300,000. The value of the common shares outstanding based on fair market value would be $250 per share calculated as follows:

Total Assets	$300,000
Less: Total Liabilities	50,000
Shareholders' Equity	$250,000
	——— = $250
Divided by Outstanding	
Common Shares	1,000

Note that the par value of the shares is $5, the book value is $50, and the fair market value of the shares is $250. Thus, the book value of a share of stock does not represent its par value or fair market value.

If at a later date, the corporation pays a 5 percent dividend on its $100 par value common stock, a shareholder will receive $5 per share even though the stock's book or fair market value may be much higher (or lower).

STOCK SPLITS AND REVERSE STOCK SPLITS

When a corporation divides up its authorized and issued shares into a greater number of shares, i.e., two shares for every old one, it is termed a stock split.

From a legal viewpoint, a stock split results in an increase in the number of shares outstanding and a corresponding *decrease* in the par or stated value (in the case of no par value stock given a stated value) per share. A stock decrease, although it results in an increase in the number of shares outstanding, does not decrease the par or stated value of the shares. Thus, when the board of directors votes to split its stock, it does not change total shareholders' equity but merely increases the number of shares owned by the shareholders.

EXAMPLE The Gin Rummy Playing Card Corporation had 1,000 shares of $10 par value common stock outstanding when its board voted to split the stock in half. This action reduces the par value of the stock to $5 and increases the shares to 2,000 shares outstanding. The corporation's shareholders' equity section both before and after the stock split, assuming retained earnings of $5,000, would appear as follows:

STOCKHOLDERS' EQUITY
BEFORE STOCK SPLIT

Common Stock:	
1,000 shares at $10 par	$10,000
Retained Earnings	5,000
	$15,000

STOCKHOLDERS' EQUITY
AFTER STOCK SPLIT

Common Stock:	
2,000 shares at $5 par	$10,000
Retained Earnings	5,000
	$15,000

A corporation can also declare a reverse stock split where outstanding shares are combined into a lesser number of the same class, i.e., one new share for every three outstanding.

A stock split and a reverse stock split require board action. In some states, it may also require advance shareholder approval. The articles of incorporation must also be amended to change the par value or stated value of the shares.

TAX CONSEQUENCES *There are no tax consequences to a stock split except to divide the cost basis of each share in case of a split, or to multiply the basis of the stock in case of a reverse stock split.*

EXAMPLE 1 Roy Hamilton bought 100 shares of the Zebra Maintenance Corp. for $1,000. One year later, the corporation votes to split the stock, i.e., two shares for every old one. The old cost basis of $10 per share ($1,000/100 shares) is reduced after the split to $5 per share ($1,000/200 shares). Should Roy later sell 100 shares for $2,000, his capital gain, for tax purposes, would be $1,500 ($2,000 sales price – $500 [100 shares sold × $5]).

EXAMPLE 2 Same facts as in **EXAMPLE 1**, except that Zebra votes a reverse stock split, i.e., one new share for every five shares outstanding. The old cost basis of $10 per share ($1,000/100 shares) is increased to $50 per share ($1,000/20 shares). Should Roy later sell ten shares for $2,000, his capital gain, for tax purposes, would be $1,500 ($2,000 sales price – $500 [10 shares sold × $50]).

Note that both a stock dividend and stock split do not involve an expenditure of corporate assets.

FRACTIONAL SHARES (OR SCRIP)

A corporation may issue fractional shares or scrip, such as a 1/10 fractional share for every share held. These fractional shares entitle the shareholder to dividends, and the right to receive a full share in return for enough scrip to equal one share (e.g., ten 1/10 fractional shares equals one full share). A corporation may also issue money equal to the value of a fractional share.

••

What the applicable RMBCA section says *Section 6.04, governing fractional shares, states that a corporation may issue fractions of shares or pay in money the value of fractions of a share. Each certificate representing scrip must be labeled "scrip." The holder of a fractional share is entitled to exercise the rights of a shareholder, including the rights to vote, receive dividends, and to participate in the assets of the corporation upon liquidation.*

••

DISCRETION OF THE DIRECTORS TO DECLARE A DIVIDEND

The determination of whether or not to declare a dividend is left to the discretion of the board of directors. Even if the corporation has sufficient funds with which to pay dividends, the law does not require that they do so. In addition, courts will not interfere with the decision of the board not to declare dividends unless there is evidence of bad faith or dishonest motives.

EXAMPLE The board of directors of The Ace Safe Company, Inc. is in the process of expanding their operations in certain foreign countries. Pursuant to this corporate expansion process, Ace Safe has accumulated surplus funds, or as accountants call it, retained earnings, far in excess of the amount needed to support its program. Wallace Brown, a major shareholder, brought a court action demanding that the board declare and pay a cash dividend charging that the corporation has ample funds for

both expansion and the payment of dividends. In reply, the corporate board feels that unknown contingencies arising from the expansion program may arise requiring additional financing. Wallace cannot win. Absent a showing of bad faith or dishonest purpose on the part of the board, courts will not compel a board of directors to declare a dividend.

WHO IS ENTITLED TO A DIVIDEND?

Once a dividend is lawfully declared, the shareholder becomes a creditor of the corporation. Holders of preferred shares have rights that take precedence over the rights of common stock. The dividend preferences may be classified as being current, cumulative, and/or participating.

The Current Preference

A current dividend preference requires that a current preferred dividend must be declared and paid before any dividends can be paid on common stock.

Cumulative Preferred Preference

This rule states that if all or part of the specified current dividend is not paid in full, the unpaid balance becomes a dividend in arrears. Cumulative dividends in arrears must be paid before any common dividends can be paid. If preferred stock is noncumulative, it can never be in arrears. Thus, if dividends are not declared on noncumulative preferred stock, they are lost forever.

Participating Preferred Preference

Participating preferred stock allows preferred shareholders to receive additional amounts of dividends after the dividends stipulated in the articles of incorporation are paid to both the preferred and common shareholders on a ratable basis.

The actual computations showing the distribution of dividends based upon the number and classes of shares outstanding was illustrated in Chap. 8.

WHEN SHAREHOLDERS ARE ENTITLED TO PAYMENT OF A DIVIDEND

The board of directors may declare a dividend payable in cash, stock, or corporate property.

A typical cash dividend declaration found in the board minutes might be as follows:

On November 30, 19XX, the Board of Directors of the Acme Refrigerator Corp. hereby declares a $1.00 per share cash dividend on the 10,000 shares of no par common stock outstanding. The dividend will be paid to stockholders on January 5, 19X1 to those listed on the corporate records at December 5, 19XX.

Note that the above declaration involves three important dates:

1. **The Declaration Date.** This is the date that the board officially declares a dividend. Upon declaration of the dividend by the board, a dividend liability is created. In the above example, the declaration date is November 30, 19XX.
2. **The Record Date.** In order to determine which shareholders are entitled to receive a dividend, the board must fix a record date in advance. The record date is generally no more than fifty days before the date of payment. In the above example, the record date is December 5, 19XX.
3. **The Date of Payment.** This is the date on which the checks are disbursed by the corporation. In the above example, the payment date is January 5, 19X1.

What Does Ex-dividend Mean?

In order to receive a dividend, an individual must have bought or owned the stock before the ex-dividend date, which is four business days before the holder of record date. Thus, if the holder of record date is May 5, the stock will go ex-dividend on May 1. Therefore, an individual must have bought the stock on the last day of April in order to get the dividend.

WHO IS ENTITLED TO THE DIVIDEND IF NO DATE OF RECORD IS SPECIFIED?

If the directors do not specify a date of record, the dividend belongs to the owner of the shares on the date that the dividend was declared.

EXAMPLE Stafford Uniforms Inc. declared a $1.00 per share cash dividend on June 1, 19XX payable on July 1, 19XX. On June 5, Mary Hume sold her shares to Clark Baylor. Mary is entitled to the dividend since she was the owner of record on the date that the dividend was declared.

THE RIGHT OF A CORPORATION TO REPURCHASE ITS OWN OUTSTANDING SHARES

A corporation has the power to repurchase its own outstanding shares. A corporation might do this to consolidate its ownership into the hands of a small group of investors or to prevent the shares from falling into the hands of individuals who might be hostile to the best interests of the corporation, such as a competitor.

To protect creditors, reacquisitions and redemptions are subject to legal restrictions similar to those applicable to dividends. A corporation can only repurchase its own shares if it has sufficient retained earnings or if the repurchase will not render the corporation insolvent.

EXAMPLE The Bayou Water Supply Company Ltd. has 10,000 common shares outstanding. It also has only $500 in retained earnings. The corporation seeks to repurchase 1,000 shares with a fair market value of $10,000 owned by Digby Mantle, a shareholder. Bayou cannot repurchase the shares since it would render the corporation insolvent.

Insolvency can also occur when a corporation's liabilities exceed its assets.

What the applicable RMBCA section says *Section 6.40 (a), governing distributions to shareholders, states that a board of directors may authorize and the corporation may make distributions to its shareholders subject to restrictions set forth in the articles of incorporation. Section 6.40 (c) states that no distribution may be made if, after giving it effect, the corporation would not be able to pay its debts as they become due in the usual course of business or the corporation's total assets would be less than the sum of its total liabilities plus the amount that would be needed to satisfy the preferential rights of a designated class of shareholders.*

CHAPTER 13

Terminating the Corporation: Dissolution, Mergers and Consolidations, and Bankruptcy

THE SALE OF CORPORATE ASSETS

A mere sale of some or even all of corporate assets, may not amount to a dissolution. Such sale might be part of a redeployment of the corporation's operations into new and more potentially lucrative areas of operations. On the other hand, if irreconcilable differences arise among persons who are active in the management of a corporation, particularly a close corporation, a dissolution might be the only solution.

What the applicable RMBCA section says *Section 12.01, governing the sale of corporate assets in the regular course of business, states that a corporation may sell, lease, or dispose of all, or substantially all, of its property in the usual or regular course of business. Unless required by the articles of incorporation, shareholder approval is not required.*

Section 12.02, governing the sale of corporate assets not in the regular course of business, states that a corporation may sell, lease, or dispose of all or substantially all, of its property otherwise than in the regular course of business on terms stipulated by its board of directors. Shareholder approval is required.

DISSOLUTION

The dissolution of a corporation requires that the entity file a certificate of dissolution. As a result, its operations are terminated, its assets distributed first to its creditors and then to its shareholders, and the corporation then ceases to exist.

OBSERVATION *If all the corporate assets are sold prior to launching new activities, the directors are permitted to declare dividends provided legal standards are met. This includes having adequate retained earnings and enough capital with which to pay off all creditors.*

Voluntary Dissolution

In virtually all states, there are two methods of dissolution: voluntary and involuntary proceedings. A voluntary proceeding can be initiated by either the corporation's board of directors or by its shareholders. A few states require that a majority of the directors approve while other states set lower requirements. Upon approval by directors' vote for voluntary dissolution and subsequent ratification by the shareholders, a certificate of dissolution is filed. Although the corporation is technically dissolved, the directors are given the power to wind up the corporation's affairs. This process involves selling the corporation's assets, paying off all corporate obligations, and making liquidating distributions to the shareholders.

EXAMPLE The Candor Fragrance Corporation, a close corporation, is composed of four shareholders who also serve as directors. Although they specialize in producing and distributing womens' toiletries, two of the shareholders wish to expand into men's fragrances while the other two owners refuse to do so. This impasse continues for several months with the result that there has been a substantial falloff of business and bankruptcy is now possible. Absent a provision in the articles permitting the use of an arbitrator (see Chap. 9) to settle director deadlock, a voluntary dissolution might be the best solution. A certificate of dissolution would be filed, the corporate assets would be sold, and the creditors and shareholders given liquidating payments.

Although the above example is extreme, it does offer the shareholders capital in the form of corporate distributions, with which to pursue their own opportunities. For example, some owners might start their own corporation specializing in both mens' and womens' toiletries. Of course, a corporate buy-sell agreement might allow one group of shareholders to sell their shares either back to the corporation or to the remaining shareholders.

Involuntary Dissolution

In an involuntary dissolution, a group of shareholders owning a specific percentage of the corporation's outstanding stock, usually less than 50 percent, petition a court of proper jurisdiction to dissolve the corporation. After review of all the facts, the court may grant dissolution and appoint a receiver to wind up the corporation's affairs.

This method, called a *judicial liquidation*, is based on one or more grounds. They include the following:

1. The corporate directors are so deadlocked that the corporation cannot continue to function in a profitable manner and is in danger of insolvency; or

2. The directors have acted in an oppressive or illegal manner, such as selling off valuable corporate assets to family and friends at a fraction of their true market value; or

3. The corporation has been abandoned by its officers and directors and has ceased to function as a viable entity; or

4. The shareholders are hopelessly deadlocked and, after several meetings, are unable to elect directors as successors to the old directors; or

5. The articles of incorporation, when the corporation was formed, specified a limited life for the corporation, and the duration of life provided for has expired. This last situation is extremely rare in today's corporate environment because virtually all new articles of incorporation designate a perpetual life for the corporation.

Note that dissolution is a potent weapon for the minority shareholder. Thus, many articles of incorporation provide that in order to avoid possible involuntary dissolution, the corporation must purchase the minority shareholder's shares at their fair value. Part of this provision also requires that an independent qualified arbitrator be employed to ascertain the fair value of the dissident's shares.

When winding up corporate affairs pursuant to either a voluntary or involuntary dissolution, directors may continue the corporation for the purposes of winding up corporate affairs.

EXAMPLE The Cedric Wine Corporation correctly continued in its operations for three years after filing its certificate of dissolution for the purposes of suing other parties and for settling lawsuits brought against the corporation as defendant.

What the applicable RMBCA section says *Section 14.30 states that a court may dissolve a corporation for any of the following reasons: it is established that the corporation obtained its articles of incorporation through fraud; the corporation has continued to exceed or abused its authority; the directors are deadlocked in the management of the corporation; the shareholders are deadlocked in voting power and have failed for a period of at least* *two consecutive meetings; a proceeding has been brought by a creditor that has been reduced to judgment and remains unpaid.*

Directors who are engaged in winding up the corporation's affairs run the risk of personal liability for any debts incurred or illegal acts performed during the process.

EXAMPLE The Klein Handbag Corporation was in the process of dissolution. Part of the procedure required that the inventory be auctioned off to pay the creditors. The auction proceeds were used to pay off only part of the corporation's obligations to its creditors. Without paying the balance due the creditors, the directors declared an illegal dividend to the shareholders. The directors can be held personally liable for payment of the dividend. Their duties as trustees required that they pay off the creditors ahead of the shareholders.

What the applicable RMBCA sections says *Section 14.01 permits dissolution by a vote of a majority of the incorporators or initial directors. Section 14.02 permits dissolution by means of a vote of the directors followed by vote of the majority shareholders entitled to vote. Section 14.03 states that once a decision to dissolve is reached, the corporation must file articles of dissolution with the secretary of state. The articles must set forth the name of the corporation, the date that dissolution was authorized, and how it was authorized. Section 14.06 requires that the dissolving corporation notify known creditors of the dissolution within 120 days following the date of dissolution. Section 14.07 requires that the dissolved corporation must publish a notice of dissolution so that unknown creditors can receive notice.*

Finally, a corporation can be dissolved by the state of incorporation for failing to pay its annual corporate and franchise taxes, for failing to file any required annual reports, for continuous ultra vires acts, for criminal activities, and for procuring articles of incorporation based on fraud.

What the applicable RMBCA section says *Section 15.30 states that the secretary of state may commence a proceeding to administratively dissolve the corporation when it does not pay its taxes, does not file its annual report, fails to employ a registered agent for service of process, fails to notify the secretary of state that it has changed its registered agent, or that the stated period of life applicable to the corporation has expired.*

MERGERS AND CONSOLIDATIONS

A merger is the absorption of one corporation (called the acquired or target corporation) by another corporation (called the acquiring corporation). A consolidation is the union of two existing corporations to form a new corporation.

In a merger, the acquired corporation ceases to exist and the acquiring corporation survives. In a consolidation, both corporations disappear and a new corporation is created.

EXAMPLE 1 Allison Gear Corporation is acquired by Blue Chip Office Machines Inc. in a merger. Allison ceases to exist after the merger is completed.

EXAMPLE 2 The Brandy Wine Corporation and Spirit Waters Inc. combine into a new corporation to be called Brandy Wine and Spirits Ltd. Both Brandy Wine and Spirit Waters cease to exist after the transaction is completed. This transaction is best described as a consolidation.

Neither a merger or consolidation can wipe out the rights of the creditors without their consent, and the continuing corporation, in case of a merger, or the new corporation, in case of a consolidation, become liable for the debts of the merged or consolidated corporations.

Whether the transaction is cast as either a merger or as a consolidation, the same corporate rules apply. This means that the board of each constituent corporation must approve the merger or consolidation by a majority vote. The proposal is then submitted, usually in abbreviated form, to the shareholders for their approval. A shareholder who disapproves of the proposed transaction is often accorded the right to receive cash for his stock based upon its appraised value.

What the applicable RMBCA sections says *Sections 13.01 through 13.31 give shareholders the right to dissent corporate actions involving shareholder approval, including mergers and consolations, sales of corporate assets, and amendments of the articles of incorporation. Section 13.01 states that a dissenter means a shareholder who is entitled to dissent from a corporate action. Section 13.21 requires that the shareholder deliver a written notice to the corporation of his intent to demand payment for his shares. Section 13.25 states that the corporation shall pay the dissenter what it estimates to be the fair value of the shares. Section 13.28 gives the dissenting shareholder the right to reject the corporation's offer. Section 13.30 states that if the demand for payment is unsettled, it may petition the court to determine the fair value of the shares plus any applicable accrued interest.*

After the plan of merger or consolidation is approved by both the directors and shareholders, it is filed with the secretary of state. When state formalities are satisfied, articles of incorporation are issued to either the surviving or newly formed consolidated corporation.

TAX IMPLICATIONS *Under the Internal Revenue Code, mergers and consolidations fall under a set of rules called "Type A" mergers and consolidations. Two classes of Type A mergers have been accepted by the IRS. The first involves the acquiring corporation transferring its shares to the acquired or "target" corporation in exchange for the acquired corporation's assets and liabilities. The stock received by the target corporation is then distributed to the shareholders of the acquired corporation in return for their stock.*

Another variation of the merger technique is to have the acquiring corporation exchange its shares for the shares held by the target corporation's shareholders. Simply stated, the Internal Revenue Code recognized either a merger of stock for assets or stock for stock.

In a Type A consolidation, the acquired corporations have their assets acquired by the *new* corporation. The stock of the new (or acquiring corporation) is then distributed to the shareholders of the acquired corporations pursuant to a plan of complete liquidation. As with a merger, an alternative plan of consolidation permits an exchange of stock for stock followed by a complete liquidation of the acquired corporations.

Provided that the parties follow a specific set of rules set down by the Internal Revenue Code, both the mergers and consolidations discussed will be tax-free.

What the applicable RMBCA sections says *Section 11.01, governing mergers, states that one or more corporations may merge into another corporation if the board of directors of each corporation adopts and its shareholders approve a plan of merger.*

Section 11.02 states that a corporation may acquire all of the outstanding shares of one or more classes or series of another corporation if the board of directors of each corporation adopts and its shareholders approve the exchange.

Note that in both mergers and consolidations, the legal obligations of the old corporations must be assumed by the successor corporation.

OBSERVATION *In today's competitive marketplace, many small corporations are finding it advantageous to seek a merger or consolidation with another corporation that is engaged in the same or similar line of business. From the perspective of management, a merger or consolidation is usually superior to a dissolution. The merger or consolidation produces a synergistic effect (i.e., the total is greater than the sum of the parts, or 2 + 2 = 5) because excess assets are sold off, overhead is reduced, superfluous employees are either retired or terminated, there is an exchange of new ideas between the combined or new corporations, and new markets are opened.*

BANKRUPTCY

There are two types of bankruptcy actions applicable to businesses. Bankruptcies filed under Chapter 7 of the federal Bankruptcy Code involve the liquidation of a business's or an individual's assets to pay outstanding debts. Typically, creditors receive only a portion of the amount that they are owed.

Chapter 11 bankruptcies allow for a restructuring of the debts of a corporation and a continuance of corporate business. Unless a trustee is appointed by the court, the debtor corporation will retain possession of the business and may continue to operate with its own management. The court may appoint a trustee for cause, such as a showing of dishonesty, incompetence, or gross mismanagement, which would work to the detriment of the creditors.

OBSERVATION *In December, 1995, Phar-Mor Inc., a discount-drugstore chain, emerged from nearly three years of bankruptcy and is now operating under new ownership as a publicly traded company. Its founder was sentenced to prison for fraud and embezzlement resulting in the corporation filing for bankruptcy protection in 1992.*[6]

Under Chapter 11, a committee is created to represent creditors during the reorganization. A plan of repayment of existing debt, or to reduce current debts, is developed and then submitted to the creditors for their approval and to the Bankruptcy Court for its confirmation. The thrust of the plan is that it be fair to all of the parties involved and that it comply with all bankruptcy laws. Once the plan is confirmed by the Bankruptcy Court, it is binding on all creditors. A bankruptcy under this chapter may also permit courts to terminate lawsuits that have not yet been filed against the corporation.

A Chapter 11 bankruptcy can, under certain circumstances, be converted to a Chapter 7 liquidation by parties other than the debtor.

A corporation that has had debts discharged in bankruptcy is barred from instituting another bankruptcy action subsequent to the current one for six years.

A more complete discussion of Bankruptcy is found in *Barron's Bankruptcy Step-by-Step.*

[6]*The Wall Street Journal*, December 4, 1995, pg. B5

CHAPTER 14

Establishing the Accounting Records

SETTING UP THE CORPORATE RECORDS

When starting up a new corporation, the Internal Revenue Code requires that a system of recordkeeping suitable for the business must be set up. Note that failure to keep proper business records can lead to tax audits, additional taxes, and in extreme cases, even criminal charges.

CHOOSING THE RIGHT TAX YEAR

A corporation must calculate its net income on the basis of a tax year. The "tax year" is the annual accounting period the corporation uses for maintaining its records and reporting income and expenses. The corporation can use either a calendar year or a fiscal year.

Calendar Year

A corporation adopts a tax year when it files its first income tax return. The corporation must adopt its first tax year by the due date, not including extensions, for filing a return for that year.

The due date for filing returns for regular corporations and S corporations is the 15th day of the 3rd month after the end of the tax year. If the 15th day of the month falls on a Saturday, Sunday, or legal holiday, the due date is the next day that is not a Saturday, Sunday, or legal holiday.

EXAMPLE The Solar Roofing Repair Corp.'s year end is December 31, 19XX. March 15 of the following year falls out on Saturday. The corporate tax return (Form 1120) is due Monday, March 17. If March 15 is a Friday, the return is due on that Friday.

The Fiscal Tax Year

A regular fiscal year is 12 consecutive months ending on the last day of any month except December. A 52–53 week year is a fiscal tax year that varies from 52 to 53 weeks. If a corporation adopts a fiscal year tax year, it must maintain its books and records and report income and expenses using the same tax year.

Generally, S corporations and personal service corporations (PSC's) or professional associations (PA's) must use a regular tax year unless the corporation has a business purpose for electing a fiscal year.

52–53 Week Tax Year

A corporation can elect to use a 52–53 week tax year if it keeps its books and records and reports its income and expenses on that basis. If the corporation makes this election, the tax year will always be 52 or 53 weeks long, and will always end on the same day of the week. The corporation may choose to have the tax year always end on either:

1. The date a specified day of the week last occurs in a particular month, or
2. The date that day of the week occurs nearest the last day of a particular calendar month.

For example, a corporation may elect a tax year that always ends on the last Monday in March.

To make the election, the corporation must file the tax return for the 52–53 week year and attach a statement showing:

1. The day of the week on which the tax year will always end,
2. Whether it will end on the last such day of the week in the calendar month or on the date such day of the week occurs nearest the end of the month, and
3. The month in which or with reference to which the tax year will end.

BUSINESS PURPOSE TAX YEAR

A business purpose for a tax year is an accounting period that has a substantial business purpose for its existence. Both tax and nontax factors must be considered in determining if there is a substantial business purpose for a requested tax year.

One nontax factor that may be sufficient to establish a business purpose for a tax year is the annual cycle of business activity, called a "natural business year." The accounting period of a natural business year includes all related income and expenses. A natural business year exists when a business has a peak period and a nonpeak period. The natural business year is considered to end at or soon after the end of the peak period. In the absence of substantial distortion of income, or other factors showing that the change is requested for purposes of tax advantage, the showing of a natural business year will ordinarily be accepted as a substantial business purpose for approval of a change in accounting period. A business whose income is steady from month to month, year-round, would not have a natural business year as such. In considering whether there is a business purpose for a tax year, significant weight is given to tax factors. A prime consideration is whether the change would create a substantial distortion of income, such

as the shifting of a substantial portion of deductions, from one year to another so as to reduce tax liability.

Other nontax factors, based on the convenience of the taxpayer, usually will not be sufficient to establish that a business purpose exists for a particular tax year. These factors include the use of a particular year for regulatory or financial accounting purposes and the hiring patterns of a particular business, such as the fact that a firm typically hires staff during certain times of the year.

CHOOSING THE RIGHT ACCOUNTING METHOD

Upon incorporation, the enterprise should set up books using an accounting method that clearly shows income for the accounting period that is the corporation's tax year. The corporation must also decide whether to use a single or a double entry bookkeeping system. The single entry system is simple and easy to maintain, but may not be suitable for every corporation. Corporations may find the double entry system better because it has built-in procedures to assure accuracy and control.

Single entry

The single entry bookkeeping system is based on the profit or loss statement and includes only the corporation's business income and expense accounts. It can be a simple and very practical system for a small corporation just starting out. For tax purposes, this system records all income and expenses through the use of a daily summary of cash receipts and a monthly summary of cash receipts and cash payments.

Double entry

The double entry bookkeeping system uses books, called journals, and is based on both the income statement and the balance sheet. Transactions are first entered in a journal and then monthly totals of the journal transactions are entered in ledger accounts. Ledger accounts include income, expense, asset, liability, and net worth (the difference between what your business owns and what it owes). These accounts are used to prepare a company's financial statements.

Many computer software packages are available to enable the new corporation to install and operate a complete set of accounting books and records.

ACCRUAL VERSUS THE CASH BASIS OF ACCOUNTING
Accrual Accounting

Accrual accounting is based on the fundamental principle that all income earned for a period must be matched with the expenses assignable to that period. This process "matches" the revenue earned for the period with the expenses incurred for the same period irrespective of when the income has been received or the expenses paid. All companies listed on the various exchanges (i.e., New York, American, etc.) use the accrual basis of accounting. Small businesses, particularly professional and service type organizations, tend to use the "cash basis" of accounting.

Cash Basis

Under the cash basis, income is recorded when received, and expenses are recorded when paid. This method is simple but does not match income and costs for a given period.

EXAMPLE Polar Contractors Inc. performed work billed at $7,300 during the month of September, 19XX. The company received payments of $4,000 on September 16 and $3,300 on October 12. Wages of $2,600, the only expense, was paid on September 30. The difference in net income for the months of September and October, would be as follows:

	Cash Basis		Accrual Basis	
	September	October	September	October
Revenue	$4,000	$3,300	$7,300	None
Expense	2,600	None	2,600	None
Net Income	$1,400	$3,300	$4,700	None

It is evident from the illustration that the accrual basis gives more accurate results because it reflects the correct net income earned in each period.

Accrual accounting is the method preferred by accountants, but many small businesses prefer the simplicity of the cash basis of accounting.

OBSERVATION *The cash receipts and disbursements method of accounting is used by most individual taxpayers and most noncorporate businesses that do not have inventories. The accrual method must be used where inventories are a material income producing factor. The hybrid method, which is really a combination of the cash and accrual methods, can be used only with approval from the IRS.*[7]

HOW TO SUPPORT ALL THE ENTRIES MADE IN THE CORPORATE BOOKS

Sales slips, invoices, canceled checks, paid bills, duplicate deposit slips, and any other documents that explain and support entries made in your books should be filed in an orderly manner and stored in a safe place. Memorandums or sketchy records that approximate income, deductions, or other items may not be allowed by the Internal Revenue Service (IRS) and may result in additional taxes and other charges.

HOW TO GET AN EMPLOYER IDENTIFICATION NUMBER (EIN)

A corporation must obtain an employer's identification number (EIN) for tax purposes by obtaining and filing Form SS–4 with its local IRS office. This form is available from IRS and Social Security Administration offices. The EIN is used on filed tax returns and correspondence with the IRS.

A sole proprietorship or partnership converting into a corporation needs a new EIN. A corporation converting to an S corporation does not need a new EIN.

PAYROLL RECORDS

An employer, regardless of the number of employees, must maintain all records pertaining to payroll taxes (income tax withholding, social security, and unemployment tax) for at least four years after the tax becomes due or is paid, whichever is later.

Employers must withhold taxes from all employees, including corporate officers. In order to do so, a new employee must fill out Form W–4

---

[7]IRC Reg. §1.446-1(c)(2)(ii).

(Employee's Withholding Allowance Certificate) listing her appropriate exemptions and then sign it. The corporation will then withhold income tax based on the IRS's withholding tables. If the employee for some reason does not prepare a W–4, the corporation must treat her as a single person with no withholding exemptions. The corporation must advise its employees to prepare a new certificate if their status changes (e.g., there is a decrease in the number of their dependents). This new certificate must be filed prior to December 1 of the next year.

On or before January 31, the corporation must provide employees, the IRS, and state and local tax agencies with copies of Form W–2 (Wage and Tax Statement) listing salary earned and taxes withheld for the last calendar year.

....

OBSERVATION *Employees who expect to have no tax liability can be exempt from income tax withholding by certifying on form W–4 to his employer that he had no federal income tax liability in the preceding year, and expects to have no tax liability for the current year as well.*

....

If an employee receives tips of $20 or more in a month, the corporation must report these tips for tax purposes on or before the tenth of the following month.

The corporation must deduct social security taxes from the employee's salary, and must also match the employee's contribution. Form 941 is used to remit withholding taxes and social security deductions to the IRS. A completed Form 941 is found in back of this book. Form 941 must filed by the last day of the month following the end of the quarter, i.e., April 30, June 30, September 30, and January 31 of the following year. For example, Form 941 for the first quarter of the year (January 1 to March 1) must be filed by April 30. The corporation must also deposit the withholding and social security deductions in a separate account. This is accomplished with Form 501 (Federal Tax Deposits, Withheld Income, and FICA taxes). This form, along with the remittances, is sent to a bank authorized to accept tax deposits. An employer is either a monthly

or semiweekly depositor. An employer is a monthly depositor if the aggregate amount of employment taxes for the lookback period, (i.e., the twelve month period ending the preceding June 30) is $50,000 or less. An employer will be a semimonthly depositor for the entire calendar year if the amount of employment taxes reported for the lookback period (i.e., the twelve month period ending the preceding June 30) exceeds $50,000.

Unemployment tax is paid to both the state and the federal government. The IRS gives a partial credit for unemployment taxes paid to the state. The corporation must first register with the state Bureau of Labor; it will then receive an identification number so that its deposits will be credited to its corporate account. The corporation's employment experience rate will partly determine how much unemployment tax it must pay; the rate will change depending on how many employees are hired and fired. For example, if the corporation terminates a large number of employees, its unemployment tax rate will increase because of the higher demand placed on the state's unemployment fund.

The federal unemployment tax (FUTA) is less than the state rate. Because wages are calculated on a December 31 basis rather than the corporation's fiscal year-end, Form 940 (and the simpler Form 940–EZ) is due no later than the following January 31. The corporation must then file Form 940 (or Form 940–EZ) with the IRS to show how the corporation computed the unemployment tax. If the amount exceeds $100, the corporation should use a Special Deposit Card 508 (Federal Unemployment Tax Deposit) and pay the tax to an authorized bank before January 31. If the tax is under $100, it may remit the amount directly with Form 940 (or Form 940–EZ). A completed Form 940–EZ is found in back of this book. Usually the corporation must have at least two full-time employees before the unemployment tax will exceed $100.

If the corporation hires individuals to perform services as independent contractors, it must file an annual information return (Form 1099) to report payments totaling $600 or more made to any individual in the course of trade or business during the calendar year. The records in support of Form 1099 must list the name, address, and social security number of every independent contractor employed, along with pertinent dates and the amounts paid each person. The reports do not have to be mailed with copies of Form 1099 but must be available for examination by the IRS if required. Each payment must be supported by an invoice submitted by the contractor.

PAYROLL TAXES

The most common types of payroll deductions are Social Security taxes, federal, state and city withholding taxes, and miscellaneous items, such as insurance premiums, employee savings, and union dues.

Social Security Taxes

All corporate employers covered are required to collect the employee's share of Social Security tax by deducting it from the employee's gross pay and to remit it to the government along with the employer's share. Both the employer and the employee are taxed at the same rate, currently 6.2 percent (1996) based on the employee's gross pay up to a $62,700 annual limit.

Medicare is a two-part program designed to alleviate the high cost of medical care for those over age 65. The Basic Plan, which provides hospital and other institutional services, is financed by a separate Hospital Insurance tax (also called the Medicare tax) paid by both the employee and the employer at the rate of 1.45 percent on the employee's total compensation. The Voluntary Plan takes care of the major part of doctors' bills and other medical and health services and is financed by monthly payments from all who enroll plus matching funds from the federal government.

The combination of the O.A.S.D.I. tax, often called Federal Insurance Contribution Act (F.I.C.A.) tax, and the federal Hospital Insurance Tax make up the Social Security tax. The combined rate for these taxes, 7.65 percent on an employee's wages to $62,700 and 1.45 percent in excess of $62,700, is changed annually by acts of Congress. The corporate employer is required to remit to the government its share of F.I.C.A. tax along with the amount of F.I.C.A. tax deducted from each employee's gross compensation.

Income Tax Withholding

Federal and some state income tax laws require employers to withhold from the pay of each employee the applicable income tax due on those wages. The amount of income tax withheld is computed by the employer according to a government-prescribed formula or withholding tax table. The amount to be withheld for the pay period depends on each employee's taxable wages, marital status, and claimed dependents.

If the income tax withheld plus the employee and the employer social security taxes exceeds specified amounts per month, the employer is required to make remittances to the government at given intervals during the month. Monthly deposits are not required if the employer's liability for the calendar quarter is less than $500. Instead, the tax liability is remitted with the employer's quarterly payroll tax return.

EXAMPLE Assume a weekly payroll of $10,000, entirely subject to F.I.C.A. and Medicare (7.65 percent), income tax withholding of $1,500, and a deduction of $100 in union dues.

The entry to record the wages and salaries paid and the employee payroll deductions would be:

Wages and Salaries		$10,000
Less:		
F.I.C.A. Taxes Payable	765	
Withholding Taxes Payable	$1,500	
Union Dues	100	2,365
Net Payroll Payable		$ 7,635

Unemployment Taxes

Another payroll tax levied by the federal government in cooperation with state governments provides a system of unemployment insurance. All employers who (1) paid wages of $1,500 or more during any calendar quarter in the year or preceding year or (2) employed at least one individual on at least one day in each of twenty weeks during the current or preceding calendar year are subject to the Federal Unemployment Tax Act (F.U.T.A.). This tax is levied *only on the employer* at a rate of 6.2 percent (1996) on the first $7,000 of compensation paid to each employee during the calendar year. However, a credit is granted for up to 5.4 percent of wages paid to the state government so that the amount paid to the federal government may be as low as 0.8 percent.

State unemployment compensation laws differ from the federal law and differ among various states. Therefore, employers must be familiar with the unemployment tax laws in each state in which they pay wages and salaries. Although the normal state tax may range from 3 percent to 7 percent or higher, all states provide for some form of merit rating under which a reduction in the state contribution rate is allowed.

In order not to penalize an employer who has earned a reduction in the state contribution rate, the federal law allows a credit of 5.4 percent even though the effective state contribution rate is less than 5.4 percent.

EXAMPLE The Cable Telephone Corporation, which has a taxable payroll of $100,000, is subject to a federal rate of 6.2 percent and a state contribution rate of 5.7 percent. But because of stable employment experience, the company's state rate is 1 percent. The computation of the federal and state unemployment taxes for Cable Telephone is as follows:

State unemployment tax payment (1%)($100,000)	$1,000
Federal unemployment tax (6.2% – 5.4%)($100,000)	800
Total federal and state unemployment tax	$1,800

The federal unemployment tax is paid annually on or before January 31 of the following taxable calendar year. State contributions generally are required to be paid quarterly.

Beginning in 1994, the IRS has established an electronic funds transfer (EFT) system for federal tax deposits by which employer withheld taxes may be transferred to a financial institution authorized to collect such funds on behalf of the government.

MISCELLANEOUS FRINGE BENEFITS

While employee compensation is taxable, the tax law encourages certain types of fringe benefits by allowing the corporation to deduct the cost of the benefit while permitting the employee to exclude the value of the benefits from her income. Some of the suggested benefits are as follows:

Pension and Profit-Sharing Plans

A newly formed corporation can set up pension, profit-sharing, and stock bonus plans, which give rise to immediate tax deductions for the corporation while enabling the corporation to attract and keep qualified individuals. Earnings in these plans are not taxable to the employees until the payments are actually received at a later date. A *pension plan* can be either contributory or noncontributory. Under a noncontributory pension plan, contributions are made solely by the corporation. Under a contributory pension plan, the employee makes additional contributions to supplement those made by the corporation.

Under a *profit-sharing plan*, the employer allocates a share of corporate profits according to some predetermined formula. Incidental benefits such as disability, death, or medical insurance can also be provided as part of a profit-sharing arrangement. A profit-sharing plan can be established in addition to or in lieu of a pension plan.

A *stock bonus plan* is a special type of arrangement whereby the employer's stock is contributed to a trust. The stock is then allocated to each participant in the trust for eventual distribution to them.

Qualified pension, profit-sharing and stock plans must meet complex rules in order to achieve their favorable tax treatment of immediate deductibility.

Cash or Deferred Arrangement Plans

Corporate executives can sign agreements calling for compensation to be paid at future dates. Such agreements result in a tax savings because the income will be spread over several future periods, thereby resulting in the income being taxed at lower rates.

EXAMPLE Wade Flag, a retired baseball player, is hired by Syndicated Restaurant Chains Inc. to represent them at all public events sponsored by the chain. Syndicated initially proposed a salary agreement calling for annual payments of $300,000 per year for three years or a total of $900,000. Instead,

Flag demanded and eventually received a contract calling for specified payments of $90,000 per year to be paid over ten years thereby allowing the income to be taxed at a lower personal rate.

Life Insurance Arrangements

The corporation can make the following programs available to its employees.

1. *Group-term.* Under this arrangement, the corporation provides group insurance coverage for its employees. The corporation gets a deduction for the premium payment, and the premiums attributable to the first $50,000 of coverage are excluded from the employee's gross income.
2. *Split-dollar.* Split-dollar insurance is an arrangement in which the corporation purchases life insurance on certain key employees. The corporation pays that part of the premium equal to the annual increase in the cash value of the policy, and the employee pays the balance of the premium.
3. *Key-employee.* Key-employee insurance is a form designed almost exclusively to compensate the corporation for the loss of a vital employee whose services are important to the success of the enterprise. The insurance proceeds received by the corporation in the event of the employee's death are nontaxable. The premiums, however, are nondeductible by the corporation.

Health Insurance Arrangements

These plans may include the following:

1. *Accident and health insurance.* A corporation may provide accident and health insurance coverage for its employees. Under the Internal Revenue Code, the employer's premium payments are deductible by the corporation and are not included in the employee's income. Moreover, the actual payment of the insurance benefit is not included in the employee's income.
2. *Medical reimbursement plans.* This type of plan allows employees to exclude from income amounts received as reimbursement for medical expenses they incur for their medical care and those of their spouses and dependents.

Death Benefits

The corporation may establish a death benefit program whereby payments are made to a family or friends of the employee who dies. The Internal Revenue Code permits a $5,000 exclusion for each deceased employee. If there is more than one beneficiary, the $5,000 exclusion is allocated among all of the beneficiaries.

EXAMPLE Randolph Brand, an employee of the Whitecomb Chair Corp., died in 19XX. According to his death benefit policy, his $10,000 death benefit was to be shared equally by his mother and his companion. Thus, each beneficiary will receive a $5,000 death benefit of which $2,500 will be excluded from taxes ($5,000/2), and each will be taxed on the remaining $2,500.

Cafeteria Plans

These are plans that offer employees the option of choosing cash or certain nontaxable fringe benefits, such as group term life insurance, accident and health benefits, or child care. If the employee chooses cash, the cash is taxable. However, if the employee instead chooses a nontaxable fringe benefit, the value of the benefit is excluded from gross income. The fact that the employee could have chosen cash will not cause the fringe benefit to be taxed. The plan cannot discriminate in favor of highly compensated employees or their dependents or spouses. Employer plans may specify what benefits are offered and may limit the amount of benefits that individual employees may receive.

Dependent Care Assistance Programs

An employer can set up a dependent care assistance program that provides for care of an employee's children or other dependents. The purpose of the program is to allow the employee to work. Payments up to $5,000 annually is excluded from the employee's gross income.

"Flextime" programs

In order to allow employees to spend more time with their families, some corporations offer "flextime" where employees can arrange their work schedules in different ways, such as four ten-hour days with three days off, work from home part of the day, etc.

The Family and Medical Leave Act of 1993

Under the Family and Medical Leave Act (FMLA), covered employers must provide access to up to twelve weeks' leave per calendar or fiscal year for the employee's own illness, the illness of a close family member, or the birth or adoption of a child. This act applies to employers with fifty or more employees in each day of twenty or more workweeks in a year in which an employee seeks to take leave.

Other Miscellaneous Benefits

Corporations may also provide such nontaxable fringe benefits as qualified employee discounts, de minimis (meaning minimal cost) fringe benefits, such as free coffee, free parking subject to a monthly statutory limit, and the use of athletic facilities, such as employer owned tennis courts.

CHAPTER 15

Taxation of Corporations

ORGANIZATIONS TAXED AS CORPORATIONS

While the sole proprietorship and general and limited partnerships are subject to a single tax at the individual or personal level, the corporation is subject to double taxation. This tax burden is frequently cited as the major disadvantage of doing business in the corporate form. Corporations are required to pay an entity-level tax on their taxable income. They file tax returns (Form 1120 or Form 1120A if they meet certain requirements) and pay tax on corporate taxable income at specific rates. Shareholders pay additional tax (at their own individual rates) on dividends that are declared and paid from the corporations earnings and profits. This means that corporate stockholders are effectively taxed twice on income, once at the corporate level and again when profits are distributed by way of a dividend. Shareholders must also eventually pay a tax on capital gains (stock losses can offset a shareholder's ordinary income up to $3,000 per year) from the subsequent sale of their shares.

Current corporate tax rates are as follows:

Rate	Taxable Income	Tax
15%	Up to $50,000	$7,500
25%	$50,000–$75,000	6,250
34%	$75,000–$100,000	8,500
39%	$100,001–$335,000	91,650
34%	$335,001–$10,000,000	3,286,100
35%	$10,000,000–$15,000,000	1,750,000
38%	$15,000,000–$18,333,333	1,266,667
35%	Over $18,333,333	

For a corporation that has taxable income in excess of $100,000 for any taxable year, the amount of the tax is increased by the lesser of (1) 5 percent of the taxable amount over $100,000 or (2) $11,750. The extra 5 percent surtax is designed to phase out the benefits of the lower rates on the first $75,000 in taxes.

Secondly, the maximum tax rate on corporate taxable income increases from 34 percent to 35 percent for corporate taxable income in excess of $10 million. In addition, in order to recapture the benefits of being subject to a lower 34 percent tax rate, corporate taxable income in excess of $15 million is subject to an additional tax equal to the lesser of (1) 3 percent of the excess or (2) $100,000.

EXAMPLE 1 For 19XX, Derby Horse Farms, Inc. has taxable income of $335,000. The corporate tax liability will be $113,900 determined as follows:

Taxable Income	Tax Rate	Tax
$ 50,000	× 15%	$ 7,500
25,000	× 25%	6,250
260,000	× 34%	88,400
235,000 ($335,000 – $100,000)	× 5%	11,750
		$113,900

EXAMPLE 2 For 19XX, Zinnia Art Galleries, Inc. had taxable income of $400,000. The tax liability for the corporation would be $136,000 calculated as follows:

Rate	Taxable Income		Tax
15%	First	$50,000	$ 7,500
25%	Next	25,000	6,250
34%	Next	325,000	110,500
			124,250
Add: Surtax $335,000 – $100,000			
= $235,000 × 5%			11,750
	Total tax		$136,000

An alternate method for calculating the corporate tax liability of $136,000 would be to multiply $400,000 × 34 percent.

EXAMPLE 3 For 19XX, The China Paint Corporation had taxable income of $14 million. The tax liability for the corporation would be $4,800,000 calculated as follows:

Rate	Bracket		Tax
15%	Up to $50,000	$	7,500
25%	$50,000–$75,000		6,250
34%	$75,000–$100,000		8,500
39%	$100,001–$335,000		91,650
34%	$335,001–$10,000,000		3,286,100
35%	$10,000,000–$14,000,000		1,400,000
			$4,800,000

An alternate method for calculating the corporate tax liability of $4,800,000 would be as follows:

$10,000,000 × 34%	$3,400,000
4,000,000 × 35%	1,400,000
$14,000,000	$4,800,000

A personal service corporation (PSC) or professional corporation (PA) does not enjoy the benefits of having the first $50,000 taxed at 15 percent and the next $25,000 at 25 percent. Instead, a PSC must pay a flat tax of 35 percent on all of its taxable income. Thus, assuming that a personal service corporation had taxable income of $80,000, its tax liability for the year would be $28,000 ($80,000 × 35 percent).

Filing Requirements

The corporate tax return filed is Form 1120 unless the corporation is a small business corporation entitled to file the shorter Form 1120-A. Form 1120-A may be filed if *all* of the following requirements are met:

1. Gross receipts or sales do not exceed $500,000.
2. Total assets do not exceed $500,000.
3. The corporation is not involved in a dissolution or liquidation.
4. The corporation is not a member of a controlled group (controlled by other corporations).
5. The corporation does not file a consolidated tax return.
6. The corporation does not have ownership in a foreign corporation.
7. The corporation does not have foreign shareholders who directly or indirectly own 50 percent or more of its stock.

AVOIDING DOUBLE TAXATION: THE S CORPORATION

S corporations can avoid paying corporate income taxes if all the shareholders consent to taxation of corporate income at the shareholder level. Although there are exceptions, most often the corporation itself is not a tax-paying entity. This is in sharp contrast to the separate taxpayer status held by regular corporations who are subject to double taxation. In effect, the election makes the S corporation a tax-reporting rather than a tax-paying entity. The income of the corporation flows through to the individuals as if the reporting entity was a partnership. Simplified, the S election treats the corporation as if it is a partnership. S corporations file Form 1120S annually.

EXAMPLE Roy Eric is the sole shareholder of the Office Design Corporation. For the year 19XX, Design earned taxable income of $400,000. Office Design's directors elected to distribute all after-tax earnings as a dividend to Roy. Assume that he is in the 39.6 percent tax bracket. The total federal taxes paid on the $400,000 of taxable earnings would be $240,544 calculated as follows:

		Taxes Paid
Taxable income	$400,000	
Less: Corporate tax at 34%	136,000	$136,000
Balance distributed as a dividend	$264,000	
Less: Individual tax at 39.6%	104,544	104,544
After-tax dollars	$159,456	
Total taxes paid		$240,544

If Roy had elected S corporation status for 19XX, his total tax liability would have been $158,400 ($400,000 × 39.6 percent) resulting in a tax savings of $82,144 ($240,544 – $158,400).

In order to qualify under Subchapter S, a corporation must be a small business corporation. The following additional requirements must be met in order to be a small business corporation.

1. Must be a domestic corporation.
2. Must not have more than 35 shareholders (75 shareholders for tax years starting in 1997).
3. Must include only eligible shareholders.
4. Must have only one class of stock.

There are other limitations as well.

OBSERVATION *The corporation may not have more than 35 (75 in 1997) shareholders. Thus, if a husband and wife own shares as joint tenants, they are considered as one shareholder for this purpose. However, should the couple later divorce, then each would count as a separate shareholder even if the stock is still held jointly. If one spouse dies while the couple is married, there is only one shareholder as long as the stock remains in the deceased shareholder's estate.*

Individuals (other than nonresident aliens), estates, and certain trusts are eligible to hold stock in an S corporation. Among the trusts, which are not eligible shareholders of S corporation stock, are trusts adopted to administer tax-qualified retirement plans.

The IRS has also ruled that a corporation cannot qualify for an S election if it has a partner as a shareholder.

POINT TO REMEMBER *To elect S corporation status, the corporation must be a domestic corporation, owned by not more than 35 shareholders. Only one class of stock may be issued, although differences in common stock voting rights are permitted. Finally, none of the shareholders can be nonresident (an individual who is not a citizen or resident of the United States) shareholders.*

Election to be Classified As an S Corporation: Time for Election

Election to be an S corporation must be filed either at any time during the taxable year that immediately precedes the first taxable year for which the election is to be effective or at any time before the 16th day of the third month of the year to be so affected. A small business corporation must file Form 2553 (Appendix 7) (Election by a Small Business Corporation). See completed form in Basic Forms and Materials in back of text. All of the shareholders who own stock on the date the S corporation election is filed must consent to the election. If the stock is jointly owned, both joint owners must sign the consent form. Persons who are shareholders during any part of the year preceding the date of the election is made must also consent to the election even though they are not shareholders on the election date. An election made after the 15th day of the third month of the election year is treated as made for the next tax year.

EXAMPLE Sundial Wheat Growers, Inc. is incorporated on January 1, 19XX and decides to be an S corporation beginning in 19XX. The election must be made no later than March 15, 19XX to be effective for the year 19XX. If the election is made *after* March 15, 19XX, Drake will not have S corporation status until 19X1.

OBSERVATION *Generally, the IRS will give notification of acceptance of an S corporation election within 60 days after Form 2553 has been filed. Form 1120S is not to be filed until notification of acceptance is received.*

When Corporation Tax Return and Remaining Tax Due Must be Paid

Filing of the corporate tax return and payment of any balance of taxes owed are due in full by the 15th of the third calendar month following the close of the tax year. If the corporation uses a December 31 year end, it files its tax return by March 15. If it uses a fiscal year end and it ends, for example, on June 30, the tax return, and any payment, is due by September 15 (two and half months later).

A corporation can also get an automatic extension to the 15th day of the sixth month after the month of the due date of the corporate tax return by filing Form 7004 by the regular due date of the tax return. This form is an application for extension in place of filing the actual corporate tax return. Any remaining taxes due with the regular tax return must be filed with the extension.

A corporation may also have to pay estimated taxes by making four installments of estimated tax each year.

TRANSFERRING PROPERTY TO THE CORPORATE ENTITY: HOW TO CREATE A TAX-FREE TRANSFER

Section 351 of the Internal Revenue Code permits the shareholders of a corporation to defer recognition of a gain or loss on the transfer of assets to a corporation. The transfer of properties may either be made when a new corporation is formed or may reflect additional capital contributions to an existing corporation. A gain recognized by transferors of assets with a low basis to a corporation will not result in a taxable event if the following three requirements are met.

1. The person or persons making the transfer to the corporation must together control the corporation immediately after the exchange.
2. Each of the transferors must receive back stock or securities of such corporation.
3. The corporation does not assume any liabilities of a particular transferor or acquire property from a particular transferor subject to a liability if the purpose is to avoid a federal income tax on the exchange.

The utilization of Section 351 results in the following tax consequences.

1. No gain or loss is recognized by the transferor or transferors after the exchange is consummated.
2. The corporation succeeds to the transferor's adjusted basis for the property received by it.
3. The transferor's basis for the stock or securities received by him is the same as his adjusted basis for the property transferred.

EXAMPLE Alex Hayden owns a machine with a cost basis of $2,000 and a fair market value of $20,000. Hanna Baron owns land with a cost basis of $40,000 and a fair market value of $20,000. They both transfer their property to a newly organized corporation in exchange for equal shares of stock. Under Section 351, Alex's $18,000 gain and Hanna's $20,000 loss are not recognized.

How to Meet the "Control" Requirements of Section 351

All the transferors will be subject to a tax on the transfer of property to a corporation unless they meet the "control" test. "Control" means at least 80 percent of the combined voting power of all classes of voting stock and, in addition, at least 80 percent of all other classes of stock of the corporation. If two or more classes of voting stock are issued, the transferors must own at least 80 percent of the total voting power, irrespective of the number of shares issued in each class of stock. Furthermore, if two or more classes of nonvoting shares are issued, the transferors must also receive at least 80 percent of the number of shares in each class of nonvoting shares.

EXAMPLE Antony Neff and Baker Mackenzie, as individuals, form Barton Fixtures Corporation. Antony transfers property with an adjusted basis of $30,000, fair market value $60,000, for 50 percent of the stock. Baker transfers property with an adjusted basis of $40,000, fair market value $60,000, for the remaining 50 percent of the stock. Gain to either individual is not recognized because immediately after the transfer, Antony and Baker own at least 80 percent of the total combined voting power of all classes of stock.

Control Must Exist "Immediately After the Exchange"

The transferors of property to the corporation must be in control "immediately after the exchange." Control is defined as ownership of at least 80 percent of the total combined voting power of all classes entitled to vote and at least 80 percent of the total number of shares of all other classes of stock.

If a partnership distributes its assets to a new corporation in exchange for the corporation's stock and immediately thereafter transfers the stock to the partners, the control requirement is met. The control requirement would even be met if the partnership first dissolved and the former partners then transferred the property to the newly formed corporation.

If the transfer possesses the characteristics of a donative intent, the control requirements will be met.

EXAMPLE David Burke transfers land, which is an appreciated asset, to a new corporation in return for 100 shares. Immediately thereafter, David makes a gift of 30 shares to his grandchildren. The control requirement will still be satisfied.

Definition of Property

As discussed in the above paragraphs, the term "property" includes cash and intangibles, such as goodwill and patents, but excludes services that will be performed in the future.

LEASING PROPERTY TO THE CORPORATION INSTEAD OF TRANSFERRING IT

There may be a tax savings to the corporation if it leases rather than purchases corporate assets. The corporation receives an immediate tax deduction while preserving its working capital so it can be invested in more profitable ventures.

THE USE OF DEBT IN THE CAPITAL STRUCTURE: THIN INCORPORATION

Under a procedure called "thinning," assets are transferred to the corporation not only for stock but also for debt securities, such as notes payable to the shareholders. The advantage is that the interest payable by the corporation to the shareholders is tax deductible by the corporation. By contrast, dividends paid on the stock are not a deductible item but represent a distribution of profits. Thinning of the capital structure also enables the shareholders to share with the general creditors of the corporation in case of insolvency. If the shareholder's entire interest in the corporation was in the form of a stock investment, the entire investment may be lost in case of an insolvency proceeding.

Thinning also allows the corporation an opportunity to distribute the cash of a prosperous corporation to its shareholders in the form of a loan repayment. This permits the shareholder to receive dollars at no tax cost.

DANGER ZONE *If the debt-to-equity ratio of a closely held corporation is excessive, some of the alleged debt might be treated as stock by the IRS. That is, so-called interest and principal payments to the shareholders may be taxed as ordinary dividends, assuming adequate earnings and profits in the corporation. The point at which a debt-to-equity ratio becomes excessive is not clear. Court cases and the IRS have suggested that ratios exceeding three to one or four to one should be treated as excessive.*

EXAMPLE 1 Robert Downs starts a new corporation and invests $100,000. He takes back $80,000 in 10 percent ten year notes and $20,000 in common stock. This situation, showing a ratio of four to one would most likely be viewed as one of thin incorporation and the notes would be treated as equity. Thus, any interest payments attributed to them would be treated as nondeductible dividends.

EXAMPLE 2 Same facts as in **EXAMPLE 1**, except that Downs takes back $50,000 in notes and $50,000 in stock. Thin incorporation would not be an issue in this case and any interest paid on the notes would be tax deductible.

Checklist for determining whether thin capitalization is a problem.

1. Is it in fact, a true debt instrument? Does it call for an unconditional promise by the

2. Is there a conversion privilege (debt to equity)?

3. Is there a fixed interest rate?

4. Is there a relationship between the proportion of stock held by an investor and the proportion of debt held by that investor?

5. Has shareholder debt been subordinated to outside creditor debt?

6. The debt-to-equity ratio of the corporation's capital structure should be examined. Although no clear-cut rule of thumb can be given, if the debt-to-equity ratio of shareholders' holdings exceeds three to one, a careful evaluation is required.

ASSURING ORDINARY LOSS DEDUCTIONS UNDER SECTION 1244

Section 1244 rules permit an ordinary loss to be claimed for qualifying stock issued by small business corporations. Clearly, an ordinary loss is more advantageous to an investor than a capital loss deduction. Original stockholders that contribute up to $1,000,000 of corporate capital are permitted to deduct realized capital losses against their other income without regard to the usual annual limitation that applies to the sale of regular stock (currently $3,000). The annual Section 1244 deduction limit is $50,000 per taxpayer ($100,000 for a joint return). Losses in excess of the dollar ceiling in any given year are considered capital losses. To qualify, the corporation must be primarily an operating company rather than a company engaged in investing.

Section 1244 stock must be common stock issued by a small business corporation. This means that the amount of money and other property received by the corporation for its stock as a contribution to capital and as paid-in surplus (retained earnings) cannot initially exceed $1 million.

EXAMPLE Helen Allen, who is married filing a joint tax return, is one of the original stock purchasers of Halo Cosmetics Ltd. whose stock qualifies for Section 1244 treatment. Two years ago, in 19XX, she bought the stock for $200,000. During 19X2, she sold all of the stock for $50,000 thereby sustaining a $150,000 loss ($200,000 – $150,000). On her joint return for 19X2, she can deduct $100,000 as an ordinary loss. The remaining portion of the loss $50,000 ($150,000 – $100,000) is treated as a long-term capital loss. Assuming that Helen has no other capital gains, she can deduct $3,000 of the remaining $50,000 capital loss in 19X2 and $47,000 ($50,000 – $3,000) will be carried forward to future years.

An S corporation can elect Section 1244 treatment.

How to Make the Election

A board resolution must be passed prior to the original issuance of the shares. The resolution would appear as follows:

Section 1244 of the Internal Revenue Code permits ordinary loss treatment when the holder of Section 1244 sells or exchanges such stock at a loss or such stock becomes worthless. The stock to be issued by this domestic corporation shall be issued as "Section 1244" stock. It is the desire of this corporation to secure for its shareholders any benefits accorded them under Section 1244.

Thus, it is hereby resolved that all stock of this corporation initially issued shall be designated "Section 1244" at the time of issuance thereof. The officers are hereby authorized and empowered to perform all acts necessary to carry out the issuance of such stock in the manner prescribed by the Internal Revenue Code.

PARTIAL CAPITAL GAIN EXCLUSION FOR SMALL BUSINESS STOCK HELD FOR FIVE YEARS

A noncorporate taxpayer who holds for more than five years qualified small business stock issued after August 10, 1993, can exclude 50 percent of any gain on the sale or exchange of the stock. The amount of gain eligible for the exclusion is limited to the greater of (1) ten times the taxpayer's basis in the stock or (2) $10 million of gain from stock in that corporation. The exclusion is on a shareholder-by-shareholder basis.

EXAMPLE Archer Corless acquired all 100 shares of the Allentown Screw Corp. common stock in 19XX (after August 10, 1993) by transferring property with a cost of $10,000 and a fair market value of $40,000.

Allentown is a qualified small business corporation. In June of the year 20XX, Archer sold all of the stock for $100,000. The excluded gain would be $45,000 calculated as follows:

Selling Price	$ 100,000
Less: Cost Basis	10,000
Realized Gain	$ 90,000
Exclusion Percentage	50%
Excluded Gain	$ 45,000

The limitation under the Internal Revenue Code is the greater of $10,000 or $400,000 ($40,000 × 10). Thus, none of the $90,000 is subject to the limitation.

The rules establishing what constitutes qualified small business stock for purposes of this rule are as follows:

1. The stock must be acquired by the taxpayer at original issuance after August 10, 1993. Thus, stock acquired by purchase from a prior stockholder is not eligible for the exclusion.
2. The corporation must be a C corporation that uses at least 80 percent of its gross assets in the active conduct of a qualified trade or business.
3. A qualified trade or business is any trade or business other than personal service type businesses, such as health, law, or engineering.
4. As of the date of issuance of the stock, the corporation's gross assets cannot exceed $50 million.

ELECTION TO AMORTIZE ORGANIZATION COSTS

Under the Internal Revenue Code, a corporation may elect to amortize its organizational expenses over a period of sixty months or more for tax purposes beginning with the first month of corporate operations. To qualify for the election, the expenditure must be incurred before the end of the taxable year in which the corporation begins doing business. These expenditures include fees paid for legal services in drafting the corporate charter, costs of merger or consolidation, bylaws, minutes of organization meetings, fees paid for accounting services, and fees paid to the state of incorporation. The costs do not include costs of issuing and selling the stock and costs incurred in the transfer of assets to a corporation.

EXAMPLE Vanko Cosmetics, Inc. a newly organized corporation, was formed on June 30, 19XX, and began doing business on July 1. The corporation will have a December 31 year end. Vanko incurred the following expenses in organizing the business:

Legal fees for drafting corporate charter	$ 600
Fees paid for accounting services	700
Fees paid to state of incorporation	500
Costs of selling shares of stock	2,000
	$ 3,800

Amortization for the six months (July 1 to December 31, 19XX) will be $180, calculated as follows:

Legal fees for corporate charter	$ 600
Accounting fees	700
Fees paid to state	500
Organization expenses	$ 1,800

$1,800 ÷ 60 months = $30 per month × 6 months = $180. The cost of selling the shares may not be amortized.

••

WARNING *Failure to elect amortization of expenses of the corporation's organization on the corporation's initial tax return will result in their permanent capitalization without the ability to deduct these expenditures. Therefore, it is imperative to properly categorize these costs as amortizable because any attempt to improperly deduct the entire cost in the first year will result in their permanent disallowance.*

••

The corporation's election is made by attaching to its initial tax return a statement indicating the amount and nature of the expenditures, the date the expenditures were incurred, the period over which it will be amortized, and date of incorporation.

ELECTION TO AMORTIZE BUSINESS START-UP EXPENSES

A distinction must be made between a corporation's organization expenses discussed in the preceding section and its start-up expenses. Start-up expenses are qualifying expenditures made in connection with the creation or acquisition of a trade or business. They include market surveys, advertising, outside consulting services, training costs prior to starting a business, and travel and entertainment. A separate election may be made to amortize start-up expenses over a period of sixty months or more starting with the first month that corporate business begins.

The corporation's election is made by attaching to its initial tax return a statement indicating the amount and nature of the expenditures, the date the expenditures were incurred, the period over which they will be amortized, and the date of incorporation.

LIMITED DEDUCTIONS: CHARITABLE CONTRIBUTIONS AND CAPITAL GAINS AND LOSSES
Introduction
Corporations making contributions to recognized charitable organizations are allowed a maximum deduction of 10 percent of their taxable income. Any charitable contributions in excess of the allowed deduction can be carried forward five years.

Accrual of Charitable Contribution Allowed
A charitable contribution can be deducted by an accrual basis corporation, even if the contribution has not been paid by year-end, as long as:

1. The contribution has been accrued by year-end, as authorized by the board of directors, and
2. The contribution is paid by March 15 of the following year for a calendar-year company, or 2½ months after the close of the corporation's fiscal year.

EXAMPLE For 19XX, Sexton Batteries, Ltd. had total sales of $100,000 and operating expenses of $35,000 before deducting charitable contributions of $20,000. Sexton may deduct $6,500 in contributions for the year calculated as follows:

Taxable Income Before Deducting	
Contributions	$ 100,000
Less: Operating Expenses	35,000
	$ 65,000
Contribution limitation	
(10% × $65,000)	$ 6,500

The remaining contributions of $13,500 ($20,000 – $6,500) are carried over for five years.

A corporation may not deduct any charitable contribution if the corporation had a net operating loss for the year.

Capital Gains and Losses
A corporation determines its capital gains and losses in the same manner as other taxpayers.
Gains
Unlike the individual, the tax rate on net capital gain for a corporation, is not limited to 28 percent.
Losses
The $3,000 deduction for capital losses in excess of capital gains available to individuals is not allowable to corporations. Thus, a corporation can only use capital losses to offset capital gains.

1. Excess capital losses may be carried back three years and then forward five years.
2. Carryback and carryforward losses are treated as short-term capital losses in the year to which they are carried.

PERSONAL HOLDING COMPANY TAX
Introduction
The personal holding company (PHC) penalty tax is imposed in order to discourage the use of the corporate form as an "incorporated pocketbook" to shelter the income of high tax bracket individuals from the individual tax rates. To be considered a personal holding company (PHC), the corporation must satisfy two tests—the "adjusted ordinary gross income" test and the stock ownership test.

The "Adjusted Ordinary Gross Income" Test
The personal holding company (PHC) income test is satisfied if the corporation's personal holding company equals or exceeds 60 percent of its total ordinary gross income. PHC income means unearned income such as interest, dividends, rents, and royalties in addition to amounts received under personal service contracts. There are exceptions to this complex rule.

The Stock Ownership Test

The stock ownership test is satisfied if at any time during the last half of the taxable year more than 50 percent of the outstanding stock of the corporation is owned, directly or indirectly, by or no more than five individuals. Individuals are regarded as constructively owning any stock owned by members of their families (called the attribution rule under the IRC). Almost all closely held corporations will meet the 50 percent ownership test.

EXAMPLE The Damon Holding Corp. which is owned by four shareholders, has adjusted ordinary gross income of $100,000 for the year. The $100,000 is composed of interest, dividends, rents, and royalties. Since the corporation is owned by less than five individuals for the entire year, and all of its income is unearned income, Damon is a personal holding company.

If a corporation is a personal holding company for a given year, it is subject to a flat rate of 39.6 percent on any undistributed PHC income *in addition* to whatever corporate income tax it already pays.

ACCUMULATED EARNINGS TAX

This tax is imposed on the accumulation of earnings beyond the reasonable business needs of the corporation. These reasonably anticipated needs include planned additions to plant facilities, planned retirement of debt, and a provision for working capital needs. Investments are generally not regarded as reasonable business needs. A corporation is allowed to accumulate $250,000 of earnings before it must prove that the accumulation is for its reasonable business needs. The accumulated earnings credit is reduced to $150,000 for corporations primarily engaged in the business of providing professional services, such as accounting, law, health, engineering, architecture, actuarial, sciences, performing arts, and consulting.

THE USE OF FOREIGN SUBSIDIARIES

A United States corporation can form a foreign subsidiary to operate in a country where the tax rates are lower than that of the United States. The foreign corporation would pay the foreign income taxes on the subsidiary's profits and accumulate the income until such time that the parent corporation deems it appropriate to make payment to the United States parent. Upon such payment, the parent would take a direct credit against its United States federal tax liability for any foreign taxes paid.

EXAMPLE In 19XX, Maryland Manufacturing Corporation, incorporated and operating in the United States, formed a subsidiary corporation in a foreign country with tax rates that were substantially lower than United States tax rates. Over the years, the subsidiary accumulated $300,000 in net income on which it paid $50,000 in foreign taxes. In 19X5, the parent corporation deemed it appropriate to have the subsidiary transfer the profits to the United States parent. The distribution was included in the combined taxable income of the parent and resulted in a final overall federal tax liability of $400,000. The parent is now permitted to take a foreign tax credit of $50,000 based on the foreign income thereby resulting in a net tax payable of $350,000 ($400,000 – $50,000).

THE USE OF MULTIPLE CORPORATIONS TO REDUCE TAXES AND TO PROTECT CORPORATE ASSETS

Some incorporators form more than one corporation to minimize their tax exposure and to protect assets. Unfortunately, minimizing taxes by forming multiple corporations does not lower taxes under current tax laws. If two or more corporations are members of a controlled group (e.g., two or more corporations that are owned directly or indirectly by the same shareholder or shareholders), all member corporations are limited to a total of $50,000 being taxed at 15 percent, $25,000 being taxed at 25 percent, and $10 million being taxed at 34 and 35 percent.

EXAMPLE Corporations A, B, C, and D are owned by Cedric Holmes, the sole shareholder. Their individual taxable income for the year 19XX is $35,000 and their tax liabilities are calculated as follows:

Corporation	Taxable Income	Tax Liability
A	$15,000	$ 2,500*
B	$15,000	2,500
C	$15,000	2,500
D	$15,000	2,500
	$60,000	$10,000

*$12,500 × 15% = $1,875
2,500 × 25% =   625
$15,000 $2,500

Note that the same tax liability of $10,000 would result if Holmes, as the sole shareholder, owned one corporation that had net income of $60,000.

As stated in Chap. 2, the use of multiple corporations might be used to simplify operations, increase efficiency, and limit the exposure of corporate assets to outside claims and lawsuits. On the other hand, multiple entities might result in increased legal and accounting costs, duplication of operations, problems when operating in different states and municipalities due to a multiplicity of state and municipal tax laws, and possible antitrust violations.

DIVIDENDS AND THE REDEMPTION OF STOCK

When a corporation repurchases its own stock, two possibilities can result.

1. First, the redemption might be treated as a taxable dividend, or
2. The redemption might be considered an exchange of stock, thereby resulting in capital gain treatment. It depends on the particular circumstances.

A tax-free recovery of the shareholder's stock basis is not permitted if the distribution is equivalent to a dividend. A distribution might be considered equivalent to a dividend if the shareholder's percentage of ownership in the corporation remains the same.

EXAMPLE Edgar Wyler, who is unmarried and has no relatives, owns all of the 100 shares outstanding of the Keller Shipping Corp. Edgar redeems 50 shares costing $1,000 for $10,000, at a time when the corporation has retained earnings of $20,000.

Since Edgar still continues to own all of the outstanding shares, thereby retaining the same percentage of control over the corporation, the proceeds from the sale are treated as dividends subject to ordinary income tax rates.

Where the redemption completely terminates the shareholder's interest in the corporation, any profits can be treated as capital gains subject to a maximum rate capital gains rate of 28 percent.

EXAMPLE Chester Benny and Ruth Marlin each own 50 shares of the Rostand Book Co. Inc. Chester redeems his 50 shares costing $1,000 for $10,000, at a time when the corporation has retained earnings of $20,000. Since the redemption completely terminated his interest in the corporation, any long-term profits can be treated as capital gains subject to a maximum tax rate of 28 percent.

Thus, from the above discussion of this complex topic, not all stock redemptions can be given capital gains treatment.

"DEATH TAX" REDEMPTIONS: CORPORATE BUY-SELL AGREEMENTS

The Internal Revenue Code has a special provision that enables estates of deceased shareholders to more easily redeem their shares that make up a significant portion of the deceased shareholder's estate. Where the value of the stock redeemed is more than 35 percent of the decedent's gross estate with certain adjustments, the estate will *not recognize gain from the redemption* if the proceeds are used to pay all estate taxes, funeral expenses, and administration expenses imposed on the estate.

EXAMPLE Jade Phillips dies in 19XX and her gross estate is valued at $1,000,000. Her death, funeral, and administration expenses totalled $300,000. At the time of her death, she owned $500,000 worth of stock of Georgia Foods, Inc., a small business corporation. She bought the stock five years ago for $100,000. Because the value of the decedent's stock exceeds 35 percent of her gross estate, in this case 50 percent ($500,000/$1,000,000), the executor of Jade's estate may redeem $300,000 of stock tax-free. This amount is necessary to pay all of the decedent's death, funeral, and administration expenses. If it were not for this provision in the Code, the estate would have to pay a tax based upon the gain due to the redemption.

Certain types of stock repurchase agreements expedite these redemptions. These arrangements, called either stock redemption or cross-purchase agreements, assure the further continuance of the corporation. These agreements may also give the corporation or shareholders the right of first refusal should the stock become available due to the death of a shareholder, or because a shareholder wishes to sell her stock.

Agreements involving the sale of stock may take the following forms.

1. **The Stock Redemption Agreement.** This type of arrangement binds both the shareholders and the corporation. On the death of the shareholder, when the shareholder wishes to sell his stock back to the corporation, or in the event of a director deadlock that cannot be broken the corporation is bound to repurchase the shares.

2. **The Cross-Purchase Agreement.** This type of agreement obligates each of the shareholders to buy each other's shares in case of the death of a shareholder or if one of the shareholders wishes to sell.

The advantages of these types of arrangements is that they guarantee a ready market for the stock in case of death or the need for immediate cash by one of the shareholders. It also enables the executor of an estate to fix the value of the stock for estate tax purposes.

The purchase price can be established by either a fixed-dollar amount subject to annual review, by book value at date of death, by an independent CPA or other qualified appraiser, or by a formula based on prior earnings of the corporation for a stated period of time.

A detailed discussion involving the contents of a buy/sell agreement for purchasing a business is in Chap. 16.

CHAPTER 16

How to Buy and/or Sell an Ongoing Business

INTRODUCTION

T here is no absolute value that can be put on a business, although value, when determined, must be translated into terms of money. A valuation is a means of justifying the premium in the asking price of a business. While net worth is a primary factor in valuing most privately owned businesses, one cannot rely entirely on balance sheet figures because they are based upon original cost and, therefore, do not purport to reflect the current replacement value of assets.

Another issue is goodwill. Goodwill may not be reflected on the balance sheet, but it may be material in amount, and the common practice of ignoring goodwill on the corporation's balance sheet might lead to a serious undervaluation of a company's assets.

CHECKLIST OF DIFFERENCES BETWEEN A LARGE AND SMALL BUSINESS AS A DETERMINANT FACTOR IN SELECTING A VALUATION TECHNIQUE

1. Small businesses are likely to be sole proprietorships, partnerships, or S corporations while a large enterprise is usually organized as a regular corporation. The inability of a large corporation to elect S corporation status may lower its resale value.
2. If a corporation is small, the owner-shareholder plays a greater role in the success of the company. This situation may call for the owner to continue her role as the manager after the purchase of the business.
3. Larger companies usually pay their managers the market rate in salaries while smaller businesses tend to pay their managers only what they can afford.
4. Larger companies tend to have a more accurate picture of their financial condition, which might increase their tax burden, while small companies tend to use the accounting policy which produces the lowest possible tax liability.
5. Large businesses tend to be sold for cash and stock while small enterprises are usually sold for a cash down payment plus monthly payments for a fixed number of years.
6. Larger businesses have usually been in business longer than smaller entities, thus making it easier to study and evaluate their financial history and potential future value.
7. Most larger companies use the accrual basis of accounting while smaller businesses tend to use the cash basis. Under the Internal Revenue Code, the cash method of accounting may not be used by any regular corporation, except by qualified personal service corporations, and entities with average annual gross receipts of $5 million or less for all prior taxable years.

8. Larger companies usually have audited financial statements while smaller companies tend to have compiled statements (financial statements where the CPA compiles the accounting data according to generally accepted accounting principles but does not express an opinion as to the accuracy of the financial statements).

9. Larger companies generally have better accounting records than smaller entities.

10. Larger companies tend to have highly paid executives whose compensation package includes a "golden parachute" (a costly severance package) given upon termination.

11. Larger companies tend to have more union problems than smaller companies.

Some of the more important and useful methods of valuation are discussed below.

HOW TO VALUE AN ONGOING BUSINESS

Suppose that you decide to purchase an ongoing business. It does have its advantages. First, there is a recognized product with established sales outlets. Second, you have experienced employees working for you. Third, there is no start-up or break-in period where costly mistakes are made in order to "learn the ropes." Of course, purchasing an ongoing business can be costly, and there is always the ongoing risk that you, as a buyer, may overpay. The other side of the coin is that you, as a seller, may risk undervaluation of, perhaps, your most valuable asset, your business. What follows is a basic discussion regarding the use of certain methods for accurately valuing an ongoing corporation.

Tangible Book Value

This value is determined by the company's last balance sheet. Basically the computation involves subtracting the entity's total liabilities from its total assets.

DANGER *Since balance sheet assets are reflected at cost, which ignores fair market value, and since goodwill may not be recorded on the balance sheet, a business with high resale value assets or unrecorded goodwill should avoid this method.*

Adjusted Tangible Book Value

This method takes the book value of all assets and liabilities and adjusts them to fair market value.

EXAMPLE Bantam Sales Company Inc. presents the following financial data:

	Reported Net Book Value	Fair Market Value
Inventory	$ 20,000	$ 25,000
Land and plant	45,000	60,000
Equipment	50,000	100,000
	$115,000	$ 185,000
Liabilities	20,000	

Assuming that there is unrecorded goodwill of $40,000, the fair market value of the company would be $205,000 ($185,000 + $40,000 – $20,000).

Liquidation Value

This method assumes that the business ceases operations, sells its assets, pays off all of its liabilities, and distributes the remaining cash to its shareholders in proportion to their stock ownership.

EXAMPLE Sundial Paper Corporation, which has 10,000 shares of common stock outstanding, plans to liquidate by selling all of its assets, paying its liabilities, and making a liquidating distribution to its shareholders. Assuming assets with a net realizable value of $200,000, and liabilities of $50,000, each shareholder would be expected to get $15 per share calculated as follows:

Estimated fair market value of assets	$ 200,000
Less: Liabilities	50,000
Net liquidation value	$ 150,000
Outstanding number of shares	10,000
Liquidation value per share	$ 15

Replacement Value

Where there is a strong possibility that many assets are undervalued, an independent appraiser or a panel of appraisers may be called in by the buyers or sellers of the stock.

Price-Earnings Multiple

This method utilizes the company's price-earnings ratio. The price-earnings (P/E) is simply the market value of the share divided by the earnings per share.

EXAMPLE Norris Road Repair Inc. has a net income of $50,000 annually and 50,000 common shares outstanding or earnings per share (EPS) of $1 per share ($50,000/50,000 shares). The market value of the shares is estimated at $20 per share. Thus, the P/E or multiple will be $20 ÷ $1 or 20. Since the company has 50,000 shares outstanding, the value of the entire company would be 50,000 shares times $20 per share or $1,000,000. Stated another way, the entire business may be valued by multiplying the total net income of $50,000 by the price earnings multiple of 20 to arrive at $1,000,000.

How to Get the Best Tax Break

Once the buyer and the seller have decided to structure the transaction as a taxable purchase of assets, they must then decide whether to allocate the total sales price among the individual assets sold or whether to merely agree on and set forth in a single lump-sum price.

••

OBSERVATION *Note that in allocating the purchase price of a business to the newly acquired assets, the capitalized cost of goodwill and most other intangibles, such as licenses, patents and covenants not to compete acquired after August 10, 1993, and used in a trade or business, are ratably amortized over a 15-year period beginning in the month of acquisition.*

••

EXAMPLE On January 2, 19XX, Lion Supermarkets Ltd. acquired all of the net assets of Iris Flower Corporation for $200,000. Among the acquired assets were the following intangible assets:

Goodwill	$ 20,000
Patents	10,000
Licenses	5,000
A covenant not to compete for five years	30,000
	$ 65,000

All of the above assets are amortizable ratably over a period of 15 years beginning with the first month of the acquisition.

SALES OF CORPORATE SHARES AND ASSETS

In disposing of a corporate business, the deal can be constructed as either a taxable or nontaxable event. In a taxable deal, the seller might be seeking the following:

1. Avoiding double taxation, once at the corporate level, and a second at the stockholder level.
2. Establishing an ordinary loss so as to offset ordinary income.
3. Controlling the timing of the loss so as to obtain the best tax advantages.
4. The spreading out of the seller's tax liability for as long as possible so as to avoid an immediate tax liability.
5. Converting ordinary gain into capital gain so as to take advantage of the lower 28 percent personal capital gains rate.

Generally, the provisions of the Internal Revenue Code governing the sale, disposition, and liquidation of regular (or C) corporation shares and assets also apply to S corporations. Several methods are available to both types of corporations for disposing of corporate assets. Some of the more common ways for either a C or S corporation are

1. Sale of the corporation's stock. This gives the seller capital gain. The buyer may then liquidate or continue to operate the business as a subsidiary.
2. Sale of the corporation's assets and either liquidates or continues as an investment company or in a new business.
3. Liquidation of the corporation followed by the sale of corporate assets. This technique requires that the corporation recognize gain on any appreciated assets distributed.
4. The shareholder or shareholders can sell part of their stock and have the corporation redeem the remainder. In effect corporation funds are used as part of the purchase price. The seller

gets capital gains treatment and the buyer or buyers get control of the corporation.

There are significant tax differences that result to both the corporation and its shareholders depending on the method selected. Our discussion will focus on the legal and tax implications resulting from disposing of and liquidating corporate shares and assets that are unique to C and S corporations and their shareholders.

OBSERVATION *A seller might want to think about making some estate tax planning steps prior to the sale. For example, the seller might consider making gifts of stock to younger family members who may be subject to lower tax rates. Thus, if notes are received by the seller, any interest income would be taxed at a lower rate. This technique should be planned with great care since the IRS may contend that the proceeds should be taxed to the original seller who is responsible for the corporate sale rather than to the owner of the stock at the time of the execution of the sales contract.*

SALE OF STOCK OF A REGULAR C CORPORATION

When a shareholder of a C corporation sells her shares, determining gain or loss is the simplest of the acquisition transactions. The shareholder's stock basis will be his original cost adjusted, if at all, only by stock dividends and splits. Stock basis is then subtracted from the proceeds of the sale to determine gain or loss.

Whether the gain or loss is treated as long-term or short-term capital gain or loss depends merely on the shareholder's holding period, i.e., more than one year is treated as long-term capital gain or loss and one year or less is treated as short-term capital gain or loss. If part or all of the consideration is deferred into a later tax year, the seller's gain can be reported using the installment method of accounting. If part of the total consideration received by the seller of the stock represents an agreement with the purchaser not to compete for a specific period of time, the consideration received for the agreement is taxed as ordinary income.

Stock sales are popular with sellers because they are less complex and costly to the seller and

there is only one level of taxation, i.e., capital gains. No adjustments are made to the basis of the assets even if the purchase price of the stock is higher than the basis of the assets reported for tax purposes. This can be a disadvantage to the purchaser since the increased costs of the assets, and the resultant higher depreciation, is not available to the purchaser.

EXAMPLE Cheryl Cain has been the sole shareholder since 19XX, of the Sharp Wire and Conduit Corp., a regular C corporation. She owns 5,000 common shares having a $10 par value. The net assets of Sharp Wire were $50,000 ($65,000 – $15,000). Cheryl sold the stock for $60,000 to Walter Bigelow. She will have a long-term capital gain of $10,000 ($60,000 – $50,000). Bigelow, the purchaser, will not adjust the basis of the assets to reflect their stepped-up basis.

SALE OF ASSETS OF A REGULAR C CORPORATION

When a corporate seller sells assets, the transaction is reported by determining the gain or loss recognized on the sale of each individual asset. The buyer simply records the assets at their acquisition cost. The corporation may be liquidated after the sale has been completed. The corporation recognizes gain or loss with respect to the assets sold. Any properties that were not sold by the corporation can be distributed to the shareholder or shareholders as part of the liquidation. The selling corporation must recognize gain at the time the distribution occurs as if the properties had been sold. The shareholders of the selling corporation report their gain on the liquidation as capital gain or loss.

SELLING S CORPORATION STOCK

An S corporation shareholder poses greater problems than those associated with a C corporation when selling stock. While the holding period rules for S corporation stock are the same as those for C corporation shareholders, an S corporation shareholder faces the tax rule that a corporation's S election will terminate if the shares are sold to an ineligible shareholder. For example, partnerships, corporations, and nonresident aliens cannot be shareholders in an S corporation.

HOW TO HANDLE THE INSTALLMENT SALE OF A BUSINESS

The installment method of reporting involves the seller's treatment of each payment received from the sale as part gain and part nontaxable recovery of her basis in the property sold. Under the Internal Revenue Code, sales of publicly traded property, including stocks and bonds, and inventory do not qualify for the installment method. However, the sale of privately held stock, *not listed on a national exchange*, would qualify. The installment method must be used to report gains (income) from installment sales of real or personal property by nondealers unless an election is made *not* to use the method.

If the sale results in a loss, the taxpayer may not use the installment method. If the loss is on an installment sale of business assets, it can be deducted only in the tax year of the sale.

WHAT AN EFFECTIVE AND COMPREHENSIVE BUY-SELL AGREEMENT SHOULD CONTAIN

Any transaction involving the purchase and sale of a corporation contains areas of potential and costly conflicts. The following checklist will enable purchasing and selling parties to deal with potential problem areas at the time the transaction is entered into so as to avoid possible future litigation.

Checklist for Buy-Sell Agreements

1. Should the buy-sell agreement apply to just current shareholders or to all new shareholders during the life of the new or existing corporation?
2. There should be a statement in the buy-sell agreement to the effect that it supersedes all other existing agreements to redeem stock or purchase stock executed by the shareholders.
3. Will the death of a shareholder in the corporation result in an automatic buy-out of his interest, or will the next of kin be allowed to become a shareholder in the corporation?
4. Will all of the death buy-out amount be funded by insurance, or just part of it? In the event of a death buy-out, will all the proceeds from the policy be used to redeem the stock of the deceased shareholder.

5. In the event of the death of a shareholder, what will be the disposition of shareholder receivables or payables?
6. What will be the price paid to an employee shareholder who resigns or is fired from the corporation?
7. In case an employee shareholder resigns or is fired from the corporation, will a covenant not to compete be involved, and if so, what will be its geographic area (fifty miles, for example) and for how long will it be in effect (for example, five years, or in conjunction with the installment payments of the buy-out if not paid in cash)?
8. How many days should the corporation have in which to pay off a terminated, disabled, or deceased shareholder?

••
OBSERVATION *As discussd in Chap. 15, certain arrangements, called either stock redemption or cross-purchase agreements, assure the further continuance of the corporation. These agreements may also give the corporation or shareholders the right of first refusal should the stock become available due to the death of a shareholder or because a shareholder wishes to sell her stock.*
••

EXAMPLE Marvin Gunn and Sima Parno are equal shareholders in Victor Heat Controls Inc. By prior written agreement, if either individual dies, retires, or becomes totally disabled, the other shareholder is required to purchase the shares, thus becoming the sole shareholder. This is an example of a cross-purchase agreement.

9. Disability buy-out is a sensitive subject for employee shareholders to discuss. However, a disabled corporate employee cannot be carried for very long in a small business. Most businesses use a disability buy-out period of between three and six months. In other words, if one of the employee shareholders becomes totally disabled for a period of three months, on the first day of the fourth month, the corporate employee's stock is automatically sold back to the corporation at a disability buy-out price.

10. The corporation needs to discuss the possibility of one of the shareholders finding a nonrelated third party to buy his stock. Does the corporation want shareholders to have the right to sell on the open market to any third party or only have the right of first refusal? Or does the corporation want to restrict rights and only allow the shareholders to sell back to the corporation itself. There is quite a danger in allowing for unrelated third parties to make offers on stock of closely held corporations. Obviously a competitor could make an offer, making it hard to tell if it was a bona fide offer or just a ploy to drive the stock price up so that the remaining shareholders would have to pay a higher price to repurchase the stock.

11. All shareholders in the corporation who sign buy-sell agreements should also have their spouses, if any, sign the agreement as well. It is best to do this at the attorney's office and have the signatures witnessed or notarized. This prevents later problems in the event of a marital dissolution.

12. Shareholders of a corporation must decide whether or not the corporation will guarantee obligations to a retiring or deceased shareholder. The obligations should be personally guaranteed by the remaining shareholders when a shareholder dies or retires because the corporation could eventually become insolvent. Since one of the most important functions of a corporation is to shield the shareholders from personal liability, the personal guarantee, in writing, of every shareholder would provide the best protection against pending obligations.

GLOSSARY

ACCOUNTING EQUATION   Assets = Liabilities + Capital (or Shareholder's Equity)

ACCRUAL ACCOUNTING   Based on the fundamental principle that all income earned for a period be matched with the expenses assignable to that period.

ACCUMULATED EARNINGS TAX   A tax imposed on the accumulation of corporate earnings beyond the reasonable business needs of the corporation. The tax applies when corporate accumulated earnings exceeds $250,000 ($150,000 for personal service corporations).

ADOPTION   In corporation law, the concept is applied when a newly formed corporation accepts a preincorporation contract made for its benefit by a promoter prior to the corporation's coming into existence. Adoption speaks only from the time such corporation agrees to accept the benefits of the preincorporation contract, in contrast to a "ratification," which relates back to the time the original contract was made.

ARTIFICIAL ENTITY   A fictitious entity (or corporation) validly formed under state statutes applicable to corporations. Being an artificial person, it can only act through its directors, officers, employees, and agents.

ARTICLES OF INCORPORATION   A certificate (or charter) filed with the state containing the name, purposes, and number of shares authorized for sale for a proposed corporation. The charter represents a contract between the state and its incorporators.

AUTHORIZED SHARES   The shares described in the articles of incorporation, which a corporation can sell. Modern corporate practice recommends authorization of more shares than the corporation initially plans to issue.

BANKRUPTCY PROCEEDINGS   A federal action permitting a corporation to either restructure itself or to liquidate. Bankruptcies filed under Chapter 7 of the federal bankruptcy code involve the liquidation of a business's or an individual's assets to pay outstanding debts. Typically, creditors receive only a portion of the amount that they are owed. Chapter 11 bankruptcies allow for a restructuring of the debts of a corporation.

BASIS   In tax law, it is roughly the equivalent of the cost of the property by the taxpayer. To compute gain or loss on the sale or exchange of property, the basis of property is generally subtracted from the amount realized from the sale or exchange.

BENEFICIAL HOLDERS OF SECURITIES   Individuals who have the equitable or legal title to shares but who have not registered the shares on the records of the corporation.

BLUE SKY LAWS   State registration statutes that regulate the sale of securities within the state. Most blue sky laws require the registration of new issues of securities with a state agency that reviews selling documents for truth and completeness. The registration does not, however, guarantee that investors will earn a profit.

BONDS   Long term (having a maturity life of more than one year) debt instruments. They can be either unsecured or secured by a lien on some or all of the corporate property. A bond, which pays interest on a semi-annual or annual basis, is payable to either its bearer or to its registered owner.

BUSINESS CORPORATION LAW (BCL) Used in New York State in place of the Model Business Corporation Act (MBCA) and the Revised Model Business Corporation Act (RMBCA).

BUSINESS JUDGMENT RULE Under this principle, a corporate director or officer can usually avoid liability for poor business judgments.

BYLAWS Govern the internal conduct of the corporation. The initial bylaws may be formulated by incorporators, shareholders, or board of directors.

C CORPORATION Internal Revenue Code, a corporation that is subject to double taxation, once at the corporate level and again if there are profits that are distributed in the form of dividends.

CAFETERIA PLANS Employee benefit plans that offer workers the option of choosing cash or certain nontaxable fringe benefits (such as group term life insurance, accident and health benefits, or child care).

CALLABLE OR REDEEMABLE PREFERRED STOCK This type of stock is subject to involuntary redemption at the option of the board of directors at a fixed price at specific future dates.

CAPITAL GAINS AND LOSSES Under the Internal Revenue Code, stock held for longer than one year that is sold results in either a long-term gain or loss.

CAPITAL GAIN EXCLUSION FOR SMALL BUSINESS STOCK A noncorporate taxpayer who holds for more than five years qualified small business stock issued after August 10, 1993, can exclude 50 percent of any gain on the investor's sale or exchange of the stock.

CASH BASIS ACCOUNTING Under this system, income is recorded when received, and expenses are recorded when paid.

COMMON STOCK Represents the residual interest of the corporation. The common shareholders are the owners of shares who bear the risk of loss and enjoy the benefits of any profits in the form of dividend payments.

COMMON SHAREHOLDERS The owners of shares who bear the risk of loss and enjoy the benefits of any profits in the form of dividend payments. Their interest is said to be residual meaning that they are the last to be paid after creditors and preferred shareholders, if any.

CONSOLIDATION A consolidation is the union of two existing corporations to form a new corporation.

CONVERTIBLE SHARES Both common and other classes of shareholders may be given the option to exchange their shares into common stock and vice versa. This is known as the *convertibility* feature applicable to a particular class of shares.

CORPORATION BY ESTOPPEL This doctrine prevents a third party from holding a corporate director or officer or shareholder personally liable by denial of the corporate existence.

CRITERIA FOR CORPORATION NAME Name must include the word "corporation," "incorporated," "company," or "limited." Abbreviations such as "Corp.," "Inc.," "Co." and "Ltd." are also permitted.

CROSS-PURCHASE AGREEMENT An agreement that obligates each of the shareholders to buy each other's shares in case of the death of the shareholder or if one of the shareholders wishes to sell.

CUMULATIVE PREFERRED STOCK Cumulative preferred stock that gives the shareholder the right to receive a dividend, usually each quarter before the payment of any common dividends. If the dividends are not paid for a particular period, they accumulate as dividends in arrears.

CUMULATIVE VOTING A technique whereby minority shareholders concentrate all of their voting strength on one or more individual directors with the hope that they are elected. It is an excellent way of helping to preserve minority shareholder representation on the board of directors. The formula is the number of shares held times the number of individual directors to be elected.

DEADLOCK Occurs when there are an equal number of directors, and there is a tie vote that cannot be broken despite several attempts to do so, which may prevent the corporation from functioning.

DEATH TAX REDEMPTION A provision in the Internal Revenue Code stating that if the value of the stock redeemed is more than 35 percent of the decedent's gross estate with certain adjustments, the estate will *not recognize gain* from the redemption if the proceeds are used to pay all estate taxes, funeral and administration expenses imposed on the estate.

DE FACTO CORPORATION Arises when there has been a good faith attempt to comply fully with the state's statutory corporate laws and an exercise of corporate powers. A de facto corporation enjoys the same benefits as a properly formed corporation and cannot be challenged by third parties except for the state.

DEFERRED ARRANGEMENT PLANS Corporate executives can sign agreements calling for compensation to be paid at future dates. Such agreements result in a tax savings because the income will be spread over several future periods thereby resulting in the income being taxed at lower rates.

DE JURE CORPORATION   A properly formed corporation that insulates the shareholders from personal liability.

DERIVATIVE ACTION   The lawsuit is brought, usually by the minority shareholders, on the name of and on behalf of the corporation. The relief sought is in the form of compelling abusive directors and officers to account to the corporation for losses caused by their negligence, breach of fiduciary duty, or any other misconduct.

DILUTION   A reduction in the percentage of outstanding shares owned, and also control of a corporation, resulting from the issuance of additional shares to other shareholders. For example, a shareholder owning 10 out of 100 common shares outstanding would own 10 percent of the corporation. If another shareholder bought an additional 100 shares, the original 10 percent shareholder would now own 5 percent (10/200) of the corporation. Dilution has occurred. Dilution also reduces earnings per share (EPS) because more shares are outstanding.

DIRECTORS   Elected by the shareholders to represent the corporation and not the shareholders, directors, acting as a board, formulate the overall general policies of the corporation. The board of directors has final authority over all of the corporation's business activities. They are not involved in the day-to-day operations of the corporation unless they also serve as corporate officers.

DISSOLUTION   The dissolution of a corporation requires that the entity file a certificate of dissolution. As a result, its operations are terminated, its assets distributed first to its creditors and then to its shareholders, and the corporation then ceases to exist.

DIVIDENDS IN ARREARS   Dividends not paid in a particular year on preferred stock are said to be in arrears. All dividends in arrears must be paid before any dividends can be distributed to the common shareholders.

DOMESTIC CORPORATION   A corporation doing business in the state where it is incorporated.

DOUBLE ENTRY BOOKKEEPING   Under this system, debits and credits reflecting business transactions are entered into both journals and ledgers. The total amounts in the ledger are then added and adjusted at the end of the accounting period to create the financial statements.

EARNINGS PER SHARE (EPS)   Net income divided by shares outstanding. Thus, if a corporation's net income is $100,000 and there are 100,000 common shares outstanding, EPS is $1 per share ($100,000/100,000).

EMPLOYER IDENTIFICATION NUMBER (EIN)   A corporation must obtain an employer identification number (EIN) for tax purposes by obtaining and filing Form SS–4 with its local IRS office. The EIN is used on filed tax returns and correspondence with the IRS.

EX-DIVIDEND   Meaning without the right to a dividend. A share goes "ex-dividend" on the date the seller becomes entitled to keep the dividend. This date is four business days before the date of record. The names of the holders of record are listed on a specific date on the corporation's books. Thus, if January 30 is the date of record, the stock goes "ex-dividend on January 26." If the purchaser buys the stock after January 26, the seller, or previous owner, is entitled to the dividend.

EXECUTIVE COMMITTEE   Directors generally have the authority to designate executive committees composed of at least two directors, to exercise board authority in such matters as executive compensation, employee pension and retirement benefits, and accounting principles to be adopted by the corporation. Executive committees generally do not have the power to approve basic fundamental changes in the operation of the corporation, such as a merger or consolidation with another corporation, nor can they authorize the payment of dividends.

FAMILY AND MEDICAL LEAVE ACT (FMLA) OF 1993   Under this federal act, covered employers must provide access to up to 12 weeks' leave per calendar or fiscal year, for the employee's own illness, the illness of a close family member; or the birth or adoption of a child.

FIDUCIARY   An individual who is in a trust relationship. Directors, officers, and majority stockholders have a fiduciary duty to the corporation. This means that they are not permitted to work on behalf of the corporation if their acts are motivated by self-interest.

FISCAL TAX YEAR   A regular fiscal year is 12 consecutive months ending on the last day of any month except December. A 52–53 week year is a fiscal tax year that varies from 52 to 53 weeks.

FOREIGN CORPORATION   A corporation doing business in a state where it is not incorporated. Thus, a corporation incorporated in Delaware but doing business in all other states is a domestic corporation if it does business in Delaware but foreign when doing business in any other state (e.g., California).

GENERAL MANAGER   The role of this person is to administer the ordinary business of the corporation. Her general functions include hiring and firing employees, setting their compensation, purchasing materials and supplies, and paying corporate debts.

GENERAL PARTNERSHIP Composed of two or more individuals who contribute their capital and skills toward ongoing profit-directed activities. In a partnership, every partner is an agent of the partnership in dealing with third parties. Each partner is jointly (meaning that each copromisor is liable for the entire debt) and/or severally liable (meaning that each party is liable alone or individually) for the debts of the partnership.

ISSUED AND OUTSTANDING Shares sold by a corporation to its shareholders are called issued and outstanding shares.

JOINT VENTURE An undertaking by two or more persons or other entities, usually to accomplish a single objective. Aside from the single-objective feature, it is identical to a general partnership.

JUDICIAL LIQUIDATION An involuntary corporate dissolution, whereby a group of shareholders owning a specific percentage of the corporation's outstanding stock, usually less than 50 percent, petition a court of proper jurisdiction to dissolve the corporation. After review of all the facts, the court may grant dissolution and appoint a receiver to wind up the corporation's affairs.

LIABILITY FOR NEGLIGENCE Directors and officers are liable to the corporation for losses sustained by the business due to negligence in office.

LIMITED LIABILITY COMPANY (LLC) A recent form of organization that may offer greater business and tax advantages than a regular corporation. Profits and losses flow through to each individual owner on the personal level (called a "member" for LLC purposes). An LLC has the advantages of a partnership's nontaxable flow-through tax treatment, a corporate shareholder's limited liability, and a general partner's control of management (called a "manager" for LLC purposes).

LIMITED PARTNERSHIP The limited partnership form of doing business can only be created according to the formalities stated in the Uniform Limited Partnership Act (ULPA), which has been adopted in virtually all states. Every limited partnership must have at least one general and one limited partner.

LIQUIDATING DIVIDENDS Paid by a corporation that is in the process of liquidation. Such dividends are generally nontaxable under the Internal Revenue Code.

MAJORITY More than half the votes cast.

MERGER The absorption of one corporation (called the acquired or target corporation) by another corporation (called the acquiring corporation).

MODEL BUSINESS CORPORATION ACT (MBCA) A codification of today's modern corporation statutes. Used in many states as their statutory corporate law.

NATURAL BUSINESS YEAR Exists when a business has a peak period and a non-peak period.

NO PAR VALUE STOCK If no amount is designed for each share of stock in the articles of incorporation, the stock is called no par value stock. No par value stock can be given a stated value by the board of directors. The rights and privileges of the owners of no par value stock are generally the same as par value shareholders.

NONCUMULATIVE PREFERRED STOCK If a dividend is not declared on this type of stock for any given year, the obligation ceases for that particular year and there is no obligation to pay the dividend in future years.

NONPARTICIPATING PREFERRED STOCK Preferred stock that is entitled to its current annual dividend only, regardless of the dividends paid to the common shareholders.

OFFICERS Officers, unlike directors, are the true agents of the corporation. Each officer, i.e., president, vice-president, etc., has the power to bind the corporation by his individual acts within the actual or apparent scope of his authority.

OWNERS' OR SHAREHOLDERS' EQUITY Another name for the capital of the corporation. The capital of a corporation is composed of its outstanding preferred and common stock, and its surplus or retained earnings.

PAID-IN CAPITAL When a corporation receives payment for its shares in excess of its par or stated value, the excess is allocated to a capital account called paid-in capital. No such account exists where the corporation issues only no par value stock.

PAR VALUE Stock that is given an arbitrary value is called par value or stated value stock.

PARTICIPATING PREFERRED STOCK Participating preferred stock allows preferred shareholders to receive additional amounts of dividends after the dividends stipulated in the articles of incorporation are paid to both the preferred and common shareholders on a ratable basis.

PERSONAL HOLDING COMPANY A tax concept. To be considered a personal holding company (PHC), the corporation must satisfy two tests—the "adjusted ordinary gross income" test and the stock ownership test. The personal holding company (PHC) penalty tax is imposed in order to discourage the use of the corporate form as an "incorporated pocketbook" to shelter the income (meaning to offset other income) for later distribution when the individuals are in a lower tax bracket.

PIERCING THE CORPORATE VEIL Courts will sweep aside the dual personality concept applicable to the corporation by concluding that the entity and its shareholders are one and the same thereby making the shareholders personally liable for all corporate debts.

PLURALITY In some states, all directors can be chosen by a plurality (meaning the largest number of votes cast) of the shareholder votes cast providing that there is a quorum present.

PREEMPTIVE RIGHTS Allows an existing shareholder to purchase a new issue of shares in proportion to the amount of shares that he currently owns before it is offered to others. Thus, if the shareholder owns 1,000 common shares out of 10,000 common shares outstanding, he is permitted to purchase 10 percent of the new issue.

PREFERRED SHARES Shares that have preferential rights as to dividend payments and in case of corporate liquidation. Dividend payments on preferred shares are generally a stated amount of par, i.e., 6 percent of $100 par value preferred shares will result in a $6 dividend per year if declared and paid by the board of directors.

PREFERRED SHARES WITH A LIQUIDATING PREFERENCE In the event that the corporation is liquidated, the preferred shareholders are to receive assets up to a specified amount, for example, up to their par value. The effect of this preference is to make the preferred shares more attractive and less of a risk than the common shares.

PREFERRED STOCK ISSUED IN A SERIES (OR BLANK SHARES) A class of preferred shares that will be issued in installments over a period of time as fixed by the board of directors.

PRESIDENT Usually has the authority to manage the business of the corporation. These dealings include the signing of contracts, stock certificates, checks, notes, hiring key personnel, instituting corporate litigation, and making all other commitments on behalf of the corporation.

PRICE EARNINGS RATIO (P/E) The market value of the corporate shares divided by the earnings per share. Thus, if a corporation's market value is $100 and earnings per share (EPS) is $10, then the P/E ration is 10 to 1. The ratio is used as a measure of a potential investor's confidence in a company.

PROFESSIONAL SERVICE CORPORATIONS (PSCs) Members of the professions (e.g., those entities engaged in the practice of law, medicine, or accountancy) can form a professional service corporation (also called a professional association or PA in some states). By incorporating their practice, professionals and their employees, can participate in employee fringe benefits and pension and profit-sharing plans. There are other legal benefits as well.

PROFIT-SHARING PLAN Under this arrangement, the employer allocates a share of corporate profits according to some predetermined formula. Incidental benefits such as disability, death, or medical insurance can also be provided. A profit-sharing plan can be established in addition to, or in lieu of, a pension plan.

PROMOTER An individual who provides the organizational initiative for forming the corporation for a specific purpose or purposes. Promoters are often called "insiders," as opposed to the "outsiders" or ultimate investors because their initial efforts and resources help establish the corporation.

PROXY A power of attorney given by a stockholder authorizing a designated person to cast the stockholder's ballot.

PUBLICLY HELD CORPORATION A corporation with shares held by numerous people. A corporation listed on an established stock exchange [e.g., New York, American, or over-the-counter (OTC)] is generally referred to as a publicly held corporation.

QUORUM The number of votes necessary to validate a meeting.

REASONABLE COMPENSATION Payments made to a shareholder-officer, such as a president or vice president, in the form of salary, bonus, or fringe benefits that are tax deductible. Compensation payments are deductible by the corporation as long as they are reasonable and necessary in amount.

RECORD OWNER The person in whose name the shares are registered on the books of the corporation.

REGISTERED AGENT A specific person who has been designated by the corporation as an agent to receive legal documents, including service of process.

RETAINED EARNINGS Another name required to be used by CPAs for listing surplus on the corporation's balance sheet. Retained earnings represents the total accumulated profits and losses of the corporation, less the payment of dividends, over the life of the corporation.

REVISED MODEL BUSINESS CORPORATION ACT (RMBCA) After several revisions, the MBCA is referred to as the Revised Model Business Corporation Act (RMBCA). Used in many states as its statutory law.

REVISED UNIFORM LIMITED PARTNERSHIP ACT (RULPA) Both the Uniform Limited Partnership Act (ULPA) and RULPA form the basis for governing the limited partnership.

RIGHT OF FIRST REFUSAL Gives the corporation, or its shareholders, the opportunity to repurchase the shares of a selling shareholder by matching the best price that the shareholder can obtain on the open marketplace.

S CORPORATION Under the Internal Revenue Code, a corporation that avoids double taxation, once at the corporate level and again at the shareholder level, by electing to be taxed as if it was a partnership. S corporations cannot have more than 35 shareholders.

SCRIP Fractional shares of stock. Fractional shares may be turned in to the corporation for an equivalent number of full shares. For example, if a shareholder has 1/10 fractional share, he would need 9 more fractional shares to receive a full share.

SECRETARY The corporate secretary exercises authority equal to that of a general manager.

SECTION 1244 STOCK Section 1244 permits a special tax treatment for losses due to the sale of certain stock. Up to $100,000 for married couples filing jointly ($50,000 for single taxpayers) in Section 1244 stock losses can be deducted in one year against ordinary income.

SECURITIES AND EXCHANGE COMMISSION (SEC) An independent governmental regulatory agency whose function it is to administer the SEC Acts of 1933 and 1934. One if its major functions is to require disclosure of facts concerning offerings listed on national stock exchanges and certain securities traded over the counter (OTC).

SINGLE ENTRY ACCOUNTING SYSTEM A single entry bookkeeping system that is based on the company's profit or loss statement and includes only the corporation's business income and expense accounts.

SMALL BUSINESS ADMINISTRATION (SBA) An agency of the federal government set up to make credit available to small businesses that cannot reasonably obtain financing from private sources. The SBA makes direct loans, participation loans, and economic opportunity loans.

SOLE OR INDIVIDUAL PROPRIETORSHIP This is a natural form of doing business at lowest initial cost. The sole proprietor is the owner and "boss."

STATED VALUE STOCK No par value stock that is given a stated value (e.g., $1, $10 per share). Directors may vote to give no par value stock a stated value to give the stock a more meaningful value in the eyes of the investing public.

STERILIZATION OF THE BOARD OF DIRECTORS A restriction of the authority of the board of directors of a nonpublic, or closely-held corporation. This limitation must be set forth in the articles of incorporation. The effect of this provision is to relieve the directors of any liability for negligence on their part and to transfer such liability on all of the shareholders.

STOCK BONUS PLAN An arrangement whereby the employer's stock is contributed to a trust. The stock is allocated to each participant in the trust for eventual distribution to them.

STOCK DIVIDENDS A dividend payable in the stock of the corporation instead of cash or property.

STOCK REDEMPTION AGREEMENT This type of arrangement binds both the shareholders and the corporation. On the death of the shareholder, or in case the shareholder wishes to sell his stock back to the corporation, or in the event of a director deadlock that cannot be broken, the corporation is bound to repurchase the shares. See also the *cross purchase agreement.*

STOCK SPLIT Occurs when a corporation increases the number of issued shares of stock and reduces the par or stated value proportionally. When a corporation's stock is selling at a very low value, the corporation may perform a reverse stock split which reduces the number of shares outstanding and increases the market price of the stock.

STOCK SUBSCRIPTION A contract whereby an individual wishing to become a shareholder in a corporation to be organized or already organized makes an offer to subscribe to a specified number of shares at a stated price both before and after incorporation.

SURPLUS If net assets grow and exceed the corporation's capital there will be a *surplus* (called retained earnings by CPAs); if the net assets fall below capital due to operating losses, the corporation will have a *deficit* in its retained earnings account.

TAX-FREE INCORPORATION Where the incorporators contribute property, but not services, to the corporation and take back control of the corporation. Control under the Internal Revenue Code means at least 80 percent of the combined voting power of all classes of voting stock and, in addition, at least 80 percent of all other classes of the corporation.

TAX YEAR A corporation must calculate its net income on the basis of a tax year. The "tax year" is the annual accounting period the corporation uses for maintaining its records and reporting income and expenses. A corporation can use either a calendar year or a fiscal year.

TREASURER Chief financial officer of the corporation. As chief custodian of the corporate funds, she is frequently designated to countersign notes, checks, miscellaneous corporate instruments, and stock certificates.

TREASURY SHARES Issued and outstanding shares that are reacquired by the corporation. The corporation may reacquire shares to fund a company pension plan, to reduce the number of shareholders who have an interest in the corporation, to eliminate dissident or unhappy shareholders, to keep outsiders from gaining control of the corporation, to use the stock to acquire other companies, and for later reissuance as circumstances dictate.

UNIFORM LIMITED PARTNERSHIP ACT (ULPA) Both this act and RULPA (Revised Uniform Limited Partnership Act) form the basis for governing the limited partnership.

ULTRA VIRES Corporate acts that exceed the powers or stated purposes of the corporation. Modern corporate states generally validate most corporate acts if they are profit directed and are not in direct contravention of civil or criminal statutes.

UNISSUED SHARES Shares authorized by the articles of incorporation but not yet issued are called *unissued* shares.

VICE PRESIDENT A person who has no authority in his individual capacity, but is empowered to act in place of the president in case of the latter's death, illness, or incapacity.

VOTING AGREEMENT Two or more shareholders may enter into an agreement to vote their shares in a certain way. This "pooling agreement," which must be in writing and signed by the shareholders, requires that the members cast their votes in a certain way, such as which directors to elect.

VOTING TRUST An agreement by which shareholders surrender their voting power and place it irrevocably into the hands of others.

WARRANTS Stock options are usually evidenced by certificates known as "warrants."

WATERED STOCK Par value stock that is issued for less than its full value (e.g., discounted stock). The stockholder receiving watered stock is liable to the corporation for the difference between the price paid and the par value of the stock.

APPENDIX 1

Where to File Incorporation Papers

T he basic instrument, which upon filing usually creates the corporation, is called, in most states, "articles of incorporation" or "certificate of incorporation" or simply "the charter." Its contents are prescribed in the general incorporation statutes. In many jurisdictions, official forms are also prescribed. In most jurisdictions, corporate existence begins with the filing, usually with the secretary of state or other appropriate state officer. The following is a list of the appropriate state addresses for filing the corporate charter and all other required papers.

State	Filing Address
Alabama	**Secretary of State**
	Business Division
	P.O. Box 5616
	Montgomery, Alabama 36103
Alaska	**State of Alaska**
	Department of Commerce
	& Economic Development
	Corporations Section
	P.O. Box 110808
	Juneau, Alaska 99811
Arizona	**Arizona Corporation Commission**
	1200 W. Washington
	Phoenix, Arizona 85007

State	Filing Address
Arkansas	**Secretary of State**
	State Capitol
	Little Rock, Arkansas 72201
California	**Secretary of State**
	1500–11th Street
	P.O. Box 944260
	Sacramento, California 94244
Colorado	**State of Colorado**
	Secretary of State
	1560 Broadway Suite 200
	Denver, Colorado 80202
Connecticut	**Office of the Secretary of State**
	State of Connecticut
	30 Trinity Street
	Hartford, Connecticut 06106
Delaware	**Department of State**
	Division of Corporations
	P.O. Box 898
	Dover, Delaware 19903

State	Filing Address	State	Filing Address
District of Columbia	*Corporations Division* Dept. of Consumer and Regulatory Affairs 614 H St., N.W., Rm. 407 Washington, D.C. 20009	*Kentucky*	*Secretary of State* P.O. Box 718 Frankfort, Kentucky 40602
Florida	*Division of Corporations* Florida Department of State P.O. Box 6327 Tallahassee, Florida 32314	*Louisiana*	*Secretary of State* P.O. Box 94125 Baton Rouge, Louisiana 70804
Georgia	*Secretary of State* Business Services and Regulation Suite 306 West Tower #2 Martin Luther King, Jr. Dr., S.E. Atlanta, Georgia 30334	*Maine*	*Bureau of Corporations, Elections & Commissions* Department of The Secretary of State State House Station #101 Augusta, Maine 04333
Hawaii	*State of Hawaii* Dept. of Commerce & Consumer Affairs Business Registration Division P.O. Box 40 Honolulu, Hawaii 96810	*Maryland*	*Department of Assessments and Taxation* Business Services and Finance Division Room 809 301 West Preston Street Baltimore, Maryland 21201
Idaho	*State of Idaho* Secretary of State Room 203, Statehouse P.O. Box 83720 Boise, Idaho 83720	*Massachusetts*	*The Commonwealth of Massachusetts* Secretary of the Commonwealth Corporations' Division One Ashburton Place Boston, Massachusetts 02108
Illinois	*Secretary of State* Springfield, Illinois 62756	*Michigan*	*State of Michigan* Department of Commerce Corporation & Securities Bureau P.O. Box 30054 Lansing, Michigan 48909
Indiana	*Secretary of State* 201 State House Indianapolis, Indiana 46204		
Iowa	*Secretary of State* State of Iowa Hoover Building Des Moines, Iowa 50319	*Minnesota*	*Secretary of State* 180 State Office Building St. Paul, Minnesota 55155
		Mississippi	*Secretary of State* Jackson, Mississippi 39200
Kansas	*Secretary of State* 2nd Floor, State Capitol 300 S.W. 10th Ave. Topeka, Kansas 66612		

State	Filing Address	State	Filing Address
Missouri	*Secretary of State* P.O. Box 778 Jefferson City, Missouri 65102	*Ohio*	*Ohio Secretary of State* 30 East Broad Street, 14th Floor Columbus, Ohio 43266
Montana	*Secretary of State* Montana State Capital P.O. Box 202801 Helena, Montana 59620	*Oklahoma*	*Secretary of State* State of Oklahoma 2300 N. Lincoln Blvd., Room 101 Oklahoma City, Oklahoma 73105
Nebraska	*Secretary of State* P.O. Box 94608 Lincoln, Nebraska 68509	*Oregon*	*Secretary of State* Corporation Division Public Service Bldg. 255 Capitol St. NE, Ste 151 Salem, Oregon 97310
Nevada	*Secretary of State* Capitol Complex Carson City, Nevada 89710		
New Hampshire	*The State of New Hampshire* Department of State State House, Room 204 107 North Main Street Concord, New Hampshire 03301	*Pennsylvania*	*Department of State* Corporation Bureau P.O. Box 8722 Harrisburg, Pennsylvania 17105
		Rhode Island	*Office of the Secretary of State* 100 North Main Street Providence, Rhode Island 02903
New Jersey	*State of New Jersey* Department of State CN 308 Trenton, New Jersey 08625	*South Carolina*	*Secretary of State* Columbia, South Carolina 29200
New Mexico	*State Corporation Commission* P.O. Drawer 1269 Santa Fe, Mexico 87504	*South Dakota*	*Secretary of State* State Capitol, Suite 204 500 E. Capitol Pierre, South Dakota 57501
New York	*Department of State* 162 Washington Ave. Albany, New York 12231	*Tennessee*	*State of Tennessee* Department of State Division of Services Suite 1800 James K. Polk Building Nashville, Tennessee 37243
North Carolina	*Secretary of State* 300 N. Salisbury Street Raleigh, North Carolina 27603	*Texas*	*Secretary of State* Statutory Filings Division Corporations Section P.O. Box 13697 Austin, Texas 78711
North Dakota	*Secretary of State* State of North Dakota 600 East Boulevard Avenue Bismarck, North Dakota 58505		

State	Filing Address	State	Filing Address
Utah	*Department of Commerce* Division of Corporations and Commercial Code Heber M. Wells Building 160 East 300 South / P.O. Box 45801 Salt Lake City, Utah 84145	*Washington*	*Secretary of State* Corporations Division P.O. Box 40234 Olympia, Washington 98504
Vermont	*Office of the Secretary of State* Corporations Division 109 State Street Montpelier, Vermont 05609	*West Virginia*	*Secretary of State* State Capitol Charleston, West Virginia 25305
		Wisconsin	*Wisconsin Secretary of State* Corporations Division P.O. Box 7846 Madison, Wisconsin 53707
Virginia	*Commonwealth of Virginia* State Corporation Commission P.O. Box 1197 Richmond, Virginia 23209	*Wyoming*	*Secretary of State* State Capitol Cheyenne, Wyoming 82002

State Incorporation Fees

A corporation doing business in the state where it is incorporated is known as a domestic corporation. All other corporations doing business in that state are foreign corporations.

For example, a Delaware corporation incorporated in Delaware and doing business in both New York State and Delaware is a domestic corporation for Delaware purposes but a foreign corporation while doing business in New York State.

A corporation wishing to do business in a state other than its state of incorporation must meet the licensing requirements of the state where it intends to do business. The usual procedure is to file an application with the secretary of state in the state where the corporation intends to operate certifying the corporation's name, date and state of incorporation, the nature if its business, the location of its principal place of business, and enclosing a copy of its certificate of incorporation and other significant data. This information is usually accompanied by a registration fee payable to the intended state. Once operations commence, the corporation is then also subject to all rules applicable to domestic corporations within the state, such as use of a corporate name and the payment of corporate income and franchise taxes.

State	Fees
Alabama	**Domestic Corporations** INCORPORATION FEES—Fee for filing articles and issuing certificate of incorporation: $40 to State; $35 to Probate Judge. Indexing fees may also apply in some counties. **Foreign Corporations** Application designating its principal office $5 payable to State.
Alaska	**Domestic Corporations** INCORPORATION FEES—Fee is $150; biennial incorporation tax is $100. **Foreign Corporations** Fee for appointing an agent for a foreign corporation established by the department by regulation.
Arizona	**Domestic Corporations** Fee for filing articles and incorporation, $50; there is no fee for appointing statutory agent. **Foreign Corporations** Must designate as agent either an individual resident of Arizona for at least three years, a domestic corporation, or a qualified foreign corporation upon whom process may be served. There are entrance fees.

State	Fees
Arkansas	**Domestic Corporations**
	Fee paid to secretary of state for certificate upon filing $50.
	Foreign Corporations
	Must designate as agent either an individual resident, a domestic corporation, or qualified foreign corporation upon whom process may be served. Filing fee $300.
California	**Domestic Corporations**
	INCORPORATION FEES—Fee for filing articles of incorporation $900 (includes $800 franchise tax "prepayment").
	Foreign Corporations
	Entrance fee of $350.
Colorado	**Domestic Corporations**
	INCORPORATION FEES—Fee for filing articles of incorporation $50. There are also incidental fees.
	Foreign Corporations
	Corporation must designate agent for service of process. If not, state will appoint one. Entrance fee of $75; corporate report $100.
Connecticut	**Domestic Corporations**
	INCORPORATION FEES—Fee for filing articles of incorporation $50.
	Foreign Corporations—Corporation certificate of authority $50.
Delaware	**Domestic Corporations**
	Filing and certification fees, approximately $55.
	Foreign Corporations
	Filing fee $150.
District of Columbia	**Domestic Corporations**
	Filing fee $100.
	Foreign Corporations
	Filing fee $100.

State	Fees
Florida	**Domestic Corporation**
	Filing fee $70.
	Foreign Corporations
	Filing fee $70.
Georgia	**Domestic Corporations**
	Fee for filing articles of incorporation $60.
	Foreign Corporations
	Corporation certificate of authority $170.
Hawaii	**Domestic Corporations**
	Filing fee $50.
	Foreign Corporations
	Filing fee $90.
Idaho	**Domestic Corporations**
	Filing fee $100 if typed, $120 if not typed.
	Foreign Corporations—Filing fee $100 if typed, $120 if not typed.
Illinois	**Domestic Corporations**
	Filing fee $75.
	Foreign Corporations
	Filing fee $75.
Indiana	**Domestic Corporations**
	Filing fee $90.
	Foreign Corporations
	Filing fee $90.
Iowa	**Domestic Corporations**
	Filing fee $50.
	Foreign Corporations
	Filing fee $100.
Kansas	**Domestic Corporations**
	Filing fee $75.
	Foreign Corporations
	Filing fee $95.

State	Fees
Kentucky	**Domestic Corporations**
	Filing fee $90; Minimum of $8 for recording by county clerk.
	Foreign Corporations—Filing fee $90.
Louisiana	**Domestic Corporations**
	Filing fee $60.
	Foreign Corporations
	Filing fee $90.
Maine	**Domestic Corporations**
	Filing fee $90.
	Foreign Corporations
	Filing fee $180.
Maryland	**Domestic Corporations**
	Filing fee $20.
	Foreign Corporations
	Filing fee to do interstate or foreign business. No Fee. Qualification to do intrastate business $50.
Massachusetts	**Domestic Corporations**
	Minimum filing fee $200.
	Foreign Corporations
	Minimum filing fee $300.
Michigan	**Domestic Corporations**
	Minimum filing fee $10. There are also other fees.
	Foreign Corporations
	Minimum filing fee $10. There are also other filing fees.
Minnesota	**Domestic Corporations**
	Minimum filing fee $35. Organization fee $100.
	Foreign Corporations
	Minimum filing fee $200.
Mississippi	**Domestic Corporations**
	Minimum filing fee $50. There is a surcharge if official form is not used.
	Foreign Corporations
	Filing fee $525.

State	Fees
Missouri	**Domestic Corporations**
	Filing fee $3. There are also other fees.
	Foreign Corporations
	Filing fee $155. There are also other fees.
Montana	**Domestic Corporations**
	Filing fee $20. There is also a license fee with a starting minimum of $50.
	Foreign Corporations
	Filing fee $20. There are also other fees.
Nebraska	**Domestic Corporations**
	The fee is based on the number of total authorized par value shares. Minimum filing fee $60 and increases according to the number of total authorized shares. On aggregate amounts exceeding $100,000, the fee is $200 plus $3 for each $1,000 in excess of $100,000. The recording fee is $3 per page.
	Foreign Corporations
	Filing fee $125 plus a recording fee.
Nevada	**Domestic Corporations**
	Filing fee $85 for officers, directors, and agents, with a maximum initial fee of $25,000.
	Foreign Corporations
	Based on the corporation's aggregate authorized capital stock or aggregate number of no-par value shares with a maximum initial incorporation fee of $25,000.
New Hampshire	**Domestic Corporations**
	Filing fee for articles of incorporation $35; required "blue sky" fee, $50.
	Foreign Corporations
	Filing fee $85.

State	Fees	State	Fees

New Jersey — *Domestic Corporations*

Filing fee for articles of incorporation $100; certification fee, $25.

Foreign Corporations—Filing fee $100.

New Mexico — *Domestic Corporations*

Filing fee $1 for each 10,000 authorized shares with a minimum fee of $100 and a maximum fee of $1,000; first report fee, $20.

Foreign Corporations

Filing fee $1 for each 1,000 shares authorized and "represented in" New Mexico with a minimum fee of $200 and a maximum fee of $1,000; first report $25.

New York — *Domestic Corporations*

Filing fee $125; for organization tax: 1/20 of 1% (.0005) on aggregate par value of authorized shares. 5 cents per authorized no par value; minimum is $10.

Foreign Corporations

Filing fee $225.

North Carolina — *Domestic Corporations*

Filing fee for incorporation is $100; initial report, $10.

Foreign Corporations

Filing fee for application of certificate of authority, $200; initial report $10.

North Dakota — *Domestic Corporations*

Filing fee for incorporation is $40; license fee based on aggregate par value of all authorized shares.

Foreign Corporations

Filing fee $50; initial license fee, $85.

Ohio — *Domestic Corporations*

Filing fee for incorporation is based on aggregate authorized shares with a minimum of $85.

Foreign Corporations

Filing fee $100; initial license fee, $5, based on shares allocated to Ohio.

Oklahoma — *Domestic Corporations*

Filing fee for articles of incorporation is 1/10 of 1% (.001) of the aggregate par value of all authorized shares, including no par value, with a minimum of $50.

Foreign Corporations

Filing fee is 1/10 of 1% (.001) of either the maximum amount of capital invested or proposed to be invested in Oklahoma "during the fiscal year" the license issued or the amount of "total authorized capital," whichever is lower (minimum $300); annual fee of secretary of state for acting as "registered" agent is $40.

Oregon — *Domestic Corporations*

Filing fee for incorporation is $50.

Foreign Corporations

Filing fee $440.

Pennsylvania — *Domestic Corporations*

Filing fee for incorporation is $100.

Foreign Corporations

Filing fee $180.

Rhode Island — *Domestic Corporations*

Filing fee for incorporation is $70; license fee based on number of aggregate authorized shares, minimum fee is $80.

Foreign Corporations

Filing fee $50; license fee based on number of aggregate authorized shares represented in Rhode Island with a minimum of $15.

State	Fees	State	Fees

South Carolina

Domestic Corporations
Filing fee
for incorporation is $10; filing tax fee,
$100, initial annual report fee, $25.

Foreign Corporations
Filing fee $10; filing tax fee, $100,
initial annual report fee, $25.

South Dakota

Domestic Corporations
Filing fee for articles of incorporation is based on authorized capital
stock with a maximum amount of
$16,000.

Foreign Corporations
Filing fee is the same as the incorporation filing fee.

Tennessee

Domestic Corporations
Filing fee $100.

Foreign Corporations
Filing fee $600.

Texas

Domestic Corporations
Filing fee $300.

Foreign Corporations
Filing fee $750.

Utah

Domestic Corporations
Filing fee $75.

Foreign Corporations
Filing fee $75.

Vermont

Domestic Corporations
Filing fee $75.

Foreign Corporations
Filing fee $100.

Virginia

Domestic Corporations
Filing fee for incorporation, $25;
charter fee based on number of
aggregate authorized shares, regardless of value.

Foreign Corporations
Filing fee $80.

Washington

Domestic Corporations
Filing fee for incorporation, $175;
fee for filing initial report, $10.

Foreign Corporations
Filing fee for incorporation, $175;
fee for filing initial report, $10.

West Virginia

Domestic Corporations
Filing fee for incorporation, $10;
initial annual fee $10.

Foreign Corporations
Filing fee for incorporation, $10;
initial annual fee $10.

Wisconsin

Domestic Corporations
Filing fee for incorporation, one cent
for each authorized share, but minimum fee is $90 and maximum fee is
$10,000.

Foreign Corporations
Filing fee $100, plus $2 for every
$1,000 or fraction thereof of the cor-
poration's capital exceeding $60,000
employed or to be employed in
Wisconsin.

Wyoming

Domestic Corporations
Filing fee is $90, but if articles of
incorporation are in order and the
Secretary of State does not file them
by the close of the next business day
after receipt, the fee is $70.

Foreign Corporations
Filing fee $80.

APPENDIX 3 Sample Tax Forms

T he forms in this appendix (accompanied by their respective instructions) represent some of the information needed to be prepared by a corporation for income tax purposes. They have been filled in with information from a fictional corporation in order to help you understand how they need to be prepared. You will, of course, need to determine which forms you will need and supply your own corporation's personal information on current tax forms, which can be obtained from your local IRS office.

Form **940-EZ**

Department of the Treasury
Internal Revenue Service   (99)

Employer's Annual Federal Unemployment (FUTA) Tax Return

OMB No. 1545-1110

1995

Name (as distinguished from trade name)	Calendar year	T
		FF
Trade name, if any		FD
		FP
Address and ZIP code	Employer identification number	I
		T

Peter Cone
362 Main Street
Pine Town VA 23000

Follow the chart under **Who May Use Form 940-EZ** *on page 2. If you cannot use Form 940-EZ, you must use Form 940 instead.*

A Enter the amount of contributions paid to your state unemployment fund. (See instructions for line A on page 4.) ▶ $ _____ 630.00

B (1) Enter the name of the state where you have to pay contributions . . . . ▶ VIRGINIA

(2) Enter your state reporting number as shown on state unemployment tax return. ▶ 98765432

If you will not have to file returns in the future, check here (see **Who Must File**, on page 2) complete, and sign the return . . . . ▶

If this is an Amended Return check here . . . . ▶

Part I   Taxable Wages and FUTA Tax

1	Total payments (including payments shown on lines 2 and 3) during the calendar year for services of employees	1		78,000.00
			Amount paid	
2	Exempt payments. (Explain all exempt payments, attaching additional sheets if necessary.) ▶	2		
3	Payments for services of more than $7,000. Enter only amounts over the first $7,000 paid to each employee. Do not include any exempt payments from line 2. Do not use your state wage limitation. The $7,000 amount is the Federal wage base. Your state wage base may be different	3	57,000 00	
4	Total exempt payments (add lines 2 and 3)	4		57,000.00
5	**Total taxable wages.** (subtract line 4 from line 1) . . . . ▶	5		21,000.00
6	FUTA tax. Multiply the wages on line 5 by .008 and enter here. (If the result is over $100, also complete Part II.)	6		168.00
7	Total FUTA tax deposited for the year, including any overpayment applied from a prior year (from your records)	7		149.60
8	**Amount you owe** (subtract line 7 from line 6). This should be $100 or less. Pay to "Internal Revenue Service" ▶	8		18.40
9	**Overpayment** (subtract line 6 from line 7). Check if it is to be: ☐ Applied to next return, or ☐ Refunded ▶	9		

Part II   Record of Quarterly Federal Unemployment Tax Liability   (Do not include state liability.) Complete only if line 6 is over $100.

Quarter	First (Jan. 1 - Mar. 31)	Second (Apr. 1 - June 30)	Third (July 1 - Sept. 30)	Fourth (Oct. 1 - Dec. 31)	Total for Year
Liability for quarter	149.60	18.40			168.00

Under penalties of perjury, I declare that I have examined this return, including accompanying schedules and statements, and, to the best of my knowledge and belief, it is true, correct, and complete, and that no part of any payment made to a state unemployment fund claimed as a credit was, or is to be, deducted from the payments to employees.

Signature ▶ *Peter Cone*   Title (Owner, etc.) ▶ *Owner*   Date ▶ 1/25/XX

Form **940-EZ** (1995)

DETACH HERE

Form **940-EZ(V)**

Department of the Treasury
Internal Revenue Service

Form 940-EZ Payment Voucher

For Paperwork Reduction Act Notice, see instructions.

OMB No. 1545-1110

1995

Complete boxes 1, 2, 3, and 4. Do not send cash and do not staple your payment to this voucher. Make your check or money order, with your employer identification number written on it, payable to the **Internal Revenue Service.**

1 Enter the amount of the payment you are making	2 Enter the first four characters of your business name	3 Enter your employer identification number
▶ $		
	4 Enter your name	
	Enter your address	
Do not staple your payment to this voucher.	Enter your city, state, and ZIP code	

5W9174 2.000   JSA

Form 941
(Rev. January 1996)
Department of the Treasury
Internal Revenue Service

4 1 4 1

Employer's Quarterly Federal Tax Return

▶ See separate instructions for information on completing this return.

Please type or print.

OMB No. 1545-0029

Enter state code for state in which deposits made ▶ (see page 3 of instructions).

Name (as distinguished from trade name) — Date quarter ended

Trade name, if any

Peter Cone
362 Main Street

Employer identification number

Address (number and street) *Pine Town*

City, state, and ZIP code

VA 23000

T
FF
FD
FP
I
T

If address is different from prior return, check here ▶

IRS Use

1 1 1 1 1 1 1 1 1 1   2   3 3 3 3 3   4 4 4

5 5 5   6   7   8 8 8 8 8   9 9 9   10 10 10 10 10 10 10 10 10 10

If you do not have to file returns in the future, check here ▶ ☐ and enter date final wages paid ▶

If you are a seasonal employer, see **Seasonal employers** on page 1 of the instructions and check here ▶

1	Number of employees (except household) employed in the pay period that includes March 12th ▶	1		
2	Total wages and tips, plus other compensation	2	*19,500.00*	
3	Total income tax withheld from wages, tips, and sick pay	3	*1,872.00*	
4	Adjustment of withheld income tax for preceding quarters of calendar year	4		
5	Adjusted total of income tax withheld (line 3 as adjusted by line 4 - see instructions)	5	*1,872.00*	
6a	Taxable social security wages . . . . $ *19,500.00* x 12.4% (.124) =	6a	*2,418.00*	
b	Taxable social security tips . . . . $ x 12.4% (.124) =	6b		
7	Taxable Medicare wages and tips . . . . $ *19,500.00* x 2.9% (.029) =	7	*565.50*	
8	Total social security and Medicare taxes (add lines 6a, 6b, and 7). Check here if wages are not subject to social security and/or Medicare tax . . . . ▶ ☐	8	*2,983.50*	
9	Adjustment of social security and Medicare taxes (see instructions for required explanation) Sick Pay $ _____ ± Fractions of Cents $ _____ ± Other $ _____ =	9		
10	Adjusted total of social security and Medicare taxes (line 8 as adjusted by line 9 - see instructions)	10	*2,983.50*	
11	**Total taxes** (add lines 5 and 10)	11	*4,855.50*	
12	Advance earned income credit (EIC) payments made to employees, if any	12		
13	Net taxes (subtract line 12 from line 11). **This should equal line 17, column (d) below** (or line D of Schedule B (Form 941))	13	*4,855.50*	
14	Total deposits for quarter, including overpayment applied from a prior quarter	14	*4,855.50*	
15	**Balance due** (subtract line 14 from line 13). See instructions	15		

16 **Overpayment,** if line 14 is more than line 13, enter excess here ▶ $ _____
and check if to be: ☐ Applied to next return **OR** ☐ Refunded.

- **All filers:** If line 13 is less than $500, you need not complete line 17 or Schedule B.
- **Semiweekly schedule depositors:** Complete Schedule B and check here . . . . ▶ ☐
- **Monthly schedule depositors:** Complete line 17, columns (a) through (d), and check here . . . . ▶ ☐

17	Monthly Summary of Federal Tax Liability.		
(a) First month liability	**(b)** Second month liability	**(c)** Third month liability	**(d)** Total liability for quarter
1,494.00	*1,867.50*	*1,494.00*	*4,855.50*

Sign Here

Under penalties of perjury, I declare that I have examined this return, including accompanying schedules and statements, and to the best of my knowledge and belief, it is true, correct, and complete.

Signature ▶ *Peter Cone*   Print Your Name and Title ▶ *PETER CONE, Owner*   Date ▶ *2/5/XX*

For Paperwork Reduction Act Notice, see page 1 of separate instructions.   Form **941** (Rev. 1-96)

1995

Department of the Treasury
Internal Revenue Service

Instructions for Forms 1120 and 1120-A

Section references are to the Internal Revenue Code unless otherwise noted.

Paperwork Reduction Act Notice

We ask for the information on these forms to carry out the Internal Revenue laws of the United States. You are required to give us the information. We need it to ensure that you are complying with these laws and to allow us to figure and collect the right amount of tax.

The time needed to complete and file the following forms will vary depending on individual circumstances. The estimated average times are:

Form	Recordkeeping	Learning about the law or the form	Preparing the form	Copying, assembling, and sending the form to the IRS
1120	71 hr., 59 min.	41 hr., 58 min.	71 hr., 59 min.	7 hr., 47 min.
1120-A	43 hr., 17 min.	23 hr., 15 min.	40 hr., 47 min.	4 hr., 34 min.
Sch. D (1120)	6 hr., 56 min.	3 hr., 31 min.	5 hr., 39 min.	32 min.
Sch. H (1120)	5 hr., 59 min.	35 min.	43 min.	0 min.
Sch. PH (1120)	15 hr., 19 min.	6 hr., 6 min.	8 hr., 29 min.	32 min.

If you have comments concerning the accuracy of these time estimates or suggestions for making these forms simpler, we would be happy to hear from you. You can write to the Tax Forms Committee, Western Area Distribution Center, Rancho Cordova, CA 95743-0001. **DO NOT** send these tax forms to this office. Instead, see **Where To File** on page 2.

Contents

Changes To Note

● Corporations that had total deposits of withheld income, social security, and Medicare taxes during calendar year 1993 or 1994 in excess of $47 million are required to use the electronic funds transfer (EFT) system for depository taxes due in 1996. Corporations required to use the EFT system in 1995 must continue to use the system in 1996. For details, see **Depository Method of Tax Payment** on page 3.

● Final regulations have been issued on the capitalization of interest expense paid or incurred during the production period of certain property. For details, see Regulations sections 1.263A-8 through 1.263A-15. These regulations, which generally are effective for tax years beginning after 1994, may require a change in accounting method. Any such change must be made under Rev. Proc. 95-19, 1995-12 I.R.B. 6.

● You can use your computer to get tax forms and publications. See **General Instructions.**

Voluntary Contributions To Reduce the Public Debt

A corporation may make a contribution to reduce the public debt. To do so, enclose with the tax return a check made payable to "Bureau of the Public Debt." Voluntary contributions to reduce the public debt are deductible subject to the rules and limitations for charitable contributions.

General Instructions

Note: *In addition to the publications listed throughout these instructions, corporations may find it helpful to get:* **Pub. 534,** *Depreciating Property Placed in Service Before 1987;* **Pub. 535,** *Business Expenses;* **Pub. 542,** *Tax Information on Corporations; and* **Pub. 946,** *How To Depreciate Property.*

You can get these publications and other forms and publications referred to in the instructions at most IRS offices. To order publications and forms, call our toll-free number 1-800-TAX-FORM (1-800-829-3676).

If you subscribe to an on-line service, ask if IRS information is available and, if so, how to access it. You can get information through IRIS, the Internal Revenue Information Services, on FedWorld, a government bulletin board. Tax forms, instructions, publications, and other IRS information are available through IRIS.

IRIS is accessible directly by calling 703-321-8020. On the Internet, telnet to fedworld.gov or, for file transfer protocol services, connect to ftp.fedworld.gov. If you are using the World-Wide Web, connect to http://www.ustreas.gov. FedWorld's help desk offers technical assistance on accessing IRIS (not tax help) during regular business hours at 703-487-4608. The IRIS menus offer information on available file formats and software needed to read and print files. You must print the forms to use them; the forms are not designed to be filled out on-screen.

Tax forms, instructions, and publications are also available on CD-ROM, including prior-year forms starting with the 1991 tax year. For ordering information and software requirements, contact the Government Printing Office's Superintendent of Documents (202-512-1800) or Federal Bulletin Board (202-512-1387).

Purpose of Form

Use **Form 1120**, U.S. Corporation Income Tax Return, and **Form 1120-A**, U.S. Corporation Short-Form Income Tax Return, to report the income, gains, losses, deductions, credits, and to figure the income tax liability of a corporation.

Cat. No. 11455T

Who Must File

Unless exempt under section 501, all domestic corporations (including corporations in bankruptcy) must file whether or not they have taxable income. Domestic corporations must file Form 1120, or, if they qualify, Form 1120-A, unless they are required to file a special return (see **Special Returns for Certain Organizations** below).

Note: *If an organization resembles a corporation more than it resembles a partnership or trust, it will be considered an association taxed as a corporation.*

Limited liability companies.—If an entity was formed as a limited liability company under state law and is treated as a partnership for Federal income tax purposes, it should not file Form 1120 or 1120-A. Instead, it should file **Form 1065,** U.S. Partnership Return of Income. For the definition of a limited liability company, see the Instructions for Form 1065.

Who May File Form 1120-A

A corporation may file Form 1120-A if it meets **all** of the following requirements:

● Its gross receipts (line 1a, page 1) are under $500,000.

● Its total income (line 11, page 1) is under $500,000.

● Its total assets (line 12, column (b), Part III on page 2) are under $500,000.

● It does not have any ownership in a foreign corporation.

● It does not have foreign shareholders who own, directly or indirectly, 50% or more of its stock.

● It is not a member of a controlled group of corporations (sections 1561 and 1563).

● It is not a personal holding company (sections 541 through 547).

● It is not a consolidated corporate return filer.

● It is not a corporation undergoing a dissolution or liquidation.

● It is not filing its final tax return.

● Its only dividend income (none of which represents debt-financed securities) is from domestic corporations, and those dividends qualify for the 70% deduction.

● It has no nonrefundable tax credits other than the general business credit and the credit for prior year minimum tax.

● It is not subject to environmental tax under section 59A.

● It has no liability for interest under section 453(l)(3) or 453A(c) (relating to certain installment sales) or installment payments of tax under section 1363(d).

● It has no liability for interest due under the look-back method of section 460(b)(2).

● It is not required to file **Form 8621,** Return by a Shareholder of a Passive Foreign Investment Company or Qualified Electing Fund.

● It has no liability for tax under section 7518 on a nonqualified withdrawal from a capital construction fund.

● It is not making an election under section 172(b)(3) to forego the carryback period of an NOL.

● It is not electing to pay tax on the gain from the sale of an intangible as described in section 197(f)(9)(B)(ii).

● It is not required to file one of the special tax returns listed below.

Special Returns for Certain Organizations

Certain organizations, as shown below, have to file special returns.

If the organization is a	File Form
Farmers' cooperative (sec. 1381)	990-C
Exempt organization with unrelated trade or business income	990-T
Entity formed as a limited liability company under state law and treated as a partnership for Federal income tax purposes	1065
Religious or apostolic organization exempt under section 501(d)	1065
Entity that elects to be treated as real estate mortgage investment conduit (REMIC) under sec. 860D	1066
Settlement fund (sec. 468B)	1120-SF
Interest charge domestic international sales corporation (sec. 992)	1120-IC-DISC
Foreign corporation (other than life and property and casualty insurance company filing Form 1120-L or Form 1120-PC)	1120-F
Foreign sales corporation (sec. 922)	1120-FSC
Condominium management association or residential real estate management association that elects to be treated as a homeowners association under sec. 528	1120-H
Life insurance company (sec. 801)	1120-L
Fund set up to pay for nuclear decommissioning costs (sec. 468A)	1120-ND
Property and casualty insurance company (sec. 831)	1120-PC
Political organization (sec. 527)	1120-POL
Real estate investment trust (sec. 856)	1120-REIT
Regulated investment company (sec. 851)	1120-RIC
S corporation (sec. 1361)	1120S

When To File

In general, a corporation must file its income tax return by the 15th day of the 3rd month after the end of the tax year. A new corporation filing a short-period return must generally file by the 15th day of the 3rd month after the short period ends. A corporation that has dissolved must generally file by the 15th day of the 3rd month after the date it dissolved.

If the due date falls on a Saturday, Sunday, or legal holiday, the corporation may file on the next business day.

Extension.—File **Form 7004,** Application for Automatic Extension of Time To File Corporation Income Tax Return, to request a 6-month extension of time to file.

Where To File

Use the preaddressed envelope. If you do not use the envelope, file your return at the applicable IRS address listed below.

If the corporation's principal business, office, or agency is located in	Use the following Internal Revenue Service Center address
New Jersey, New York (New York City and counties of Nassau, Rockland, Suffolk, and Westchester)	Holtsville, NY 00501-0012
New York (all other counties), Connecticut, Maine, Massachusetts, New Hampshire, Rhode Island, Vermont	Andover, MA 05501-0012
Florida, Georgia, South Carolina	Atlanta, GA 39901-0012
Indiana, Kentucky, Michigan, Ohio, West Virginia	Cincinnati, OH 45999-0012
Kansas, New Mexico, Oklahoma, Texas	Austin, TX 73301-0012
Alaska, Arizona, California (counties of Alpine, Amador, Butte, Calaveras, Colusa, Contra Costa, Del Norte, El Dorado, Glenn, Humboldt, Lake, Lassen, Marin, Mendocino, Modoc, Napa, Nevada, Placer, Plumas, Sacramento, San Joaquin, Shasta, Sierra, Siskiyou, Solano, Sonoma, Sutter, Tehama, Trinity, Yolo, and Yuba), Colorado, Idaho, Montana, Nebraska, Nevada, North Dakota, Oregon, South Dakota, Utah, Washington, Wyoming	Ogden, UT 84201-0012
California (all other counties), Hawaii	Fresno, CA 93888-0012
Illinois, Iowa, Minnesota, Missouri, Wisconsin	Kansas City, MO 64999-0012
Alabama, Arkansas, Louisiana, Mississippi, North Carolina, Tennessee	Memphis, TN 37501-0012
Delaware, District of Columbia, Maryland, Pennsylvania, Virginia	Philadelphia, PA 19255-0012

Corporations with their principal place of business outside the United States or claiming a possessions tax credit (section 936) must file with the Internal Revenue Service Center, Philadelphia, PA 19255-0012.

Page 2

A group of corporations located in several service center regions will often keep all the books and records at the principal office of the managing corporation. In this case, the income tax returns of the corporations may be filed with the service center for the region in which the principal office is located.

Who Must Sign

The return must be signed and dated by the president, vice president, treasurer, assistant treasurer, chief accounting officer, or any other corporate officer (such as tax officer) authorized to sign. Receivers, trustees, or assignees must also sign and date any return filed on behalf of a corporation.

If a corporate officer completes Form 1120 or Form 1120-A, the Paid Preparer's space should remain blank. Anyone who prepares Form 1120 or Form 1120-A but does not charge the corporation should not sign the return. Generally, anyone who is paid to prepare the return must sign it and fill in the Paid Preparer's Use Only area.

The paid preparer must complete the required preparer information and—

● Sign the return, by hand, in the space provided for the preparer's signature (signature stamps and labels are not acceptable).

● Give a copy of the return to the taxpayer.

Accounting Methods

Figure taxable income using the method of accounting regularly used in keeping the corporation's books and records. Permissible methods include the cash, accrual, or any other method authorized by the Internal Revenue Code. In all cases, the method used must clearly show taxable income.

Generally, a corporation (other than a qualified personal service corporation) must use the accrual method of accounting if its average annual gross receipts exceed $5 million. See section 448(c). A corporation engaged in farming operations must also use the accrual method. For exceptions, see section 447.

Under the accrual method, an amount is includible in income when all the events have occurred that fix the right to receive the income and the amount can be determined with reasonable accuracy. See Regulations section 1.451-1(a) for details.

Generally, an accrual basis taxpayer can deduct accrued expenses in the tax year in which (1) all events that determine the liability have occurred, (2) the amount of the liability can be figured with reasonable accuracy, and (3) economic performance takes place with respect to the expense. There are exceptions to the economic performance rule for certain items, including recurring expenses. See section 461(h) and the related regulations for the rules for determining when economic performance takes place.

Long-term contracts (except for certain real property construction contracts) must generally be accounted for using the percentage of completion method described in section 460. See section 460 for general rules on long-term contracts.

Generally, the corporation may change the method of accounting used to report taxable income (for income as a whole or for any material item) only by getting consent on **Form 3115,** Application for Change in Accounting Method. For more information, get **Pub. 538,** Accounting Periods and Methods.

Mark-to-market accounting method for dealers in securities.—Dealers in securities must use the mark-to-market accounting method described in section 475 for tax years ending on or after December 31, 1993. Under this method, any security that is inventory to the dealer must be included in inventory at its fair market value. Any security held by a dealer that is not inventory and that is held at the close of the tax year is treated as sold at its fair market value on the last business day of the tax year. Any gain or loss must be taken into account in determining gross income. The gain or loss taken into account is generally treated as ordinary gain or loss.

Dealers required to change their accounting method to comply with the new law are considered as having initiated the change with the consent of the IRS. Generally, the net amount of the section 481(a) adjustment (reported on line 10, page 1) is taken into account ratably over a 5-year period, beginning with the first tax year ending on or after December 31, 1993. For details, including exceptions, see section 475, the related temporary regulations, and Rev. Rul. 94-7, 1994-1 C.B. 151.

Change in Accounting Period

Generally, before changing an accounting period, a corporation must get the Commissioner's approval (Regulations section 1.442-1) by filing **Form 1128,** Application To Adopt, Change, or Retain a Tax Year. Also see Pub. 538.

Personal service corporations, as defined in Temporary Regulations section 1.441-4T (see the instructions for Item A on page 6), must use a calendar year unless:

● The corporation can establish to the satisfaction of the Commissioner that there is a business purpose for having a different tax year, or

● The corporation elects under section 444 to have a tax year other than a calendar year.

Personal service corporations that wish to establish a business purpose for having a different tax year should see Rev. Rul. 87-57, 1987-2 C.B. 117. See Rev. Proc. 87-32, 1987-2 C.B. 396, for procedures to use in adopting, retaining, or changing the corporation's tax year. Personal service corporations that wish to adopt or retain a noncalendar tax year must file Form 1128.

Personal service corporations that wish to elect under section 444 to have a tax year other than a calendar year must file **Form 8716,** Election To Have a Tax Year Other Than a Required Tax Year.

Generally, Form 8716 must be filed by the earlier of:

● The 15th day of the 5th month following the month that includes the 1st day of the tax year for which the election will be effective, or

● The due date (not including extensions) of the income tax return resulting from the section 444 election.

Electing corporations are subject to minimum distribution requirements under section 280H(c) for each year the election is in effect. If the requirements are not met, the deduction allowable for certain amounts paid to employee-owners is limited. Disallowed amounts are carried over to the following tax year. Get **Schedule H (Form 1120),** Section 280H Limitations for a Personal Service Corporation (PSC), to figure the required minimum distributions and the maximum deductible amount.

If a section 444 election is terminated and the termination results in a short tax year, type or print at the top of the first page of Form 1120 or 1120-A for the short tax year "SECTION 444 ELECTION TERMINATED." See Temporary Regulations section 1.444-1T(a)(5) for more information.

Rounding Off to Whole Dollars

The corporation may show amounts on the return and accompanying schedules as whole dollars. To do so, drop amounts less than 50 cents and increase amounts from 50 cents through 99 cents to the next higher dollar.

Recordkeeping

Keep the corporation's records for as long as they may be needed for the administration of any provision of the Internal Revenue Code. Usually, records that support an item of income, deduction, or credit on the return must be kept for 3 years from the date the return is due or filed, whichever is later. Keep records that verify the corporation's basis in property for as long as they are needed to figure the basis of the original or replacement property.

The corporation should keep copies of all filed returns. They help in preparing future returns and amended returns.

Depository Method of Tax Payment

The corporation must pay the tax due in full no later than the 15th day of the 3rd month after the end of the tax year. If the corporation does not use the electronic funds transfer (EFT) system, deposit corporation income tax payments (and estimated tax payments) with **Form 8109,** Federal Tax Deposit Coupon. Do not send deposits directly to an IRS office. Mail or deliver the completed Form 8109 with the payment to a qualified depository for Federal taxes or to the Federal Reserve bank (FRB) servicing the corporation's geographic area. Make checks or money orders payable to that depository or FRB.

Page 3

To help ensure proper crediting, write the corporation's EIN, the tax period to which the deposit applies, and "Form 1120" on the check or money order. Be sure to darken the "1120" box on the coupon. Records of these deposits will be sent to the IRS.

A penalty may be imposed if the deposits are mailed or delivered to an IRS office rather than to an authorized depository or FRB.

For more information on deposits, see the instructions in the coupon booklet (Form 8109) and **Pub. 583,** Starting a Business and Keeping Records.

Caution: *If the corporation owes tax when it files Form 1120 or Form 1120-A, do not include the payment with the tax return. Instead, mail or deliver the payment with Form 8109 to a qualified depository or FRB, or use the EFT system, if applicable.*

Generally, corporations that had total deposits of withheld income, social security, and Medicare taxes during calendar year 1993 or 1994 that exceeded $47 million are required to deposit all depository taxes due in 1996 by electronic funds transfer (EFT). TAXLINK, an electronic remittance processing system, must be used to make deposits by EFT. Corporations that are not required to make deposits by EFT may voluntarily participate in TAXLINK. For more details on TAXLINK, call the toll-free TAXLINK HELPLINE at 1-800-829-5469 (for TAXLINK information only), or write to:

Internal Revenue Service
Cash Management Office
P.O. Box 47669, Stop 295
Doraville, GA 30362

Estimated Tax Payments

Generally, a corporation must make installment payments of estimated tax if it expects its estimated tax (income tax minus credits) to be $500 or more. For a calendar or fiscal year corporation, the installments are due by the 15th day of the 4th, 6th, 9th, and 12th months of the tax year. If any date falls on a Saturday, Sunday, or legal holiday, the installment is due on the next regular business day. Use **Form 1120-W,** Estimated Tax for Corporations, as a worksheet to compute estimated tax. Use the deposit coupons (Forms 8109) to make deposits of estimated tax. For more information on estimated tax payments, including penalties that apply if the corporation fails to make required payments, see the instructions for line 33 on page 12.

If the corporation overpaid estimated tax, it may be able to get a quick refund by filing **Form 4466,** Corporation Application for Quick Refund of Overpayment of Estimated Tax. The overpayment must be at least 10% of the corporation's expected income tax liability and at least $500. To apply for a quick refund, file Form 4466 before the 16th day of the 3rd month after the end of the tax year, but before the corporation files its income tax return. Do not file Form 4466 before the end of the corporation's tax year.

Interest and Penalties

Interest.—Interest is charged on taxes paid late even if an extension of time to file is granted. Interest is also charged on penalties imposed for failure to file, negligence, fraud, gross valuation overstatements, and substantial understatements of tax from the due date (including extensions) to the date of payment. The interest charge is figured at a rate determined under section 6621.

Penalty for late filing of return.—A corporation that does not file its tax return by the due date, including extensions, may be penalized 5% of the unpaid tax for each month or part of a month the return is late, up to a maximum of 25% of the unpaid tax. The minimum penalty for a return that is over 60 days late is the smaller of the tax due or $100. The penalty will not be imposed if the corporation can show that the failure to file on time was due to reasonable cause. Corporations that file late must attach a statement explaining the reasonable cause.

Penalty for late payment of tax.—A corporation that does not pay the tax when due may have to pay a penalty of ½ of 1% of the unpaid tax for each month or part of a month the tax is not paid, up to a maximum of 25% of the unpaid tax. The penalty will not be imposed if the corporation can show that the failure to pay on time was due to reasonable cause.

Other penalties.—Other penalties can be imposed for negligence, substantial understatement of tax, and fraud. See sections 6662 and 6663.

Unresolved Tax Problems

The IRS has a Problem Resolution Program for taxpayers who have been unable to resolve their problems with the IRS. If the corporation has a tax problem it has been unable to resolve through normal channels, write to the corporation's local IRS district director or call the corporation's local IRS office and ask for Problem Resolution Assistance. Hearing-impaired persons who have access to TDD equipment may call 1-800-829-4059 to ask for help. The Problem Resolution office will ensure that your problem receives proper attention. Although the office cannot change the tax law or make technical decisions, it can help clear up problems that resulted from previous contacts.

Other Forms, Returns, and Statements That May Be Required

Forms

The corporation may have to file:

Form W-2, Wage and Tax Statement, and **Form W-3,** Transmittal of Income and Tax Statements.

Form 720, Quarterly Federal Excise Tax Return. Use Form 720 to report the luxury tax on passenger vehicles, environmental excise taxes, communications and air transportation taxes, fuel taxes, manufacturers taxes, ship passenger tax,

and certain other excise taxes. Also, see **Trust fund recovery penalty** on page 5.

Form 926, Return by a U.S. Transferor of Property to a Foreign Corporation, Foreign Estate or Trust, or Foreign Partnership. Use this form to report transfers of property to a foreign corporation, foreign estate or trust, or foreign partnership, to pay any excise tax due under section 1491, and to report information required under section 6038B. For details, see Form 926.

Form 940 or **Form 940-EZ,** Employer's Annual Federal Unemployment (FUTA) Tax Return. The corporation may be liable for FUTA tax and may have to file Form 940 or 940-EZ if it paid wages of $1,500 or more in any calendar quarter during the calendar year (or the preceding calendar year) or one or more employees worked for the corporation for some part of a day in any 20 different weeks during the calendar year (or the preceding calendar year).

Form 941, Employer's Quarterly Federal Tax Return. Employers must file this form quarterly to report income tax withheld and employer and employee social security and Medicare taxes. Agricultural employers must file **Form 943,** Employer's Annual Tax Return for Agricultural Employees, instead of Form 941, to report income tax withheld and employer and employee social security and Medicare taxes for farmworkers. Also see **Trust fund recovery penalty** on page 5.

Form 945, Annual Return of Withheld Federal Income Tax. File Form 945 to report income tax withholding from nonpayroll distributions or payments. Nonpayroll payments include pensions, annuities, IRAs, military retirement, gambling winnings, Indian gaming profits, and backup withholding. Also see **Trust fund recovery penalty** on page 5.

Form 952, Consent To Extend Period of Limitation on Assessment of Income Taxes, is used to extend the period of assessment of all income taxes of the receiving corporation on the complete liquidation of a subsidiary under section 332. File Form 952 if the liquidation will be completed within the 3-year period following the end of the subsidiary's tax year in which the first distribution was made.

Form 966, Corporate Dissolution or Liquidation.

Form 1042, Annual Withholding Tax Return for U.S. Source Income of Foreign Persons, and **Form 1042-S,** Foreign Person's U.S. Source Income Subject to Withholding. Use these forms to report and send withheld tax on payments or distributions made to nonresident alien individuals, foreign partnerships, or foreign corporations, to the extent payments or distributions constitute gross income from sources within the United States (see sections 861 through 865). For more information, see sections 1441 and 1442, and **Pub. 515,** Withholding of Tax on Nonresident Aliens and Foreign Corporations.

Form 1096, Annual Summary and Transmittal of U.S. Information Returns.

Page 4

122

Form 1098, Mortgage Interest Statement. This form is used to report the receipt from any individual of $600 or more of mortgage interest and points in the course of the corporation's trade or business for any calendar year.

Forms 1099-A, B, C, DIV, INT, MISC, OID, PATR, R, and **S.** Use these information returns to report abandonments; acquisitions through foreclosure; proceeds from broker and barter exchange transactions; discharges of indebtedness; certain dividends and distributions; interest payments; payments for certain fishing boat crew members; medical and dental health care payments; direct sales of consumer goods for resale; miscellaneous income payments and nonemployee compensation; original issue discount; patronage dividends; distributions from profit-sharing plans, retirement plans, individual retirement arrangements, insurance contracts, etc.; and proceeds from real estate transactions. Also use these returns to report amounts received as a nominee for another person.

For more information, see the Instructions for Forms 1099, 1098, 5498, and W-2G.

Note: *Every corporation must file Form 1099-MISC if, in the course of its trade or business, it makes payments of rents, commissions, or other fixed or determinable income (see section 6041) totaling $600 or more to any one person during the calendar year.*

Form 2553, Election by a Small Business Corporation. Corporations use this form to elect to be an S corporation.

Form 5452, Corporate Report of Nondividend Distributions.

Form 5498, Individual Retirement Arrangement Information. Use this form to report contributions (including rollover contributions) to an individual retirement arrangement (IRA) and the value of an IRA or simplified employee pension (SEP) account.

Form 5713, International Boycott Report, for persons having operations in or related to "boycotting" countries. Also, persons who participate in or cooperate with an international boycott may have to complete Schedule A or Schedule B and Schedule C of Form 5713 to compute their loss of the following items: the foreign tax credit, the deferral of earnings of a controlled foreign corporation, IC-DISC benefits, and FSC benefits.

Form 8264, Application for Registration of a Tax Shelter. Tax shelter organizers use Form 8264 to register tax shelters with the IRS to get a tax shelter registration number.

Form 8271, Investor Reporting of Tax Shelter Registration Number. Taxpayers who have acquired an interest in a tax shelter which is required to be registered use this form to report the tax shelter's registration number. Form 8271 must be attached to any tax return (including an application for tentative refund (Form 1139) and an amended return (Form 1120X)) on which a deduction, credit, loss, or other tax benefit attributable to a tax shelter is

taken or any income attributable to a tax shelter is reported.

Form 8275, Disclosure Statement. Taxpayers and income tax return preparers file Form 8275 to disclose items or positions (except those contrary to a regulation—see **Form 8275-R** below) that are not otherwise adequately disclosed on a tax return. The disclosure is made to avoid parts of the accuracy-related penalty imposed for disregard of rules or substantial understatement of tax. Form 8275 is also used for disclosures relating to preparer penalties for understatements due to unrealistic positions or disregard of rules.

Form 8275-R, Regulation Disclosure Statement, is used to disclose any item on a tax return for which a position has been taken that is contrary to Treasury regulations.

Form 8281, Information Return for Publicly Offered Original Issue Discount Instruments. Issuers of public offerings of debt instruments generally must file this form within 30 days of the issuance of the debt instrument.

Form 8300, Report of Cash Payments Over $10,000 Received in a Trade or Business. File this form to report the receipt of more than $10,000 in cash or foreign currency in one transaction or in a series of related transactions.

Cashier's checks, bank drafts, and money orders with face amounts of $10,000 or less are considered cash under certain circumstances. For more information, see Form 8300 and Regulations section 1.6050I-1(c).

Form 8594, Asset Acquisition Statement under Section 1060, must be filed by both the purchaser and seller of a group of assets constituting a trade or business if section 197 intangibles attach to such assets and if the purchaser's basis in the assets is determined only by the amount paid for the assets.

Form 8621, Return by a Shareholder of a Passive Foreign Investment Company or Qualified Electing Fund. A corporation that was a shareholder in a passive foreign investment company (as defined in section 1296) at any time during the tax year must complete and attach this form to its return.

Form 8697, Interest Computation Under the Look-Back Method for Completed Long-Term Contracts. Use this form to figure the interest due or to be refunded under the look-back method of section 460(b)(2) on certain long-term contracts accounted for under either the percentage of completion-capitalized cost method or the percentage of completion method.

Form 8810, Corporate Passive Activity Loss and Credit Limitations. Closely held corporations and personal service corporations that are subject to the passive activity limitations of section 469 use this form to compute their allowable passive activity loss and credit.

Form 8817, Allocation of Patronage and Nonpatronage Income and Deductions. Taxable cooperatives with gross receipts of $10 million or more that have both patronage and nonpatronage source

income and deductions must complete and attach this form to the return.

Form 8842, Election To Use Different Annualization Periods for Corporate Estimated Tax. Corporations use Form 8842 for each year they want to elect one of the annualization periods in section 6655(e)(2)(C) for figuring estimated tax payments under the annualized income installment method.

Form 8849, Claim for Refund of Excise Taxes. Use this form in the first three quarters of the tax year to claim a refund of excise taxes paid on Form 720, Form 730, or Form 2290. See the instructions to Form 8849 and **Pub. 378,** Fuel Tax Credits and Refunds, for more information.

Trust fund recovery penalty.—This penalty may apply if certain excise, income, social security, and Medicare taxes that must be collected or withheld are not collected or withheld, or these taxes are not paid to the IRS. These taxes are generally reported on Forms 720, 941, 943, or 945. The trust fund recovery penalty may be imposed on all persons who are determined by the IRS to have been responsible for collecting, accounting for, and paying over these taxes, and who acted willfully in not doing so. The penalty is equal to the unpaid trust fund tax. See the instructions for Form 720, **Pub. 15** (Circular E), Employer's Tax Guide, or **Pub. 51** (Circular A), Agricultural Employer's Tax Guide, for details, including the definition of responsible persons.

Consolidated Return

The parent corporation of an affiliated group of corporations must attach **Form 851,** Affiliations Schedule, to the consolidated return. For the first year a consolidated return is filed, each subsidiary must attach **Form 1122,** Authorization and Consent of Subsidiary Corporation to be Included in a Consolidated Income Tax Return.

File supporting statements for each corporation included in the consolidated return. Do not use Form 1120 as a supporting statement. On the supporting statement, use columns to show the following, both before and after adjustments:

● Items of gross income and deductions.

● A computation of taxable income.

● Balance sheets as of the beginning and end of the tax year.

● A reconciliation of income per books with income per return.

● A reconciliation of retained earnings.

Enter the totals for the consolidated group on Form 1120. Attach consolidated balance sheets and a reconciliation of consolidated retained earnings. For more information on consolidated returns, see the regulations under section 1502.

Farm Return

Do not file **Schedule F (Form 1040),** Profit or Loss From Farming. Instead, enter income on lines 1a through 10, page 1, Form 1120 (Form 1120-A) and read the related instructions. Forms 1120 and 1120-A have entry lines for many of the

Page 5

expenses deducted by farming corporations. Expenses not listed on the form should be entered on the line for "Other deductions." Attach a schedule, listing by type and amount, all deductions shown on this line. Also, see the instructions for lines 12 through 26, Form 1120 (lines 12 through 22, Form 1120-A).

Amended Return

Use **Form 1120X,** Amended U.S. Corporation Income Tax Return, to correct any error in a previously filed Form 1120 or Form 1120-A.

Statements

Stock ownership in foreign corporations.—Attach the statement required by section 551(c) if **(a)** the corporation owned 5% or more in value of the outstanding stock of a foreign personal holding company and **(b)** the corporation was required to include in its gross income any undistributed foreign personal holding company income from a foreign personal holding company.

A corporation may have to file **Form 5471,** Information Return of U.S. Persons With Respect to Certain Foreign Corporations, if any of the following applies:

1. It controls a foreign corporation.

2. It acquires, disposes of, or owns 5% or more in value of the outstanding stock of a foreign corporation.

3. It owns stock in a foreign corporation that is a controlled foreign corporation for an uninterrupted period of 30 days or more during the tax year of the foreign corporation that ends with or within its tax year, and it owned that stock on the last day of the foreign corporation's tax year.

Foreign ownership in a domestic corporation.—A domestic corporation that is 25% or more foreign-owned may have to file **Form 5472,** Information Return of a 25% Foreign-Owned U.S. Corporation or a Foreign Corporation Engaged in a U.S. Trade or Business. See the instructions on page 18 for more information.

Transfers to a corporation controlled by the transferor.—If a person receives stock of a corporation in exchange for property, and no gain or loss is recognized under section 351, the person (transferor) and the transferee must each attach to their tax returns the information required by Regulations section 1.351-3.

Dual consolidated losses.—If a domestic corporation incurs a dual consolidated loss (as defined in Regulations section 1.1503-2(c)(5)), the corporation (or consolidated group) may need to attach an elective relief agreement and/or an annual certification as provided in Regulations section 1503-2(g)(2).

Attachments

Attach **Form 4136,** Credit for Federal Tax Paid on Fuels, after page 4, Form 1120, or page 2, Form 1120-A. Attach schedules in alphabetical order and other forms in numerical order after Form 4136.

Complete every applicable entry space on Form 1120 or Form 1120-A. Do not

Page 6

write "See attached" instead of completing the entry spaces. If you need more space on the forms or schedules, attach separate sheets, using the same size and format as the printed forms. Show the totals on the printed forms. Attach these separate sheets after all the schedules and forms. Be sure to put the corporation's name and EIN on each sheet.

Specific Instructions

Period Covered

File the 1995 return for calendar year 1995 and fiscal years that begin in 1995 and end in 1996. For a fiscal year, fill in the tax year space at the top of the form.

Note: *The 1995 Form 1120 may also be used if **(1)** the corporation has a tax year of less than 12 months that begins and ends in 1996 and **(2)** the 1996 Form 1120 is not available at the time the corporation is required to file its return. However, the corporation must show its 1996 tax year on the 1995 Form 1120 and incorporate any tax law changes that are effective for tax years beginning after December 31, 1995.*

Name, Address, and Employer Identification Number (EIN)

Use the label on the package that was mailed to the corporation. Cross out any errors and print the correct information on the label. If the corporation doesn't have a label, print or type the corporation's true name (as set forth in the charter or other legal document creating it), address, and EIN on the appropriate lines.

Address.—Include the suite, room, or other unit number after the street address. If a preaddressed label is used, include this information on the label.

If the Post Office does not deliver mail to the street address and the corporation has a P.O. box, show the box number instead of the street address.

Note: *If a change in address occurs after the return is filed, use **Form 8822,** Change of Address, to notify the IRS of the new address.*

Employer identification number (EIN).— Show the correct EIN in item B on page 1 of Form 1120 or Form 1120-A. If the corporation does not have an EIN, it should apply for one on **Form SS-4,** Application for Employer Identification Number. Form SS-4 can be obtained at most IRS or Social Security Administration (SSA) offices. If the corporation has not received its EIN by the time the return is due, write "Applied for" in the space for the EIN. See Pub. 583 for details.

Item A—Personal Service Corporation

The term "personal service corporation" means a corporation whose principal activity during the testing period for the tax year is the performance of personal services that are substantially performed by employee-owners who own more than 10% of the fair market value of the corporation's outstanding stock as of the last day of the testing period for the tax year.

The testing period for a tax year is the tax year preceding the tax year. The testing period for a new corporation in its first tax year is the period beginning on the first day of its first tax year and ending on the earlier of the last day of its first tax year or the last day of the calendar year in which the first tax year began.

Activities that are treated as the performance of personal services are those that involve the performance of services in the fields of health, law, engineering, architecture, accounting, actuarial science, performing arts, or consulting (as such fields are defined in Temporary Regulations section 1.448-1T(e)).

Personal services are substantially performed by employee-owners if more than 20% of the corporation's compensation cost for the testing period attributable to the performance of personal services is attributable to personal services performed by employee-owners.

A person is considered to be an employee-owner if the person is an employee of the corporation on any day of the testing period and the person owns any outstanding stock of the corporation on any day of the testing period. Stock ownership is determined under the attribution rules of section 318 (except that "any" is substituted for "50%" in section 318(a)(2)(C)).

For details, see Temporary Regulations section 1.441-4T.

Item D—Total Assets

Enter the corporation's total assets (as determined by the accounting method regularly used in keeping the corporation's books and records) at the end of the tax year. If there are no assets at the end of the tax year, enter the total assets as of the beginning of the tax year.

Item E—Initial Return, Final Return, or Change of Address

If this is the corporation's first return, check the "Initial return" box. If the corporation ceases to exist, file Form 1120 and check the "Final return" box. Do not file Form 1120-A.

If the corporation has changed its address since it last filed a return, check the box for "Change of address."

Income

Note: *Generally, income from all sources, whether U.S. or foreign, must be included.*

Line 1

Gross Receipts

Enter gross receipts or sales from all business operations except those that must be reported on lines 4 through 10. For reporting advance payments, see Regulations section 1.451-5. To report income from long-term contracts, see section 460.

Installment sales.—Generally, the installment method cannot be used for dealer dispositions of property. A "dealer disposition" means any disposition of personal property by a person who regularly sells or otherwise disposes of property of the same type on the installment plan. The disposition of property used or produced in the farming business is not included as a dealer disposition. See section 453(l) for details and exceptions.

Enter on line 1 (and carry to line 3), the gross profit on collections from installment sales for any of the following:

● Dealer dispositions of property before March 1, 1986.

● Dispositions of property used or produced in the trade or business of farming.

● Certain dispositions of timeshares and residential lots reported under the installment method.

Attach a schedule showing the following information for the current and the 3 preceding years: **(a)** gross sales, **(b)** cost of goods sold, **(c)** gross profits, **(d)** percentage of gross profits to gross sales, **(e)** amount collected, and **(f)** gross profit on the amount collected.

For sales of timeshares and residential lots reported under the installment method, the corporation's income tax is increased by the interest payable under section 453(l)(3). To report this addition to the tax, see the instructions for line 10, Schedule J, Form 1120.

Accrual method taxpayers need not accrue certain amounts to be received from the performance of services that, on the basis of their experience, will not be collected (section 448(d)(5)). This provision does not apply to any amount if interest is required to be paid on the amount or if there is any penalty for failure to timely pay the amount. Corporations that fall under this provision should attach a schedule showing total gross receipts, the amount not accrued as a result of the application of section 448(d)(5), and the net amount accrued. Enter the net amount on line 1a. For more information and guidelines on this "non-accrual experience method," see Temporary Regulations section 1.448-2T.

Line 2

Cost of Goods Sold

Enter the cost of goods sold on line 2, page 1. Before making this entry, a Form 1120 filer must complete Schedule A on page 2 of Form 1120. Form 1120-A filers may use the worksheet on page 12 to figure the amount to enter on line 2. Both Form 1120 and Form 1120-A filers should see the instructions for Schedule A and the worksheet.

Line 4

Dividends

Form 1120 filers.—See the instructions for Schedule C. Then, complete Schedule C and enter on line 4 the amount from Schedule C, line 19.

Form 1120-A filers.—Enter the total dividends received (that are not from debt-financed stock) from domestic corporations that qualify for the 70% dividends-received deduction.

Line 5

Interest

Enter taxable interest on U.S. obligations and on loans, notes, mortgages, bonds, bank deposits, corporate bonds, tax refunds, etc.

Do not offset interest expense against interest income.

Special rules apply to interest income from certain below-market-rate loans. See section 7872 for more information.

Line 6

Gross Rents

Enter the gross amount received for the rent of property. Deduct expenses such as repairs, interest, taxes, and depreciation on the proper lines for deductions. A rental activity held by a closely held corporation or a personal service corporation may be subject to the passive activity loss rules. See Form 8810 and its instructions.

Line 8

Capital Gain Net Income

Every sale or exchange of a capital asset must be reported in detail on **Schedule D (Form 1120)**, Capital Gains and Losses, even though no gain or loss is indicated.

Line 9

Net Gain or (Loss)

Enter the net gain or (loss) from line 20, Part II, **Form 4797**, Sales of Business Property.

Line 10

Other Income

Enter any other taxable income not reported on lines 1 through 9. List the type and amount of income on an attached schedule. If the corporation has only one item of other income, describe it in parentheses on line 10. Examples of other income to report on line 10 are:

● Any adjustment under section 481(a) required to be included in income during the current tax year due to a change in a method of accounting.

● Recoveries of bad debts deducted in prior years under the specific charge-off method.

● The amount of credit for alcohol used as fuel (determined without regard to the limitation based on tax) that was entered on **Form 6478**, Credit for Alcohol Used as Fuel.

● Refunds of taxes deducted in prior years to the extent they reduced income subject to tax in the year deducted (see section 111). Do not offset current year taxes against tax refunds.

● The amount of any deduction previously taken under section 179A that is subject to recapture. The corporation must recapture the benefit of any allowable deduction for clean-fuel vehicle property (or clean-fuel vehicle refueling property), if, within 3 years of the date the property was placed in

service, the property ceases to qualify. See Regulations section 1.179A-1 for details.

● Ordinary income from trade or business activities of a partnership (from Schedule K-1 (Form 1065), line 1).

Deductions

Limitations on Deductions

Section 263A uniform capitalization rules.—These rules require corporations to capitalize or include in inventory certain costs incurred in connection with the production of real and tangible personal property held in inventory or held for sale in the ordinary course of business. Tangible personal property produced by a corporation includes a film, sound recording, videotape, book, or similar property. The rules also apply to personal property (tangible and intangible) acquired for resale. Corporations subject to the rules are required to capitalize not only direct costs but an allocable portion of most indirect costs (including taxes) that relate to the assets produced or acquired for resale. Interest expense paid or incurred during the production period of certain property must be capitalized and is governed by special rules. For more information, see Regulations sections 1.263A-8 through 1.263A-15. The uniform capitalization rules also apply to the production of property constructed or improved by a taxpayer for use in its trade or business or in an activity engaged in for profit.

Section 263A does not apply to personal property acquired for resale if the taxpayer's annual average gross receipts for the 3 prior tax years are $10 million or less. It does not apply to timber or to most property produced under a long-term contract. Special rules apply for farmers. The rules do not apply to property that is produced for use by the corporation if substantial construction occurred before March 1, 1986.

In the case of inventory, some of the indirect costs that must be capitalized are administration expenses; taxes; depreciation; insurance; compensation paid to officers attributable to services; rework labor; and contributions to pension, stock bonus, and certain profit-sharing, annuity, or deferred compensation plans.

The costs that must be capitalized under section 263A are not deductible until the property to which the costs relate is sold, used, or otherwise disposed of by the corporation.

Current deductions may still be claimed for reasonable research and experimental costs under section 174, intangible drilling costs for oil and gas and geothermal property, and mining and exploration and development costs. Regulations section 1.263A-1(e)(3) specifies other indirect costs that may be currently deducted and those that must be capitalized with respect to production or resale activities. For more information, see Regulations sections 1.263A-1 through 1.263A-3.

Transactions between related taxpayers.—Generally, an accrual basis taxpayer may only deduct business

Page 7

expenses and interest owed to a related party in the year the payment is included in the income of the related party. See sections 163(e)(3), 163(j), and 267 for limitations on deductions for unpaid interest and expenses.

Section 291 limitations.—Corporations may be required to adjust deductions for depletion of iron ore and coal, intangible drilling and exploration and development costs, certain deductions for financial institutions, and the amortizable basis of pollution control facilities. See section 291 to determine the amount of adjustment. Also see section 43.

Golden parachute payments.—A portion of the payments made by a corporation to key personnel that exceeds their usual compensation may not be deductible. This occurs when the corporation has an agreement (golden parachute) with these key employees to pay them these excessive amounts if control of the corporation changes. See section 280G.

Business startup expenses.—Business startup expenses must be capitalized unless an election is made to amortize them over a period of 60 months. See section 195.

Passive activity limitations.—Limitations on passive activity losses and credits under section 469 apply to personal service corporations as defined in Temporary Regulations section 1.441-4T (see **Item A—Personal Service Corporation** on page 6) and closely held corporations.

For this purpose, a corporation is a closely held corporation if at any time during the last half of the tax year more than 50% in value of its outstanding stock is owned, directly or indirectly, by or for not more than five individuals, and the corporation is not a personal service corporation. Certain organizations are treated as individuals for purposes of this test. (See section 542(a)(2).) For rules of determining stock ownership, see section 544 (as modified by section 465(a)(3)).

Generally, there are two kinds of passive activities: trade or business activities in which the corporation did not materially participate (see Temporary Regulations section 1.469-1T(g)(3)) for the tax year, and rental activities regardless of its participation. For exceptions, see Form 8810. An activity is a trade or business activity if the activity involves the conduct of a trade or business (i.e., deductions from the activity would be allowable under section 162 if other limitations, such as the passive loss rules, did not apply), or the activity involves research and experimental costs that are deductible under section 174 (or would be deductible if the corporation chose to deduct rather than capitalize them), and the activity is not a rental activity.

Corporations subject to the passive activity limitations must complete Form 8810 to compute their allowable passive activity loss and credit. Before completing Form 8810, see Temporary Regulations section 1.163-8T, which provides rules for allocating interest expense among activities. If a passive activity is also subject to the at-risk rules of section 465,

Page 8

the at-risk rules apply before the passive loss rules. For more information, see section 469, the related regulations, and **Pub. 925,** Passive Activity and At-Risk Rules.

Reducing certain expenses for which credits are allowable.—For each credit listed below, the corporation must reduce the otherwise allowable deductions for expenses used to figure the credit by the amount of the current year credit:

1. The credit for increasing research activities.

2. The enhanced oil recovery credit.

3. The disabled access credit.

4. The jobs credit.

5. The employer credit for social security and Medicare taxes paid on tips.

6. The empowerment zone employment credit.

7. The Indian employment credit.

If the corporation has any of these credits, be sure to figure each current year credit before figuring the deduction for expenses on which the credit is based.

Line 12

Compensation of Officers

Enter deductible officers' compensation on line 12. Before entering an amount on line 12, Form 1120 filers must complete Schedule E if their total receipts (line 1a, plus lines 4 through 10) are $500,000 or more. Do not include compensation deductible elsewhere on the return, such as amounts included in cost of goods sold, elective contributions to a section 401(k) cash or deferred arrangement, or amounts contributed under a salary reduction SEP agreement.

Include only the deductible part of officers' compensation on Schedule E. (See **Disallowance of deduction for employee compensation in excess of $1 million** below.) Complete Schedule E, line 1, columns (a) through (f), for all officers. The corporation determines who is an officer under the laws of the state where incorporated.

If a consolidated return is filed, each member of an affiliated group must furnish this information.

Disallowance of deduction for employee compensation in excess of $1 million.—Publicly held corporations may not deduct compensation to a "covered employee" to the extent that the compensation exceeds $1 million. Generally, a covered employee is:

● The chief executive officer of the corporation (or an individual acting in that capacity) as of the end of the tax year, or

● An employee whose total compensation must be reported to shareholders under the Securities Exchange Act of 1934 because the employee is among the four highest compensated officers for that tax year (other than the chief executive officer).

For this purpose, compensation does not include the following:

● Income from certain employee trusts, annuity plans, or pensions;

● Any benefit paid to an employee that is excluded from the employee's income.

The deduction limit does not apply to:

● Commissions based on individual performance;

● Qualified performance-based compensation; and,

● Income payable under a written, binding contract in effect on February 17, 1993.

The $1 million limit is reduced by amounts disallowed as excess parachute payments under section 280G.

For details, see section 162(m) and Notice 94-68, 1994-1 C.B. 376.

Line 13

Salaries and Wages

Enter the amount of salaries and wages paid for the tax year, less the amount of any jobs credit from Form 5884, empowerment zone employment credit from Form 8844, and Indian employment credit from Form 8845. See the instructions for these forms for more information. Do not include salaries and wages deductible elsewhere on the return, such as amounts included in cost of goods sold, elective contributions to a section 401(k) cash or deferred arrangement, or amounts contributed under a salary reduction SEP agreement.

Caution: *If the corporation provided taxable fringe benefits to its employees, such as personal use of a car, do not deduct as wages the amount allocated for depreciation and other expenses claimed on lines 20 and 26, Form 1120, or lines 20 and 22, Form 1120-A.*

Line 14

Repairs and Maintenance

Enter the cost of incidental repairs and maintenance not claimed elsewhere on the return, such as labor and supplies, that do not add to the value of the property or appreciably prolong its life. New buildings, machinery, or permanent improvements that increase the value of the property are not deductible. They must be depreciated or amortized.

Line 15

Bad Debts

Enter the total debts that became worthless in whole or in part during the tax year. A small bank or thrift institution using the reserve method should attach a schedule showing how it arrived at the current year's provision.

Caution: *A cash basis taxpayer may not claim a bad debt deduction unless the amount was previously included in income.*

Line 16

Rents

If the corporation rented or leased a vehicle, enter the total annual rent or lease expense paid or incurred during the year. Also complete Part V of **Form 4562,** Depreciation and Amortization. If the corporation leased a vehicle for a term of 30 days or more, the deduction for vehicle lease expense may have to be reduced by an amount called the **inclusion amount.** The corporation may have an inclusion amount if:

The lease term began:	And the vehicle's fair market value on the first day of the lease exceeded:
After 12/31/94	$15,500
After 12/31/93 but before 1/1/95 . .	$14,600
After 12/31/92 but before 1/1/94 . .	$14,300
After 12/31/91 but before 1/1/93 . .	$13,700
After 12/31/90 but before 1/1/92 . .	$13,400
After 12/31/86 but before 1/1/91 . .	$12,800

If the lease term began after June 18, 1984, but before January 1, 1987, see **Pub. 917,** Business Use of a Car, to find out if the corporation has an inclusion amount. Also see Pub. 917 for instructions on figuring the inclusion amount.

Line 17

Taxes and Licenses

Enter taxes paid or accrued during the tax year, but do not include the following:

• Federal income taxes (except the environmental tax under section 59A).

• Foreign or U.S. possession income taxes if a tax credit is claimed (however, see the Instructions for Form 5735 for special rules for possession income taxes).

• Taxes not imposed on the corporation.

• Taxes, including state or local sales taxes, that are paid or incurred in connection with an acquisition or disposition of property (these taxes must be treated as a part of the cost of the acquired property or, in the case of a disposition, as a reduction in the amount realized on the disposition).

• Taxes assessed against local benefits that increase the value of the property assessed (such as for paving, etc.).

• Taxes deducted elsewhere on the return, such as those reflected in cost of goods sold.

See section 164(d) for apportionment of taxes on real property between seller and purchaser.

If the corporation is liable for the environmental tax under section 59A, get **Form 4626,** Alternative Minimum Tax—Corporations, for computation of the environmental tax deduction.

Line 18

Interest

If the proceeds of a loan were used for more than one purpose (e.g., to purchase a portfolio investment and to acquire an interest in a passive activity), an interest allocation must be made. See Temporary Regulations section 1.163-8T for the interest allocation rules.

Do not include interest on indebtedness incurred or continued to purchase or carry obligations if the interest is wholly exempt from income tax. For exceptions, see section 265(b).

Mutual savings banks, building and loan associations, and cooperative banks can deduct the amounts paid or credited to the accounts of depositors as dividends, interest, or earnings. See section 591.

Generally, a cash basis taxpayer cannot deduct prepaid interest allocable to years following the current tax year. For example, a cash basis calendar year taxpayer who in 1995 prepaid interest allocable to any period after 1995 can deduct only the amount allocable to 1995.

Generally, the interest and carrying charges on straddles cannot be deducted and must be capitalized. See section 263(g).

See section 163(e)(5) for special rules for the disqualified portion of original issue discount on a high yield discount obligation.

Certain interest paid or accrued by the corporation (directly or indirectly) to a related person may be limited if no tax is imposed on that interest. See section 163(j) for more information.

Do not deduct interest on debt allocable to the production of qualified property. Interest that is allocable to property produced by a corporation for its own use or for sale must be capitalized. A corporation must also capitalize any interest on debt allocable to an asset used to produce the above property. See section 263A and Regulations section 1.263A-8 through 1.263A-15 for definitions and more information.

See section 7872 for special rules on the deductibility of foregone interest on certain below-market-rate loans.

Line 19

Charitable Contributions

Enter contributions or gifts actually paid within the tax year to or for the use of charitable and governmental organizations described in section 170(c) and any unused contributions carried over from prior years.

The total amount claimed may not be more than 10% of taxable income (line 30, Form 1120, or line 26, Form 1120-A) computed without regard to the following:

• Any deduction for contributions,

• The special deductions on line 29b, Form 1120 (line 25b, Form 1120-A),

• The deduction allowed under section 249,

• Any net operating loss (NOL) carryback to the tax year under section 172, and

• Any capital loss carryback to the tax year under section 1212(a)(1).

Charitable contributions over the 10% limitation may not be deducted for the tax year but may be carried over to the next 5 tax years.

Special rules apply if the corporation has an NOL carryover to the tax year. In figuring the charitable contributions deduction for the tax year, the 10% limit is applied using the taxable income after taking into account any deduction for the NOL.

To figure the amount of any remaining NOL carryover to later years, taxable income must be modified (see section 172(b)). To the extent that contributions are used to reduce taxable income for this purpose and increase an NOL carryover, a contributions carryover is not allowed. See section 170(d)(2)(B).

Corporations on the accrual basis may elect to deduct contributions paid by the 15th day of the 3rd month after the end of the tax year if the contributions are authorized by the board of directors during the tax year. Attach a declaration to the return, signed by an officer, stating that the resolution authorizing the contributions was adopted by the board of directors during the tax year. Also attach a copy of the resolution.

Substantiation requirements.—Generally, no deduction is allowed for any contribution of $250 or more unless the corporation gets a written acknowledgment from the donee organization that shows the amount of cash contributed, describes any property contributed, and gives an estimate of the value of any goods or services provided in return for the contribution. The acknowledgment must be obtained by the due date (including extensions) of the corporation's return, or, if earlier, the date the return is filed. Do not attach the acknowledgment to the tax return, but keep it with the corporation's records. These rules apply in addition to the filing requirements for Form 8283 described below.

For more information on substantiation and recordkeeping requirements, see the regulations under section 170 and **Pub. 526,** Charitable Contributions.

Contributions of property other than cash.—If a corporation (other than a closely held or personal service corporation) contributes property other than cash and claims over a $500 deduction for the property, it must attach a schedule to the return describing the kind of property contributed and the method used to determine its fair market value. Closely held corporations and personal service corporations must complete **Form 8283,** Noncash Charitable Contributions, and attach it to their returns. All other corporations generally must complete and attach Form 8283 to their returns for contributions of property other than money if the total claimed deduction for all property contributed was more than $5,000.

If the corporation made a "qualified conservation contribution" under section 170(h), also include the fair market value of the underlying property before and after the donation, as well as the type of legal interest contributed, and describe the conservation purpose benefited by the donation. If a contribution carryover is included, show the amount and how it was determined.

Special rule for contributions of certain property.—For a charitable contribution of property, the corporation must reduce the contribution by the sum of:

• The ordinary income, short-term capital gain that would have resulted if the property were sold at its fair market value, and

• For certain contributions, all of the long-term capital gain that would have

Page 9

resulted if the property were sold at its fair market value.

The reduction for the long-term capital gain applies to:

• Contributions of tangible personal property for use by an exempt organization for a purpose or function unrelated to the basis for its exemption, and

• Contributions of any property to or for the use of certain private foundations. See section 170(e) and Regulations section 1.170A-4.

For special rules for contributions of inventory and other property to certain organizations, see section 170(e)(3) and Regulations section 1.170A-4A.

Charitable contributions of scientific property used for research.—A corporation (other than a personal holding company or a service organization) can receive a larger deduction for contributing scientific property used for research to an institution of higher education. For more details, see section 170(e).

Contributions to organizations conducting lobbying activities.— Contributions made to an organization that conducts lobbying activities are not deductible if:

• The lobbying activities relate to matters of direct financial interest to the donor's trade or business, and

• The principal purpose of the contribution was to avoid Federal income tax by obtaining a deduction for activities that would have been nondeductible under the lobbying expense rules if conducted directly by the donor.

Line 20

Depreciation

Besides depreciation, include on line 20 the part of the cost that the corporation elected to expense under section 179 for certain tangible property placed in service during tax year 1995 or carried over from 1994. See **Form 4562,** Depreciation and Amortization, and its instructions.

Line 22 (Form 1120 only)

Depletion

See sections 613 and 613A for percentage depletion rates applicable to natural deposits. Also, see section 291 for the limitation on the depletion deduction for iron ore and coal (including lignite).

Foreign intangible drilling costs and foreign exploration and development costs must either be added to the corporation's basis for cost depletion purposes or be deducted ratably over a 10-year period. See sections 263(i), 616, and 617 for details.

Attach **Form T (Timber),** Forest Activities Schedules, if a deduction for depletion of timber is taken.

Line 24 (Form 1120 only)

Pension, Profit-Sharing, etc., Plans

Enter the deduction for contributions to qualified pension, profit-sharing, or other funded deferred compensation plans.

Page 10

Employers who maintain such a plan generally must file one of the forms listed below, even if the plan is not a qualified plan under the Internal Revenue Code. The filing requirement applies even if the corporation does not claim a deduction for the current tax year. There are penalties for failure to file these forms on time and for overstating the pension plan deduction. See sections 6652(e) and 6662(f).

Form 5500.—File this form for each plan with 100 or more participants.

Form 5500-C/R.—File this form for each plan with fewer than 100 participants.

Form 5500-EZ.—File this form for a one-participant plan. The term "one-participant plan" also means a plan that covers the owner and his or her spouse, or a plan that covers partners in a business partnership (or the partners and their spouses).

Line 25 (Form 1120 only)

Employee Benefit Programs

Enter contributions to employee benefit programs not claimed elsewhere on the return (e.g., insurance, health and welfare programs) that are not an incidental part of a pension, profit-sharing, etc., plan included on line 24.

Line 26, Form 1120 (Line 22, Form 1120-A)

Other Deductions

Note: *Do not deduct fines or penalties paid to a government for violating any law.*

Attach a schedule, listing by type and amount, all allowable deductions that are not deductible elsewhere on Form 1120 or Form 1120-A. Form 1120-A filers should include amounts described in the instructions above for lines 22, 24, and 25 of Form 1120. Enter the total on line 26, Form 1120 (line 22, Form 1120-A).

Include on this line the deduction for amortization of pollution control facilities, organization expenses, etc. See Form 4562.

Also include ordinary losses from trade or business activities of a partnership (from Schedule K-1 (Form 1065), line 1).

A corporation may deduct dividends it pays in cash on stock held by an employee stock ownership plan. However, a deduction may only be taken if, according to the plan, the dividends are:

• Paid in cash directly to the plan participants or beneficiaries;

• Paid to the plan, which distributes them in cash to the plan participants or their beneficiaries no later than 90 days after the end of the plan year in which the dividends are paid; or

• Used to make payments on a loan described in section 404(a)(9).

See section 404(k) for more details and the limitation on certain dividends.

Generally, a deduction may not be taken for any amount that is allocable to a class of exempt income. See section 265(b) for exceptions.

Meals, travel, and entertainment.— Generally, the corporation can deduct only 50% of the amount otherwise allowable for meals and entertainment expenses paid or incurred in its trade or business. Also, meals must not be lavish or extravagant; a bona fide business discussion must occur during, immediately before, or immediately after the meal; and an employee of the corporation must be present at the meal. See section 274(k)(2) for exceptions. If the corporation claims a deduction for unallowable meal expenses, it may have to pay a penalty.

Additional limitations apply to deductions for gifts, skybox rentals, luxury water travel, convention expenses, and entertainment tickets. For details, see section 274 and **Pub. 463,** Travel, Entertainment, and Gift Expenses.

No deduction is allowed for dues paid or incurred for membership in any club organized for business, pleasure, recreation, or other social purpose. This includes country clubs, golf and athletic clubs, airline and hotel clubs, and clubs operated to provide meals under conditions favorable to business discussion. But it does not include civic or public service organizations, professional organizations (such as bar and medical associations), business leagues, trade associations, chambers of commerce, boards of trade, and real estate boards, unless a principal purpose of the organization is to entertain or provide entertainment facilities for members or their guests.

Also, no deduction is allowed for travel expenses paid or incurred for a spouse, dependent, or other individual accompanying an officer or employee of the corporation on business travel, unless that spouse, dependent, or other individual is an employee of the corporation and the travel is for a bona fide business purpose and would otherwise be deductible by that person.

Generally, a corporation can deduct all other ordinary and necessary travel and entertainment expenses paid or incurred in its trade or business. However, it cannot deduct an expense paid or incurred for a facility (such as a yacht or hunting lodge) used for an activity that is usually considered entertainment, amusement, or recreation.

Note: *The corporation may be able to deduct otherwise nondeductible meals, travel, and entertainment expenses if the amounts are treated as compensation and reported on Form W-2 for an employee or on Form 1099-MISC for an independent contractor.*

Deduction for clean-fuel vehicles and certain refueling property.—Section 179A allows a deduction for part of the cost of qualified clean-fuel vehicle property and qualified clean-fuel vehicle refueling property placed in service after June 30, 1993. For more information, see Pub. 535.

Lobbying expenses.—Generally, lobbying expenses are not deductible. These expenses include amounts paid or incurred in connection with influencing Federal or state legislation (but not local legislation), or amounts paid or incurred in connection with any communication with certain Federal executive branch officials in an attempt to influence the official actions or positions of the officials. See Regulations section 1.162-29 for the definition of "influencing legislation." If certain in-house lobbying expenditures do not exceed $2,000, they are deductible. Dues and other similar amounts paid to certain tax-exempt organizations may not be deductible. See section 162(e)(3). For information on contributions to charitable organizations that conduct lobbying activities, see the instructions for line 19. For more information on lobbying expenses, see section 162(e).

Line 28, Form 1120 (Line 24, Form 1120-A)

Taxable Income Before NOL Deduction and Special Deductions

At-risk rules.—Generally, special at-risk rules under section 465 apply to closely held corporations (see **Passive activity limitations** on page 8) engaged in any activity as a trade or business or for the production of income. These corporations may have to adjust the amount on line 28, Form 1120, or line 24, Form 1120-A. (See below.)

But the at-risk rules do not apply to:

• Holding real property placed in service by the taxpayer before 1987;

• Equipment leasing under sections 465(c)(4), (5), and (6); or

• Any qualifying business of a qualified corporation under section 465(c)(7).

However, the at-risk rules do apply to the holding of mineral property.

If the at-risk rules apply, adjust the amount on this line for any section 465(d) losses. These losses are limited to the amount for which the corporation is at risk for each separate activity at the close of the tax year. If the corporation is involved in one or more activities, any of which incurs a loss for the year, report the losses for each activity separately. Attach **Form 6198,** At-Risk Limitations, showing the amount at risk and gross income and deductions for the activities with the losses.

If the corporation sells or otherwise disposes of an asset or its interest (either total or partial) in an activity to which the at-risk rules apply, determine the net profit or loss from the activity by combining the gain or loss on the sale or disposition with the profit or loss from the activity. If the corporation has a net loss, it may be limited because of the at-risk rules.

Treat any loss from an activity not allowed for the tax year as a deduction allocable to the activity in the next tax year.

Line 29a, Form 1120 (Line 25a, Form 1120-A)

Net Operating Loss Deduction

A corporation may use the net operating loss (NOL) incurred in one tax year to reduce its taxable income in another year. Generally, a corporation may carry an NOL back to each of the 3 years preceding the year of the loss and then carry any remaining amount over to each of the 15 years following the year of the loss (but Form 1120 filers see **Exceptions to carryback rules** below). Enter on line 29a (line 25a, Form 1120-A), the total NOL carryovers from prior tax years, but do not enter more than the corporation's taxable income (after special deductions). An NOL deduction cannot be taken in a year in which the corporation has a negative taxable income. Attach a schedule showing the computation of the NOL deduction. Form 1120 filers must also complete question 15 on Schedule K.

For details on the NOL deduction, get **Pub. 536,** Net Operating Losses.

Carryback and carryover rules.—Generally, an NOL first must be carried back to the third tax year preceding the year of the loss. To carry back the loss and obtain a quick refund of taxes, use **Form 1139,** Corporation Application for Tentative Refund. Form 1139 must be filed within 12 months after the close of the tax year of the loss. See section 6411 for details. Do not attach Form 1139 to the corporation's income tax return. Mail it in a separate envelope to the service center where the corporation files its income tax return.

For carryback claims filed later than 12 months after the close of the tax year of the loss, file **Form 1120X,** Amended U.S. Corporation Income Tax Return, instead of Form 1139.

After the corporation applies the NOL to the first tax year to which it may be carried, the taxable income of that year is modified (as described in section 172(b)) to determine how much of the remaining loss may be carried to other years. See section 172(b) and the related regulations for details.

Special rules apply when an ownership change occurs (i.e., for any tax year ending after a post-1986 ownership change, the amount of the taxable income of a loss corporation that can be offset by pre-change NOL carryovers is limited). See section 382 and the related regulations. Also see Temporary Regulations section 1.382-2T(a)(2)(ii), which requires that a loss corporation file an information statement with its income tax return for each tax year that it is a loss corporation and certain shifts in ownership occurred. Also see Regulations section 1.382-6(b) for details on how to make the closing-of-the-books election.

See section 384 for the limitation on the use of preacquisition losses of one corporation to offset recognized built-in gains of another corporation.

Exceptions to carryback rules (Form 1120 filers only).—A corporation may make an irrevocable election to forego the carryback period and instead carry the NOL over to each of the 15 years following the year of the loss. To make this election, check the box in question 14 on Schedule K. The return must be timely filed (including extensions).

Different carryback periods apply for certain losses. The part of an NOL that is attributable to a specified liability loss, including a product liability loss, may be carried back 10 years (section 172(b)(1)(C)). See Regulations section 1.172-13(c) for the statement that must be attached to Form 1120 if the corporation is claiming the 10-year carryback period for a product liability loss.

Special rules apply to the carryback of losses that are attributable to interest paid in connection with corporate equity reduction transactions (CERTs). The rules apply if a corporation has a corporate equity reduction interest loss in a loss limitation year ending after August 2, 1989. See section 172(b)(1)(E).

Personal service corporations may not carry back an NOL to or from any tax year to which a section 444 election applies.

Line 29b, Form 1120 (Line 25b, Form 1120-A)

Special Deductions

Form 1120 filers.—See the Instructions for Schedule C.

Form 1120-A filers.—Generally, enter 70% of line 4, page 1, on line 25b. However, this deduction may not be more than 70% of line 24, page 1. Compute line 24 without regard to any adjustment under section 1059 and without regard to any capital loss carryback to the tax year under section 1212(a)(1).

In a year in which an NOL occurs, this 70% limitation does not apply even if the loss is created by the dividends-received deduction. See sections 172(d) and 246(b).

Line 30, Form 1120 (Line 26, Form 1120-A)

Taxable Income

Capital construction fund.—To take a deduction for amounts contributed to a capital construction fund, reduce the amount that would otherwise be entered on line 30 (line 26, Form 1120-A) by the amount of the deduction. On the dotted line next to the entry space, write "CCF" and the amount of the deduction. For more information, get **Pub. 595,** Tax Guide for Commercial Fishermen.

Line 32b, Form 1120 (Line 28b, Form 1120-A)

Estimated Tax Payments

Enter any estimated tax payments the corporation made for the tax year.

Beneficiaries of trusts.—If the corporation is the beneficiary of a trust, and the trust makes a section 643(g) election to credit its estimated tax payments to its beneficiaries, include the corporation's share of the payment in the total for line 32b, Form 1120 (line 28b, Form 1120-A). Write "T" and the amount on the dotted line next to the entry space.

Special estimated tax payments for certain life insurance companies.—If the corporation is required to make or apply special estimated tax payments (SETP) under section 847 in addition to its regular estimated tax payments, enter on line 32b (line 28b, Form 1120-A), the corporation's total estimated tax payments. On the

Page 11

dotted line next to the entry space, write "SETP" and the amount. Attach a schedule showing your computation of estimated tax payments. See section 847(2) and **Form 8816,** Special Loss Discount Account and Special Estimated Tax Payments for Insurance Companies, for more information.

Line 32g, Form 1120 (Line 28g, Form 1120-A)

Credit for Federal Tax on Fuels

Complete Form 4136 if the corporation qualifies to take this credit. Attach Form 4136 after page 4, Form 1120, or page 2, Form 1120-A.

Credit for ozone-depleting chemicals.— Include on line 32g (line 28g, Form 1120-A) any credit the corporation is claiming under section 4682(g)(4) for tax on ozone-depleting chemicals. Write "ODC" to the left of the entry space.

Line 32h, Form 1120 (Line 28h, Form 1120-A)

Total Payments

On Form 1120, add the amounts on lines 32d through 32g and enter the total on line 32h. On Form 1120-A, add the amounts on lines 28d through 28g and enter the total on line 28h.

Backup withholding.—If the corporation had income tax withheld from any payments it received, because, for example, it failed to give the payer its correct EIN, include the amount withheld in the total for line 32h, Form 1120 (line 28h, Form 1120-A). This type of withholding is called backup withholding. On Form 1120, show the amount withheld in the blank space in the right-hand column between lines 31 and 32h, and write "backup withholding." On Form 1120-A, show the amount withheld on the dotted line to the left of line 28h, and write "backup withholding."

Line 33, Form 1120 (Line 29, Form 1120-A)

Estimated Tax Penalty

A corporation that does not make estimated tax payments when due may be subject to an underpayment penalty for the period of underpayment. Generally, a corporation is subject to the penalty if its tax liability is $500 or more, and it did not timely pay the smaller of **(a)** 100% of its tax liability for 1995, or **(b)** 100% of its prior year's tax. See section 6655 for details and exceptions, including special rules for large corporations.

Form 2220, Underpayment of Estimated Tax by Corporations, is used to see if the corporation owes a penalty and to figure the amount of the penalty. Generally, the corporation does not have to file this form because the IRS can figure the amount of any penalty and bill the corporation for it. However, even if the corporation does not owe the penalty you must complete and attach Form 2220 if:

● The annualized income or adjusted seasonal installment method is used, or

● The corporation is a large corporation computing its first required installment based on the prior year's tax. (See the Form 2220 instructions for the definition of a large corporation.)

If you attach Form 2220, check the box on line 33, Form 1120 (line 29, Form 1120-A), and enter the amount of any penalty on this line.

Schedule A, Form 1120 (Worksheet, Form 1120-A)

Cost of Goods Sold

Inventories are required at the beginning and end of each tax year if the production, purchase, or sale of merchandise is an income-producing factor. See Regulations section 1.471-1. If inventories are not used, enter zero on lines 1 and 7 of Schedule A, Form 1120, or the worksheet.

All filers should see **Section 263A uniform capitalization rules** on page 7 before completing Schedule A or the worksheet below. The instructions for lines 4 through 7 below apply to both Schedule A and the worksheet.

Line 4

Additional Section 263A Costs

An entry is required on this line only for corporations that have elected a simplified method of accounting.

For corporations that have elected the simplified production method, additional section 263A costs are generally those costs, other than interest, that were not capitalized under the corporation's method of accounting immediately prior to the effective date of section 263A that are now required to be capitalized under section 263A. For details, see Regulations section 1.263A-2(b).

For corporations that have elected the simplified resale method, additional section 263A costs are generally those costs incurred with respect to the following categories: off-site storage or warehousing; purchasing; handling, processing, assembly, and repackaging; and general and administrative costs (mixed service costs). For details, see Regulations section 1.263A-3(d).

Enter on line 4 the balance of section 263A costs paid or incurred during the tax year not included on lines 2, 3, and 5.

Line 5

Other Costs

Enter on line 5 any costs paid or incurred during the tax year not entered on lines 2 through 4.

Line 7

Inventory at End of Year

See Regulations section 1.263A-1 through 1.263A-3 for details on figuring the amount of additional section 263A costs to be included in ending inventory.

Lines 9a Through 9f (Schedule A)

Inventory Valuation Methods

Inventories can be valued at:

● Cost;

● Cost or market value (whichever is lower); or

● Any other method approved by the IRS that conforms to the requirements of the applicable regulations cited below.

The average cost (rolling average) method of valuing inventories generally does not conform to the requirements of the regulations. See Rev. Rul. 71-234, 1971-1 C.B. 148.

Corporations that use erroneous valuation methods must change to a method permitted for Federal income tax purposes. To make this change, use Form 3115.

On line 9a, check the method(s) used for valuing inventories. Under lower of cost or market, the term "market" (for normal goods) means the current bid price prevailing on the inventory valuation date for the particular merchandise in the volume usually purchased by the taxpayer. For a manufacturer, market applies to the basic elements of cost--raw materials, labor, and burden. If section 263A applies to the taxpayer, the basic elements of cost must reflect the current bid price of all direct costs and all indirect costs properly allocable to goods on hand at the inventory date.

Inventory may be valued below cost when the merchandise is unsaleable at normal prices or unusable in the normal

---

Cost of Goods Sold Worksheet

Form 1120-A
(Keep for your records.)

1. Inventory at start of year. Enter here and in Part III, line 3, column (a), Form 1120-A . . . . 1. _____
2. Purchases. Enter here and in Part II, line 5a(1), Form 1120-A . . . . . 2. _____
3. Cost of labor. Enter here and include in total in Part II, line 5a(3), Form 1120-A 3. _____
4. Additional section 263A costs. Enter here and in Part II, line 5a(2), Form 1120-A (see instructions) . . . . 4. _____
5. Other costs. Enter here and include in Part II, line 5a(3), Form 1120-A . . 5. _____
6. Total. Add lines 1 through 5 . . . . 6. _____
7. Inventory at end of year. Enter here and in Part III, line 3, column (b), Form 1120-A . . . . 7. _____
8. Cost of goods sold. Subtract line 7 from line 6. Enter the result here and on page 1, line 2, Form 1120-A . . . . 8. _____

way because the goods are subnormal due to damage, imperfections, shopwear, etc., within the meaning of Regulations section 1.471-2(c). The goods may be valued at the current bona fide selling price, minus direct cost of disposition (but not less than scrap value) if such a price can be established.

If this is the first year the Last-in, First-out (LIFO) inventory method was either adopted or extended to inventory goods not previously valued under the LIFO method provided in section 472, attach **Form 970**, Application To Use LIFO Inventory Method, or a statement with the information required by Form 970. Also check the LIFO box on line 9c. On line 9d, enter the amount or the percent of total closing inventories covered under section 472. Estimates are acceptable.

If the corporation changed or extended its inventory method to LIFO and had to write up the opening inventory to cost in the year of election, report the effect of the writeup as other income (line 10, page 1), proportionately over a 3-year period that begins with the year of the LIFO election (section 472(d)).

Note: *Corporations using the LIFO method that make an S corporation election or transfer LIFO inventory to an S corporation in a nonrecognition transaction may be subject to an additional tax attributable to the LIFO recapture amount. See the instructions for line 10, Schedule J.*

For more information on inventory valuation methods, get **Pub. 538**, Accounting Periods and Methods.

Schedule C (Form 1120 Only)

Dividends and Special Deductions

For purposes of the 20% ownership test on lines 1 through 7, the percentage of stock owned by the corporation is based on voting power and value of the stock. Preferred stock described in section 1504(a)(4) is not taken into account. Corporations filing a consolidated return should see Regulations sections 1.1502-13 (1.1502-14 for filers with tax years that begin before July 12, 1995), 1.1502-26, and 1.1502-27 before completing Schedule C.

Line 1, Column (a)

Enter dividends (except those received on debt-financed stock acquired after July 18, 1984—see section 246A) that are received from less-than-20%-owned domestic corporations subject to income tax and that are subject to the 70% deduction under section 243(a)(1). Include on this line taxable distributions from an IC-DISC or former DISC that are designated as eligible for the 70% deduction and certain dividends of Federal Home Loan Banks. See section 246(a)(2).

Also include on line 1 dividends (except those received on debt-financed stock acquired after July 18, 1984) from a regulated investment company (RIC). The amount of dividends eligible for the

dividends-received deduction under section 243 is limited by section 854(b). The corporation should receive a notice from the RIC specifying the amount of dividends that qualify for the deduction.

Report so-called dividends or earnings received from mutual savings banks, etc., as interest. Do not treat them as dividends.

Line 2, Column (a)

Enter dividends (except those received on debt-financed stock acquired after July 18, 1984) that are received from 20%-or-more-owned domestic corporations subject to income tax and that are subject to the 80% deduction under section 243(c). Include on this line taxable distributions from an IC-DISC or former DISC that are considered eligible for the 80% deduction.

Line 3, Column (a)

Enter dividends on debt-financed stock acquired after July 18, 1984, received from domestic and foreign corporations subject to income tax that would otherwise be subject to the dividends-received deduction under section 243(a)(1), 243(c), or 245(a). Generally, debt-financed stock is stock that the corporation acquired by incurring a debt (e.g., it borrowed money to buy the stock).

Include on line 3 dividends received from a regulated investment company (RIC) on debt-financed stock. The amount of dividends eligible for the dividends-received deduction is limited by section 854(b). The corporation should receive a notice from the RIC specifying the amount of dividends that qualify for the deduction.

Line 3, Columns (b) and (c)

Dividends received on debt-financed stock acquired after July 18, 1984, are not entitled to the full 70% or 80% dividends-received deduction. The 70% or 80% deduction is reduced by a percentage that is related to the amount of debt incurred to acquire the stock. See section 246A. Also see section 245(a) before making this computation for an additional limitation that applies to dividends received from foreign corporations. Attach a schedule to Form 1120 showing how the amount on line 3, column (c), was figured.

Line 4, Column (a)

Enter dividends received on the preferred stock of a less-than-20%-owned public utility that is subject to income tax and is allowed the deduction provided in section 247 for dividends paid.

Line 5, Column (a)

Enter dividends received on preferred stock of a 20%-or-more-owned public utility that is subject to income tax and is allowed the deduction provided in section 247 for dividends paid.

Line 6, Column (a)

Enter the U.S.-source portion of dividends that are received from less-than-20%-owned foreign corporations and that qualify for the 70% deduction

under section 245(a). To qualify for the 70% deduction, the corporation must own at least 10% of the stock of the foreign corporation by vote and value. Also include dividends received from a less-than-20%-owned FSC that are attributable to income treated as effectively connected with the conduct of a trade or business within the United States (excluding foreign trade income) and that qualify for the 70% deduction provided in section 245(c)(1)(B).

Line 7, Column (a)

Enter the U.S.-source portion of dividends that are received from 20%-or-more-owned foreign corporations that qualify for the 80% deduction under section 245(a). Also include dividends received from a 20%-or-more-owned FSC that are attributable to income treated as effectively connected with the conduct of a trade or business within the United States (excluding foreign trade income) and qualify for the 80% deduction provided in section 245(c)(1)(B).

Line 8, Column (a)

Enter dividends received from wholly owned foreign subsidiaries that are eligible for the 100% deduction provided in section 245(b).

In general, the deduction under section 245(b) applies to dividends paid out of the earnings and profits of a foreign corporation for a tax year during which:

- All of its outstanding stock is owned (directly or indirectly) by the domestic corporation receiving the dividends, and
- All of its gross income from all sources is effectively connected with the conduct of a trade or business within the United States.

Line 9, Column (c)

Limitation on Dividends-Received Deduction

Generally, line 9, column (c) may not exceed the amount from the worksheet on page 14. However, in a year in which an NOL occurs, this limitation does not apply even if the loss is created by the dividends-received deduction. See sections 172(d) and 246(b). Certain financial institutions to which section 593(a) applies should see section 596 for the special limitation on the dividends-received deduction.

Line 10, Columns (a) and (c)

Small business investment companies operating under the Small Business Investment Act of 1958 (15 U.S.C. 661 and following) must enter dividends that are received from domestic corporations subject to income tax even though a deduction is allowed for the entire amount of those dividends. To claim the 100% deduction on line 10, column (c), the company must file with its return a statement that it was a Federal licensee under the Small Business Investment Act of 1958 at the time it received the dividends.

Page 13

Worksheet for Schedule C, line 9

(Keep for your records.)

1. Refigure line 28, page 1, Form 1120, without any adjustment under section 1059 and without any capital loss carryback to the tax year under section 1212(a)(1) . . . . 1. _____
2. Complete lines 10, 11, and 12, column (c), and enter the total here . . . 2. _____
3. Subtract line 2 from line 1 . . . . 3. _____
4. Multiply line 3 by 80% . . . . 4. _____
5. Add lines 2, 5, 7, and 8, column (c), and the part of the deduction on line 3, column (c), that is attributable to dividends from 20%-or-more-owned corporations . . . . 5. _____
6. Enter the smaller of line 4 or 5. If line 5 is greater than line 4, stop here; enter the amount from line 6 on line 9, column (c), and do not complete the rest of this worksheet . . . . 6. _____
7. Enter the total amount of dividends from 20%-or-more-owned corporations that are included on lines 2, 3, 5, 7, and 8, column (a) . . . . 7. _____
8. Subtract line 7 from line 3 . . . . 8. _____
9. Multiply line 8 by 70% . . . . 9. _____
10. Subtract line 5 above from line 9, column (c) . . . . 10. _____
11. Enter the smaller of line 9 or line 10 . . . . 11. _____
12. Dividends-received deduction after limitation (sec. 246(b)). Add lines 6 and 11. Enter the result here and on line 9, column (c) . . . . 12. _____

Line 11, Column (a)

Enter dividends from FSCs that are attributable to foreign trade income and that are eligible for the 100% deduction provided in section 245(c)(1)(A).

Line 12, Columns (a) and (c)

Enter only those dividends that qualify under section 243(b) for the 100% dividends-received deduction described in section 243(3). Corporations taking this deduction are subject to the provisions of section 1561.

Note: *The 100% deduction does not apply to affiliated group members that are joining in the filing of a consolidated return.*

Line 13, Column (a)

Enter foreign dividends not reportable on lines 3, 6, 7, 8, or 11 of column (a). Include on line 13 the corporation's share of the ordinary earnings of a qualified electing fund from Form 8621, line 6c, or the amount of any excess distribution from a passive foreign investment company from Form 8621, line 11b. Exclude distributions of amounts constructively taxed in the current year or in prior years under subpart F (sections 951 through 964).

Line 14, Column (a)

Include income constructively received from controlled foreign corporations under subpart F. This amount should equal the total Subpart F income reported on Schedule I, Form 5471.

Line 15, Column (a)

Include gross-up for taxes deemed paid under sections 902 and 960.

Line 16, Column (a)

Enter taxable distributions from an IC-DISC or former DISC that are designated as not eligible for a dividends-received deduction.

No deduction is allowed under section 243 for a dividend from an IC-DISC or former DISC (as defined in section 992(a)) to the extent the dividend:

1. Is paid out of the corporation's accumulated IC-DISC income or previously taxed income, or

2. Is a deemed distribution under section 995(b)(1).

Line 17, Column (a)

Include the following:

1. Dividends (other than capital gain dividends and exempt-interest dividends) that are received from regulated investment companies and that are not subject to the 70% deduction.

2. Dividends from tax-exempt organizations.

3. Dividends (other than capital gain dividends) received from a real estate investment trust that, for the tax year of the trust in which the dividends are paid, qualifies under sections 856 through 860.

4. Dividends not eligible for a dividends-received deduction because of the holding period of the stock or an obligation to make corresponding payments with respect to similar stock.

Two situations in which the dividends-received deduction will not be allowed on any share of stock are:

● If the corporation held it 45 days or less (see section 246(c)(1)(A)), or

● To the extent the corporation is under an obligation to make related payments for substantially similar or related property.

5. Any other taxable dividend income not properly reported above (including distributions under section 936(h)(4)).

If patronage dividends or per-unit retain allocations are included on line 17, identify the total of these amounts in a schedule attached to Form 1120.

Line 18, Column (c)

Section 247 allows public utilities a deduction of 40% of the smaller of:

● Dividends paid on their preferred stock during the tax year, or

● Taxable income computed without regard to this deduction.

In a year in which an NOL occurs, compute the deduction without regard to section 247(a)(1)(B). See section 172(d).

Schedule J, Form 1120 (Part I, Form 1120-A)

Tax Computation

Note: *Members of a controlled group must attach a statement showing the computation of the tax entered on line 3.*

Lines 1 and 2a, Form 1120

Members of a controlled group (Form 1120 only).—A member of a controlled group, as defined in section 1563, must check the box on line 1 and complete lines 2a and 2b of Schedule J, Form 1120.

Members of a controlled group are entitled to one $50,000, one $25,000, and one $9,925,000 taxable income bracket amount (in that order) on line 2a.

When a controlled group adopts or later amends an apportionment plan, each member must attach to its tax return a copy of its consent to this plan. The copy (or an attached statement) must show the part of the amount in each taxable income bracket apportioned to that member. See Regulations section 1.1561-3(b) for other requirements and for the time and manner of making the consent.

Equal apportionment plan.—If no apportionment plan is adopted, members of a controlled group must divide the amount in each taxable income bracket equally among themselves. For example, Controlled Group AB consists of Corporation A and Corporation B. They do not elect an apportionment plan. Therefore, Corporation A and Corporation B are each entitled to:

● $25,000 (one-half of $50,000) in the $50,000 taxable income bracket on line 2a(1),

● $12,500 (one-half of $25,000) in the $25,000 taxable income bracket on line 2a(2), and

● $4,962,500 (one-half of $9,925,000) in the $9,925,000 taxable income bracket on line 2a(3).

Unequal apportionment plan.— Members of a controlled group may elect an unequal apportionment plan and divide the taxable income brackets as they want. There is no need for consistency among taxable income brackets. Any member of the controlled group may be entitled to all, some, or none of the taxable income bracket. However, the total amount for all members of the controlled group cannot be more than the total amount in each taxable income bracket.

Line 2b, Form 1120

Additional 5% tax.—Members of a controlled group are treated as one corporation to figure the applicability of the additional 5% tax that must be paid by corporations with taxable income over $100,000. If the additional tax applies, each member of the controlled group will pay that tax based on the part of the

Page 14

Tax Computation Worksheet for Members of a Controlled Group
(Keep for your records.)

Note: *Each member of a controlled group (except a qualified personal service corporation) must compute the tax using this worksheet.*

1. Enter taxable income (line 30, page 1, Form 1120) . . . . **1.** _____
2. Enter line 1 or the corporation's share of the $50,000 taxable income bracket, whichever is less . . . . **2.** _____
3. Subtract line 2 from line 1 . . . . **3.** _____
4. Enter line 3 or the corporation's share of the $25,000 taxable income bracket, whichever is less . . . . **4.** _____
5. Subtract line 4 from line 3 . . . . **5.** _____
6. Enter line 5 or the corporation's share of the $9,925,000 taxable income bracket, whichever is less . . . . **6.** _____
7. Subtract line 6 from line 5 . . . . **7.** _____
8. Multiply line 2 by 15% . . . . **8.** _____
9. Multiply line 4 by 25% . . . . **9.** _____
10. Multiply line 6 by 34% . . . . **10.** _____
11. Multiply line 7 by 35% . . . . **11.** _____
12. If the taxable income of the controlled group exceeds $100,000, enter this member's share of the smaller of: 5% of the taxable income in excess of $100,000, or $11,750 (See **Additional 5% tax,** on page 14.) . . . . . **12.** _____
13. If the taxable income of the controlled group exceeds $15,000,000, enter this member's share of the smaller of: 3% of the taxable income in excess of $15 million, or $100,000 (See **Additional 3% tax,** below.) . . . . . . **13.** _____
14. Add lines 8 through 13. Enter here and on line 3, Schedule J, Form 1120 . **14.** _____

amount used in each taxable income bracket to reduce that member's tax. See section 1561(a). Each member of the group must enter its share of the additional 5% tax on line 2b(1) and attach to its tax return a schedule that shows the taxable income of the entire group as well as how it figured its share of the additional 5% tax.

Additional 3% tax.—Members of a controlled group are treated as one corporation to figure the additional 3% tax that must be paid by corporations with taxable income over $15 million. If the additional tax applies, each member of the controlled group will pay that tax based on the part of the amount used in each taxable income bracket to reduce that member's tax. See section 1561(a). Each member of the group must enter its share of the additional 3% tax on line 2b(2) and attach to its tax return a schedule that shows the taxable income of the entire group as well as how it figured its share of the additional 3% tax.

Line 3, Form 1120
(Line 1, Form 1120-A)

Most corporations figure their tax by using the Tax Rate Schedule below. Exceptions apply to members of a controlled group (see worksheet above) and qualified personal service corporations. (See the instructions below for more information.)

Tax Rate Schedule

If taxable income (line 30, Form 1120, or line 26, Form 1120-A) on page 1 is:

Over—	But not over—	Tax is:	Of the amount over—
$0	$50,000	15%	$0
50,000	75,000	$7,500 + 25%	50,000
75,000	100,000	13,750 + 34%	75,000
100,000	335,000	22,250 + 39%	100,000
335,000	10,000,000	113,900 + 34%	335,000
10,000,000	15,000,000	3,400,000 + 35%	10,000,000
15,000,000	18,333,333	5,150,000 + 38%	15,000,000
18,333,333	- - - - -	35%	0

Qualified personal service corporation.—A qualified personal service corporation is taxed at a flat rate of 35% on taxable income. A corporation is a qualified personal service corporation if it meets **BOTH** of the following tests:

● Substantially all of the corporation's activities involve the performance of services in the fields of health, law, engineering, architecture, accounting, actuarial science, performing arts, or consulting, and

● At least 95% of the corporation's stock, by value, is owned, directly or indirectly, by **(1)** employees performing the services, **(2)** retired employees who had performed the services listed above, **(3)** any estate of the employee or retiree described above, or **(4)** any person who acquired the stock of the corporation as a result of the death of an employee or retiree (but only for the 2-year period beginning on the date of the employee's or retiree's death). See Temporary Regulations section 1.448-1T(e) for details.

Note: *If the corporation meets these tests, check the box on line 3, Schedule J, Form 1120 (line 1, Part I, Form 1120-A).*

Mutual savings bank conducting life insurance business.—The tax under section 594 consists of the sum of **(a)** a partial tax computed on Form 1120 on the taxable income of the bank determined without regard to income or deductions allocable to the life insurance department, and **(b)** a partial tax on the taxable income computed on Form 1120-L of the life insurance department. Enter the combined tax on line 3 of Schedule J, Form 1120. Attach Form 1120-L as a schedule and identify it as such.

Deferred tax of a shareholder in a passive foreign investment company (section 1291).—If the corporation was a shareholder in a passive foreign investment company (PFIC) and received an excess distribution or disposed of its investment in the PFIC during the year, it must include the increase in taxes due under section 1291(c)(2) in the total for line 3, Schedule J, Form 1120. On the dotted line next to line 3, Schedule J, write "Section 1291" and the amount.

Do not include on line 3 any interest due under section 1291(c)(3). Instead, show the amount of interest owed in the bottom margin of page 1, Form 1120, and write "Section 1291 interest." For details, see **Form 8621,** Return by a Shareholder of a Passive Foreign Investment Company or Qualified Electing Fund.

Additional tax under section 197(f).—A corporation that elects to pay tax on the gain from the sale of an intangible under the related person exception to the anti-churning rules, should include any additional tax due under section 197(f)(9)(B) in the total for line 3. On the dotted line next to line 3, write "Section 197" and the amount. For more information, see **Pub. 535,** Business Expenses.

Line 4a (Form 1120 only)

Foreign Tax Credit

To find out when a corporation can take the credit for payment of income tax to a foreign country or U.S. possession, see **Form 1118,** Foreign Tax Credit—Corporations.

Line 4b (Form 1120 only)

Possessions Tax Credit

For rules on how to elect to claim the possessions tax credit (section 936), see **Form 5712,** Election To Be Treated as a Possessions Corporation Under Section 936. Figure the credit on **Form 5735,** Possessions Corporation Tax Credit Allowed Under Section 936.

Line 4c (Form 1120 only)

Complete line 4c if the corporation can take either of the following credits. Be sure to check the appropriate box.

Nonconventional source fuel credit.—A credit is allowed for the sale of qualified fuels produced from a nonconventional source. Section 29 contains a definition of qualified fuels, provisions for figuring the credit, and other special rules. Attach a separate schedule to the return showing the computation of the credit.

Page 15

Also see **Form 8827** if any of the 1994 credit was disallowed solely because of the tentative minimum tax limitation. See section 53(d).

Qualified electric vehicle (QEV) credit.— Include on line 4c any credit from **Form 8834**, Qualified Electric Vehicle Credit. Vehicles that qualify for this credit are not eligible for the deduction for clean-fuel vehicles under section 179A.

Line 4d, Form 1120
(Line 2a, Form 1120-A)

General Business Credit

Complete this line if the corporation can take any of the following credits. Complete **Form 3800**, General Business Credit, if the corporation has two or more of these credits, a credit carryforward or carryback (including an ESOP credit), a trans-Alaska pipeline liability fund credit, or a passive activity credit. Enter the amount of the general business credit on line 4d (line 2a, Form 1120-A), and check the box for Form 3800. If the corporation has only one credit, enter on line 4d (line 2a, Form 1120-A), the amount of the credit from the form. Also be sure to check the appropriate box for that form.

Investment credit. The corporation may claim the investment credit for property placed in service that is qualified rehabilitation, energy, timber, or transition property. See **Form 3468**, Investment Credit, for definitions and other details.

Jobs credit. The corporation may qualify to take this credit if it hired members of special targeted groups during the tax year. See **Form 5884**, Jobs Credit, for more information.

Credit for alcohol used as fuel. Use **Form 6478**, Credit for Alcohol Used as Fuel, to figure the credit.

Credit for increasing research activities. See **Form 6765**, Credit for Increasing Research Activities, and section 41.

Low-income housing credit. See **Form 8586**, Low-Income Housing Credit, and section 42.

Enhanced oil recovery credit. A corporation may claim a credit for 15% of its qualified enhanced oil recovery costs. Use **Form 8830**, Enhanced Oil Recovery Credit.

Disabled access credit. A corporation may be able to take a credit for certain expenditures paid or incurred to help individuals with disabilities. See **Form 8826**, Disabled Access Credit, and section 44.

Renewable electricity production credit. A corporation may be able to take a credit for electricity produced by the corporation using closed-loop biomass or wind and sold to an unrelated person. See **Form 8835**, Renewable Electricity Production Credit, for details.

Indian employment credit. A corporation may be able to claim a credit of 20% of a limited amount of the wages and health insurance costs it pays or incurs for qualified employees. A qualified employee is a member (or whose spouse is a member) of an enrolled Indian tribe, who

also meets certain other qualifications. See **Form 8845**, Indian Employment Credit, and section 45A.

Credit for employer social security and Medicare taxes paid on certain employee tips. Food and beverage establishments may claim a credit equal to the employer's social security and Medicare obligations attributable to tips in excess of those treated as wages for purposes of the minimum wage laws. See **Form 8846**, Credit for Employer Social Security and Medicare Taxes Paid on Certain Employee Tips, and section 45B.

Credit for contributions to certain community development corporations. Corporations may claim a credit of 5% of qualified cash contributions to certain community development corporations (CDCs) selected by the Secretary of Housing and Urban Development. See **Form 8847**, Credit for Contributions to Selected Community Development Corporations.

Note: *The empowerment zone employment credit (described below) is a component of the general business credit, but is figured separately and is not carried to Form 3800.*

Empowerment zone employment credit. A corporation that has employees that live and work for the corporation in an area designated by the Federal government as an "empowerment zone" may be able to take a credit for wages paid to certain employees. The credit is equal to 20% of the first $15,000 of qualified wages and is limited to $3,000 per year per employee. See **Form 8844**, Empowerment Zone Employment Credit, and section 1396.

Line 4e, Form 1120
(Line 2b, Form 1120-A)

Credit for Prior Year Minimum Tax

To figure the minimum tax credit and any carryforward of that credit, use **Form 8827**, Credit for Prior Year Minimum Tax—Corporations.

Line 5 (Form 1120 only)

Include on line 5 any orphan drug credit. On the dotted line next to the entry space, write "ODC" and the amount.

Also include on line 5 any trans-Alaska pipeline liability fund credit. On the dotted line next to the entry space, write "TAP" and the amount.

Line 7 (Form 1120 only)

Personal Holding Company Tax

A corporation is taxed as a personal holding company under section 542 if:

● At least 60% of its adjusted ordinary gross income for the tax year is personal holding company income, and

● At any time during the last half of the tax year more than 50% in value of its outstanding stock is owned, directly or indirectly, by five or fewer individuals.

See **Schedule PH (Form 1120)**, U.S. Personal Holding Company Tax, for definitions and details on how to figure the tax.

Line 8, Form 1120
(Line 5, Form 1120-A)

Recapture Taxes

Recapture of investment credit. If the corporation disposed of investment credit property or changed its use before the end of its useful life or recovery period, it may owe a tax. See **Form 4255**, Recapture of Investment Credit, for details.

Recapture of low-income housing credit. If the corporation disposed of property (or there was a reduction in the qualified basis of the property) for which it took the low-income housing credit, it may owe a tax. See **Form 8611**, Recapture of Low-Income Housing Credit, and section 42(j) for details.

Recapture of qualified electric vehicle (QEV) credit. The corporation must recapture part of the QEV credit it claimed in a prior year, if, within 3 years of the date the vehicle was placed in service, it ceases to qualify for the credit. See Regulations section 1.30-1 for details on how to figure the recapture. Include the amount of the recapture in the total for line 8, Schedule J, Form 1120 (line 5, Part I, Form 1120-A). On the dotted line next to the entry space, write "QEV recapture" and the amount.

Recapture of Indian employment credit. Generally, if an employer terminates the employment of a qualified employee less than 1 year after the date of initial employment, any Indian employment credit allowed for a prior tax year by reason of wages paid or incurred to that employee must be recaptured. For details, see **Form 8845**, Indian Employment Credit, and section 45A. Include the amount of the recapture in the total for line 8, Schedule J, Form 1120 (line 5, Part I, Form 1120-A). On the dotted line next to the entry space, write "45" and the amount.

Line 9a, Form 1120
(Line 6, Form 1120-A)

Alternative Minimum Tax

The corporation may owe the alternative minimum tax if it has any of the adjustments and tax preference items listed on **Form 4626**, Alternative Minimum Tax—Corporations. The corporation must file Form 4626 if its taxable income (loss) combined with these adjustments and tax preference items is more than the smaller of $40,000, or the corporation's allowable exemption amount (from Form 4626).

For this purpose, taxable income does not include the NOL deduction. Get Form 4626 for details.

Reduce alternative minimum tax by any amounts from Form 3800, Schedule A, line 34 and Form 8844, line 21. On the dotted line next to line 9a (line 6, Form 1120-A), write "Section 38(c)(2)" ("EZE" if from Form 8844) and the amounts.

Line 9b (Form 1120 only)

Environmental Tax

The corporation may be liable for the environmental tax if the modified alternative minimum taxable income of the

Page 16

corporation exceeds $2 million. See Form 4626 for details.

Line 10 (Form 1120 only)

Interest on tax attributable to payments received on installment sales of certain timeshares and residential lots. If the corporation elected to pay interest on the amount of tax attributable to payments received on installment obligations arising from the disposition of property under section 453(l)(3), include the interest due in the total for line 10, Schedule J. On the dotted line to the left of line 10, write "Section 453(l)(3) interest" and the amount. Attach a schedule showing the computation.

Interest on tax deferred under the installment method for certain nondealer installment obligations. If an obligation arising from the disposition of property to which section 453A applies is outstanding at the close of the tax year, the corporation must include the interest due under section 453A(c) in the total for line 10, Schedule J. Write on the dotted line to the left of line 10, "Section 453A(c) interest" and the amount. Attach a schedule showing the computation.

Interest under the look-back method for completed long-term contracts. Include the interest due under the look-back method of section 460(b)(2) on line 10, Schedule J. On the dotted line to the left of the entry space, write "From Form 8697" and the amount of interest due.

Deferred tax and interest on undistributed earnings of a qualified electing fund under section 1294. Complete Form 8621 to determine the corporation's share of tax attributable to the undistributed earnings of a qualified electing fund, or the deferred tax due, if any, as a result of the termination of a section 1294 election. See the instructions for Form 8621 to figure the amount of tax to include in, or subtract from the total on line 10. The instructions for Form 8621 also explain how to report any interest due under section 1294 on the deferred tax.

Installment payment of tax attributable to LIFO recapture by corporations that make an S corporation election or transfer LIFO inventory to an S corporation in a nonrecognition transaction. A C corporation must include in gross income the LIFO recapture amount (defined below) if:

1. It uses the LIFO method for its last tax year before the first tax year for which an election to be taxed as an S corporation becomes effective, or

2. It transferred LIFO inventory assets to an S corporation in a nonrecognition transaction (within the meaning of section 7701(a)(45)) in which the transferred assets constitute transferred basis property (within the meaning of section 7701(a)(43)).

The LIFO recapture amount is the amount by which the C corporation's inventory under the FIFO method (determined by using cost or market, whichever is lower) authorized by section 471 exceeds the inventory amount under the LIFO method at the close of the C corporation's last tax year as a

C corporation (or for the year of the transfer, if "2" above applies).

The additional tax due to LIFO recapture is paid in four equal installments. The corporation must pay the first installment by the due date (not including extensions) of Form 1120 for the corporation's last tax year as a C corporation or for the tax year of the transfer, whichever applies.

To determine the additional tax due to LIFO recapture, complete lines 1 through 9b of Schedule J based on income that includes the LIFO recapture amount. On a separate worksheet, using the Schedule J format, complete the entire worksheet (lines 1 through 10) based on taxable income not including the LIFO recapture amount. Compare the total of lines 1 through 9b of Schedule J to line 10 of the worksheet. The difference is the additional tax due to LIFO recapture.

Since the total of lines 1 through 9b Schedule J will include all the additional tax due to LIFO recapture, the amount that may be deferred (¾ of the additional tax) must first be subtracted to arrive at line 10, total tax. On the dotted line to the left of line 10, Schedule J, write "Section 1363(d) deferral" and the amount. Attach a schedule showing the computation. See section 1363(d) for more information.

Note: *The remaining three installments of deferred tax must be paid by the due date of Form 1120S for the next 3 tax years. No interest is payable on the deferred tax if paid on time.*

For details, see Regulations section 1.1363-2 and Rev. Proc. 94-61, 1994-2 C.B. 775.

Tax on a nonqualified withdrawal from a capital construction fund. If the corporation owes tax under section 7518 on a nonqualified withdrawal from a capital construction fund, include the tax and interest in the total for line 10. On the dotted line next to line 10, write "CCF" and the amounts of tax and interest. For more information, see **Pub. 595,** Tax Guide for Commercial Fishermen.

Schedule K, Form 1120 (Part II, Form 1120-A)

Other Information

The following instructions apply to questions 1 through 15 on Form 1120, page 3, Schedule K, or questions 1 through 6 on Form 1120-A, page 2, Part II. Be sure to answer all the questions that apply to the corporation.

Question 4 (Form 1120 only)

Check the "Yes" box for question 4 if:

● The corporation is a subsidiary in an affiliated group (defined below), but is not filing a consolidated return for the tax year with that group, or

● The corporation is a subsidiary in a parent-subsidiary controlled group (defined below).

Any corporation that meets either of the requirements above should check the "Yes" box. This applies even if the

corporation is a subsidiary member of one group and the parent corporation of another.

Note: *If the corporation is an "excluded member" of a controlled group (see section 1563(b)(2)), it is still considered a member of a controlled group for this purpose.*

Affiliated group.—The term "affiliated group" means one or more chains of includible corporations (section 1504(a)) connected through stock ownership with a common parent corporation. The common parent must be an includible corporation and the following requirements must be met:

1. The common parent must own directly stock that represents at least 80% of the total voting power and at least 80% of the total value of the stock of at least one of the other includible corporations.

2. Stock that represents at least 80% of the total voting power, and at least 80% of the total value of the stock of each of the other corporations (except for the common parent) must be owned directly by at least one of the other includible corporations.

For this purpose, the term "stock" generally does not include any stock that **(a)** is nonvoting, **(b)** is nonconvertible, **(c)** is limited and preferred as to dividends and does not participate significantly in corporate growth, and **(d)** has redemption and liquidation rights that do not exceed the issue price of the stock (except for a reasonable redemption or liquidation premium). See section 1504(a)(4).

Parent-subsidiary controlled group.—The term "parent-subsidiary controlled group" means one or more chains of corporations connected through stock ownership (section 1563(a)(1)). Both of the following requirements must be met:

1. 80% of the total combined voting power of all classes of stock entitled to vote or at least 80% of the total value of all classes of stock of each corporation in the group (except the parent) must be owned by one or more of the other corporations in the group.

2. The common parent must own at least 80% of the total combined voting power of all classes of stock entitled to vote or at least 80% of the total value of all classes of stock of at least one of the other corporations in the group. Stock owned directly by other members of the group is not counted when computing the voting power or value.

See section 1563(d)(1) for the definition of "stock" for purposes of determining stock ownership above.

Question 8, Form 1120 (Question 6, Form 1120-A)

Foreign financial accounts.—Check the "Yes" box if either **1** or **2** below applies to the corporation. Otherwise, check the "No" box:

1. At any time during the 1995 calendar year the corporation had an interest in or signature or other authority over a bank, securities, or other financial account in a foreign country; and

Page 17

- The combined value of the accounts was more than $10,000 at any time during the calendar year, and

- The account was NOT with a U.S. military banking facility operated by a U.S. financial institution.

2. The corporation owns more than 50% of the stock in any corporation that would answer "Yes" to item **1** above.

Get **Form TD F 90-22.1,** Report of Foreign Bank and Financial Accounts, to see if the corporation is considered to have an interest in or signature or other authority over a financial account in a foreign country.

If "Yes" is checked for this question, file Form TD F 90-22.1 by June 30, 1996, with the Department of the Treasury at the address shown on the form. Form TD F 90-22.1 is not a tax return, so do not file it with Form 1120 (or Form 1120-A).

You can get Form TD F 90-22.1 from an IRS Distribution Center or by calling 1-800-TAX-FORM (1-800-829-3676).

Also, if "Yes" is checked for this question, enter the name of the foreign country or countries. Attach a separate sheet if more space is needed.

Question 10 (Form 1120 only)

Check the "Yes" box if one foreign person owned at least 25% of **(a)** the total voting power of all classes of stock of the corporation entitled to vote or **(b)** the total value of all classes of stock of the corporation.

The constructive ownership rules of section 318 apply in determining if a corporation is foreign owned. See section 6038A(c)(5) and the related regulations.

Enter on line 10a the percentage owned by the foreign person specified in question 10. On line 10b, write the name of the owner's country.

Note: *If there is more than one 25%-or-more foreign owner, complete lines 10a and 10b for the foreign person with the highest percentage of ownership.*

Foreign person.—The term "foreign person" means:

- A foreign citizen or nonresident alien.

- An individual who is a citizen of a U.S. possession (but who is not a U.S. citizen or resident).

- A foreign partnership.

- A foreign corporation.

- Any foreign estate or trust within the meaning of section 7701(a)(31).

- A foreign government (or one of its agencies or instrumentalities) to the extent that it is engaged in the conduct of a commercial activity as described in section 892.

Owner's country.—For individuals, the term "owner's country" means the country of residence. For all others, it is the country where incorporated, organized, created, or administered.

Requirement to file Form 5472.—If the corporation checked "Yes" to Question 10, it may have to file **Form 5472,** Information Return of a 25% Foreign-Owned U.S. Corporation or a Foreign Corporation Engaged in a U.S. Trade or Business. Generally, a 25% foreign-owned corporation that had a reportable transaction with a foreign or domestic related party during the tax year must file Form 5472.

See Form 5472 for filing instructions and penalties for failure to file.

Question 12, Form 1120 (Question 3, Form 1120-A)

Show any tax-exempt interest received or accrued. Include any exempt-interest dividends received as a shareholder in a mutual fund or other regulated investment company.

Question 14 (Form 1120 only)

Check the box on line 14 if the corporation elects under section 172(b)(3) to forego the carryback period for a net operating loss (NOL). If you check this box, do not attach the statement described in Temporary Regulations section 301.9100-12T(d).

Question 15 (Form 1120 only)

Enter the amount of the net operating loss (NOL) carryover to the tax year from prior years, regardless of whether any of the loss is used to offset income on this return. The amount to enter is the total of all NOLs generated in prior years but not used to offset income (either as a carryback or carryover) to a tax year prior to 1995. Do not reduce the amount by any NOL deduction reported on line 29a.

Pub. 536 has a worksheet for figuring a corporation's NOL carryover.

Schedule L, Form 1120 (Part III, Form 1120-A)

Balance Sheets

The balance sheet should agree with the corporation's books and records. Include certificates of deposit as cash on line 1, Schedule L.

Line 5

Tax-Exempt Securities

Include on this line:

1. State and local government obligations, the interest on which is excludable from gross income under section 103(a), and

2. Stock in a mutual fund or other regulated investment company that distributed exempt-interest dividends during the tax year of the corporation.

Schedule M-1, Form 1120 (Part IV, Form 1120-A)

Reconciliation of Income (Loss) per Books With Income per Return

Line 5c, Form 1120 (Line 5, Form 1120-A)

Travel and Entertainment

Include on line 5c (line 5, Form 1120-A) any of the following:

- 50% of the meals and entertainment not allowed under section 274(n).

- Expenses for the use of an entertainment facility.

- The part of business gifts over $25.

- Expenses of an individual over $2,000, which are allocable to conventions on cruise ships.

- Employee achievement awards over $400.

- The cost of entertainment tickets over face value (also subject to 50% disallowance under section 274(n)).

- The cost of skyboxes over the face value of nonluxury box seat tickets.

- The part of luxury water travel not allowed under section 274(m).

- Expenses for travel as a form of education.

- Other travel and entertainment expenses not allowed as a deduction.

For more information, see Pub. 542.

Line 7, Form 1120 (Line 6, Form 1120-A)

Tax-Exempt Interest

Include as interest on line 7 (line 6, Form 1120-A), any exempt-interest dividends received as a shareholder in a mutual fund or other regulated investment company.

Codes for Principal Business Activity

These codes for the Principal Business Activity are designed to classify enterprises by the type of activity in which they are engaged to facilitate the administration of the Internal Revenue Code. Though similar in format and structure to the Standard Industrial Classification (SIC) codes, they should not be used as SIC codes.

Using the list below, enter on Form 1120, Schedule K, line 2a (Form 1120-A, Part II, line 1a) the code number for the specific industry group from which the largest percentage of "total receipts" is derived. "Total receipts" means gross receipts (line 1a, page 1) plus all other income (lines 4 through 10, page 1).

On Form 1120, Schedule K, lines 2b and 2c (Form 1120-A, Part II, lines 1b and 1c), state the principal business activity and principal product or service that account for the largest percentage of total receipts. For example, if the principal business activity is "Grain mill products," the principal product or service may be "Cereal preparations."

If, as its principal business activity, the corporation: (1) purchases raw materials, (2) subcontracts out for labor to make a finished product from the raw materials, and (3) retains title to the goods, the corporation is considered to be a manufacturer and must enter one of the codes (2010-3998) under "Manufacturing."

Agriculture, Forestry, and Fishing
Code
0400 Agricultural production
0600 Agricultural services (except veterinarians), forestry, fishing, hunting, and trapping

Mining
Metal mining
1010 Iron ores
1070 Copper, lead and zinc, gold and silver ores
1098 Other metal mining
1150 Coal mining
Oil and gas extraction
1330 Crude petroleum, natural gas, and natural gas liquids
1380 Oil and gas field services
Nonmetallic minerals, except fuels
1430 Dimension, crushed and broken stone; sand and gravel
1498 Other nonmetallic minerals, except fuels

Construction
General building contractors and operative builders
1510 General building contractors
1531 Operative builders
1600 Heavy construction contractors
Special trade contractors
1711 Plumbing, heating, and air conditioning
1731 Electrical work
1798 Other special trade contractors

Manufacturing
Food and kindred products
2010 Meat products
2020 Dairy products
2030 Preserved fruits and vegetables
2040 Grain mill products
2050 Bakery products
2060 Sugar and confectionary products
2081 Malt liquors and malt
2088 Alcoholic beverages, except malt liquors and malt
2089 Bottled soft drinks, and flavorings
2096 Other food and kindred products
2100 Tobacco manufacturers
Textile mill products
2228 Weaving mills and textile finishing
2250 Knitting mills
2298 Other textile mill products
Apparel and other textile products
2315 Men's and boys' clothing
2345 Women's and children's clothing
2388 Other apparel and accessories
2390 Miscellaneous fabricated textile products
Lumber and wood products
2415 Logging, sawmills, and planing mills
2430 Millwork, plywood, and related products
2498 Other wood products, including wood buildings and mobile homes
2500 Furniture and fixtures

Code
Paper and allied products
2625 Pulp, paper, and board mills
2699 Other paper products
Printing and publishing
2710 Newspapers
2720 Periodicals
2735 Books, greeting cards, and miscellaneous publishing
2799 Commercial and other printing, and printing trade services
Chemicals and allied products
2815 Industrial chemicals, plastics materials, and synthetics
2830 Drugs
2840 Soap, cleaners, and toilet goods
2850 Paints and allied products
2898 Agricultural and other chemical products
Petroleum refining and related industries (including those integrated with extraction)
2910 Petroleum refining (including integrated)
2998 Other petroleum and coal products
Rubber and misc. plastics products
3050 Rubber products, plastics footwear, hose and belting
3070 Misc. plastics products
Leather and leather products
3140 Footwear, except rubber
3198 Other leather and leather products
Stone, clay, and glass products
3225 Glass products
3240 Cement, hydraulic
3270 Concrete, gypsum, and plaster products
3298 Other nonmetallic mineral products
Primary metal industries
3370 Ferrous metal industries; misc. primary metal products
3380 Nonferrous metal industries
Fabricated metal products
3410 Metal cans and shipping containers
3428 Cutlery, hand tools, and hardware; screw machine products, bolts, and similar products
3430 Plumbing and heating, except electric and warm air
3440 Fabricated structural metal products
3460 Metal forgings and stampings
3470 Coating, engraving, and allied services
3480 Ordnance and accessories, except vehicles and guided missiles
3490 Misc. fabricated metal products
Machinery, except electrical
3520 Farm machinery
3530 Construction and related machinery
3540 Metalworking machinery
3550 Special industry machinery
3560 General industrial machinery
3570 Office, computing, and accounting machines
3598 Other machinery except electrical

Code
Electrical and electronic equipment
3630 Household appliances
3665 Radio, television, and communication equipment
3670 Electronic components and accessories
3698 Other electrical equipment
3710 Motor vehicles and equipment
Transportation equipment, except motor vehicles
3725 Aircraft, guided missiles and parts
3730 Ship and boat building and repairing
3798 Other transportation equipment, except motor vehicles
Instruments and related products
3815 Scientific instruments and measuring devices; watches and clocks
3845 Optical, medical, and ophthalmic goods
3860 Photographic equipment and supplies
3998 Other manufacturing products

Transportation and Public Utilities
Transportation
4000 Railroad transportation
4100 Local and interurban passenger transit
4200 Trucking and warehousing
4400 Water transportation
4500 Transportation by air
4600 Pipe lines, except natural gas
4700 Miscellaneous transportation services
Communication
4825 Telephone, telegraph, and other communication services
4830 Radio and television broadcasting
Electric, gas, and sanitary services
4910 Electric services
4920 Gas production and distribution
4930 Combination utility services
4990 Water supply and other sanitary services

Wholesale Trade
Durable
5008 Machinery, equipment, and supplies
5010 Motor vehicles and automotive equipment
5020 Furniture and home furnishings
5030 Lumber and construction materials
5040 Sporting, recreational, photographic, and hobby goods, toys and supplies
5050 Metals and minerals, except petroleum and scrap
5060 Electrical goods
5070 Hardware, plumbing and heating equipment and supplies
5098 Other durable goods
Nondurable
5110 Paper and paper products
5129 Drugs, drug proprietaries, and druggists' sundries
5130 Apparel, piece goods, and notions
5140 Groceries and related products
5150 Farm-product raw materials
5160 Chemicals and allied products
5170 Petroleum and petroleum products
5180 Alcoholic beverages
5190 Misc. nondurable goods

Retail Trade
Building materials, garden supplies, and mobile home dealers
5220 Building materials dealers
5251 Hardware stores
5265 Garden supplies and mobile home dealers
5300 General merchandise stores
Food stores
5410 Grocery stores
5490 Other food stores
Automotive dealers and service stations
5515 Motor vehicle dealers
5541 Gasoline service stations
5598 Other automotive dealers
5600 Apparel and accessory stores
5700 Furniture and home furnishings stores

Code
5800 Eating and drinking places
Misc. retail stores
5912 Drug stores and proprietary stores
5921 Liquor stores
5995 Other retail stores

Finance, Insurance, and Real Estate
Banking
6030 Mutual savings banks
6060 Bank holding companies
6090 Banks, except mutual savings banks and bank holding companies
Credit agencies other than banks
6120 Savings and loan associations
6140 Personal credit institutions
6150 Business credit institutions
6199 Other credit agencies
Security, commodity brokers and services
6210 Security brokers, dealers, and flotation companies
6299 Commodity contracts brokers and dealers; security and commodity exchanges; and allied services
Insurance
6355 Life insurance
6356 Mutual insurance, except life or marine and certain fire or flood insurance companies
6359 Other insurance companies
6411 Insurance agents, brokers, and service
Real estate
6511 Real estate operators and lessors of buildings
6516 Lessors of mining, oil, and similar property
6518 Lessors of railroad property and other real property
6530 Condominium management and cooperative housing associations
6550 Subdividers and developers
6599 Other real estate
Holding and other investment companies, except bank holding companies
6744 Small business investment companies
6749 Other holding and investment companies except bank holding companies

Services
7000 Hotels and other lodging places
7200 Personal services
Business services
7310 Advertising
7389 Business services, except advertising
Auto repair; misc. repair services
7500 Auto repair and services
7600 Misc. repair services
Amusement and recreation services
7812 Motion picture production, distribution, and services
7830 Motion picture theaters
7900 Amusement and recreation services, except motion pictures
Other services
8015 Offices of physicians, including osteopathic physicians
8021 Offices of dentists
8040 Offices of other health practitioners
8050 Nursing and personal care facilities
8060 Hospitals
8071 Medical laboratories
8099 Other medical services
8111 Legal services
8200 Educational services
8300 Social services
8600 Membership organizations
8911 Architectural and engineering services
8930 Accounting, auditing, and bookkeeping
8980 Miscellaneous services (including veterinarians)

Page 19

Index to Instructions for Forms 1120 and 1120-A

 Printed on recycled paper

Form 1120
Department of the Treasury
Internal Revenue Service

U.S. Corporation Income Tax Return

For calendar year 1995 or tax year beginning .... , 1995, ending .... , 19 ...
▶ Instructions are separate. See page 1 for Paperwork Reduction Act Notice.

OMB No. 1545-0123

1995

A Check if a:	**Use IRS label. Other-wise, print or type.**	Name **Tentex Toys, Inc.**	**B** Employer identification number
1 Consolidated return (attach Form 851) ☐		Number, street, and room or suite no. (If a P.O. box, see page 6 of instructions.) **36 Division Street**	**C** Date incorporated **3-1-72**
2 Personal holding co. (attach Sch. PH) ☐		City or town, state, and ZIP code **Anytown IL 60930**	**D** Total assets (see page 6 of instructions)
3 Personal service corp. (as defined in Temporary Regs. sec. 1.441-4T— see instructions) ☐			$ **879,417**

E Check applicable boxes: (1) ☐ Initial return (2) ☐ Final return (3) ☐ Change of address

Income

1a	Gross receipts or sales **2,010,000**	b Less returns and allowances **20,000**	c Bal ▶ 1c **1,990,000**
2	Cost of goods sold (Schedule A, line 8)		2 **1,520,000**
3	Gross profit. Subtract line 2 from line 1c		3 **470,000**
4	Dividends (Schedule C, line 19)		4 **10,000**
5	Interest		5 **5,500**
6	Gross rents		6
7	Gross royalties		7
8	Capital gain net income (attach Schedule D (Form 1120))		8
9	Net gain or (loss) from Form 4797, Part II, line 20 (attach Form 4797)		9
10	Other income (see page 7 of instructions—attach schedule)		10
11	**Total income.** Add lines 3 through 10 ▶		11 **485,500**

Deductions (See instructions for limitations on deductions.)

12	Compensation of officers (Schedule E, line 4)			12 **70,000**
13	Salaries and wages (less employment credits)			13 **38,000**
14	Repairs and maintenance			14 **800**
15	Bad debts			15 **1,600**
16	Rents			16 **9,200**
17	Taxes and licenses			17 **15,000**
18	Interest			18 **27,200**
19	Charitable contributions (see page 9 of instructions for 10% limitation)			19 **23,150**
20	Depreciation (attach Form 4562)	20 **17,600**		
21	Less depreciation claimed on Schedule A and elsewhere on return	21a **12,400**		21b **5,200**
22	Depletion			22
23	Advertising			23 **8,700**
24	Pension, profit-sharing, etc., plans			24
25	Employee benefit programs			25
26	Other deductions (attach schedule)			26 **78,300**
27	**Total deductions.** Add lines 12 through 26 ▶			27 **277,150**
28	Taxable income before net operating loss deduction and special deductions. Subtract line 27 from line 11			28 **208,350**
29	**Less:** a Net operating loss deduction (see page 11 of instructions)	29a		
	b Special deductions (Schedule C, line 20)	29b **8,000**		29c **8,000**

Tax and Payments

30	**Taxable income.** Subtract line 29c from line 28			30 **200,350**
31	**Total tax** (Schedule J, line 10)			31 **55,387**
32	Payments: a 1994 overpayment credited to 1995	32a		
	b 1995 estimated tax payments	32b **69,117**		
	c Less 1995 refund applied for on Form 4466	32c ( )	d Bal ▶ 32d **69,117**	
	e Tax deposited with Form 7004		32e	
	f Credit from regulated investment companies (attach Form 2439)		32f	
	g Credit for Federal tax on fuels (attach Form 4136). See instructions		32g	32h **69,117**
33	Estimated tax penalty (see page 12 of instructions). Check if Form 2220 is attached ▶ ☐			33
34	**Tax due.** If line 32h is smaller than the total of lines 31 and 33, enter amount owed			34
35	**Overpayment.** If line 32h is larger than the total of lines 31 and 33, enter amount overpaid			35 **13,730**
36	Enter amount of line 35 you want: **Credited to 1996 estimated tax** ▶ **13,730** **Refunded** ▶			36

Sign Here

Under penalties of perjury, I declare that I have examined this return, including accompanying schedules and statements, and to the best of my knowledge and belief, it is true, correct, and complete. Declaration of preparer (other than taxpayer) is based on all information of which preparer has any knowledge.

▶ *James O. Barclay* Signature of officer | *3/7/xx* Date | ▶ *President* Title

Paid Preparer's Use Only

Preparer's signature ▶		Date	Check if self-employed ☐	Preparer's social security number
Firm's name (or yours if self-employed) and address			EIN ▶
			ZIP code ▶

Cat. No. 11450Q

Form 1120 (1995)   Page **2**

Schedule A   Cost of Goods Sold (See page 12 of instructions.)

1	Inventory at beginning of year	1	126,000
2	Purchases	2	1,127,100
3	Cost of labor	3	402,000
4	Additional section 263A costs (attach schedule)	4	40,000
5	Other costs (attach schedule)	5	123,000
6	**Total.** Add lines 1 through 5	6	1,818,400
7	Inventory at end of year	7	298,400
8	**Cost of goods sold.** Subtract line 7 from line 6. Enter here and on page 1, line 2	8	1,520,000

9a   Check all methods used for valuing closing inventory:

(i) ☐ Cost as described in Regulations section 1.471-3

(ii) ☑ Lower of cost or market as described in Regulations section 1.471-4

(iii) ☐ Other (Specify method used and attach explanation.) ▶ ....

b   Check if there was a writedown of subnormal goods as described in Regulations section 1.471-2(c) . . . . ▶ ☐

c   Check if the LIFO inventory method was adopted this tax year for any goods (if checked, attach Form 970) . . . . . . ▶ ☐

d   If the LIFO inventory method was used for this tax year, enter percentage (or amounts) of closing inventory computed under LIFO . . . . `9d`

e   Do the rules of section 263A (for property produced or acquired for resale) apply to the corporation? . . . . . ☑ Yes ☐ No

f   Was there any change in determining quantities, cost, or valuations between opening and closing inventory? If "Yes," attach explanation . . . . ☐ Yes ☑ No

Schedule C   Dividends and Special Deductions (See page 13 of instructions.)

		(a) Dividends received	(b) %	(c) Special deductions (a) × (b)
1	Dividends from less-than-20%-owned domestic corporations that are subject to the 70% deduction (other than debt-financed stock)		70	
2	Dividends from 20%-or-more-owned domestic corporations that are subject to the 80% deduction (other than debt-financed stock)	10,000	80	8,000
3	Dividends on debt-financed stock of domestic and foreign corporations (section 246A)		see instructions	
4	Dividends on certain preferred stock of less-than-20%-owned public utilities		42	
5	Dividends on certain preferred stock of 20%-or-more-owned public utilities		48	
6	Dividends from less-than-20%-owned foreign corporations and certain FSCs that are subject to the 70% deduction		70	
7	Dividends from 20%-or-more-owned foreign corporations and certain FSCs that are subject to the 80% deduction		80	
8	Dividends from wholly owned foreign subsidiaries subject to the 100% deduction (section 245(b))		100	
9	**Total.** Add lines 1 through 8. See page 13 of instructions for limitation			8,000
10	Dividends from domestic corporations received by a small business investment company operating under the Small Business Investment Act of 1958		100	
11	Dividends from certain FSCs that are subject to the 100% deduction (section 245(c)(1))		100	
12	Dividends from affiliated group members subject to the 100% deduction (section 243(a)(3))		100	
13	Other dividends from foreign corporations not included on lines 3, 6, 7, 8, or 11			
14	Income from controlled foreign corporations under subpart F (attach Form(s) 5471)			
15	Foreign dividend gross-up (section 78)			
16	IC-DISC and former DISC dividends not included on lines 1, 2, or 3 (section 246(d))			
17	Other dividends			
18	Deduction for dividends paid on certain preferred stock of public utilities			
19	**Total dividends.** Add lines 1 through 17. Enter here and on line 4, page 1 ▶	10,000		
20	**Total special deductions.** Add lines 9, 10, 11, 12, and 18. Enter here and on line 29b, page 1 ▶			8,000

Schedule E   Compensation of Officers (See instructions for line 12, page 1.)

Complete Schedule E only if total receipts (line 1a plus lines 4 through 10 on page 1, Form 1120) are $500,000 or more.

(a) Name of officer	(b) Social security number	(c) Percent of time devoted to business	Percent of corporation stock owned		(f) Amount of compensation
			(d) Common	(e) Preferred	
1 James O. Barclay	581-00-0936	100 %	45 %	%	55,000
		%	%	%	
George M. Collins	447-00-2604	100 %	15 %	%	31,000
		%	%	%	
Samuel Adams	401-00-2611	50 %	2 %	%	14,000
2	Total compensation of officers				100,000
3	Compensation of officers claimed on Schedule A and elsewhere on return				30,000
4	Subtract line 3 from line 2. Enter the result here and on line 12, page 1				70,000

Form 1120 (1995)   Page **3**

Schedule J   Tax Computation (See page 14 of instructions.)

1   Check if the corporation is a member of a controlled group (see sections 1561 and 1563) . . . . ▶ ☐

   Important: Members of a controlled group, see instructions on page 14.

2a   If the box on line 1 is checked, enter the corporation's share of the $50,000, $25,000, and $9,925,000 taxable income brackets (in that order):

   (1) $ _____   **(2)** $ _____   **(3)** $ _____

b   Enter the corporation's share of:

   (1) Additional 5% tax (not more than $11,750) $ _____

   (2) Additional 3% tax (not more than $100,000) $ _____

3   Income tax. Check this box if the corporation is a qualified personal service corporation as defined in section 448(d)(2) (see instructions on page 15). . . . . ▶ ☐ | **3** | 61,387 |

4a   Foreign tax credit (attach Form 1118) . | **4a** | |

b   Possessions tax credit (attach Form 5735) . . . . | **4b** | |

c   Check: ☐ Nonconventional source fuel credit ☐ QEV credit (attach Form 8834) | **4c** | |

d   General business credit. Enter here and check which forms are attached:

   ☐ 3800 ☐ 3468 ☑ 5884 ☐ 6478 ☐ 6765 ☐ 8586 ☐ 8830

   ☐ 8826 ☐ 8835 ☐ 8844 ☐ 8845 ☐ 8846 ☐ 8847 . . . . | **4d** | 6,000 |

e   Credit for prior year minimum tax (attach Form 8827) . . . . . . | **4e** | |

5   **Total credits.** Add lines 4a through 4e . . . . | **5** | 6,000 |

6   Subtract line 5 from line 3 . . . . | **6** | 55,387 |

7   Personal holding company tax (attach Schedule PH (Form 1120)) . . . . . | **7** | |

8   Recapture taxes. Check if from: ☐ Form 4255 ☐ Form 8611 . . . . . | **8** | |

9a   Alternative minimum tax (attach Form 4626) . . . . | **9a** | |

b   Environmental tax (attach Form 4626) . . . . | **9b** | |

10   **Total tax.** Add lines 6 through 9b. Enter here and on line 31, page 1 . . . . | **10** | 55,387 |

Schedule K   Other Information (See page 17 of instructions.)

		Yes	No
1	Check method of accounting: **a** ☐ Cash		
	b ☑ Accrual **c** ☐ Other (specify) ▶		
2	See page 19 of the instructions and state the principal:		
a	Business activity code no. ▶ *3998*		
b	Business activity ▶ *Manufacturing*		
c	Product or service ▶ *Toys*		
3	Did the corporation at the end of the tax year own, directly or indirectly, 50% or more of the voting stock of a domestic corporation? (For rules of attribution, see section 267(c).)		✓
	If "Yes," attach a schedule showing: (a) name and identifying number, (b) percentage owned, and (c) taxable income or (loss) before NOL and special deductions of such corporation for the tax year ending with or within your tax year.		
4	Is the corporation a subsidiary in an affiliated group or a parent-subsidiary controlled group?		✓
	If "Yes," enter employer identification number and name of the parent corporation ▶		
5	Did any individual, partnership, corporation, estate or trust at the end of the tax year own, directly or indirectly, 50% or more of the corporation's voting stock? (For rules of attribution, see section 267(c).)	✓	
	If "Yes," attach a schedule showing name and identifying number. (Do not include any information already entered in **4** above.) Enter percentage owned ▶		
6	During this tax year, did the corporation pay dividends (other than stock dividends and distributions in exchange for stock) in excess of the corporation's current and accumulated earnings and profits? (See secs. 301 and 316.)		✓
	If "Yes," file Form 5452. If this is a consolidated return, answer here for the parent corporation and on **Form 851**, Affiliations Schedule, for each subsidiary.		

		Yes	No
7	Was the corporation a U.S. shareholder of any controlled foreign corporation? (See sections 951 and 957.) . . .		✓
	If "Yes," attach Form 5471 for each such corporation. Enter number of Forms 5471 attached ▶		
8	At any time during the 1995 calendar year, did the corporation have an interest in or a signature or other authority over a financial account in a foreign country (such as a bank account, securities account, or other financial account)? . .		✓
	If "Yes," the corporation may have to file Form TD F 90-22.1. If "Yes," enter name of foreign country ▶		
9	Was the corporation the grantor of, or transferor to, a foreign trust that existed during the current tax year, whether or not the corporation has any beneficial interest in it? If "Yes," the corporation may have to file Forms 926, 3520, or 3520-A		✓
10	Did one foreign person at any time during the tax year own, directly or indirectly, at least 25% of: **(a)** the total voting power of all classes of stock of the corporation entitled to vote, or **(b)** the total value of all classes of stock of the corporation? If "Yes,"		✓
a	Enter percentage owned ▶		
b	Enter owner's country ▶		
c	The corporation may have to file Form 5472. Enter number of Forms 5472 attached ▶		
11	Check this box if the corporation issued publicly offered debt instruments with original issue discount . ▶ ☐		
	If so, the corporation may have to file Form 8281.		
12	Enter the amount of tax-exempt interest received or accrued during the tax year ▶ $ ....*5,000*....		
13	If there were 35 or fewer shareholders at the end of the tax year, enter the number ▶		
14	If the corporation has an NOL for the tax year and is electing to forego the carryback period, check here ▶ ☐		
15	Enter the available NOL carryover from prior tax years (Do not reduce it by any deduction on line 29a.) ▶ $		

Form 1120 (1995)   Page **4**

Schedule L — Balance Sheets

Assets	Beginning of tax year (a)	(b)	End of tax year (c)	(d)
1 Cash		14,700		28,331
2a Trade notes and accounts receivable	98,400		103,700	
b Less allowance for bad debts	( )	98,400	( )	103,700
3 Inventories		126,000		298,400
4 U.S. government obligations				
5 Tax-exempt securities (see instructions)		100,000		120,000
6 Other current assets (attach schedule)		26,300		17,266
7 Loans to stockholders				
8 Mortgage and real estate loans				
9 Other investments (attach schedule)		100,000		80,000
10a Buildings and other depreciable assets	272,400		296,700	
b Less accumulated depreciation	(88,300)	184,100	(104,280)	192,400
11a Depletable assets				
b Less accumulated depletion	( )		( )	
12 Land (net of any amortization)		20,000		20,000
13a Intangible assets (amortizable only)				
b Less accumulated amortization	( )		( )	
14 Other assets (attach schedule)		14,800		19,300
15 Total assets		684,300		879,417
Liabilities and Stockholders' Equity				
16 Accounts payable		28,500		34,834
17 Mortgages, notes, bonds payable in less than 1 year		4,300		4,300
18 Other current liabilities (attach schedule)		6,800		7,400
19 Loans from stockholders				
20 Mortgages, notes, bonds payable in 1 year or more		176,700		264,100
21 Other liabilities (attach schedule)				
22 Capital stock: a Preferred stock				
b Common stock	200,000	200,000	200,000	200,000
23 Paid-in or capital surplus				
24 Retained earnings—Appropriated (attach schedule)		30,000		40,000
25 Retained earnings—Unappropriated		238,000		328,783
26 Less cost of treasury stock		( )		( )
27 Total liabilities and stockholders' equity		684,300		879,417

Note: You are not required to complete Schedules M-1 and M-2 below if the total assets on line 15, column (d) of Schedule L are less than $25,000.

Schedule M-1 — Reconciliation of Income (Loss) per Books With Income per Return (See page 18 of instructions.)

1	Net income (loss) per books	147,783	7	Income recorded on books this year not included on this return (itemize):	
2	Federal income tax	55,387		Tax-exempt interest $ 5,000	
3	Excess of capital losses over capital gains	3,600		Insurance proceeds— 9,500	14,500
4	Income subject to tax not recorded on books this year (itemize):		8	Deductions on this return not charged against book income this year (itemize):	
5	Expenses recorded on books this year not deducted on this return (itemize):		a	Depreciation . . . . $ 1,620	
a	Depreciation . . . . $		b	Contributions carryover $	
b	Contributions carryover $ 850				
c	Travel and entertainment $ See itemized statement attached (not shown)- 16,850	17,700	9	Add lines 7 and 8	1,620 / 16,120
6	Add lines 1 through 5	224,470	10	Income (line 28, page 1)—line 6 less line 9	208,350

Schedule M-2 — Analysis of Unappropriated Retained Earnings per Books (Line 25, Schedule L)

1	Balance at beginning of year	238,000	5	Distributions: a Cash	65,000
2	Net income (loss) per books	147,783		b Stock	
3	Other increases (itemize): Refund of 1991 income tax due to IRS examination	18,000		c Property	
			6	Other decreases (itemize): Reserve arrangements	10,000
			7	Add lines 5 and 6	75,000
4	Add lines 1, 2, and 3	403,783	8	Balance at end of year (line 4 less line 7)	328,783

Printed on recycled paper

SCHEDULE D (Form 1120)	Capital Gains and Losses	OMB No. 1545-0123
Department of the Treasury Internal Revenue Service	To be filed with Forms 1120, 1120-A, 1120-IC-DISC, 1120-F, 1120-FSC, 1120-H, 1120-L, 1120-ND, 1120-PC, 1120-POL, 1120-REIT, 1120-RIC, 1120-SF, 990-C, and certain Forms 990-T	1995

Name | Employer identification number

Part I — Short-Term Capital Gains and Losses—Assets Held One Year or Less

(a) Kind of property and description (Example, 100 shares of "Z" Co.)	(b) Date acquired (mo., day, yr.)	(c) Date sold (mo., day, yr.)	(d) Sales price (see instructions)	(e) Cost or other basis (see instructions)	(f) Gain or (loss) ((d) less (e))
1					

2	Short-term capital gain from installment sales from Form 6252, line 26 or 37	2
3	Short-term gain or (loss) from like-kind exchanges from Form 8824	3
4	Unused capital loss carryover (attach computation)	4 ( )
5	Net short-term capital gain or (loss). Combine lines 1 through 4	5

Part II — Long-Term Capital Gains and Losses—Assets Held More Than One Year

6					

7	Enter gain from Form 4797, line 8 or 10	7
8	Long-term capital gain from installment sales from Form 6252, line 26 or 37	8
9	Long-term gain or (loss) from like-kind exchanges from Form 8824	9
10	Net long-term capital gain or (loss). Combine lines 6 through 9	10

Part III — Summary of Parts I and II

11	Enter excess of net short-term capital gain (line 5) over net long-term capital loss (line 10). . .	11
12	Net capital gain. Enter excess of net long-term capital gain (line 10) over net short-term capital loss (line 5)	12
13	Add lines 11 and 12. Enter here and on Form 1120, page 1, line 8, or the proper line on other returns.	13

Note: If losses exceed gains, see instructions on capital losses for explanation of capital loss carrybacks.

Instructions

Section references are to the Internal Revenue Code unless otherwise noted.

Caution: *At the time these instructions were printed, Congress was considering legislation that would change the tax treatment of capital gains. Get Pub. 553, Highlights of 1995 Tax Changes, for more information. You can get it by calling 1-800-TAX-FORM (1-800-829-3676). It is also available electronically through our bulletin board or via the Internet (see page 1 of the Form 1120 instructions).*

Purpose of Schedule

Use Schedule D to report sales and exchanges of capital assets and gains on distributions to shareholders of appreciated capital assets.

Report sales, exchanges, and distributions of property other than capital assets on **Form 4797,** Sales of Business Property. Include on Form 4797 a sale, exchange, or distribution of property used in a trade or business; involuntary conversions (from other than casualties or thefts); gain from the disposition of oil, gas, or geothermal property; and the section 291 adjustment to section 1250 gains. See the instructions for Form 4797 for more details.

If property is involuntarily converted because of a casualty or theft, use **Form 4684,** Casualties and Thefts.

Parts I and II

Generally, a corporation must report sales and exchanges even if there is no gain or loss. Use Part I to report the sale, exchange, or distribution of capital assets held 1 year or less. Use Part II to report the sale, exchange, or distribution of capital assets held more than 1 year. Use the trade dates for the dates of acquisition and sale of stocks and bonds on an exchange or over-the-counter market.

What Is a Capital Asset?—Each item of property the corporation held (whether or not connected with its trade or business) is a capital asset **except:**

1. Assets that can be inventoried or property held mainly for sale to customers.

2. Depreciable or real property used in the trade or business.

3. Certain copyrights; literary, musical, or artistic compositions; letters or memoranda; or similar property.

4. Accounts or notes receivable acquired in the ordinary course of trade or business for services rendered or from the sale of property described in 1 above.

5. U.S. Government publications, including the Congressional Record, that the corporation received from the Government, other than by purchase at the normal sales price, or that the corporation got from another taxpayer who had received it in a similar way, if the corporation's basis is determined by reference to the previous owner's basis.

Capital Losses.—Capital losses are allowed only to the extent of capital gains. A net

For Paperwork Reduction Act Notice, see page 1 of the Instructions for Forms 1120 and 1120-A. Cat. No. 11460M **Schedule D (Form 1120) 1995** capital loss may be carried back 3 years and forward 5 years as a short-term capital loss. Carry back a capital loss to the extent it does not increase or produce a net operating loss in the tax year to which it is carried. Foreign expropriation capital losses may not be carried back, but may be carried forward 10 years. A net capital loss for a regulated investment company may be carried forward 8 years.

Special Rules for the Treatment of Certain Gains and Losses

Note: *For more information, get* **Pub. 544,** *Sales and Other Dispositions of Assets, and* **Pub. 542,** *Tax Information on Corporations.*

● **Loss from a sale or exchange between the corporation and a related person.—** Except for distributions in complete liquidation of a corporation, no loss is allowed from the sale or exchange of property between the corporation and certain related persons. See section 267 for details.

● **Loss from a wash sale.—**The corporation cannot deduct a loss from a wash sale of stock or securities (including contracts or options to acquire or sell stock or securities) unless the corporation is a dealer in stock or securities and the loss was sustained in a transaction made in the ordinary course of the corporation's trade or business. A wash sale occurs if the corporation acquires (by purchase or exchange), or has a contract or option to acquire, substantially identical stock or securities within 30 days before or after the date of the sale or exchange. See section 1091 for more information.

● **Like-kind exchanges.—**An exchange of business or investment property for property of a like kind is reported on **Form 8824,** Like-Kind Exchanges.

● **At-risk limitations (section 465).—**If the corporation sold or exchanged a capital asset used in an activity to which the at-risk rules apply, combine the gain or loss on the sale or exchange with the profit or loss from the activity. If the result is a net loss, complete **Form 6198,** At-Risk Limitations. Report any gain from the capital asset on Schedule D and on Form 6198.

● **Gains and losses from passive activities.—**A closely held or personal service corporation that has a gain or loss that relates to a passive activity (section 469) may be required to complete **Form 8810,** Corporate Passive Activity Loss and Credit Limitations, before completing Schedule D. A Schedule D loss may be limited under the passive activity rules. See Form 8810 for more detailed information.

● **Gain on distributions of appreciated property.—** Generally, gain (but not loss) is recognized on a nonliquidating distribution of appreciated property to the extent that the property's fair market value exceeds its adjusted basis. See section 311 for more information.

● **Gain or loss on distribution of property in complete liquidation.—** Generally, gain or loss is recognized on property distributed in a complete liquidation. Treat the property as if it had been sold at its fair market value. An exception to this rule applies for liquidations of certain subsidiaries. See sections 336 and 337 for more information and other exceptions to the general rules.

● **Gains and losses on section 1256 contracts and straddles.—**Use **Form 6781,** Gains and Losses From Section 1256 Contracts and Straddles, to report these gains and losses.

● **Gain or loss on certain short-term Federal, state, and municipal obligations.—** Such obligations are treated as capital assets in determining gain or loss. On any gain realized, a portion is treated as ordinary income and the balance as a short-term capital gain. See section 1271.

● **Gain from installment sales.—**If the corporation has a gain this year from the casual sale of real or personal property (other than inventory) and is to receive any payment in a later year, it must use the installment method (unless it elects not to—see below) and file **Form 6252,** Installment Sale Income. Also use Form 6252 if a payment is received this year from a sale made in an earlier year on the installment method.

The corporation may elect out of the installment method by reporting the full amount of the gain on a timely filed return (including extensions).

The installment method may not be used for sales of stock or securities (or certain other property described in the regulations) traded on an established securities market. See section 453(k).

● **Rollover of publicly traded securities gain into specialized small business investment companies (SSBICs).—**A corporation that sells publicly traded securities at a gain may elect under section 1044 to postpone all or part of the gain if the seller buys stock or a partnership interest in an SSBIC during the 60-day period that begins on the date the securities are sold.

An SSBIC is any partnership or corporation licensed by the Small Business Administration under section 301(d) of the Small Business Investment Act of 1958. The corporation must recognize gain on the sale to the extent the proceeds from the sale exceed the cost of the SSBIC stock or partnership interest purchased during the 60-day period that began on the date of the sale (and not previously taken into account). The gain a corporation may postpone each tax year is limited to the lesser of **(a)** $250,000 or **(b)** $1 million, reduced by the gain previously excluded under section 1044. The basis of the SSBIC stock or partnership interest is reduced by any postponed gain.

To make the election to postpone gain, complete line 1 or line 6, whichever applies, showing the entire gain realized in column (f). Directly below the line on which the gain is reported, enter "SSBIC Rollover" in column (a). Enter the amount of the postponed gain (in parentheses) in column (f). Also, attach a schedule showing **(a)** how you figured the postponed gain, **(b)** the name of the SSBIC in which you purchased common stock or a partnership interest, **(c)** the date of that purchase, and **(d)** the new basis in that SSBIC stock or partnership interest.

For more details, see section 1044.

● **Gain or loss on an option to buy or sell property.—**See sections 1032 and 1234 for the rules that apply to a purchaser or grantor of an option.

● **Gain or loss from a short sale of property.—**Report the gain or loss to the extent that the property used to close the

short sale is considered a capital asset in the hands of the taxpayer.

● **Gains and losses of foreign corporations from the disposition of investment in U.S. real property.—**Foreign corporations are required to report gains and losses from the disposition of U.S. real property interests. See section 897 for details.

● **Gains on certain insurance property.—** Form 1120-L filers with gains on property held on December 31, 1958, and certain substituted property acquired after 1958 should see section 818(c).

● **Loss from the sale or exchange of capital assets of an insurance company taxable under section 831.—**Under the provisions of section 834(c)(6), capital losses of a casualty insurance company are deductible to the extent that the assets were sold to meet abnormal insurance losses or to provide for the payment of dividend and similar distributions to policyholders.

● **Loss from securities that are capital assets that become worthless during the year.—**Except for securities held by a bank, treat the loss as a capital loss as of the last day of the tax year. (See section 582 for the rules on the treatment of securities held by a bank.)

● **Disposition of market discount bonds.—** See section 1276 for rules on the disposition of market discount bonds.

● **Capital gain distributions.—**Report capital gain distributions paid by mutual funds as long-term capital gains on line 6 regardless of how long the corporation owned stock in the fund.

Specific Instructions

Line 1, column (d).—Enter either the gross sales price or the net sales price. If the net sales price is entered, do not increase the cost or other basis in column (e) by any expense of sale.

Line 1, column (e).—In determining gain or loss, the basis of property will generally be its cost. See section 1012 and the related regulations. Exceptions to the general rule are provided in sections in subchapters C, K, O, and P of the Code. For example, if the corporation acquired the property by dividend, liquidation of a corporation, transfer from a shareholder, reorganization, bequest, contribution or gift, tax-free exchange, involuntary conversion, certain asset acquisitions, or wash sale of stock, see sections 301 (or 1059), 334, 362 (or 358), 1014, 1015, 1031, 1033, 1060, and 1091, respectively. Attach an explanation if the corporation uses a basis other than actual cash cost of the property.

If the gross sales price is reported in column (d), increase the cost or other basis by any expense of sale such as broker's fees, commissions, or option premiums before entering an amount in column (e).

If the corporation is allowed a charitable contribution deduction because it sold property in a bargain sale to a charitable organization, figure the adjusted basis for determining gain from the sale by dividing the amount realized by the fair market value and multiplying that result by the adjusted basis.

See section 852(f) for the treatment of certain load charges incurred in acquiring stock in a mutual fund with a reinvestment right.

 Printed on recycled paper

Form 1120-A

Department of the Treasury
Internal Revenue Service

U.S. Corporation Short-Form Income Tax Return

See separate instructions to make sure the corporation qualifies to file Form 1120-A.
For calendar year 1995 or tax year beginning ...., 1995, ending............., 19.....

OMB No. 1545-0890

1995

A Check this box if the corp. is a personal service corp. (as defined in Temporary Regs. section 1.441-4T—see instructions) ▶ ☐

Use IRS label. Otherwise, print or type.

Name Rose Flower Shop, Inc.

Number, street, and room or suite no. (If a P.O. box, see page 6 of instructions.) 38 Superior Lane

City or town, state, and ZIP code Fair City MD 20715

B Employer identification number

C Date incorporated 7-1-82

D Total assets (see page 6 of instructions) $ 65,987

E Check applicable boxes: **(1)** ☐ Initial return **(2)** ☐ Change of address

F Check method of accounting: **(1)** ☐ Cash **(2)** ☑ Accrual **(3)** ☐ Other (specify) . . ▶

Income

1a Gross receipts or sales 248,000 **b** Less returns and allowances 7,500 **c** Balance ▶		1c	240,500
2 Cost of goods sold (see page 12 of instructions)		2	144,000
3 Gross profit. Subtract line 2 from line 1c		3	96,500
4 Domestic corporation dividends subject to the 70% deduction		4	
5 Interest		5	942
6 Gross rents		6	
7 Gross royalties		7	
8 Capital gain net income (attach Schedule D (Form 1120))		8	
9 Net gain or (loss) from Form 4797, Part II, line 20 (attach Form 4797)		9	
10 Other income (see page 7 of instructions)		10	
11 **Total income.** Add lines 3 through 10 ▶		11	97,442

Deductions (See instructions for limitations on deductions.)

12 Compensation of officers (see page 8 of instructions)		12	23,000
13 Salaries and wages (less employment credits)		13	24,320
14 Repairs and maintenance		14	
15 Bad debts		15	
16 Rents		16	6,000
17 Taxes and licenses		17	3,320
18 Interest		18	1,340
19 Charitable contributions (see page 9 of instructions for 10% limitation)		19	1,820
20 Depreciation (attach Form 4562)	20		
21 Less depreciation claimed elsewhere on return	21a	21b	
22 Other deductions (attach schedule) Advertising		22	3,000
23 **Total deductions.** Add lines 12 through 22 ▶		23	62,800
24 Taxable income before net operating loss deduction and special deductions. Subtract line 23 from line 11		24	34,642
25 **Less: a** Net operating loss deduction (see page 11 of instructions)	25a		
b Special deductions (see page 11 of instructions)	25b	25c	

Tax and Payments

26 **Taxable income.** Subtract line 25c from line 24		26	34,642
27 **Total tax** (from page 2, Part I, line 7)		27	5,196
28 Payments:			
a 1994 overpayment credited to 1995	28a		
b 1995 estimated tax payments	28b 6,000		
c Less 1995 refund applied for on Form 4466	28c ( ) Bal ▶ 28d 6,000		
e Tax deposited with Form 7004	28e		
f Credit from regulated investment companies (attach Form 2439)	28f		
g Credit for Federal tax on fuels (attach Form 4136). See instructions	28g		
h **Total payments.** Add lines 28d through 28g		28h	6,000
29 Estimated tax penalty (see page 12 of instructions). Check if Form 2220 is attached ▶ ☐		29	
30 **Tax due.** If line 28h is smaller than the total of lines 27 and 29, enter amount owed		30	
31 **Overpayment.** If line 28h is larger than the total of lines 27 and 29, enter amount overpaid		31	804
32 Enter amount of line 31 you want: **Credited to 1996 estimated tax** ▶ Refunded ▶		32	

Sign Here

Under penalties of perjury, I declare that I have examined this return, including accompanying schedules and statements, and to the best of my knowledge and belief, it is true, correct, and complete. Declaration of preparer (other than taxpayer) is based on all information of which preparer has any knowledge.

▶ George Rose *(Signature of officer)* | 2-15-XX *(Date)* | ▶ President *(Title)*

Paid Preparer's Use Only

| Preparer's signature ▶ | Date | Check if self-employed ▶ ☐ | Preparer's social security number |
| Firm's name (or yours if self-employed) and address ▶ | | EIN ▶ | ZIP code ▶ |

For Paperwork Reduction Act Notice, see page 1 of the instructions.   Cat. No. 11456E   Form **1120-A** (1995)

Form 1120-A (1995)   Page **2**

Part I Tax Computation (See page 14 of instructions.)

1	Income tax. If the corporation is a qualified personal service corporation (see page 15), check here ▶ ☐	1	5,196
2a	General business credit. Check if from: ☐ Form 3800 ☐ Form 3468 ☐ Form 5884		
	☐ Form 6478 ☐ Form 6765 ☐ Form 8586 ☐ Form 8830 ☐ Form 8826 ☐ Form 8835		
	☐ Form 8844 ☐ Form 8845 ☐ Form 8846 ☐ Form 8847 . . . . . 2a		
b	Credit for prior year minimum tax (attach Form 8827) 2b		
3	**Total credits.** Add lines 2a and 2b	3	
4	Subtract line 3 from line 1	4	5,196
5	Recapture taxes. Check if from: ☐ Form 4255 ☐ Form 8611 . . .	5	
6	Alternative minimum tax (attach Form 4626)	6	
7	**Total tax.** Add lines 4 through 6. Enter here and on line 27, page 1 . . .	7	5,196

Part II Other Information (See page 17 of instructions.)

1 See page 19 of the instructions and state the principal:
a Business activity code no. ▶ ...5995......
b Business activity ▶ Flower shop
c Product or service ▶ Flowers

2 Did any individual, partnership, estate, or trust at the end of the tax year own, directly or indirectly, 50% or more of the corporation's voting stock? (For rules of attribution, see section 267(c).) Schedule not shown ☑ Yes ☐ No

If "Yes," attach a schedule showing name and identifying number.

3 Enter the amount of tax-exempt interest received or accrued during the tax year . . . . ▶ |$ -0-|

4 Enter amount of cash distributions and the book value of property (other than cash) distributions made in this tax year . . . . ▶ |$ -0-|

5a If an amount is entered on line 2, page 1, see the worksheet on page 12 for amounts to enter below:

(1)	Purchases	134,014
(2)	Additional sec. 263A costs (attach schedule)	
(3)	Other costs (attach schedule) .	9,466

b Do the rules of section 263A (for property produced or acquired for resale) apply to the corporation? . . . . . . ☐ Yes ☑ No

6 At any time during the 1995 calendar year, did the corporation have an interest in or a signature or other authority over a financial account in a foreign country (such as a bank account, securities account, or other financial account)? If "Yes," the corporation may have to file Form TD F 90-22.1 . . . . ☐ Yes ☑ No
If "Yes," enter the name of the foreign country ▶ ....

Part III Balance Sheets

		(a) Beginning of tax year	(b) End of tax year
	Assets		
1	Cash	20,540	18,498
2a	Trade notes and accounts receivable .		
b	Less allowance for bad debts . . .	( )	( )
3	Inventories	2,530	2,010
4	U.S. government obligations	13,807	45,479
5	Tax-exempt securities (see instructions) .		
6	Other current assets (attach schedule) . .		
7	Loans to stockholders		
8	Mortgage and real estate loans . . .		
9a	Depreciable, depletable, and intangible assets . . .		
b	Less accumulated depreciation, depletion, and amortization	( )	( )
10	Land (net of any amortization)		
11	Other assets (attach schedule)		
12	Total assets	36,877	65,987
	Liabilities and Stockholders' Equity		
13	Accounts payable	6,415	6,079
14	Other current liabilities (attach schedule) . .		
15	Loans from stockholders		
16	Mortgages, notes, bonds payable . . .		
17	Other liabilities (attach schedule) . . .		
18	Capital stock (preferred and common stock) . . .	20,000	20,000
19	Paid-in or capital surplus		
20	Retained earnings	10,462	39,908
21	Less cost of treasury stock	( )	( )
22	Total liabilities and stockholders' equity .	36,877	65,987

Part IV Reconciliation of Income (Loss) per Books With Income per Return (You are not required to complete Part IV if the total assets on line 12, column (b), Part III are less than $25,000.)

1	Net income (loss) per books	29,446	6 Income recorded on books this year not included on this return (itemize)	
2	Federal income tax	5,196		
3	Excess of capital losses over capital gains . .		7 Deductions on this return not charged against book income this year (itemize)	
4	Income subject to tax not recorded on books this year (itemize)		....	
5	Expenses recorded on books this year not deducted on this return (itemize)		8 Income (line 24, page 1). Enter the sum of lines 1 through 5 less the sum of lines 6 and 7 . .	34,642

✱ Printed on recycled paper

1995

Department of the Treasury
Internal Revenue Service

Instructions for Form 1120S
U.S. Income Tax Return for an S Corporation

Section references are to the Internal Revenue Code unless otherwise noted.

Paperwork Reduction Act Notice

We ask for the information on these forms to carry out the Internal Revenue laws of the United States. You are required to give us the information. We need it to ensure that you are complying with these laws and to allow us to figure and collect the right amount of tax.

The time needed to complete and file this form and related schedules will vary depending on individual circumstances. The estimated average times are:

Form	Recordkeeping	Learning about the law or the form	Preparing the form	Copying, assembling, and sending the form to the IRS
1120S	62 hr., 40 min.	20 hr., 8 min.	35 hr., 59 min.	4 hr., 1 min.
Sch. D (1120S)	9 hr., 20 min.	4 hr., 8 min.	9 hr., 7 min.	1 hr., 20 min.
Sch. K-1 (1120S)	14 hr., 50 min.	10 hr., 7 min.	14 hr., 31 min.	1 hr., 4 min.

If you have comments concerning the accuracy of these time estimates or suggestions for making these forms simpler, we would be happy to hear from you. You can write to the Tax Forms Committee, Western Area Distribution Center, Rancho Cordova, CA 95743-0001. **DO NOT** send the tax form to this address. Instead, see **Where To File** on page 2.

Contents

Cat. No. 11515K

Voluntary Contributions To Reduce the Public Debt

Quite often, inquiries are received about how to make voluntary contributions to reduce the public debt. A corporation may contribute by enclosing with the tax return a check made payable to "Bureau of the Public Debt."

A Change To Note

Final regulations under section 263A(f) have been issued on the capitalization of interest expense paid or incurred during the production period of certain property. Regulations sections 1.263A-8 through 1.263A-15, which generally are effective for tax years beginning after 1994, may require a change in accounting method. Any such change must be made under Rev. Proc. 95-19, 1995-12 I.R.B. 6.

General Instructions

Note: *In addition to the publications listed throughout these instructions, you may wish to get **Pub. 334,** Tax Guide for Small Business; **Pub. 535,** Business Expenses; **Pub. 550,** Investment Income and Expenses; **Pub. 556,** Examination of Returns, Appeal Rights, and Claims for Refund; and **Pub. 589,** Tax Information on S Corporations.*

You can get these and other publications referenced throughout these instructions at most IRS offices. To order publications and forms, call 1-800-TAX-FORM (1-800-829-3676). If you have a personal computer and a modem, you can also get forms and publications electronically. For details, see page 34 of the Instructions for Form 1040.

Purpose of Form

Form 1120S is used to report the income, deductions, gains, losses, etc., of a domestic corporation that has elected to be an S corporation by filing **Form 2553,** Election by a Small Business Corporation, and whose election is in effect for the tax year.

Who Must File

A corporation must file Form 1120S if **(a)** it elected to be an S corporation by filing Form 2553, **(b)** the IRS accepted the election, and **(c)** the election remains in effect. Do not file Form 1120S until the corporation has been notified by the IRS that the election has been accepted.

Termination of Election

Once the election is made, it stays in effect until it is terminated. During the 5 years after the election is terminated, the corporation (or a successor corporation) may make another election on Form 2553 only with IRS consent. See Regulations section 1.1362-5 for more details.

An election terminates **automatically** in any of the following cases:

1. The corporation is no longer a small business corporation as defined in section 1361(b). The termination of an election in this manner is effective as of the day on which the corporation no longer meets the definition of a small business corporation. If the election terminates for this reason, attach to Form 1120S for the final year of the S corporation a statement notifying the IRS of the termination and the date it occurred.

2. The corporation, for each of three consecutive tax years, **(a)** has subchapter C earnings and profits and **(b)** derives more than 25% of its gross receipts from passive investment income as defined in section 1362(d)(3)(D). The election terminates on the first day of the first tax year beginning after the third consecutive tax year. The corporation must pay a tax for each year it has excess net passive income. See the instructions for line 22a for details on how to figure the tax.

3. The election is revoked. An election may be revoked only with the consent of shareholders who, at the time the revocation is made, hold more than 50% of the number of issued and outstanding shares of stock (including non-voting stock). The revocation may specify an effective revocation date that is on or after the day the revocation is filed. If no date is specified, the revocation is effective at the start of a tax year if the revocation is made on or before the 15th day of the 3rd month of that tax year. If no date is specified and the revocation is made after the 15th day of the 3rd month of the tax year, the revocation is effective at the start of the next tax year.

To revoke the election, the corporation must file a statement with the service center where it filed its election to be an S corporation. In the statement, the corporation must notify the IRS that it is revoking its election to be an S corporation. The statement must be signed by each shareholder who consents to the revocation and contain the information required by Regulations section 1.1362-6(a)(3). A revocation may be rescinded before the revocation takes effect. See Regulations section 1.1362-6(a)(4) for details.

For rules on allocating income and deductions between an S short year and a C short year and other special rules that apply when an election is terminated, see section 1362(e) and Regulations section 1.1362-3.

If an election was terminated under **1** or **2** above, and the corporation believes the termination was inadvertent, the corporation may request permission from the IRS to continue to be treated as an S corporation. See Regulations section 1.1362-4 for the specific requirements that must be met to qualify for inadvertent termination relief.

When To File

In general, file Form 1120S by the 15th day of the 3rd month following the date the corporation's tax year ended as shown at the top of Form 1120S. For calendar year corporations, the due date is March 15, 1996. If the due date falls on a Saturday, Sunday, or legal holiday, file on the next business day. A business day is any day that is not a Saturday, Sunday, or legal holiday.

If the S election was terminated during the tax year, file Form 1120S for the S short year by the due date (including extensions) of the C short year return.

Extension

Use **Form 7004,** Application for Automatic Extension of Time To File Corporation Income Tax Return, to request an automatic 6-month extension of time to file Form 1120S.

Period Covered

File the 1995 return for calendar year 1995 and fiscal years beginning in 1995 and ending in 1996. If the return is for a fiscal year or a short tax year, fill in the tax year space at the top of the form.

Note: *The 1995 Form 1120S may also be used if **(a)** the corporation has a tax year of less than 12 months that begins and ends in 1996 and **(b)** the 1996 Form 1120S is not available by the time the corporation is required to file its return. However, the corporation must show its 1996 tax year on the 1995 Form 1120S and incorporate any tax law changes that are effective for tax years beginning after December 31, 1995.*

Where To File

Use the preaddressed envelope. If you do not have the envelope, file your return at the applicable IRS address listed below.

If the corporation's principal business, office, or agency is located in ▼	Use the following Internal Revenue Service Center address ▼
New Jersey, New York (New York City and counties of Nassau, Rockland, Suffolk, and Westchester)	Holtsville, NY 00501-0013
New York (all other counties), Connecticut, Maine, Massachusetts, New Hampshire, Rhode Island, Vermont	Andover, MA 05501-0013
Florida, Georgia, South Carolina	Atlanta, GA 39901-0013
Indiana, Kentucky, Michigan, Ohio, West Virginia	Cincinnati, OH 45999-0013
Kansas, New Mexico, Oklahoma, Texas	Austin, TX 73301-0013
Alaska, Arizona, California (counties of Alpine, Amador, Butte, Calaveras, Colusa, Contra Costa, Del Norte, El Dorado, Glenn, Humboldt, Lake, Lassen, Marin, Mendocino, Modoc, Napa, Nevada, Placer, Plumas, Sacramento, San Joaquin, Shasta, Sierra, Siskiyou, Solano, Sonoma, Sutter, Tehama, Trinity, Yolo, and Yuba), Colorado, Idaho, Montana, Nebraska, Nevada, North Dakota, Oregon, South Dakota, Utah, Washington, Wyoming	Ogden, UT 84201-0013
California (all other counties), Hawaii	Fresno, CA 93888-0013
Illinois, Iowa, Minnesota, Missouri, Wisconsin	Kansas City, MO 64999-0013
Alabama, Arkansas, Louisiana, Mississippi, North Carolina, Tennessee	Memphis, TN 37501-0013
Delaware, District of Columbia, Maryland, Pennsylvania, Virginia	Philadelphia, PA 19255-0013

Who Must Sign

The return must be signed and dated by the president, vice president, treasurer, assistant treasurer, chief accounting officer, or any other corporate officer (such as tax officer) authorized to sign. A receiver, trustee, or assignee must sign and date any return he or she is required to file on behalf of a corporation.

If a corporate officer filled in Form 1120S, the Paid Preparer's space under "Signature of officer" should remain blank. If someone prepares Form 1120S and does not charge the corporation, that person should not sign the return. Certain others who prepare Form 1120S should not sign. For example, a regular, full-time employee of the corporation such as a clerk, secretary, etc., should not sign.

Generally, anyone paid to prepare Form 1120S must sign the return and fill in the other blanks in the Paid Preparer's Use Only area of the return.

The preparer required to sign the return MUST complete the required preparer information and:

● Sign it, by hand, in the space provided for the preparer's signature. (Signature stamps or labels are not acceptable.)

● Give a copy of Form 1120S to the taxpayer in addition to the copy filed with the IRS.

Accounting Methods

Figure ordinary income using the method of accounting regularly used in keeping the corporation's books and records. Generally, permissible methods include the cash method, the accrual method, or any other method permitted by the Internal Revenue Code. In all cases, the method adopted must clearly reflect income.

Page 2

Generally, an S corporation may not use the cash method of accounting if the corporation is a tax shelter (as defined in section 448(d)(3)). See section 448 for details.

Under the accrual method, an amount is includible in income when all the events have occurred that fix the right to receive the income and the amount can be determined with reasonable accuracy. See Regulations section 1.451-1(a) for details.

Generally, an accrual basis taxpayer can deduct accrued expenses in the tax year in which all events that determine liability have occurred, the amount of the liability can be figured with reasonable accuracy, and economic performance takes place with respect to the expense. There are exceptions for recurring items and items involving transactions between related taxpayers described in section 267.

Except for certain home construction contracts and other real property small construction contracts, long-term contracts must generally be accounted for using the percentage of completion method described in section 460.

Dealers in securities must use the "mark-to-market" accounting method described in section 475. Under this method, any security that is inventory to the dealer must be included in inventory at its fair market value. Any security that is not inventory and that is held at the close of the tax year is treated as sold at its fair market value on the last business day of the tax year, and any gain or loss must be taken into account in determining gross income. The gain or loss taken into account is generally treated as ordinary gain or loss. For details, including exceptions, see section 475.

Generally, the corporation may change its method of accounting used to report taxable income (for income as a whole or for any material item) only by getting consent on **Form 3115,** Application for Change in Accounting Method. For more information, get **Pub. 538,** Accounting Periods and Methods.

Accounting Periods

Generally, an S corporation may not change its accounting period to a tax year that is not a permitted year. A "permitted year" is a calendar year or any other accounting period for which the corporation can establish to the satisfaction of the IRS that there is a business purpose for the tax year.

To change an accounting period, see Regulations section 1.442-1 and **Form 1128,** Application to Adopt, Change, or Retain a Tax Year. Also see Pub. 538.

Election of a tax year other than a required year.—Under the provisions of section 444, an S corporation may elect to have a tax year other than a permitted year, but only if the deferral period of the tax year is not longer than 3 months. This election is made by filing **Form 8716,** Election To Have a Tax Year Other Than a Required Tax Year.

An S corporation may not make or continue an election under section 444 if it is a member of a tiered structure, other than a tiered structure that consists entirely of partnerships and S corporations that have the same tax year. For the S corporation to have a section 444 election in effect, it must make the payments required by section 7519 and file **Form 8752,** Required Payment or Refund Under Section 7519.

A section 444 election ends if an S corporation changes its accounting period to a calendar year or some other permitted year, it willfully fails to comply with the requirements of section 7519, or its S election is terminated (unless it immediately becomes a personal service corporation). If the termination results in a short tax year, type or legibly print at the top of the first page of Form 1120S for the short tax year, "SECTION 444 ELECTION TERMINATED."

Rounding Off to Whole Dollars

You may round off cents to whole dollars on your return and accompanying schedules. To do so, drop amounts under 50 cents and increase amounts from 50 to 99 cents to the next higher dollar.

Recordkeeping

The corporation's records must be kept as long as they may be needed for the administration of any provision of the Internal Revenue Code. If the consolidated audit procedures of sections 6241 through 6245 apply to the corporation, records that support an item of income, deduction, or credit on the corporation's return usually must be kept for 3 years from the date the return is due or is filed, whichever is later. If the consolidated audit procedures do not apply, these records usually must be kept for 3 years from the date each shareholder's return is due or is filed, whichever is later. Keep records that verify the corporation's basis in property for as long as they are needed to figure the basis of the original or replacement property.

The corporation should also keep copies of any returns it has filed. They help in preparing future returns and in making computations when filing an amended return.

Depositary Method of Tax Payment

The corporation must pay the tax due in full no later than the 15th day of the 3rd month after the end of the tax year.

Deposit corporation income tax payments (and estimated tax payments) with **Form 8109,** Federal Tax Deposit Coupon. Do not submit deposits directly to an IRS office; otherwise, the corporation may have to pay a penalty. Mail or deliver the completed Form 8109 with the payment to a qualified depositary for Federal taxes or to the Federal Reserve bank (FRB) servicing your geographic area.

Make your checks or money orders payable to that depositary or FRB.

To help ensure proper crediting, write the corporation's employer identification number, the tax period to which the deposit applies, and "Form 1120S" on your check or money order. Be sure to darken the "1120" box on the coupon. These records of deposit will be sent to the IRS.

For more information on deposits, see the instructions in the coupon booklet (Form 8109) and **Pub. 583,** Starting a Business and Keeping Records.

Estimated Tax

Generally, the corporation must make estimated tax payments for the following taxes if the total of these taxes is $500 or more: **(a)** the tax on certain capital gains, **(b)** the tax on built-in gains, **(c)** the excess net passive income tax, and **(d)** the investment credit recapture tax.

The amount of estimated tax required to be paid annually is the lesser of **(a)** the total of the above taxes shown on the return for the tax year (or if no return is filed, the total of these taxes for the year); or **(b)** the sum of **(i)** the investment credit recapture tax and the built-in gains tax (or the tax on certain capital gains) shown on the return for the tax year (or if no return is filed, the total of these taxes for the year), and **(ii)** any excess net passive income tax shown on the corporation's return for the preceding tax year. If the preceding tax year was less than 12 months, the estimated tax must be determined under **(a)**.

The estimated tax is generally payable in four equal installments. However, the corporation may be able to lower the amount of one or more installments by using the annualized income installment method or adjusted seasonal installment method under section 6655(e).

For a calendar year corporation, the payments are due for 1996 by April 15, June 17, September 16, and December 16. For a fiscal year corporation, they are due by the 15th day of the 4th, 6th, 9th, and 12th months of the fiscal year.

The corporation must make the payments using the depositary method described above.

Interest and Penalties

Interest

Interest is charged on taxes not paid by the due date, even if an extension of time to file is granted. Interest is also charged from the due date (including extensions) to the date of payment on the failure to file penalty, the accuracy-related penalty, and the fraud penalty. The interest charge is figured at a rate determined under section 6621.

Late Filing of Return

A corporation that does not file its tax return by the due date, including extensions, may have to pay a penalty of 5% a month, or part of a month, up to a

Page 3

maximum of 25%, for each month the return is not filed. The penalty is imposed on the net amount due. The minimum penalty for filing a return more than 60 days late is the smaller of the tax due or $100. The penalty will not be imposed if the corporation can show that the failure to file on time was due to reasonable cause. If the failure is due to reasonable cause, attach an explanation to the return.

Late Payment of Tax

A corporation that does not pay the tax when due generally may have to pay a penalty of ½ of 1% a month or part of a month, up to a maximum of 25%, for each month the tax is not paid. The penalty is imposed on the net amount due.

The penalty will not be imposed if the corporation can show that failure to pay on time was due to reasonable cause.

Failure To Furnish Information Timely

Section 6037(b) requires an S corporation to furnish to each shareholder a copy of the information shown on Schedule K-1 (Form 1120S) that is attached to Form 1120S. Provide Schedule K-1 to each shareholder on or before the day on which the corporation files Form 1120S.

For each failure to furnish Schedule K-1 to a shareholder when due and each failure to include on Schedule K-1 all the information required to be shown (or the inclusion of incorrect information), a $50 penalty may be imposed with regard to each Schedule K-1 for which a failure occurs. If the requirement to report correct information is intentionally disregarded, each $50 penalty is increased to $100 or, if greater, 10% of the aggregate amount of items required to be reported. See sections 6722 and 6724 for more information.

The penalty will not be imposed if the corporation can show that not furnishing information timely was due to reasonable cause and not due to willful neglect.

Unresolved Tax Problems

The IRS has a Problem Resolution Program for taxpayers who have been unable to resolve their problems with the IRS. If the corporation has a tax problem it has been unable to resolve through normal channels, write to the corporation's local IRS District Director or call the corporation's local IRS office and ask for Problem Resolution assistance. Hearing-impaired persons who have access to TDD equipment may call 1-800-829-4059 to ask for help. The Problem Resolution office will ensure that your problem receives proper attention. Although the office cannot change the tax law or make technical decisions, it can help clear up problems that resulted from previous contacts.

Other Forms and Statements That May Be Required

● **Forms W-2** and **W-3,** Wage and Tax Statement; and Transmittal of Income and Tax Statements.

● **Form 720,** Quarterly Federal Excise Tax Return. Use Form 720 to report environmental excise taxes, communications and air transportation taxes, fuel taxes, luxury tax on passenger vehicles, manufacturers taxes, ship passenger tax, and certain other excise taxes.

Caution: *See* **Trust fund recovery penalty** *on page 5.*

● **Form 940** or **Form 940-EZ,** Employer's Annual Federal Unemployment (FUTA) Tax Return. The corporation may be liable for FUTA tax and may have to file Form 940 or 940-EZ if it paid wages of $1,500 or more in any calendar quarter during the calendar year (or the preceding calendar year) or one or more employees worked for the corporation for some part of a day in any 20 different weeks during the calendar year (or the preceding calendar year). A corporate officer who performs substantial services is considered an employee. Except as provided in section 3306(a), reasonable compensation for these services is subject to FUTA tax, no matter what the corporation calls the payments.

● **Form 941,** Employer's Quarterly Federal Tax Return. Employers must file this form quarterly to report income tax withheld on wages and employer and employee social security and Medicare taxes. A corporate officer who performs substantial services is considered an employee. Except as provided in sections 3121(a) and 3401(a), reasonable compensation for these services is subject to employer and employee social security and Medicare taxes and income tax withholding, no matter what the corporation calls the payments. Agricultural employers must file **Form 943,** Employer's Annual Tax Return for Agricultural Employees, instead of Form 941, to report income tax withheld and employer and employee social security and Medicare taxes on farmworkers.

Caution: *See* **Trust fund recovery penalty** *on page 5.*

● **Form 945,** Annual Return of Withheld Federal Income Tax. Use this form to report income tax withheld from nonpayroll payments, including pensions, annuities, IRAs, gambling winnings, and backup withholding.

Caution: *See* **Trust fund recovery penalty** *on page 5.*

● **Form 966,** Corporate Dissolution or Liquidation.

● **Forms 1042** and **1042-S,** Annual Withholding Tax Return for U.S. Source Income of Foreign Persons; and Foreign Person's U.S. Source Income Subject to Withholding. Use these forms to report and transmit withheld tax on payments made to nonresident alien individuals, foreign partnerships, or foreign corporations to the extent such payments constitute gross income from sources within the United

States (see sections 861 through 865). For more information, see sections 1441 and 1442, and **Pub. 515,** Withholding of Tax on Nonresident Aliens and Foreign Corporations.

● **Form 1096,** Annual Summary and Transmittal of U.S. Information Returns.

● **Form 1098,** Mortgage Interest Statement. Use this form to report the receipt from any individual of $600 or more of mortgage interest and points in the course of the corporation's trade or business.

● **Forms 1099-A, B, DIV, INT, MISC, OID, PATR, R,** and **S.** You may have to file these information returns to report abandonments; acquisitions through foreclosure; proceeds from broker and barter exchange transactions; certain dividends; interest payments; medical and dental health care payments; miscellaneous income payments; original issue discount; patronage dividends; distributions from pensions, annuities, retirement or profit-sharing plans, IRAs, insurance contracts, etc.; and proceeds from real estate transactions. Also use certain of these returns to report amounts that were received as a nominee on behalf of another person.

Use Form 1099-DIV to report actual dividends paid by the corporation. Only distributions from accumulated earnings and profits are classified as dividends. Do not issue Form 1099-DIV for dividends received by the corporation that are allocated to shareholders on line 4b of Schedule K-1.

For more information, see the separate **Instructions for Forms 1099, 1098, 5498, and W-2G.**

Note: *Every corporation must file Forms 1099-MISC if it makes payments of rents, commissions, or other fixed or determinable income (see section 6041) totaling $600 or more to any one person in the course of its trade or business during the calendar year.*

● **Form 5713,** International Boycott Report. Every corporation that had operations in, or related to, a "boycotting" country, company, or national of a country must file Form 5713. In addition, persons who participate in or cooperate with an international boycott may have to complete Schedule A or Schedule B and Schedule C of Form 5713 to figure their loss of the foreign tax credit, the deferral of earnings of a controlled foreign corporation, IC-DISC benefits, and FSC benefits.

● **Form 8264,** Application for Registration of a Tax Shelter. Tax shelter organizers must file Form 8264 to register tax shelters with the IRS for the purpose of receiving a tax shelter registration number.

● **Form 8271,** Investor Reporting of Tax Shelter Registration Number. Corporations that have acquired an interest in a tax shelter that is required to be registered use Form 8271 to report the tax shelter's registration number. Attach Form 8271 to any return on which a deduction, credit, loss, or other tax benefit attributable to a tax shelter is taken or any income attributable to a tax shelter is reported.

- **Form 8275,** Disclosure Statement. File Form 8275 to disclose items or positions, except those contrary to a regulation, that are not otherwise adequately disclosed on a tax return. The disclosure is made to avoid the parts of the accuracy-related penalty imposed for disregard of rules or substantial understatement of tax. Form 8275 is also used for disclosures relating to preparer penalties for understatements due to unrealistic positions or disregard of rules.

- **Form 8275-R,** Regulation Disclosure Statement, is used to disclose any item on a tax return for which a position has been taken that is contrary to Treasury regulations.

- **Form 8281,** Information Return for Publicly Offered Original Issue Discount Instruments. This form is used by issuers of publicly offered debt instruments having OID to provide the information required by section 1275(c).

- **Forms 8288** and **8288-A,** U.S. Withholding Tax Return for Dispositions by Foreign Persons of U.S. Real Property Interests; and Statement of Withholding on Dispositions by Foreign Persons of U.S. Real Property Interests. Use these forms to report and transmit withheld tax on the sale of U.S. real property by a foreign person. See section 1445 and the related regulations for additional information.

- **Form 8300,** Report of Cash Payments Over $10,000 Received in a Trade or Business. File this form to report the receipt of more than $10,000 in cash or foreign currency in one transaction (or a series of related transactions).

- **Form 8594,** Asset Acquisition Statement. Both the purchaser and seller of a group of assets constituting a trade or business must file this form if section 197 intangibles attach, or could attach, to such assets and if the purchaser's basis in the assets is determined only by the amount paid for the assets.

- **Form 8697,** Interest Computation Under the Look-Back Method for Completed Long-Term Contracts. Certain S corporations that are not closely held may have to file Form 8697. Form 8697 is used to figure the interest due or to be refunded under the look-back method of section 460(b)(2) on certain long-term contracts that are accounted for under either the percentage of completion-capitalized cost method or the percentage of completion method. Closely held corporations should see the instructions on page 22 for line 23, item 10, of Schedule K-1 for details on the Form 8697 information they must provide to their shareholders.

Stock ownership in foreign corporations.—If the corporation owned at least 5% in value of the outstanding stock of a foreign personal holding company, and the corporation was required to include in its gross income any undistributed foreign personal holding company income, attach the statement required by section 551(c).

A corporation may have to file **Form 5471,** Information Return of U.S. Persons With Respect to Certain Foreign Corporations, if any of the following applies:

1. It controls a foreign corporation.

2. It acquires, disposes of, or owns 5% or more in value of the outstanding stock of a foreign corporation.

3. It is a 10%-or-more shareholder of a foreign personal holding company.

4. It owns stock in a controlled foreign corporation for an uninterrupted period of 30 days or more during any tax year of the foreign corporation, and it owned that stock on the last day of that year.

Transfers to a corporation controlled by the transferor.—If a person receives stock of a corporation in exchange for property, and no gain or loss is recognized under section 351, the transferor and transferee must each attach to their tax returns the information required by Regulations section 1.351-3.

Trust fund recovery penalty.—This penalty may apply if certain excise, income, social security, and Medicare taxes that must be collected or withheld are not collected or withheld, or these taxes are not paid to the IRS. These taxes are generally reported on Forms 720, 941, 943, or 945. The trust fund recovery penalty may be imposed on all persons who are determined by the IRS to have been **responsible** for collecting, accounting for, and paying over these taxes, and who acted willfully in not doing so. The penalty is equal to the unpaid trust fund tax. See the instructions for Form 720, **Pub. 15 (Circular E),** Employer's Tax Guide, or **Pub. 51 (Circular A),** Agricultural Employer's Tax Guide, for more details, including the definition of responsible persons.

Attachments

Attach **Form 4136,** Credit for Federal Tax Paid on Fuels, after page 4, Form 1120S. Attach schedules in alphabetical order and other forms in numerical order after Form 4136.

To assist us in processing the return, **please complete every applicable entry space on Form 1120S and Schedule K-1.** If you attach statements, do not write "See attached" instead of completing the entry spaces on Form 1120S and Schedule K-1.

If you need more space on the forms or schedules, attach separate sheets. Use the same size and format as on the printed forms. **But show the totals on the printed forms.** Attach these separate sheets after all the schedules and forms. Be sure to put the corporation's name and employer identification number (EIN) on each sheet.

Amended Return

To correct an error on a Form 1120S already filed, file an amended Form 1120S and check box F(4). If the amended return results in a change to income, or a change in the distribution of any income or other information provided any shareholder, an amended Schedule K-1 (Form 1120S) must also be filed with the amended Form 1120S and given to that shareholder. Be sure to check box D(2) on each Schedule K-1 to indicate that it is an amended Schedule K-1.

Note: *If an S corporation does not meet the small S corporation exception under Temporary Regulations section 301.6241-1T or if it is a small S corporation that has made the election described in Temporary Regulations section 301.6241-1T(c)(2)(v), and it files an amended return, the amended return will be a request for administrative adjustment and the tax matters person must file Form 8082, Notice of Inconsistent Treatment or Amended Return (Administrative Adjustment Request (AAR)). See the temporary regulations under section 6241 for more information.*

A change to the corporation's Federal return may affect its state return. This includes changes made as the result of an IRS examination of Form 1120S. For more information, contact the state tax agency for the state in which the corporation's return was filed.

Passive Activity Limitations

In general, section 469 limits the amount of losses, deductions, and credits that shareholders may claim from "passive activities." The passive activity limitations do not apply to the corporation. Instead, they apply to each shareholder's share of any income or loss and credit attributable to a passive activity. Because the treatment of each shareholder's share of corporate income or loss and credit depends upon the nature of the activity that generated it, the corporation must report income or loss and credits separately for each activity.

The instructions below (pages 5 through 9) and the instructions for Schedules K and K-1 (pages 15 through 22) explain the applicable passive activity limitation rules and specify the type of information the corporation must provide to its shareholders for each activity. If the corporation had more than one activity, it must report information for each activity on an attachment to Schedules K and K-1.

Generally, passive activities include **(a)** activities that involve the conduct of a trade or business in which the shareholder does not materially participate and **(b)** any rental activity (defined on page 6) even if the shareholder materially participates. For exceptions, see **Activities That Are Not Passive Activities** on page 6. The level of each shareholder's participation in an activity must be determined by the shareholder.

The passive activity rules provide that losses and credits from passive activities can be generally be applied only against income and tax from passive activities. Thus, passive losses and credits cannot be applied against income from salaries, wages, professional fees, or a business in which the shareholder materially participates; against "portfolio income"

Page 5

(defined on page 7); or against the tax related to any of these types of income.

Special rules require that net income from certain activities that would otherwise be treated as passive income must be recharacterized as nonpassive income for purposes of the passive activity limitations.

To allow each shareholder to apply the passive activity limitations at the individual level, the corporation must report income or loss and credits separately for each of the following: trade or business activities, rental real estate activities, rental activities other than rental real estate, and portfolio income.

Activities That Are Not Passive Activities

Passive activities do not include:

1. Trade or business activities in which the shareholder materially participated for the tax year.

2. Any rental real estate activity in which the shareholder materially participated and met both of the following conditions for the tax year:

a. More than half of the personal services the shareholder performed in trades or businesses were performed in real property trades or businesses in which he or she materially participated, and

b. The shareholder performed more than 750 hours of services in real property trades or businesses in which he or she materially participated.

For purposes of this rule, each interest in rental real estate is a separate activity unless the shareholder elects to treat all interests in rental real estate as one activity.

If the shareholder is married filing jointly, either the shareholder or his or her spouse must separately meet both of the above conditions, without taking into account services performed by the other spouse.

A real property trade or business is any real property development, redevelopment, construction, reconstruction, acquisition, conversion, rental, operation, management, leasing, or brokerage trade or business. Services the shareholder performed as an employee are not treated as performed in a real property trade or business unless he or she owned more than 5% of the stock in the employer.

3. The rental of a dwelling unit used by a shareholder for personal purposes during the year for more than the greater of 14 days or 10% of the number of days that the residence was rented at fair rental value.

4. An activity of trading personal property for the account of owners of interests in the activity. See Temporary Regulations section 1.469-1T(e)(6).

Note: *The section 469(c)(3) exception for a working interest in oil and gas properties is not applicable to an S corporation because state law generally limits the liability of corporate shareholders.*

Trade or Business Activities

A trade or business activity is an activity (other than a rental activity or an activity treated as incidental to an activity of holding property for investment) that—

1. Involves the conduct of a trade or business (within the meaning of section 162),

2. Is conducted in anticipation of starting a trade or business, or

3. Involves research or experimental expenditures deductible under section 174 (or that would be if you chose to deduct rather than capitalize them).

If the shareholder does not materially participate in the activity, a trade or business activity of the corporation is a passive activity for the shareholder.

Each shareholder must determine if he or she materially participated in an activity. As a result, while the corporation's overall trade or business income (loss) is reported on page 1 of Form 1120S, the specific income and deductions from each separate trade or business activity must be reported on attachments to Form 1120S. Similarly, while each shareholder's allocable share of the corporation's overall trade or business income (loss) is reported on line 1 of Schedule K-1, each shareholder's allocable share of the income and deductions from each trade or business activity must be reported on attachments to each Schedule K-1. See **Passive Activity Reporting Requirements** on page 8 for more information.

Rental Activities

Generally, except as noted below, if the gross income from an activity consists of amounts paid principally for the use of real or personal tangible property held by the corporation, the activity is a rental activity.

There are several exceptions to this general rule. Under these exceptions, an activity involving the use of real or personal tangible property is not a rental activity if **(a)** the average period of customer use (defined below) for such property is 7 days or less; **(b)** the average period of customer use for such property is 30 days or less and significant personal services (defined below) are provided by or on behalf of the corporation; **(c)** extraordinary personal services (defined below) are provided by or on behalf of the corporation; **(d)** rental of the property is treated as incidental to a nonrental activity of the corporation under Temporary Regulations section 1.469-1T(e)(3)(vi) and Regulations section 1.469-1(e)(3)(vi); or **(e)** the corporation customarily makes the property available during defined business hours for nonexclusive use by various customers.

In addition, if the corporation provides property for use in a nonrental activity of a partnership in its capacity as an owner of an interest in such partnership, the provision of the property is not a rental activity. Consequently, the corporation's distributive share of income from the activity is not income from a rental activity. A guaranteed payment described in section 707(c) is not income from a rental

activity under any circumstances. Whether the corporation provides property used in an activity of a partnership in the corporation's capacity as an owner of an interest in the partnership is based on all the facts and circumstances.

Average period of customer use.— Figure the average period of customer use of property by dividing the total number of days in all rental periods by the number of rentals during the tax year. If the activity involves renting more than one class of property, multiply the average period of customer use of each class by the ratio of the gross rental income from that class to the activity's total gross rental income. The activity's average period of customer use equals the sum of these class-by-class average periods weighted by gross income. See Regulations section 1.469-1(e)(3)(iii).

Significant personal services.—Personal services include only services performed by individuals. In determining whether personal services are significant personal services, consider all of the relevant facts and circumstances. Relevant facts and circumstances include how often the services are provided, the type and amount of labor required to perform the services, and the value of the services in relation to the amount charged for the use of the property.

The following services are not considered in determining whether personal services are significant: **(a)** services necessary to permit the lawful use of the rental property; **(b)** services performed in connection with improvements or repairs to the rental property that extend the useful life of the property substantially beyond the average rental period; and **(c)** services provided in connection with the use of any improved real property that are similar to those commonly provided in connection with long-term rentals of high-grade commercial or residential property (e.g., cleaning and maintenance of common areas, routine repairs, trash collection, elevator service, and security at entrances).

Extraordinary personal services.— Services provided in connection with making rental property available for customer use are extraordinary personal services only if the services are performed by individuals and the customers' use of the rental property is incidental to their receipt of the services. For example, a patient's use of a hospital room generally is incidental to the care that the patient receives from the hospital's medical staff. Similarly, a student's use of a dormitory room in a boarding school is incidental to the personal services provided by the school's teaching staff.

Rental property incidental to a nonrental activity.—An activity is not a rental activity if the rental of the property is incidental to a nonrental activity, such as the activity of holding property for investment, a trade or business activity, or the activity of dealing in property.

Rental property is incidental to an activity of holding property for investment if the main purpose for holding the property is to realize a gain from the appreciation of the property and the gross rental income from such property for the tax year is less than 2% of the smaller of the property's unadjusted basis or its fair market value.

Rental property is incidental to a trade or business activity if **(a)** the corporation owns an interest in the trade or business at all times during the year; **(b)** the rental property was mainly used in the trade or business activity during the tax year or during at least 2 of the 5 preceding tax years; and **(c)** the gross rental income from the property is less than 2% of the smaller of the property's unadjusted basis or its fair market value.

The sale or exchange of property that is also rented during the tax year (where the gain or loss is recognized) is treated as incidental to the activity of dealing in property if, at the time of the sale or exchange, the property was held primarily for sale to customers in the ordinary course of the corporation's trade or business.

See Temporary Regulations section 1.469-1T(e)(3) and Regulations section 1.469-1(e)(3) for more information on the definition of rental activities for purposes of the passive activity limitations.

Reporting of rental activities.—In reporting the corporation's income or losses and credits from rental activities, the corporation must separately report **(a)** rental real estate activities and **(b)** rental activities other than rental real estate activities.

Shareholders who actively participate in a rental real estate activity may be able to deduct part or all of their rental real estate losses (and the deduction equivalent of rental real estate credits) against income (or tax) from nonpassive activities. Generally, the combined amount of rental real estate losses and the deduction equivalent of rental real estate credits from all sources (including rental real estate activities not held through the corporation) that may be claimed is limited to $25,000.

Report rental real estate activity income (loss) on **Form 8825,** Rental Real Estate Income and Expenses of a Partnership or an S Corporation, and on line 2 of Schedules K and K-1 rather than on page 1 of Form 1120S. Report credits related to rental real estate activities on lines 12c and 12d and low-income housing credits on line 12b of Schedules K and K-1.

Report income (loss) from rental activities other than rental real estate on line 3 and credits related to rental activities other than rental real estate on line 12e of Schedules K and K-1.

Portfolio Income

Generally, portfolio income includes all gross income, other than income derived in the ordinary course of a trade or business, that is attributable to interest; dividends; royalties; income from a real estate investment trust, a regulated investment company, a real estate mortgage investment conduit, a common trust fund, a controlled foreign corporation, a qualified

electing fund, or a cooperative; income from the disposition of property that produces income of a type defined as portfolio income; and income from the disposition of property held for investment.

Solely for purposes of the preceding paragraph, gross income derived in the ordinary course of a trade or business includes **(and portfolio income, therefore, does not include)** only the following types of income: **(a)** interest income on loans and investments made in the ordinary course of a trade or business of lending money; **(b)** interest on accounts receivable arising from the performance of services or the sale of property in the ordinary course of a trade or business of performing such services or selling such property, but only if credit is customarily offered to customers of the business; **(c)** income from investments made in the ordinary course of a trade or business of furnishing insurance or annuity contracts or reinsuring risks underwritten by insurance companies; **(d)** income or gain derived in the ordinary course of an activity of trading or dealing in any property if such activity constitutes a trade or business (unless the dealer held the property for investment at any time before such income or gain is recognized); **(e)** royalties derived by the taxpayer in the ordinary course of a trade or business of licensing intangible property; **(f)** amounts included in the gross income of a patron of a cooperative by reason of any payment or allocation to the patron based on patronage occurring with respect to a trade or business of the patron; and **(g)** other income identified by the IRS as income derived by the taxpayer in the ordinary course of a trade or business.

See Temporary Regulations section 1.469-2T(c)(3) for more information on portfolio income.

Report portfolio income on line 4 of Schedules K and K-1, rather than on page 1 of Form 1120S.

Report expenses related to portfolio income on line 9 of Schedules K and K-1.

Grouping Activities

Generally, one or more trade or business activities or rental activities may be treated as a single activity if the activities make up an appropriate economic unit for measurement of gain or loss under the passive activity rules. Whether activities make up an appropriate economic unit depends on all the relevant facts and circumstances. The factors given the greatest weight in determining whether activities make up an appropriate economic unit are—

1. Similarities and differences in types of trades or businesses,

2. The extent of common control,

3. The extent of common ownership,

4. Geographical location, and

5. Reliance between or among the activities.

Example: The corporation has a significant ownership interest in a bakery and a movie theater in Baltimore and in a bakery and a movie theater in Philadelphia.

Depending on the relevant facts and circumstances, there may be more than one reasonable method for grouping the corporation's activities. For instance, the following groupings may or may not be permissible: a single activity, a movie theater activity and a bakery activity, a Baltimore activity and a Philadelphia activity, or four separate activities.

Once the corporation chooses a grouping under these rules, it must continue using that grouping in later tax years unless a material change in the facts and circumstances makes it clearly inappropriate.

The IRS may regroup the corporation's activities if the corporation's grouping fails to reflect one or more appropriate economic units and one of the primary purposes for the grouping is to avoid the passive activity limitations.

Limitation on grouping certain activities.—The following activities may not be grouped together—

1. A rental activity with a trade or business activity unless the activities being grouped together make up an appropriate economic unit, and

a. The rental activity is insubstantial relative to the trade or business activity or vice versa, or

b. Each owner of the trade or business activity has the same proportionate ownership interest in the rental activity. If so, the portion of the rental activity involving the rental of property to be used in the trade or business activity may be grouped with the trade or business activity.

2. An activity involving the rental of real property with an activity involving the rental of personal property (except for personal property provided in connection with real property), or vice versa.

3. Any activity with another activity in a different type of business and in which the corporation holds an interest as a limited partner or as a limited entrepreneur (as defined in section 464(e)(2)) if that other activity engages in holding, producing, or distributing motion picture films or videotapes; farming; leasing section 1245 property; or exploring for (or exploiting) oil and gas resources or geothermal deposits.

Activities conducted through partnerships.—Once a partnership determines its activities under these rules, the corporation as a partner may use these rules to group those activities with each other, with activities conducted directly by the corporation, and with activities conducted through other partnerships. The corporation may not treat as separate activities those activities grouped together by the partnership.

Recharacterization of Passive Income

Under Temporary Regulations section 1.469-2T(f) and Regulations section 1.469-2(f), net passive income from certain passive activities must be treated as nonpassive income. Net passive income is the excess of an activity's passive activity gross income over its passive activity

Page 7

deductions (current year deductions and prior year unallowed losses).

Income from the following six sources is subject to recharacterization. Note that any net passive income recharacterized as nonpassive income is treated as investment income for purposes of figuring investment interest expense limitations if it is from **(a)** an activity of renting substantially nondepreciable property from an equity-financed lending activity or **(b)** an activity related to an interest in a pass-through entity that licenses intangible property.

1. Significant participation passive activities.—A significant participation passive activity is any trade or business activity in which the shareholder both participates for more than 100 hours during the tax year and does not materially participate. Because each shareholder must determine his or her level of participation, the corporation will not be able to identify significant participation passive activities.

2. Certain nondepreciable rental property activities.—Net passive income from a rental activity is nonpassive income if less than 30% of the unadjusted basis of the property used or held for use by customers in the activity is subject to depreciation under section 167.

3. Passive equity-financed lending activities.—If the corporation has net income from a passive equity-financed lending activity, the smaller of the net passive income or equity-financed interest income from the activity is nonpassive income.

Note: *The amount of income from the activities in items 1 through 3 above that any shareholder will be required to recharacterize as nonpassive income may be limited under Temporary Regulations section 1.469-2T(f)(8). Because the corporation will not have information regarding all of a shareholder's activities, it must identify all corporate activities meeting the definitions in items 2 and 3 as activities that may be subject to recharacterization.*

4. Rental activities incidental to a development activity.—Net rental activity income is nonpassive income for a shareholder if all of the following apply: **(a)** the corporation recognizes gain from the sale, exchange, or other disposition of the rental property during the tax year; **(b)** the use of the item of property in the rental activity started less than 12 months before the date of disposition (the use of an item of rental property begins on the first day on which (i) the corporation owns an interest in the property, (ii) substantially all of the property is either rented or held out for rent and ready to be rented, and (iii) no significant value-enhancing services remain to be performed); and **(c)** the shareholder materially participated or significantly participated for any tax year in an activity that involved the performance of services for the purpose of enhancing the value of the property (or any other item of property, if the basis of the property disposed of is determined in whole or in

part by reference to the basis of that item of property). Net rental activity income is the excess of passive activity gross income from renting or disposing of property over passive activity deductions (current year deductions and prior year unallowed losses) that are reasonably allocable to the rented property.

Because the corporation cannot determine a shareholder's level of participation, the corporation must identify net income from property described in items **(a)** and **(b)** above as income that may be subject to recharacterization.

5. Activities involving property rented to a nonpassive activity.—If a taxpayer rents property to a trade or business activity in which the taxpayer materially participates, the taxpayer's net rental activity income (defined above) from the property is nonpassive income.

6. Acquisition of an interest in a pass-through entity that licenses intangible property.—Generally, net royalty income from intangible property is nonpassive income if the taxpayer acquired an interest in the pass-through entity after it created the intangible property or performed substantial services or incurred substantial costs in developing or marketing the intangible property. Net royalty income is the excess of passive activity gross income from licensing or transferring any right in intangible property over passive activity deductions (current year deductions and prior year unallowed losses) that are reasonably allocable to the intangible property.

See Temporary Regulations section 1.469-2T(f)(7)(iii) for exceptions to this rule.

Passive Activity Reporting Requirements

To allow shareholders to correctly apply the passive activity loss and credit limitation rules, any corporation that carries on more than one activity must:

1. Provide an attachment for each activity conducted through the corporation that identifies the type of activity conducted (trade or business, rental real estate, rental activity other than rental real estate, or investment).

2. On the attachment for each activity, provide a schedule, using the same line numbers as shown on Schedule K-1, detailing the net income (loss), credits, and all items required to be separately stated under section 1366(a)(1) from each trade or business activity, from each rental real estate activity, from each rental activity other than a rental real estate activity, and from investments.

3. Identify the net income (loss) and the shareholder's share of corporation interest expense from each activity of renting a dwelling unit that any shareholder uses for personal purposes during the year for more than the greater of 14 days or 10% of the number of days that the residence is rented at fair rental value.

4. Identify the net income (loss) and the shareholder's share of interest expense from each activity of trading personal

property conducted through the corporation.

5. For any gain (loss) from the disposition of an interest in an activity or of an interest in property used in an activity (including dispositions before 1987 from which gain is being recognized after 1986):

a. Identify the activity in which the property was used at the time of disposition;

b. If the property was used in more than one activity during the 12 months preceding the disposition, identify the activities in which the property was used and the adjusted basis allocated to each activity; and

c. For gains only, if the property was substantially appreciated at the time of the disposition and the applicable holding period specified in Regulations section 1.469-2(c)(2)(iii)(A) was not satisfied, identify the amount of the nonpassive gain and indicate whether or not the gain is investment income under Regulations section 1.469-2(c)(2)(iii)(F).

6. Specify the amount of gross portfolio income, the interest expense properly allocable to portfolio income, and expenses other than interest expense that are clearly and directly allocable to portfolio income.

7. Identify the ratable portion of any section 481 adjustment (whether a net positive or a net negative adjustment) allocable to each corporate activity.

8. Identify any gross income from sources specifically excluded from passive activity gross income, including:

a. Income from intangible property, if the shareholder is an individual whose personal efforts significantly contributed to the creation of the property;

b. Income from state, local, or foreign income tax refunds; and

c. Income from a covenant not to compete, if the shareholder is an individual who contributed the covenant to the corporation.

9. Identify any deductions that are not passive activity deductions.

10. If the corporation makes a full or partial disposition of its interest in another entity, identify the gain (loss) allocable to each activity conducted through the entity, and the gain allocable to a passive activity that would have been recharacterized as nonpassive gain had the corporation disposed of its interest in property used in the activity (because the property was substantially appreciated at the time of the disposition, and the gain represented more than 10% of the shareholder's total gain from the disposition).

11. Identify the following items that may be subject to the recharacterization rules under Temporary Regulations section 1.469-2T(f) and Regulations section 1.469-2(f):

a. Net income from an activity of renting substantially nondepreciable property;

b. The smaller of equity-financed interest income or net passive income from an equity-financed lending activity;

c. Net rental activity income from property developed (by the shareholder or the corporation), rented, and sold within 12 months after the rental of the property commenced;

d. Net rental activity income from the rental of property by the corporation to a trade or business activity in which the shareholder had an interest (either directly or indirectly); and

e. Net royalty income from intangible property if the shareholder acquired the shareholder's interest in the corporation after the corporation created the intangible property or performed substantial services or incurred substantial costs in developing or marketing the intangible property.

12. Identify separately the credits from each activity conducted by or through the corporation.

Specific Instructions

General Information

Name, Address, and Employer Identification Number

Use the label on the postcard that was mailed to the corporation. Cross out any errors and print the correct information on the label.

Name.—If the corporation did not receive a label, print or type the corporation's true name (as set forth in the corporate charter or other legal document creating it).

Address.—Include the suite, room, or other unit number after the street address. If a preaddressed label is used, please include the information on the label. If the Post Office does not deliver to the street address and the corporation has a P.O. box, show the box number instead of the street address.

If the corporation changes its mailing address after filing its return, it can notify the IRS by filing **Form 8822,** Change of Address.

Employer identification number (EIN).— Show the correct EIN in Item C on page 1 of Form 1120S.

Item B—Business Code No.

See **Codes for Principal Business Activity** on page 24 of these instructions.

Item E—Total Assets

Enter the corporation's total assets at the end of the tax year, as determined by the accounting method regularly used in maintaining the corporation's books and records. If there were no assets at the end of the tax year, enter the total assets as of the beginning of the tax year.

Item F—Initial Return, Final Return, Change in Address, and Amended Return

If this is the corporation's first return, check box F(1). If the corporation has ceased to exist, check box F(2). Also check box D(1) on each Schedule K-1 to indicate that it is a final Schedule K-1.

Indicate a change in address by checking box F(3). If this amends a previously filed return, check box F(4). If Schedules K-1 are also being amended, check box D(2) on each Schedule K-1.

Item G—Consolidated Audit Procedures

With certain exceptions, the tax treatment of S corporation items is determined at the corporate level in a consolidated audit proceeding, rather than in separate proceedings with individual shareholders. Check the box for item G if any of the following apply.

● The S corporation had more than five shareholders at any time during the tax year (for this purpose a husband and wife, and their estates, are treated as one shareholder).

● Any shareholder was other than a natural person or estate.

● The small S corporation (five or fewer shareholders) has elected as provided in Temporary Regulations section 301.6241-1T(c)(2)(v) to be subject to the rules for consolidated proceedings.

Note: The S corporation does not make the section 301.6241-1T(c)(2)(v) election when it checks the box for item G. This election must be made separately.

For more information on the consolidated audit procedures for S corporations, see sections 6241 through 6245, Temporary Regulations section 301.6241-1T, and **Pub. 556,** Examination of Returns, Appeal Rights, and Claims for Refund.

Income

Caution: Report only trade or business activity income or loss on lines 1a through 6. ***Do not report rental activity income or portfolio income or loss on these lines.*** *(See the instructions on* **Passive Activity Limitations** *beginning on page 5 for definitions of rental income and portfolio income.) Rental activity income and portfolio income are reported on Schedules K and K-1 (rental real estate activities are also reported on Form 8825).*

Do not include any tax-exempt income on lines 1 through 5. A corporation that receives any exempt income other than interest, or holds any property or engages in an activity that produces exempt income, reports the amount of this income on line 18 of Schedules K and K-1.

Report tax-exempt interest income, including exempt-interest dividends received as a shareholder in a mutual fund or other regulated investment company, on line 17 of Schedules K and K-1.

See **Deductions** on page 10 for information on how to report expenses related to tax-exempt income.

If the S corporation has had debt discharged resulting from a title 11 bankruptcy proceeding, or while insolvent, see **Form 982,** Reduction of Tax Attributes Due to Discharge of Indebtedness, and **Pub. 908,** Tax Information on Bankruptcy.

Line 1—Gross Receipts or Sales

Enter gross receipts or sales from all trade or business operations except those you report on lines 4 and 5. For reporting advance payments, see Regulations section 1.451-5. To report income from long-term contracts, see section 460.

Installment sales.—Generally, the installment method cannot be used for dealer dispositions of property. A dealer disposition is any disposition of personal property by a person who regularly sells or otherwise disposes of property of the same type on the installment plan or any disposition of real property held for sale to customers in the ordinary course of the taxpayer's trade or business. The disposition of property used or produced in the farming business is not included as a dealer disposition. See section 453(l) for details and exceptions.

Enter on line 1a the gross profit on collections from installment sales for any of the following:

● Dealer dispositions of property before March 1, 1986.

● Dispositions of property used or produced in the trade or business of farming.

● Certain dispositions of timeshares and residential lots reported under the installment method.

Attach a schedule showing the following information for the current and the 3 preceding years: **(a)** gross sales, **(b)** cost of goods sold, **(c)** gross profits, **(d)** percentage of gross profits to gross sales, **(e)** amount collected, and **(f)** gross profit on the amount collected.

Line 2—Cost of Goods Sold

See the instructions for Schedule A.

Line 4—Net Gain (Loss) From Form 4797

Caution: Include only ordinary gains or losses from the sale, exchange, or involuntary conversion of assets used in a trade or business activity. Ordinary gains or losses from the sale, exchange, or involuntary conversions of assets used in rental activities are reported separately on Schedule K as part of the net income (loss) from the rental activity in which the property was used.

A corporation that is a partner in a partnership must include on **Form 4797,** Sales of Business Property, its share of ordinary gains (losses) from sales, exchanges, or involuntary or compulsory conversions (other than casualties or thefts) of the partnership's trade or business assets.

Do not include any recapture of the section 179 expense deduction. See the instructions on page 21 for Schedule K-1, line 23, item 3, and the Instructions for Form 4797 for more information.

Line 5—Other Income (Loss)

Enter on line 5 trade or business income (loss) that is not included on lines 1a

Page 9

resulted if the property were sold at its fair market value.

The reduction for the long-term capital gain applies to:

• Contributions of tangible personal property for use by an exempt organization for a purpose or function unrelated to the basis for its exemption, and

• Contributions of any property to or for the use of certain private foundations. See section 170(e) and Regulations section 1.170A-4.

For special rules for contributions of inventory and other property to certain organizations, see section 170(e)(3) and Regulations section 1.170A-4A.

Charitable contributions of scientific property used for research.—A corporation (other than a personal holding company or a service organization) can receive a larger deduction for contributing scientific property used for research to an institution of higher education. For more details, see section 170(e).

Contributions to organizations conducting lobbying activities.—Contributions made to an organization that conducts lobbying activities are not deductible if:

• The lobbying activities relate to matters of direct financial interest to the donor's trade or business, and

• The principal purpose of the contribution was to avoid Federal income tax by obtaining a deduction for activities that would have been nondeductible under the lobbying expense rules if conducted directly by the donor.

Line 20

Depreciation

Besides depreciation, include on line 20 the part of the cost that the corporation elected to expense under section 179 for certain tangible property placed in service during tax year 1995 or carried over from 1994. See **Form 4562,** Depreciation and Amortization, and its instructions.

Line 22 (Form 1120 only)

Depletion

See sections 613 and 613A for percentage depletion rates applicable to natural deposits. Also, see section 291 for the limitation on the depletion deduction for iron ore and coal (including lignite).

Foreign intangible drilling costs and foreign exploration and development costs must either be added to the corporation's basis for cost depletion purposes or be deducted ratably over a 10-year period. See sections 263(i), 616, and 617 for details.

Attach **Form T (Timber),** Forest Activities Schedules, if a deduction for depletion of timber is taken.

Line 24 (Form 1120 only)

Pension, Profit-Sharing, etc., Plans

Enter the deduction for contributions to qualified pension, profit-sharing, or other funded deferred compensation plans.

Employers who maintain such a plan generally must file one of the forms listed below, even if the plan is not a qualified plan under the Internal Revenue Code. The filing requirement applies even if the corporation does not claim a deduction for the current tax year. There are penalties for failure to file these forms on time and for overstating the pension plan deduction. See sections 6652(e) and 6662(f).

Form 5500.—File this form for each plan with 100 or more participants.

Form 5500-C/R.—File this form for each plan with fewer than 100 participants.

Form 5500-EZ.—File this form for a one-participant plan. The term "one-participant plan" also means a plan that covers the owner and his or her spouse, or a plan that covers partners in a business partnership (or the partners and their spouses).

Line 25 (Form 1120 only)

Employee Benefit Programs

Enter contributions to employee benefit programs not claimed elsewhere on the return (e.g., insurance, health and welfare programs) that are not an incidental part of a pension, profit-sharing, etc., plan included on line 24.

Line 26, Form 1120 (Line 22, Form 1120-A)

Other Deductions

Note: *Do not deduct fines or penalties paid to a government for violating any law.*

Attach a schedule, listing by type and amount, all allowable deductions that are not deductible elsewhere on Form 1120 or Form 1120-A. Form 1120-A filers should include amounts described in the instructions above for lines 22, 24, and 25 of Form 1120. Enter the total on line 26, Form 1120 (line 22, Form 1120-A).

Include on this line the deduction for amortization of pollution control facilities, organization expenses, etc. See Form 4562.

Also include ordinary losses from trade or business activities of a partnership (from Schedule K-1 (Form 1065), line 1).

A corporation may deduct dividends it pays in cash on stock held by an employee stock ownership plan. However, a deduction may only be taken if, according to the plan, the dividends are:

• Paid in cash directly to the plan participants or beneficiaries;

• Paid to the plan, which distributes them in cash to the plan participants or their beneficiaries no later than 90 days after the end of the plan year in which the dividends are paid; or

• Used to make payments on a loan described in section 404(a)(9).

See section 404(k) for more details and the limitation on certain dividends.

Generally, a deduction may not be taken for any amount that is allocable to a class of exempt income. See section 265(b) for exceptions.

Meals, travel, and entertainment.—Generally, the corporation can deduct only 50% of the amount otherwise allowable for meals and entertainment expenses paid or incurred in its trade or business. Also, meals must not be lavish or extravagant; a bona fide business discussion must occur during, immediately before, or immediately after the meal; and an employee of the corporation must be present at the meal. See section 274(k)(2) for exceptions. If the corporation claims a deduction for unallowable meal expenses, it may have to pay a penalty.

Additional limitations apply to deductions for gifts, skybox rentals, luxury water travel, convention expenses, and entertainment tickets. For details, see section 274 and **Pub. 463,** Travel, Entertainment, and Gift Expenses.

No deduction is allowed for dues paid or incurred for membership in any club organized for business, pleasure, recreation, or other social purpose. This includes country clubs, golf and athletic clubs, airline and hotel clubs, and clubs operated to provide meals under conditions favorable to business discussion. But it does not include civic or public service organizations, professional organizations (such as bar and medical associations), business leagues, trade associations, chambers of commerce, boards of trade, and real estate boards, unless a principal purpose of the organization is to entertain or provide entertainment facilities for members or their guests.

Also, no deduction is allowed for travel expenses paid or incurred for a spouse, dependent, or other individual accompanying an officer or employee of the corporation on business travel, unless that spouse, dependent, or other individual is an employee of the corporation and the travel is for a bona fide business purpose and would otherwise be deductible by that person.

Generally, a corporation can deduct all other ordinary and necessary travel and entertainment expenses paid or incurred in its trade or business. However, it cannot deduct an expense paid or incurred for a facility (such as a yacht or hunting lodge) used for an activity that is usually considered entertainment, amusement, or recreation.

Note: *The corporation may be able to deduct otherwise nondeductible meals, travel, and entertainment expenses if the amounts are treated as compensation and reported on Form W-2 for an employee or on Form 1099-MISC for an independent contractor.*

Deduction for clean-fuel vehicles and certain refueling property.—Section 179A allows a deduction for part of the cost of qualified clean-fuel vehicle property and qualified clean-fuel vehicle refueling property placed in service after June 30, 1993. For more information, see Pub. 535.

Lobbying expenses.—Generally, lobbying expenses are not deductible. These expenses include amounts paid or incurred in connection with influencing Federal or state legislation (but not local legislation), or amounts paid or incurred in connection

Page 10

with any communication with certain Federal executive branch officials in an attempt to influence the official actions or positions of the officials. See Regulations section 1.162-29 for the definition of "influencing legislation." If certain in-house lobbying expenditures do not exceed $2,000, they are deductible. Dues and other similar amounts paid to certain tax-exempt organizations may not be deductible. See section 162(e)(3). For information on contributions to charitable organizations that conduct lobbying activities, see the instructions for line 19. For more information on lobbying expenses, see section 162(e).

Line 28, Form 1120
(Line 24, Form 1120-A)

Taxable Income Before NOL Deduction and Special Deductions

At-risk rules.—Generally, special at-risk rules under section 465 apply to closely held corporations (see **Passive activity limitations** on page 8) engaged in any activity as a trade or business or for the production of income. These corporations may have to adjust the amount on line 28, Form 1120, or line 24, Form 1120-A. (See below.)

But the at-risk rules do not apply to:

● Holding real property placed in service by the taxpayer before 1987;

● Equipment leasing under sections 465(c)(4), (5), and (6); or

● Any qualifying business of a qualified corporation under section 465(c)(7).

However, the at-risk rules do apply to the holding of mineral property.

If the at-risk rules apply, adjust the amount on this line for any section 465(d) losses. These losses are limited to the amount for which the corporation is at risk for each separate activity at the close of the tax year. If the corporation is involved in one or more activities, any of which incurs a loss for the year, report the losses for each activity separately. Attach **Form 6198,** At-Risk Limitations, showing the amount at risk and gross income and deductions for the activities with the losses.

If the corporation sells or otherwise disposes of an asset or its interest (either total or partial) in an activity to which the at-risk rules apply, determine the net profit or loss from the activity by combining the gain or loss on the sale or disposition with the profit or loss from the activity. If the corporation has a net loss, it may be limited because of the at-risk rules.

Treat any loss from an activity not allowed for the tax year as a deduction allocable to the activity in the next tax year.

Line 29a, Form 1120
(Line 25a, Form 1120-A)

Net Operating Loss Deduction

A corporation may use the net operating loss (NOL) incurred in one tax year to reduce its taxable income in another year. Generally, a corporation may carry an NOL back to each of the 3 years preceding the year of the loss and then carry any remaining amount over to each of the 15 years following the year of the loss (but Form 1120 filers see **Exceptions to carryback rules** below). Enter on line 29a (line 25a, Form 1120-A), the total NOL carryovers from prior tax years, but do not enter more than the corporation's taxable income (after special deductions). An NOL deduction cannot be taken in a year in which the corporation has a negative taxable income. Attach a schedule showing the computation of the NOL deduction. Form 1120 filers must also complete question 15 on Schedule K.

For details on the NOL deduction, get **Pub. 536,** Net Operating Losses.

Carryback and carryover rules.—Generally, an NOL first must be carried back to the third tax year preceding the year of the loss. To carry back the loss and obtain a quick refund of taxes, use **Form 1139,** Corporation Application for Tentative Refund. Form 1139 must be filed within 12 months after the close of the tax year of the loss. See section 6411 for details. Do not attach Form 1139 to the corporation's income tax return. Mail it in a separate envelope to the service center where the corporation files its income tax return.

For carryback claims filed later than 12 months after the close of the tax year of the loss, file **Form 1120X,** Amended U.S. Corporation Income Tax Return, instead of Form 1139.

After the corporation applies the NOL to the first tax year to which it may be carried, the taxable income of that year is modified (as described in section 172(b)) to determine how much of the remaining loss may be carried to other years. See section 172(b) and the related regulations for details.

Special rules apply when an ownership change occurs (i.e., for any tax year ending after a post-1986 ownership change, the amount of the taxable income of a loss corporation that can be offset by pre-change NOL carryovers is limited). See section 382 and the related regulations. Also see Temporary Regulations section 1.382-2T(a)(2)(ii), which requires that a loss corporation file an information statement with its income tax return for each tax year that it is a loss corporation and certain shifts in ownership occurred. Also see Regulations section 1.382-6(b) for details on how to make the closing-of-the-books election.

See section 384 for the limitation on the use of preacquistion losses of one corporation to offset recognized built-in gains of another corporation.

Exceptions to carryback rules (Form 1120 filers only).—A corporation may make an irrevocable election to forego the carryback period and instead carry the NOL over to each of the 15 years following the year of the loss. To make this election, check the box in question 14 on Schedule K. The return must be timely filed (including extensions).

Different carryback periods apply for certain losses. The part of an NOL that is attributable to a specified liability loss, including a product liability loss, may be carried back 10 years (section 172(b)(1)(C)). See Regulations section 1.172-13(c) for the statement that must be attached to Form 1120 if the corporation is claiming the 10-year carryback period for a product liability loss.

Special rules apply to the carryback of losses that are attributable to interest paid in connection with corporate equity reduction transactions (CERTs). The rules apply if a corporation has a corporate equity reduction interest loss in a loss limitation year ending after August 2, 1989. See section 172(b)(1)(E).

Personal service corporations may not carry back an NOL to or from any tax year to which a section 444 election applies.

Line 29b, Form 1120
(Line 25b, Form 1120-A)

Special Deductions

Form 1120 filers.—See the Instructions for Schedule C.

Form 1120-A filers.—Generally, enter 70% of line 4, page 1, on line 25b. However, this deduction may not be more than 70% of line 24, page 1. Compute line 24 without regard to any adjustment under section 1059 and without regard to any capital loss carryback to the tax year under section 1212(a)(1).

In a year in which an NOL occurs, this 70% limitation does not apply even if the loss is created by the dividends-received deduction. See sections 172(d) and 246(b).

Line 30, Form 1120
(Line 26, Form 1120-A)

Taxable Income

Capital construction fund.—To take a deduction for amounts contributed to a capital construction fund, reduce the amount that would otherwise be entered on line 30 (line 26, Form 1120-A) by the amount of the deduction. On the dotted line next to the entry space, write "CCF" and the amount of the deduction. For more information, get **Pub. 595,** Tax Guide for Commercial Fishermen.

Line 32b, Form 1120
(Line 28b, Form 1120-A)

Estimated Tax Payments

Enter any estimated tax payments the corporation made for the tax year.

Beneficiaries of trusts.—If the corporation is the beneficiary of a trust, and the trust makes a section 643(g) election to credit its estimated tax payments to its beneficiaries, include the corporation's share of the payment in the total for line 32b, Form 1120 (line 28b, Form 1120-A). Write "T" and the amount on the dotted line next to the entry space.

Special estimated tax payments for certain life insurance companies.—If the corporation is required to make or apply special estimated tax payments (SETP) under section 847 in addition to its regular estimated tax payments, enter on line 32b (line 28b, Form 1120-A), the corporation's total estimated tax payments. On the

Page 11

157

an S corporation may have to be capitalized by a shareholder for the shareholder's own production expenditures. The information required by the shareholder to properly capitalize interest for this purpose must be provided by the corporation in an attachment for line 23 of Schedule K-1 (see the instructions on page 22 for Schedule K-1, line 23, item 9). See section 263A(f) and Regulations sections 1.263A-8 through 1.263A-15 for additional information.

Temporary Regulations section 1.163-8T gives rules for allocating interest expense among activities so that the limitations on passive activity losses, investment interest, and personal interest can be properly figured. Generally, interest expense is allocated in the same manner as debt is allocated. Debt is allocated by tracing disbursements of the debt proceeds to specific expenditures. These regulations give rules for tracing debt proceeds to expenditures.

Generally, prepaid interest can only be deducted over the period to which the prepayment applies. See section 461(g) for details.

Line 14—Depreciation

Enter on line 14a only the depreciation claimed on assets used in a trade or business activity. See the Instructions for Form 4562 or **Pub. 946,** How To Depreciate Property, to figure the amount of depreciation to enter on this line. Complete and attach Form 4562 only if the corporation placed property in service during 1995 or claims depreciation on any car or other listed property.

Do not include any section 179 expense deduction on this line. This amount is not deductible by the corporation. Instead, it is passed through to the shareholders on line 8 of Schedule K-1.

Line 15—Depletion

If the corporation claims a deduction for timber depletion, complete and attach **Form T,** Forest Activities Schedules.

Caution: *Do not deduct depletion for oil and gas properties. Each shareholder figures depletion on these properties under section 613A(c)(11). See the instructions on page 21 for Schedule K-1, line 23, item 2, for information on oil and gas depletion that must be supplied to the shareholders by the corporation.*

Line 17—Pension, Profit-Sharing, etc., Plans

Enter the deductible contributions not claimed elsewhere on the return made by the corporation for its employees under a qualified pension, profit-sharing, annuity, or simplified employee pension (SEP) plan, and under any other deferred compensation plan.

If the corporation contributes to an individual retirement arrangement (IRA) for employees, include the contribution in salaries and wages on page 1, line 8, or Schedule A, line 3, and not on line 17.

Employers who maintain a pension, profit-sharing, or other funded deferred compensation plan, whether or not qualified under the Internal Revenue Code and whether or not a deduction is claimed for the current tax year, generally must file one of the forms listed below:

Form 5500, Annual Return/Report of Employee Benefit Plan (With 100 or more participants).

Form 5500-C/R, Return/Report of Employee Benefit Plan (With fewer than 100 participants).

Form 5500-EZ, Annual Return of One-Participant (Owners and Their Spouses) Retirement Plan.

There are penalties for failure to file these forms on time and for overstating the pension plan deduction.

Line 18—Employee Benefit Programs

Enter amounts for fringe benefits paid or incurred on behalf of employees owning 2% or less of the corporation's stock. These fringe benefits include **(a)** up to $5,000 paid by reason of an employee's death to his estate or beneficiary, **(b)** employer contributions to certain accident and health plans, **(c)** the cost of up to $50,000 of group-term life insurance on an employee's life, and **(d)** meals and lodging furnished for the employer's convenience.

Do not deduct amounts that are an incidental part of a pension, profit-sharing, etc., plan included on line 17 or amounts reported elsewhere on the return.

Report amounts paid on behalf of more than 2% shareholders on line 7 or 8, whichever applies. A shareholder is considered to own more than 2% of the corporation's stock if that person owns on any day during the tax year more than 2% of the outstanding stock of the corporation or stock possessing more than 2% of the combined voting power of all stock of the corporation. See section 318 for attribution rules.

Line 19—Other Deductions

Attach your own schedule listing by type and amount all allowable deductions related to a trade or business activity for which there is no separate line on page 1 of Form 1120S. Enter the total on this line. Do not include items that must be reported separately on Schedules K and K-1.

An S corporation may not take the deduction for net operating losses provided by section 172 or the special deductions in sections 241 through 249 (except the election to amortize organizational expenditures under section 248). Subject to limitations, the corporation's net operating loss is allowed as a deduction from the shareholders' gross income. See section 1366.

Do not include qualified expenditures to which an election under section 59(e) may apply. See the instructions on page 21 for lines 16a and 16b of Schedule K-1 for details on treatment of these items.

Include on line 19 the deduction taken for amortization. See the instructions for Form 4562 for more information. Complete and attach Form 4562 if the corporation is claiming amortization of costs that began during its 1995 tax year.

Section 464(f) limits the deduction for certain expenditures of S corporations engaged in farming that use the cash method of accounting, and whose prepaid farm supplies are more than 50% of other deductible farming expenses. Prepaid farm supplies include expenses for feed, seed, fertilizer, and similar farm supplies not used or consumed during the year. They also include the cost of poultry that would be allowable as a deduction in a later tax year if the corporation were to **(a)** capitalize the cost of poultry bought for use in its farm business and deduct it ratably over the lesser of 12 months or the useful life of the poultry, and **(b)** deduct the cost of poultry bought for resale in the year it sells or otherwise disposes of it. If the limit applies, the corporation can deduct prepaid farm supplies that do not exceed 50% of its other deductible farm expenses in the year of payment. The excess is deductible only in the year the corporation uses or consumes the supplies (other than poultry, which is deductible as explained above). For exceptions and more details on these rules, get **Pub. 225,** Farmer's Tax Guide.

Do not deduct amounts paid or incurred to participate or intervene in any political campaign on behalf of a candidate for public office, or to influence the general public regarding legislative matters, elections, or referendums. In addition, corporations generally cannot deduct expenses paid or incurred to influence Federal or state legislation, or to influence the actions or positions of certain Federal executive branch officials. However, certain in-house lobbying expenditures that do not exceed $2,000 are deductible. See section 162(e) for more details.

Do not deduct fines or penalties paid to a government for violating any law.

A deduction is allowed for part of the cost of qualified clean-fuel vehicle property and qualified clean-fuel vehicle refueling property. For more details, see section 179A.

Meals, travel, and entertainment.— Generally, the corporation can deduct only 50% of the amount otherwise allowable for meals and entertainment expenses paid or incurred in its trade or business. In addition, meals must not be lavish or extravagant; a bona fide business discussion must occur during, immediately before, or immediately after the meal; and an employee of the corporation must be present at the meal. See section 274(k)(2) for exceptions.

Additional limitations apply to deductions for gifts, skybox rentals, luxury water travel, convention expenses, and entertainment tickets. See section 274 and **Pub. 463,** Travel, Entertainment, and Gift Expenses, for details.

Corporations are not allowed to deduct amounts paid or incurred for membership

Page 12

dues in any club organized for business, pleasure, recreation, or other social purpose. This includes country clubs, golf and athletic clubs, airline and hotel clubs, and clubs operated to provide meals under conditions favorable to business discussion. But it does not include civic or public service organizations, professional organizations (such as bar and medical associations), business leagues, trade associations, chambers of commerce, boards of trade, and real estate boards, unless a principal purpose of the organization is to entertain, or provide entertainment facilities for, members or their guests.

In addition, no deduction is allowed for travel expenses paid or incurred for an officer's or employee's spouse or dependent or other individual accompanying an officer or employee of the corporation, unless that spouse, dependent, or other individual is an employee of the corporation, and that person's travel is for a bona fide business purpose and would otherwise be deductible by that person.

Generally, a corporation can deduct all other ordinary and necessary travel and entertainment expenses paid or incurred in its trade or business. However, it cannot deduct an expense paid or incurred for a facility (such as a yacht or hunting lodge) used for an activity usually considered entertainment, amusement, or recreation.

Note: *The corporation may be able to deduct otherwise nondeductible meals, travel, and entertainment expenses if the amounts are treated as compensation and reported on Form W-2 for an employee or on Form 1099-MISC for an independent contractor.*

See Pub. 463 for more details.

Line 21—Ordinary Income (Loss)

Enter this income or loss on line 1 of Schedule K. Line 21 income is not used in figuring the tax on line 22a or 22b. See the instructions for line 22a for figuring taxable income for purposes of line 22a or 22b tax.

Tax and Payments

Line 22a—Excess Net Passive Income Tax

If the corporation has always been an S corporation, the excess net passive income tax does not apply. If the corporation has subchapter C earnings and profits (defined in section 1362(d)(3)(B)) at the close of its tax year, has passive investment income for the tax year that is in excess of 25% of gross receipts, **and** has taxable income at year end, the corporation must pay a tax on the excess net passive income. Complete lines 1 through 3 and line 9 of the worksheet below to make this determination. If line 2 is greater than line 3 and the corporation has taxable income (see instructions for line 9 of worksheet), it must pay the tax. Complete a separate schedule using the format of lines 1 through 11 of the worksheet below to figure the tax. Enter the tax on line 22a, page 1, Form 1120S, and attach the computation schedule to Form 1120S.

Reduce each item of passive income passed through to shareholders by its portion of tax on line 22a. See section 1366(f)(3).

Line 22b—Tax From Schedule D (Form 1120S)

If the corporation elected to be an S corporation before 1987 (or elected to be an S corporation during 1987 or 1988 and qualifies for transitional relief from the built-in gains tax), see instructions for Part III of Schedule D (Form 1120S) to determine if the corporation is liable for the capital gains tax.

If the corporation made its election to be an S corporation after 1986, see the instructions for Part IV of Schedule D to determine if the corporation is liable for the built-in gains tax.

Note: *For purposes of line 19 of Part III and line 25 of Part IV of Schedule D, taxable income is defined in section 1375(b)(1)(B) and is generally figured in the same manner as taxable income for line 9 of the line 22a worksheet below.*

Line 22c

Include in the total for line 22c the following:

Investment credit recapture tax.— The corporation is liable for investment credit recapture attributable to credits allowed for tax years for which the corporation was not an S corporation. Figure the corporation's investment credit recapture tax by completing **Form 4255,** Recapture of Investment Credit. Include the tax in the total amount to be entered on line 22c. Write to the left of the line 22c total the amount of recapture tax and the words "Tax From Form 4255," and attach Form 4255 to Form 1120S.

LIFO recapture tax.—The corporation may be liable for the additional tax due to LIFO recapture under Regulations section 1.1363-2 if:

● The corporation used the LIFO inventory pricing method for its last tax year as a C corporation, or

● A C corporation transferred LIFO inventory after August 18, 1993, to the corporation in a nonrecognition transaction in which those assets were transferred basis property.

The additional tax due to LIFO recapture is figured for the corporation's last tax year as a C corporation or for the tax year of the transfer, whichever applies. See the Instructions for Forms 1120 and 1120-A to figure the tax. The tax is paid in four equal installments. The C corporation must pay the first installment by the due date (not including extensions) of Form 1120 for the corporation's last tax year as a C corporation or for the tax year of the transfer, whichever applies. The S corporation must pay each of the remaining installments by the due date (not including extensions) of Form 1120S for the 3 succeeding tax years. Include this year's installment in the total amount to be entered on line 22c. Write to the left of the total on line 22c the installment amount and the words "LIFO tax."

Interest due under the look-back method for completed long-term contracts.—If the corporation completed **Form 8697,** Interest Computation Under the Look-Back Method for Completed Long-Term Contracts, and owes interest,

---

Worksheet for Line 22a

1. Enter gross receipts for the tax year (see section 1362(d)(3)(C) for gross receipts from the sale of capital assets)* . . . . _____

2. Enter passive investment income as defined in Regulations section 1.1362-2(c)(5)* . . . . _____

3. Enter 25% of line 1 (If line 2 is less than line 3, stop here. You are not liable for this tax.) . . . . _____

4. Excess passive investment income— Subtract line 3 from line 2 . . . _____

5. Enter deductions directly connected with the production of income on line 2 (see section 1375(b)(2))* . . . _____

6. Net passive income—Subtract line 5 from line 2 . . . . _____

7. Divide amount on line 4 by amount on line 2 . . . . ____ %

8. Excess net passive income—Multiply line 6 by line 7 . . . . . . _____

9. Enter taxable income (see instructions for taxable income below) . . . _____

10. Enter smaller of line 8 or line 9 . . _____

11. Excess net passive income tax—Enter 35% of line 10. Enter here and on line 22a, page 1, Form 1120S . . . _____

*Income and deductions on lines 1, 2, and 5 are from total operations for the tax year. This includes applicable income and expenses from page 1, Form 1120S, as well as those reported separately on Schedule K. See section 1375(b)(4) for an exception regarding lines 2 and 5.

Line 9 of Worksheet—Taxable income

Line 9 taxable income is defined in Regulations section 1.1374-1(d). Figure this income by completing lines 1 through 28 of **Form 1120,** U.S. Corporation Income Tax Return. Include the Form 1120 computation with the worksheet computation you attach to Form 1120S. You do not have to attach the schedules, etc., called for on Form 1120. However, you may want to complete certain Form 1120 schedules, such as Schedule D (Form 1120) if you have capital gains or losses.

Page 13

write to the left of the line 22c total the amount of interest and "From Form 8697." Attach the completed form to Form 1120S.

Line 23d

If the S corporation is a beneficiary of a trust and the trust makes a section 643(g) election to credit its estimated tax payments to its beneficiaries, include the corporation's share of the payment (reported to the corporation on Schedule K-1 (Form 1041)) in the total amount entered on line 23d. Also, to the left of line 23d, write "T" and the amount of the payment.

Line 24—Estimated Tax Penalty

A corporation that fails to make estimated tax payments when due may be subject to an underpayment penalty for the period of underpayment. Use **Form 2220,** Underpayment of Estimated Tax by Corporations, to see if the corporation owes a penalty and to figure the amount of the penalty. If you attach Form 2220 to Form 1120S, be sure to check the box on line 24 and enter the amount of any penalty on this line.

Schedule A—Cost of Goods Sold

Inventories are required at the beginning and end of each tax year if the production, purchase, or sale of merchandise is an income-producing factor. See Regulations section 1.471-1.

Section 263A Uniform Capitalization Rules

The uniform capitalization rules of section 263A are discussed under **Limitations on Deductions** on page 10. See those instructions before completing Schedule A.

Line 4—Additional Section 263A Costs

An entry is required on this line only for corporations that have elected a simplified method of accounting.

For corporations that have elected the simplified production method, additional section 263A costs are generally those costs, other than interest, that were not capitalized under the corporation's method of accounting immediately prior to the effective date of section 263A that are required to be capitalized under section 263A. For new corporations, additional section 263A costs are the costs, other than interest, that must be capitalized under section 263A, but which the corporation would not have been required to capitalize if it had existed before the effective date of section 263A. For more details, see Regulations section 1.263A-2(b).

For corporations that have elected the simplified resale method, additional section 263A costs are generally those costs incurred with respect to the following categories: off-site storage or warehousing; purchasing; handling, processing, assembly, and repackaging; and general

Page 14

and administrative costs (mixed service costs). For more details, see Regulations section 1.263A-3(d).

Enter on line 4 the balance of section 263A costs paid or incurred during the tax year not included on lines 2, 3, and 5.

Line 5—Other Costs

Enter on line 5 any other inventoriable costs paid or incurred during the tax year not entered on lines 2 through 4.

Line 7—Inventory at End of Year

See Regulations sections 1.263A-1 through 1.263A-3 for details on figuring the costs to be included in ending inventory.

Lines 9a through 9e—Inventory Valuation Methods

Inventories can be valued at **(a)** cost, **(b)** cost or market value (whichever is lower), or **(c)** any other method approved by the IRS that conforms to the requirements of the applicable regulations.

The average cost (rolling average) method of valuing inventories generally does not conform to the requirements of the regulations. See Rev. Rul. 71-234, 1971-1 C.B. 148.

Corporations that use erroneous valuation methods must change to a method permitted for Federal income tax purposes. To make this change, use Form 3115.

On line 9a, check the method(s) used for valuing inventories. Under "lower of cost or market," *market* (for normal goods) means the current bid price prevailing on the inventory valuation date for the particular merchandise in the volume usually purchased by the taxpayer. For a manufacturer, market applies to the basic elements of cost—raw materials, labor and burden. If section 263A applies to the taxpayer, the basic elements of cost must reflect the current bid price of all direct costs and all indirect costs properly allocable to goods on hand at the inventory date.

Inventory may be valued below cost when the merchandise is unsalable at normal prices or unusable in the normal way because the goods are "subnormal" due to damage, imperfections, shop wear, etc., within the meaning of Regulations section 1.471-2(c). These goods may be valued at a current bona fide selling price minus direct cost of disposition (but not less than scrap value) if such a price can be established.

If this is the first year the last-in, first-out (LIFO) inventory method was either adopted or extended to inventory goods not previously valued under the LIFO method provided in section 472, attach **Form 970,** Application To Use LIFO Inventory Method, or a statement with the information required by Form 970. Also check the LIFO box on line 9c. On line 9d, enter the amount or the percent of total closing inventories covered under section 472. Estimates are acceptable.

If the corporation has changed or extended its inventory method to LIFO and

has had to "write up" its opening inventory to cost in the year of election, report the effect of this write-up as income (line 5, page 1) proportionately over a 3-year period that begins with the tax year of the election (section 472(d)).

See Pub. 538 for more information on inventory valuation methods.

Schedule B—Other Information

Be sure to answer the questions and provide other information in items 1 through 10.

Line 5—Foreign Financial Accounts

Answer "Yes" to question 5 if either **1** or **2** below applies to the corporation. Otherwise, check the "No" box.

1. At any time during calendar year 1995, the corporation had an interest in or signature or other authority over a bank account, securities account, or other financial account in a foreign country; AND

● The combined value of the accounts was more than $10,000 during the calendar year; AND

● The accounts were NOT with a U.S. military banking facility operated by a U.S. financial institution.

2. The corporation owns more than 50% of the stock in any corporation that would answer the question "Yes" based on item **1** above.

Get **Form TD F 90-22.1,** Report of Foreign Bank and Financial Accounts, to see if the corporation is considered to have an interest in or signature or other authority over a bank account, securities account, or other financial account in a foreign country.

If you answered "Yes" to question 5, file Form TD F 90-22.1 by June 30, 1996, with the Department of the Treasury at the address shown on the form. Form TD F 90-22.1 is not a tax return, so do not file it with Form 1120S. Form TD F 90-22.1 may be ordered by calling 1-800-TAX-FORM (1-800-829-3676).

Line 9

Complete line 9 if the corporation **(a)** filed its election to be an S corporation after 1986; **(b)** was a C corporation before it elected to be an S corporation **or** the corporation acquired an asset with a basis determined by reference to its basis (or the basis of any other property) in the hands of a C corporation; and **(c)** has net unrealized built-in gain (defined below) in excess of the net recognized built-in gain from prior years.

The corporation is liable for section 1374 tax if **(a), (b),** and **(c)** above apply and it has a net recognized built-in gain (section 1374(d)(2)) for its tax year.

Section 633(d)(8) of the Tax Reform Act of 1986 provides transitional relief from the built-in gains tax for certain corporations that elected to be S corporations in 1987 or 1988. See the instructions for Part IV of

Schedule D (Form 1120S) for more information.

The corporation's net unrealized built-in gain is the amount, if any, by which the fair market value of the assets of the corporation at the beginning of its first S corporation year (or as of the date the assets were acquired, for any asset with a basis determined by reference to its basis (or the basis of any other property) in the hands of a C corporation) exceeds the aggregate adjusted basis of such assets at that time.

Enter on line 9 the corporation's net unrealized built-in gain reduced by the net recognized built-in gain for prior years. See sections 1374(c)(2) and (d)(1).

Line 10

Check the box on line 10 if the corporation was a C corporation in a prior year and has subchapter C earnings and profits (E&P) at the close of its 1995 tax year. For this purpose, subchapter C E&P is E&P of any corporation for any tax year when it was not an S corporation. See sections 1362(d)(3)(B) and 312 for other details. If the corporation has subchapter C E&P, it may be liable for tax imposed on excess net passive income. See the instructions for line 22a, page 1, of Form 1120S for details on this tax.

Designation of Tax Matters Person (TMP)

If the S corporation is subject to sections 6241 through 6245 (consolidated audit procedures), it may designate a shareholder as the TMP for the tax year for which the return is filed by completing the **Designation of Tax Matters Person** section at the bottom of page 2 of Form 1120S. Temporary Regulations section 301.6241-1T provides an exception to the consolidated provisions for small S corporations with five or fewer shareholders each of whom is a natural person or an estate. See the instructions for item G on page 9 for other details.

General Instructions for Schedules K and K-1— Shareholders' Shares of Income, Credits, Deductions, etc.

Purpose of Schedules

The corporation is liable for taxes on lines 22a, b, and c, page 1, Form 1120S. Shareholders are liable for income tax on their shares of the corporation's income (reduced by any taxes paid by the corporation on income) and must include their share of the income on their tax return whether or not it is distributed to them. Unlike most partnership income, S corporation income is **not** self-employment income and is not subject to self-employment tax.

Schedule K is a summary schedule of all the shareholders' shares of the corporation's income, deductions, credits, etc. Schedule K-1 shows each shareholder's separate share. Attach a copy of each shareholder's Schedule K-1 to the Form 1120S filed with the IRS. Keep a copy as a part of the corporation's records, and give each shareholder a separate copy.

The total pro rata share items (column (b)) of all Schedules K-1 should equal the amount reported on the same line of Schedule K. Lines 1 through 20 of Schedule K correspond to lines 1 through 20 of Schedule K-1. Other lines do not correspond, but instructions explain the differences.

Be sure to give each shareholder a copy of the Shareholder's Instructions for Schedule K-1 (Form 1120S). These instructions are available separately from Schedule K-1 at most IRS offices.

Note: *Instructions that apply only to line items reported on Schedule K-1 may be prepared and given to each shareholder instead of the instructions printed by the IRS.*

Substitute Forms

The corporation **does not** need IRS approval to use a substitute Schedule K-1 if it is an exact copy of the IRS schedule, **or** if it contains only those lines the taxpayer is required to use, and the lines have the same numbers and titles and are in the same order as on the IRS Schedule K-1. In either case, the substitute schedule must include the OMB number and either **(a)** the Shareholder's Instructions for Schedule K-1 (Form 1120S) or **(b)** instructions that apply to the items reported on Schedule K-1 (Form 1120S).

The corporation must request IRS approval to use other substitute Schedules K-1. To request approval, write to Internal Revenue Service, Attention: Substitute Forms Program Coordinator, T:FP:S, 1111 Constitution Avenue, N.W., Washington, DC 20224.

The corporation may be subject to a penalty if it files a substitute Schedule K-1 that does not conform to the specifications of Rev. Proc. 94-34, 1994-1 C.B. 628.

Shareholder's Pro Rata Share Items

General Rule

Items of income, loss, deductions, etc., are allocated to a shareholder on a daily basis, according to the number of shares of stock held by the shareholder on each day during the tax year of the corporation. See the instructions for item A on page 16.

A transferee shareholder (rather than the transferor) is considered to be the owner of stock on the day it is transferred.

Special Rules

Termination of shareholder's interest.—If a shareholder terminates his or her interest in a corporation during the tax year, the

corporation, with the consent of all shareholders (including the one whose interest is terminated), may elect to allocate income and expenses, etc., as if the corporation's tax year consisted of 2 tax years, the first of which ends on the date of the shareholder's termination. To make the election, the corporation must attach a statement to Form 1120S for the tax year for which the election is made. In the statement, the corporation must state that it is electing under section 1377(a)(2) to have the rules of section 1377(a)(1) applied as if the tax year consisted of 2 tax years. The statement must give the date and manner of the termination (e.g., sale of the shareholder's entire interest), and it must be signed by a corporate officer on behalf of the corporation. Also, the corporation must attach a statement of consent signed by each person who was a shareholder at any time during the tax year. If the election is made, write "Section 1377(a)(2) Election Made" at the top of each Schedule K-1.

Qualifying dispositions.—If a qualifying disposition takes place during the tax year, the corporation may make an irrevocable election to allocate income and expenses, etc., as if the corporation's tax year consisted of 2 tax years, the first of which ends on the close of the day on which the qualifying disposition occurs. A qualifying disposition is:

1. A disposition by a shareholder of at least 20% of the corporation's outstanding stock in one or more transactions in any 30-day period during the tax year,

2. A redemption treated as an exchange under section 302(a) or 303(a) of at least 20% of the corporation's outstanding stock in one or more transactions in any 30-day period during the tax year, or

3. An issuance of stock that equals at least 25% of the previously outstanding stock to one or more new shareholders in any 30-day period during the tax year.

To make the election, the corporation must attach a statement to a timely filed original or amended Form 1120S for the tax year for which the election is made. In the statement, the corporation must state that it is electing under Regulations section 1.1368-1(g)(2)(i) to treat the tax year as if it consisted of separate tax years. The statement must also give the facts relating to the qualifying disposition (e.g., sale, gift, stock issuance, or redemption), and state that each shareholder who held stock in the corporation during the tax year consents to the election. A corporate officer must sign the statement under penalties of perjury on behalf of the corporation. A single election statement may be filed for all elections made under this special rule for the tax year.

For more details on the election, see Regulations section 1.1368-1(g)(2).

Specific Instructions (Schedule K Only)

Enter the total pro rata share amount for each applicable line item on Schedule K.

Page 15

Specific Instructions (Schedule K-1 Only)

General Information

On each Schedule K-1, complete the date spaces at the top; enter the names, addresses, and identifying numbers of the shareholder and corporation; complete items A through D; and enter the shareholder's pro rata share of each item. **Schedule K-1 must be prepared and given to each shareholder on or before the day on which Form 1120S is filed.**

Note: *Space has been provided on line 23 (Supplemental Information) of Schedule K-1 for the corporation to provide additional information to shareholders. This space, if sufficient, should be used in place of any attached schedules required for any lines on Schedule K-1, or other amounts not shown on lines 1 through 22 of Schedule K-1. Please be sure to identify the applicable line number next to the information entered below line 23.*

Special Reporting Requirements for Corporations With Multiple Activities

If items of income, loss, deduction, or credit from more than one activity (determined for purposes of the passive activity loss and credit limitations) are reported on lines 1, 2, or 3 of Schedule K-1, the corporation must provide information for each activity to its shareholders. See **Passive Activity Reporting Requirements** on page 8 for details on the reporting requirements.

Special Reporting Requirements for At-Risk Activities

If the corporation is involved in one or more at-risk activities for which a loss is reported on Schedule K-1, the corporation must report information separately for each at-risk activity. See section 465(c) for a definition of at-risk activities.

For each at-risk activity, the following information must be provided on an attachment to Schedule K-1:

1. A statement that the information is a breakdown of at-risk activity loss amounts.

2. The identity of the at-risk activity; the loss amount for the activity; other income and deductions; and other information that relates to the activity.

Specific Items

Item A

If there was no change in shareholders or in the relative interest in stock the shareholders owned during the tax year, enter the percentage of total stock owned by each shareholder during the tax year. For example, if shareholders X and Y each owned 50% for the entire tax year, enter

Page 16

50% in item A for each shareholder. Each shareholder's pro rata share items (lines 1 through 20 of Schedule K-1) are figured by multiplying the Schedule K amount on the corresponding line of Schedule K by the percentage in item A.

If there was a change in shareholders or in the relative interest in stock the shareholders owned during the tax year, each shareholder's percentage of ownership is weighted for the number of days in the tax year that stock was owned. For example, A and B each held 50% for half the tax year and A, B, and C held 40%, 40%, and 20%, respectively, for the remaining half of the tax year. The percentage of ownership for the year for A, B, and C is figured as follows and is then entered in item A.

	a % of total stock owned	b % of tax year held	c (a × b) % of ownership for the year
A	50 40	50 50	25 +20	45
B	50 40	50 50	25 +20	45
C	20	50	10	10
Total			100%

If there was a change in shareholders or in the relative interest in stock the shareholders owned during the tax year, each shareholder's pro rata share items generally are figured by multiplying the Schedule K amount by the percentage in item A. However, if a shareholder terminated his or her entire interest in the corporation during the year or a qualifying disposition took place, the corporation may elect to allocate income and expenses, etc., as if the tax year consisted of 2 tax years, the first of which ends on the day of the termination or qualifying disposition. See **Special Rules** on page 15 for more details. Each shareholder's pro rata share items are figured separately for each period on a daily basis, based on the percentage of stock held by the shareholder on each day.

Item B

Enter the Internal Revenue Service Center address where the Form 1120S, to which a copy of this K-1 was attached, was or will be filed.

Item C

If the corporation is a registration-required tax shelter, it must enter its tax shelter registration number in item C. If the corporation invested in a registration-required shelter, the corporation must also furnish a copy of its Form 8271 to its shareholders. See Form 8271 for more information.

Specific Instructions (Schedules K and K-1, Except as Noted)

Income (Loss)

Reminder: Before entering income items on Schedule K or K-1, be sure to reduce the items of income for the following:

1. Built-in gains tax (Schedule D, Part IV, line 31).—Each recognized built-in gain item (within the meaning of section 1374(d)(3)) is reduced by its proportionate share of the built-in gains tax.

2. Capital gains tax (Schedule D, Part III, line 23).—The section 1231 gain included on line 5 or 6 of Schedule K is reduced by this tax.

3. Excess net passive income tax (line 22a, page 1, Form 1120S).—Each item of passive investment income (within the meaning of Regulations section 1.1362-2(c)(5)) is reduced by its proportionate share of the net passive income tax.

Line 1—Ordinary Income (Loss) From Trade or Business Activities

Enter the amount from line 21, page 1. Enter the income or loss without reference to **(a)** shareholders' basis in the stock of the corporation and in any indebtedness of the corporation to the shareholders (section 1366(d)), **(b)** shareholders' at-risk limitations, and **(c)** shareholders' passive activity limitations. These limitations, if applicable, are determined at the shareholder level.

If the corporation is involved in more than one trade or business activity, see **Passive Activity Reporting Requirements** on page 8 for details on the information to be reported for each activity. If an at-risk activity loss is reported on line 1, see **Special Reporting Requirements for At-Risk Activities** above.

Line 2—Net Income (Loss) From Rental Real Estate Activities

Enter the net income or loss from rental real estate activities of the corporation from **Form 8825,** Rental Real Estate Income and Expenses of a Partnership or an S Corporation. Each Form 8825 has space for reporting the income and expenses of up to eight properties.

If the corporation has income or loss from more than one rental real estate activity reported on line 2, see **Passive Activity Reporting Requirements** on page 8 for details on the information to be reported for each activity. If an at-risk activity loss is reported on line 2, see **Special Reporting Requirements for At-Risk Activities** above.

Line 3—Income and Expenses of Other Rental Activities

Enter on lines 3a and 3b of Schedule K (line 3 of Schedule K-1) the income and expenses of rental activities other than the income and expenses reported on Form

8825. If the corporation has more than one rental activity reported on line 3, see **Passive Activity Reporting Requirements** on page 8 for details on the information to be reported for each activity. If an at-risk activity loss is reported on line 3, see **Special Reporting Requirements for At-Risk Activities** on page 16. Also see **Rental activities** on page 6 for a definition and other details on other rental activities.

Lines 4a Through 4f—Portfolio Income (Loss)

Enter portfolio income (loss) on lines 4a through 4f. See **Portfolio income** on page 7 for the definition of portfolio income. Do not reduce portfolio income by deductions allocated to it. Report such deductions (other than interest expense) on line 9 of Schedules K and K-1. Interest expense allocable to portfolio income is generally investment interest expense and is reported on line 11a of Schedules K and K-1.

Lines 4a and 4b.—Enter only taxable interest and dividends that are portfolio income. Interest income derived in the ordinary course of the corporation's trade or business, such as interest charged on receivable balances, is reported on line 5, page 1, Form 1120S. See Temporary Regulations section 1.469-2T(c)(3).

Lines 4d and 4e.—Enter on line 4d the net short-term capital gain or loss from line 6 of Schedule D (Form 1120S) that is portfolio income. Enter on line 4e the net long-term capital gain or loss from line 12 of Schedule D (Form 1120S) that is portfolio income. If any gain or loss from lines 6 and 12 of Schedule D is not portfolio income (e.g., gain or loss from the disposition of nondepreciable personal property used in a trade or business), do not report this income or loss on lines 4d and 4e. Instead, report it on line 6 of Schedules K and K-1. If the income or loss is attributable to more than one activity, report the income or loss amount separately for each activity on an attachment to Schedule K-1 and identify the activity to which the income or loss relates.

Line 4f.—Enter any other portfolio income not reported on lines 4a through 4e.

If the corporation holds a residual interest in a REMIC, report on an attachment for line 4f each shareholder's share of taxable income (net loss) from the REMIC (line 1b of Schedule Q (Form 1066)); excess inclusion (line 2c of Schedule Q (Form 1066)); and section 212 expenses (line 3b of Schedule Q (Form 1066)). Because Schedule Q (Form 1066) is a quarterly statement, the corporation must follow the Schedule Q (Form 1066) Instructions for Residual Interest Holder to figure the amounts to report to shareholders for the corporation's tax year.

Line 5—Net Gain (Loss) Under Section 1231 (Other Than Due to Casualty or Theft)

Enter the gain (loss) under section 1231 shown on line 8 of Form 4797. Do not

include net gains or losses from involuntary conversions due to casualties or thefts on this line. Instead, report them on line 6.

If the corporation is involved in more than one trade or business or rental activity, see **Passive Activity Reporting Requirements** on page 8 for details on the information to be reported for each activity. If an at-risk activity loss is reported on line 5, see **Special Reporting Requirements for At-Risk Activities** on page 16.

Line 6—Other Income (Loss)

Enter any other item of income or loss not included on lines 1 through 5, such as:

1. Recoveries of tax benefit items (section 111).

2. Gambling gains and losses (section 165(d)).

3. Net gain (loss) from involuntary conversions due to casualty or theft. The amount for this item is shown on **Form 4684,** Casualties and Thefts, line 38a or 38b.

4. Any net gain or loss from section 1256 contracts from **Form 6781,** Gains and Losses From Section 1256 Contracts and Straddles.

If the corporation is involved in more than one trade or business or rental activity, see **Passive Activity Reporting Requirements** on page 8 for details on the information to be reported for each activity. If an at-risk activity loss is reported on line 6, see **Special Reporting Requirements for At-Risk Activities** on page 16.

Deductions

Line 7—Charitable Contributions

Enter the amount of charitable contributions paid by the corporation during its tax year. On an attachment to Schedules K and K-1, show separately the dollar amount of contributions subject to each of the 50%, 30%, and 20% of adjusted gross income limits.

Generally, no deduction is allowed for any contribution of $250 or more unless the corporation obtains a written acknowledgement from the charitable organization that shows the amount of cash contributed, describes any property contributed, and gives an estimate of the value of any goods or services provided in return for the contribution. The acknowledgment must be obtained by the due date (including extensions) of the corporation's return, or if earlier, the date the corporation files its return. Do not attach the acknowledgment to the tax return, but keep it with the corporation's records. These rules apply in addition to the filing requirements for Form 8283 described below.

Certain contributions made to an organization conducting lobbying activities are not deductible. See section 170(f)(9) for more details.

If the corporation contributes property other than cash and the deduction claimed for such property exceeds $500, complete **Form 8283,** Noncash Charitable

Contributions, and attach it to Form 1120S. The corporation must give a copy of its Form 8283 to every shareholder if the deduction for any item or group of similar items of contributed property exceeds $5,000, even if the amount allocated to any shareholder is $5,000 or less.

If the deduction for an item or group of similar items of contributed property is $5,000 or less, the corporation must report each shareholder's pro rata share of the amount of noncash contributions to enable individual shareholders to complete their own Forms 8283. See the Instructions for Form 8283 for more information.

If the corporation made a qualified conservation contribution under section 170(h), also include the fair market value of the underlying property before and after the donation, as well as the type of legal interest contributed, and describe the conservation purpose furthered by the donation. Give a copy of this information to each shareholder.

Line 8—Section 179 Expense Deduction

An S corporation may elect to expense part of the cost of certain tangible property that the corporation purchased during the tax year for use in its trade or business or certain rental activities. See the Instructions for Form 4562 for more information.

Complete Part I of Form 4562 to figure the corporation's section 179 expense deduction. The corporation does not claim the deduction itself, but instead passes it through to the shareholders. Attach Form 4562 to Form 1120S and show the total section 179 expense deduction on Schedule K, line 8. Report each individual shareholder's pro rata share on Schedule K-1, line 8. Do not complete line 8 of Schedule K-1 for any shareholder that is an estate or trust.

If the corporation is an enterprise zone business, also report on an attachment to Schedules K and K-1 the cost of section 179 property placed in service during the year that is qualified zone property.

See the instructions for line 23 of Schedule K-1, item 3, for any recapture of a section 179 amount.

Line 9—Deductions Related to Portfolio Income (Loss)

Enter on line 9 the deductions clearly and directly allocable to portfolio income (other than interest expense). Interest expense related to portfolio income is investment interest expense and is reported on line 11a of Schedules K and K-1. Generally, the line 9 expenses are section 212 expenses and are subject to section 212 limitations at the shareholder level.

Note: *No deduction is allowed under section 212 for expenses allocable to a convention, seminar, or similar meeting. Because these expenses are not deductible by shareholders, the corporation does not report these expenses on line 9 or line 10. The expenses are nondeductible*

Page 17

and are reported as such on line 19 of Schedules K and K-1.

Line 10—Other Deductions

Enter any other deductions not included on lines 7, 8, 9, and 15e. On an attachment, identify the deduction and amount, and if the corporation has more than one activity, the activity to which the deduction relates.

Examples of items to be reported on an attachment to line 10 include:

• Amounts (other than investment interest required to be reported on line 11a of Schedules K and K-1) paid by the corporation that would be allowed as itemized deductions on a shareholder's income tax return if they were paid directly by a shareholder for the same purpose. These amounts include, but are not limited to, expenses under section 212 for the production of income other than from the corporation's trade or business.

• Any penalty on early withdrawal of savings not reported on line 9 because the corporation withdrew funds from its time savings deposit before its maturity.

• Soil and water conservation expenditures (section 175).

• Expenditures paid or incurred for the removal of architectural and transportation barriers to the elderly and disabled that the corporation has elected to treat as a current expense. See section 190.

• Interest expense allocated to debt-financed distributions. See Notice 89-35, 1989-1 C.B. 675, for more information.

• If there was a gain (loss) from a casualty or theft to property not used in a trade or business or for income producing purposes, provide each shareholder with the needed information to complete Form 4684.

Investment Interest

Lines 11a and 11b must be completed for all shareholders.

Line 11a—Investment Interest Expense

Include on this line the interest properly allocable to debt on property held for investment purposes. Property held for investment includes property that produces income (unless derived in the ordinary course of a trade or business) from interest, dividends, annuities, or royalties; and gains from the disposition of property that produces those types of income or is held for investment.

Investment interest expense **does not** include interest expense allocable to a passive activity.

Report investment interest expense only on line 11a of Schedules K and K-1.

The amount on line 11a will be deducted by individual shareholders on Schedule A (Form 1040), line 13, after applying the investment interest expense limitations of section 163(d).

For more information, see **Form 4952,** Investment Interest Expense Deduction.

Page 18

Lines 11b(1) and 11b(2)—Investment Income and Expenses

Enter on line 11b(1) only the investment income included on lines 4a, b, c, and f of Schedule K-1. Do not include other portfolio gains or losses on this line.

Enter on line 11b(2) only the investment expense included on line 9 of Schedule K-1.

If there are other items of investment income or expense included in the amounts that are required to be passed through separately to the shareholders on Schedule K-1, such as net short-term capital gain or loss, net long-term capital gain or loss, and other portfolio gains or losses, give each shareholder a schedule identifying these amounts.

Investment income includes gross income from property held for investment, the excess of net gain attributable to the disposition of property held for investment over net capital gain from the disposition of property held for investment, and any net capital gain from the disposition of property held for investment that each shareholder elects to include in investment income under section 163(d)(4)(B)(iii). Generally, investment income and investment expenses do not include any income or expenses from a passive activity. See Regulations section 1.469-2(f)(10) for exceptions.

Property subject to a net lease is not treated as investment property because it is subject to the passive loss rules. Do not reduce investment income by losses from passive activities.

Investment expenses are deductible expenses (other than interest) directly connected with the production of investment income. See the Instructions for Form 4952 for more information on investment income and expenses.

Credits

Note: *If the corporation has credits from more than one trade or business activity on line 12a or 13, or from more than one rental activity on line 12b, 12c, 12d, or 12e, it must report separately on an attachment to Schedule K-1, the amount of each credit and provide any other applicable activity information listed in* **Passive Activity Reporting Requirements** *on page 8.*

Line 12a—Credit for Alcohol Used as Fuel

Enter on line 12a of Schedule K the credit for alcohol used as fuel attributable to trade or business activities. Enter on line 12d or 12e the credit for alcohol used as fuel attributable to rental activities. Figure the credit on **Form 6478,** Credit for Alcohol Used as Fuel, and attach it to Form 1120S. The credit must be included in income on page 1, line 5, of Form 1120S. See section 40(f) for an election the corporation can make to have the credit not apply.

Enter each shareholder's share of the credit for alcohol used as fuel on line 12a, 12d, or 12e of Schedule K-1.

If this credit includes the small ethanol producer credit, identify on a statement attached to each Schedule K-1 **(a)** the amount of the small producer credit included in the total credit allocated to the shareholder, **(b)** the number of gallons of qualified ethanol fuel production allocated to the shareholder, and **(c)** the shareholder's pro rata share in gallons of the corporation's productive capacity for alcohol.

Line 12b—Low-Income Housing Credit

Section 42 provides for a credit that may be claimed by owners of low-income residential rental buildings. If shareholders are eligible to claim the low-income housing credit, complete the applicable parts of **Form 8586,** Low-Income Housing Credit, and attach it to Form 1120S. Enter the credit figured by the corporation on Form 8586, and any low-income housing credit received from other entities in which the corporation is allowed to invest, on the applicable line as explained below. The corporation must also complete and attach **Form 8609,** Low-Income Housing Credit Allocation Certification, and **Schedule A (Form 8609),** Annual Statement, to Form 1120S. See the Instructions for Form 8586 and Form 8609 for information on completing these forms.

Line 12b(1).—If the corporation invested in a partnership to which the provisions of section 42(j)(5) apply, report on line 12b(1) the credit the partnership reported to the corporation on line 13a(1) of Schedule K-1 (Form 1065). If the corporation invested **before 1990** in a section 42(j)(5) partnership, also include on this line any credit the partnership reported to the corporation on line 13a(3) of Schedule K-1 (Form 1065).

Line 12b(2).—Report on line 12b(2) any low-income housing credit for property placed in service before 1990 and not reported on line 12b(1). This includes any credit from a building placed in service before 1990 in a project owned by the corporation and any credit from a partnership reported to the corporation on line 13a(2) of Schedule K-1 (Form 1065). Also include on this line any credit from a partnership reported to the corporation on line 13a(4) of Schedule K-1 (Form 1065), if the corporation invested in that partnership **before 1990.**

Line 12b(3).—If the corporation invested **after 1989** in a partnership to which the provisions of section 42(j)(5) apply, report on line 12b(3) the credit the partnership reported to the corporation on line 13a(3) of Schedule K-1 (Form 1065).

Line 12b(4).—Report on line 12b(4) any low-income housing credit for property placed in service after 1989 and not reported on any other line. This includes any credit from a building placed in service after 1989 in a project owned by the corporation and any credit from a partnership reported to the corporation on line 13a(4) of Schedule K-1 (Form 1065), if the corporation invested in that partnership **after 1989.**

Line 12c—Qualified Rehabilitation Expenditures Related to Rental Real Estate Activities

Enter total qualified rehabilitation expenditures related to rental real estate activities of the corporation. For line 12c of Schedule K, complete the applicable lines of **Form 3468**, Investment Credit, that apply to qualified rehabilitation expenditures for property related to rental real estate activities of the corporation for which income or loss is reported on line 2 of Schedule K. See Form 3468 for details on qualified rehabilitation expenditures. Attach Form 3468 to Form 1120S.

For line 12c of Schedule K-1, enter each shareholder's pro rata share of the expenditures. On the dotted line to the left of the entry space for line 12c, enter the line number of Form 3468 on which the shareholder should report the expenditures. If there is more than one type of expenditure, or the expenditures are from more than one line 2 activity, report this information separately for each expenditure or activity on an attachment to Schedules K and K-1.

Note: *Qualified rehabilitation expenditures **not** related to rental real estate activities must be listed separately on line 23 of Schedule K-1.*

Line 12d—Credits (Other Than Credits Shown on Lines 12b and 12c) Related to Rental Real Estate Activities

Enter on line 12d any other credit (other than credits on lines 12b and 12c) related to rental real estate activities. On the dotted line to the left of the entry space for line 12d, identify the type of credit. If there is more than one type of credit or the credit is from more than one line 2 activity, report this information separately for each credit or activity on an attachment to Schedules K and K-1. These credits may include any type of credit listed in the instructions for line 13.

Line 12e—Credits Related to Other Rental Activities

Enter on line 12e any credit related to other rental activities for which income or loss is reported on line 3 of Schedules K and K-1. On the dotted line to the left of the entry space for line 12e, identify the type of credit. If there is more than one type of credit or the credit is from more than one line 3 activity, report this information separately for each credit or activity on an attachment to Schedules K and K-1. These credits may include any type of credit listed in the instructions for line 13.

Line 13—Other Credits

Enter on line 13 any other credit, except credits or expenditures shown or listed for lines 12a through 12e of Schedules K and K-1 or the credit for Federal tax paid on fuels (which is reported on line 23c of page 1). On the dotted line to the left of the entry space for line 13, identify the type of credit. If there is more than one type of credit or the credit is from more than one activity, report this information separately for each credit or activity on an attachment to Schedules K and K-1.

The credits to be reported on line 13 and other required attachments are as follows:

● Nonconventional source fuel credit. Figure this credit on a separate schedule and attach it to Form 1120S. See section 29 for rules on figuring the credit.

● Unused investment credit from cooperatives. If the corporation is a member of a cooperative that passes an unused investment credit through to its members, the credit is in turn passed through to the corporation's shareholders.

● Credit for backup withholding on dividends, interest, or patronage dividends.

● Credit for increasing research activities (Form 6765).

● Jobs credit (Form 5884).

● Disabled access credit (Form 8826).

● Enhanced oil recovery credit (Form 8830).

● Qualified electric vehicle credit (Form 8834).

● Renewable electricity production credit (Form 8835).

● Empowerment zone employment credit (Form 8844).

● Indian employment credit (Form 8845).

● Credit for employer social security and Medicare taxes paid on certain employee tips (Form 8846).

● Credit for contributions to selected community development corporations (Form 8847).

See the instructions on pages 21 and 22 for line 21 (Schedule K) and line 23 (Schedule K-1) to report expenditures qualifying for the **(a)** rehabilitation credit not related to rental real estate activities, **(b)** energy credit, or **(c)** reforestation credit.

Adjustments and Tax Preference Items

Lines 14a through 14e must be completed for all shareholders.

Enter items of income and deductions that are adjustments or tax preference items. Get **Form 6251**, Alternative Minimum Tax—Individuals, or Schedule I of **Form 1041**, U.S. Income Tax Return for Estates and Trusts, to determine the amounts to enter and for other information.

Do not include as a tax preference item any qualified expenditures to which an election under section 59(e) may apply. Because these expenditures are subject to an election by each shareholder, the corporation cannot figure the amount of any tax preference related to them. Instead, the corporation must pass through to each shareholder on lines 16a and 16b of Schedule K-1 the information needed to figure the deduction.

Line 14a—Depreciation Adjustment on Property Placed in Service After 1986

Figure the adjustment for line 14a based only on tangible property placed in service after 1986 (and tangible property placed in service after July 31, 1986, and before 1987 for which the corporation elected to use the General Depreciation System). **Do not** make an adjustment for motion picture films, videotapes, sound recordings, certain public utility property (as defined in section 168(f)(2)), or property depreciated under the unit-of-production method (or any other method not expressed in a term of years).

Using the same convention the corporation used for regular tax purposes, refigure depreciation as follows:

● For property that is neither real property nor property depreciated using the straight line method, use the 150% declining balance method over the property's class life (instead of the recovery period), switching to straight line for the first tax year that method gives a better result. See Pub. 946 for a table of class lives. For property having no class life, use 12 years.

● For property depreciated using the straight line method (other than real property), use the straight line method over the property's class life (instead of the recovery period). For property having no class life, use 12 years.

● For residential rental and nonresidential real property, use the straight line method over 40 years.

Determine the depreciation adjustment by subtracting the refigured depreciation from the depreciation claimed on Form 4562. If the refigured depreciation exceeds the depreciation claimed on Form 4562, enter the difference as a negative amount. See the instructions for Form 6251 and Form 4562 for more information.

Line 14b—Adjusted Gain or Loss

If the corporation disposed of any tangible property placed in service after 1986 (or after July 31, 1986, if an election was made to use the General Depreciation System), or if it disposed of a certified pollution control facility placed in service after 1986, refigure the gain or loss from the disposition using the adjusted basis for alternative minimum tax (AMT) purposes. The property's adjusted basis for AMT purposes is its cost or other basis minus all depreciation or amortization deductions allowed or allowable for AMT purposes during the current tax year and previous tax years. Enter on this line the difference between the regular tax gain (or loss) and the AMT gain (or loss). If the AMT gain is less than the regular tax gain, OR the AMT loss is more than the regular tax loss, OR there is an AMT loss and a regular tax gain, enter the difference as a negative amount.

Page 19

Line 14c—Depletion (Other Than Oil and Gas)

Do not include any depletion on oil and gas wells. The shareholders must figure their depletion deductions separately under section 613A.

In the case of mines, wells, and other natural deposits, other than oil and gas wells, enter the amount by which the deduction for depletion under section 611 (including percentage depletion for geothermal deposits) is more than the adjusted basis of such property at the end of the tax year. Figure the adjusted basis without regard to the depletion deduction and figure the excess separately for each property.

Lines 14d(1) and 14d(2)

Generally, the amounts to be entered on these lines are only the income and deductions for oil, gas, and geothermal properties that are used to figure the amount on line 21, page 1, Form 1120S.

If there are any items of income or deductions for oil, gas, and geothermal properties included in the amounts that are required to be passed through separately to the shareholders on Schedule K-1, give each shareholder a schedule that shows, for the line on which the income or deduction is included, the amount of income or deductions included in the total amount for that line. Do not include any of these direct passthrough amounts on line 14d(1) or 14d(2). The shareholder is told in the Shareholder's Instructions for Schedule K-1 (Form 1120S) to adjust the amounts on lines 14d(1) and 14d(2) for any other income or deductions from oil, gas, or geothermal properties included on lines 2 through 10 and 23 of Schedule K-1 in order to determine the total income and deductions from oil, gas, and geothermal properties for the corporation.

Figure the amounts for lines 14d(1) and 14d(2) separately for oil and gas properties which are not geothermal deposits and for all properties that are geothermal deposits.

Give the shareholders a schedule that shows the separate amounts included in the computation of the amounts on lines 14d(1) and 14d(2).

Line 14d(1). Gross income from oil, gas, and geothermal properties.—Enter the total amount of gross income (within the meaning of section 613(a)) from all oil, gas, and geothermal properties received or accrued during the tax year and included on page 1, Form 1120S.

Line 14d(2). Deductions allocable to oil, gas, and geothermal properties.—Enter the amount of any deductions allocable to oil, gas, and geothermal properties reduced by the excess intangible drilling costs included on page 1, Form 1120S, on properties for which the corporation made an election to expense intangible drilling costs in tax years beginning before 1983. Do not include nonproductive well costs included on page 1.

Figure excess intangible drilling costs as follows: From the allowable intangible drilling and development costs (except for

costs in drilling a nonproductive well), subtract the amount that would have been allowable if the corporation had capitalized these costs and either amortized them over the 120 months that started when production began, or treated them according to any election the corporation made under section 57(b)(2).

See section 57(a)(2) for more information.

Line 14e—Other Adjustments and Tax Preference Items

Attach a schedule that shows each shareholder's share of other items not shown on lines 14a through 14d(2) that are adjustments or tax preference items or that the shareholder needs to complete Form 6251 or Schedule I of Form 1041. See these forms and their instructions to determine the amount to enter. Other adjustments or tax preference items include the following:

● Accelerated depreciation of real property under pre-1987 rules.

● Accelerated depreciation of leased personal property under pre-1987 rules.

● Long-term contracts entered into after February 28, 1986. Except for certain home construction contracts, the taxable income from these contracts must be figured using the percentage of completion method of accounting for alternative minimum tax purposes.

● Installment sales after March 1, 1986, of property held primarily for sale to customers in the ordinary course of the corporation's trade or business. Generally, the installment method may not be used for these sales in figuring alternative minimum taxable income.

● Losses from tax shelter farm activities. No loss from any tax shelter farm activity is allowed for alternative minimum tax purposes.

Foreign Taxes

Lines 15a through 15g must be completed whether or not a shareholder is eligible for the foreign tax credit, if the corporation has foreign income, deductions, or losses, or has paid or accrued foreign taxes.

In addition to the instructions below, see **Form 1116**, Foreign Tax Credit (Individual, Estate, Trust, or Nonresident Alien Individual), and the related instructions.

Line 15a—Type of Income

Enter the type of income from outside the United States as follows:

● Passive income.

● High withholding tax interest.

● Financial services income.

● Shipping income.

● Dividends from a DISC or former DISC.

● Certain distributions from a foreign sales corporation (FSC) or former FSC.

● Dividends from each noncontrolled section 902 corporation.

● Taxable income attributable to foreign trade income (within the meaning of section 923(b)).

● General limitation income (all other income from sources outside the United States, including income from sources within U.S. possessions).

If, for the country or U.S. possession shown on line 15b, the corporation had more than one type of income, enter "See attached" and attach a schedule for each type of income for lines 15c through 15g.

Line 15b—Foreign Country or U.S. Possession

Enter the name of the foreign country or U.S. possession. If, for the type of income shown on line 15a, the corporation had income from, or paid taxes to, more than one foreign country or U.S. possession, enter "See attached" and attach a schedule for each country for lines 15a and 15c through 15g.

Line 15c—Total Gross Income From Sources Outside the United States

Enter in U.S. dollars the total gross income from sources outside the United States. Attach a schedule that shows each type of income listed in the instructions for line 15a.

Line 15d—Total Applicable Deductions and Losses

Enter in U.S. dollars the total applicable deductions and losses attributable to income on line 15c. Attach a schedule that shows each type of deduction or loss as follows:

● Expenses directly allocable to each type of income listed above.

● Pro rata share of all other deductions not directly allocable to specific items of income.

● Pro rata share of losses from other separate limitation categories.

Line 15e—Total Foreign Taxes

Enter in U.S. dollars the total foreign taxes (described in section 901) paid or accrued by the corporation to foreign countries or U.S. possessions. Attach a schedule that shows the dates the taxes were paid or accrued, and the amount in both foreign currency and in U.S. dollars, as follows:

● Taxes withheld at source on dividends.

● Taxes withheld at source on rents and royalties.

● Other foreign taxes paid or accrued.

Line 15f—Reduction in Taxes Available for Credit

Enter in U.S. dollars the total reduction in taxes available for credit. Attach a schedule that shows separately the:

● Reduction for foreign mineral income.

● Reduction for failure to furnish returns required under section 6038.

● Reduction for taxes attributable to boycott operations (section 908).

● Reduction for foreign oil and gas extraction income (section 907(a)).

- Reduction for any other items (specify).

Line 15g—Other Foreign Tax Information

Enter in U.S. dollars any items not covered on lines 15c through 15f that shareholders need to complete Form 1116 (e.g., gross income from all sources).

Other

Lines 16a and 16b—Section 59(e)(2) Expenditures

Generally, section 59(e) allows each shareholder to make an election to deduct the shareholder's pro rata share of the corporation's otherwise deductible qualified expenditures ratably over 10 years (3 years for circulation expenditures), beginning with the tax year in which the expenditures were made (or for intangible drilling and development costs, over the 60-month period beginning with the month in which such costs were paid or incurred). The term "qualified expenditures" includes only the following types of expenditures paid or incurred during the tax year: circulation expenditures, research and experimental expenditures, intangible drilling and development costs, and mining exploration and development costs. If a shareholder makes this election, these items are not treated as tax preference items.

Because the shareholders are generally allowed to make this election, the corporation cannot deduct these amounts or include them as adjustments or tax preference items on Schedule K-1. Instead, on lines 16a and 16b of Schedule K-1, the corporation passes through the information the shareholders need to figure their separate deductions.

On line 16a, enter the type of expenditures claimed on line 16b. Enter on line 16b the qualified expenditures paid or incurred during the tax year to which an election under section 59(e) may apply. Enter this amount for all shareholders whether or not any shareholder makes an election under section 59(e). If the expenditures are for intangible drilling and development costs, enter the month in which the expenditures were paid or incurred (after the type of expenditures on line 16a). If there is more than one type of expenditure included in the total shown on line 16b (or intangible drilling and development costs were paid or incurred for more than 1 month), report this information separately for each type of expenditure (or month) on an attachment to Schedules K and K-1.

Line 17—Tax-Exempt Interest Income

Enter on line 17 tax-exempt interest income, including any exempt-interest dividends received from a mutual fund or other regulated investment company. This information must be reported by individuals on line 8b of Form 1040. Generally, the basis of the shareholder's stock is increased by the amount shown on this line under section 1367(a)(1)(A).

Line 18—Other Tax-Exempt Income

Enter on line 18 all income of the corporation exempt from tax other than tax-exempt interest (e.g., life insurance proceeds). Generally, the basis of the shareholder's stock is increased by the amount shown on this line under section 1367(a)(1)(A).

Line 19—Nondeductible Expenses

Enter on line 19 nondeductible expenses paid or incurred by the corporation. Do not include separately stated deductions shown elsewhere on Schedules K and K-1, capital expenditures, or items the deduction for which is deferred to a later tax year. Generally, the basis of the shareholder's stock is decreased by the amount shown on this line under section 1367(a)(2)(D).

Line 20

Enter total distributions made to each shareholder other than dividends reported on line 22 of Schedule K. Noncash distributions of appreciated property are valued at fair market value. See **Distributions** on page 23 for the ordering rules on distributions.

Line 21 (Schedule K Only)

Attach a statement to Schedule K to report the corporation's total income, expenditures, or other information for items 1 through 15 of the line 23 (Schedule K-1 Only) instruction below.

Line 22 (Schedule K Only)

Enter total dividends paid to shareholders from accumulated earnings and profits. Report these dividends to shareholders on Form 1099-DIV. Do not report them on Schedule K-1.

Lines 22a and 22b (Schedule K-1 Only)—Recapture of Low-Income Housing Credit

If recapture of part or all of the low-income housing credit is required because **(a)** prior year qualified basis of a building decreased or **(b)** the corporation disposed of a building or part of its interest in a building, get **Form 8611,** Recapture of Low-Income Housing Credit. The instructions for Form 8611 indicate when Form 8611 is completed by the corporation and what information is provided to shareholders when recapture is required.

Note: *If a shareholder's ownership interest in a building decreased because of a transaction at the shareholder level, the corporation must provide the necessary information to the shareholder to enable the shareholder to figure the recapture.*

If the corporation filed **Form 8693,** Low-Income Housing Credit Disposition Bond, to avoid recapture of the low-income housing credit, no entry should be made on line 22 of Schedule K-1.

See Form 8586, Form 8611, and section 42 for more information.

Supplemental Information

Line 23 (Schedule K-1 Only)

Enter in the line 23 Supplemental Information space of Schedule K-1, or on an attached schedule if more space is needed, each shareholder's share of any information asked for on lines 1 through 22 that is required to be reported in detail, and items **1** through **15** below. Please identify the applicable line number next to the information entered in the Supplemental Information space. Show income or gains as a positive number. Show losses in parentheses.

1. Taxes paid on undistributed capital gains by a regulated investment company. As a shareholder of a regulated investment company, the corporation will receive notice on **Form 2439,** Notice to Shareholder of Undistributed Long-Term Capital Gains, that the company paid tax on undistributed capital gains.

2. Gross income and other information relating to oil and gas well properties that are reported to shareholders to allow them to figure the depletion deduction for oil and gas well properties. See section 613A(c)(11) for details.

The corporation cannot deduct depletion on oil and gas wells. Each shareholder must determine the allowable amount to report on his or her return. See Pub. 535 for more information.

3. Recapture of section 179 expense deduction. For property placed in service after 1986, the section 179 deduction is recaptured at any time the business use of property drops to 50% or less. Enter the amount originally passed through and the corporation's tax year in which it was passed through. Inform the shareholder if the recapture amount was caused by the disposition of the section 179 property. See section 179(d)(10) for more information. Do not include this amount on line 4 or 5, page 1, Form 1120S.

4. Recapture of certain mining exploration expenditures (section 617).

5. Any information or statements the corporation is required to furnish to shareholders to allow them to comply with requirements under section 6111 (registration of tax shelters) or section 6662(d)(2)(B)(ii) (regarding adequate disclosure of items that may cause an understatement of income tax).

6. If the corporation is involved in farming or fishing activities, report the gross income from these activities to shareholders.

7. Any information needed by a shareholder to compute the interest due under section 453(l)(3). If the corporation elected to report the dispositions of certain timeshares and residential lots on the installment method, each shareholder's tax liability must be increased by the shareholder's pro rata share of the interest on tax attributable to the installment payments received during the tax year.

Page 21

8. Any information needed by a shareholder to compute the interest due under section 453A(c). If an obligation arising from the disposition of property to which section 453A applies is outstanding at the close of the year, each shareholder's tax liability must be increased by the tax due under section 453A(c) on the shareholder's pro rata share of the tax deferred under the installment method.

9. Any information needed by a shareholder to properly capitalize interest as required by section 263A(f). See **Section 263A uniform capitalization rules** on page 10 for more information.

10. If the corporation is a closely held S corporation (defined in section 460(b)) and it entered into any long-term contracts after February 28, 1986, that are accounted for under either the percentage of completion-capitalized cost method or the percentage of completion method, it must attach a schedule to Form 1120S showing the information required in items (a) and (b) of the instructions for lines 1 and 3 of Part II for **Form 8697,** Interest Computation Under the Look-Back Method for Completed Long-Term Contracts. It must also report the amounts for Part II, lines 1 and 3, to its shareholders. See the instructions for Form 8697 for more information.

11. Expenditures qualifying for the **(a)** rehabilitation credit not related to rental real estate activities, **(b)** energy credit, or **(c)** reforestation credit. Complete and attach Form 3468 to Form 1120S. See Form 3468 and related instructions for information on eligible property and the lines on Form 3468 to complete. Do not include that part of the cost of the property the corporation has elected to expense under section 179. Attach to each Schedule K-1 a separate schedule in a format similar to that shown on Form 3468 detailing each shareholder's pro rata share of qualified expenditures. Also indicate the lines of Form 3468 on which the shareholders should report these amounts.

12. Recapture of investment credit. Complete and attach **Form 4255,** Recapture of Investment Credit, when investment credit property is disposed of, or it no longer qualifies for the credit, before the end of the recapture period or the useful life applicable to the property. State the type of property at the top of Form 4255, and complete lines 2, 3, 4, and 8, whether or not any shareholder is subject to recapture of the credit. Attach to each Schedule K-1 a separate schedule providing the information the corporation is required to show on Form 4255, but list only the shareholder's pro rata share of the cost of the property subject to recapture. Also indicate the lines of Form 4255 on which the shareholders should report these amounts.

The corporation itself is liable for investment credit recapture in certain cases. See the instructions for line 22c, page 1, Form 1120S, for details.

13. Any information needed by a shareholder to compute the recapture of

the qualified electric vehicle credit. See Pub. 535 for more information.

14. Any information a shareholder may need to figure recapture of the Indian employment credit. Generally, if the corporation terminates a qualified employee less than 1 year after the date of initial employment, any Indian employment credit allowed for a prior tax year by reason of wages paid or incurred to that employee must be recaptured. For details, see section 45A(d).

15. Any other information the shareholders need to prepare their tax returns.

Specific Instructions

Schedule L—Balance Sheets

The balance sheets should agree with the corporation's books and records. Include certificates of deposit as cash on line 1 of Schedule L.

Line 5—Tax-Exempt Securities

Include on this line—

1. State and local government obligations, the interest on which is excludible from gross income under section 103(a), and

2. Stock in a mutual fund or other regulated investment company that distributed exempt-interest dividends during the tax year of the corporation.

Line 24—Retained Earnings

If the corporation maintains separate accounts for appropriated and unappropriated retained earnings, it may want to continue such accounting for purposes of preparing its financial balance sheet. Also, if the corporation converts to C corporation status in a subsequent year, it will be required to report its appropriated and unappropriated retained earnings on separate lines of Schedule L of Form 1120.

Schedule M-1— Reconciliation of Income (Loss) per Books With Income (Loss) per Return

Line 3b—Travel and Entertainment

Include on this line 50% of meals and entertainment not allowed under section 274(n); expenses for the use of an entertainment facility; the part of business gifts over $25; expenses of an individual allocable to conventions on cruise ships over $2,000; employee achievement awards over $400; the part of the cost of entertainment tickets that exceeds face value (also subject to 50% disallowance); the part of the cost of skyboxes that exceeds the face value of nonluxury box seat tickets; the part of the cost of luxury water travel not allowed under section 274(m); expenses for travel as a form of education; nondeductible club dues; and other travel and entertainment expenses not allowed as a deduction.

Schedule M-2—Analysis of Accumulated Adjustments Account, Other Adjustments Account, and Shareholders' Undistributed Taxable Income Previously Taxed

Column (a)—Accumulated Adjustments Account

The accumulated adjustments account (AAA) is an account of the S corporation that generally reflects the accumulated undistributed net income of the corporation for the corporation's post-1982 years. S corporations with accumulated earnings and profits must maintain the AAA to determine the tax effect of distributions during S years and the post-termination transition period. An S corporation without accumulated earnings and profits does not need to maintain the AAA in order to determine the tax effect of distributions. Nevertheless, if an S corporation without accumulated earnings and profits engages in certain transactions to which section 381(a) applies, such as a merger into an S corporation with accumulated earnings and profits, the S corporation must be able to calculate its AAA at the time of the merger for purposes of determining the tax effect of post-merger distributions. Therefore, it is recommended that the AAA be maintained by all S corporations.

At the end of the tax year, the AAA is determined by taking into account the taxable income, deductible losses and expenses, and nondeductible losses and expenses for the tax year (other than expenses related to tax-exempt income and Federal taxes attributable to a C corporation tax year). See Regulations section 1.1368-2. After the year-end income and expense adjustments are made, the AAA is reduced by distributions made during the tax year. See **Distributions** on page 23 for distribution rules. For adjustments to the AAA for redemptions, reorganizations, and corporate separations, see Regulations section 1.1368-2(d).

Note: The AAA may have a negative balance at year end. See section 1368(e).

Column (b)—Other Adjustments Account

The other adjustments account is adjusted for tax-exempt income (and related expenses) and Federal taxes attributable to a C corporation tax year. After these adjustments are made, the account is reduced for any distributions made during the year. See **Distributions** on page 23.

Column (c)—Shareholders' Undistributed Taxable Income Previously Taxed

The shareholders' undistributed taxable income previously taxed account, also called previously taxed income (PTI), is maintained only if the corporation had a balance in this account at the start of its 1995 tax year. If there is a beginning balance for the 1995 tax year, no adjustments are made to the account except to reduce the account for distributions made under section 1375(d) (as in effect before the enactment of the Subchapter S Revision Act of 1982). See **Distributions** below for the order of distributions from the account.

Each shareholder's right to nontaxable distributions from PTI is personal and cannot be transferred to another person. The corporation is required to keep records of each shareholder's net share of PTI.

Distributions

General rule.—Unless the corporation makes one of the elections described below, property distributions (including cash) are applied in the following order to reduce accounts of the S corporation that are used to figure the tax effect of distributions made by the corporation to its shareholders:

1. Reduce AAA (but not below zero). If distributions during the tax year exceed the AAA at the close of the tax year, the AAA is allocated pro rata to each distribution made during the tax year. See section 1368(c).

2. Reduce shareholders' PTI account for any section 1375(d) (as in effect before 1983) distributions. A distribution from the PTI account is tax free to the extent of a shareholder's basis in his or her stock in the corporation.

3. Reduce accumulated E&P. Generally, the S corporation has accumulated E&P only if it has not distributed E&P accumulated in prior years when the S corporation was a C corporation (section 1361(a)(2)) or a small business corporation prior to 1983 (section 1371 of prior law). See section 312 for information on E&P. The only adjustments that can be made to the accumulated E&P of an S corporation are **(a)** reductions for dividend distributions; **(b)** adjustments for redemptions, liquidations, reorganizations, etc.; and **(c)** reductions for investment credit recapture tax for which the corporation is liable. See sections 1371(c) and (d)(3).

4. Reduce the other adjustments account.

5. Reduce any remaining shareholders' equity accounts.

Elections relating to source of distributions.—The corporation may modify the above ordering rules by making one or more of the following elections:

1. Election to distribute accumulated E&P first.—If the corporation has accumulated E&P and wants to distribute this E&P before making distributions from the AAA, it may elect to do so with the consent of all its affected shareholders (section 1368(e)(3)(B)). This election is irrevocable and applies only for the tax year for which it is made. For details on making the election, see **Statement regarding elections** below.

2. Election to make a deemed dividend.—If the corporation wants to distribute all or part of its subchapter C E&P through a deemed dividend, it may elect to do so with the consent of all its affected shareholders (section 1368(e)(3)(B)). Under this election, the corporation will be treated as also having made the election to distribute accumulated E&P first. The amount of the deemed dividend cannot exceed the subchapter C E&P at the end of the tax year, reduced by any actual distributions of subchapter C E&P made during the tax year. A deemed dividend is treated as if it were a pro rata distribution of money to the shareholders, received by the shareholders, and immediately contributed back to the corporation, all on the last day of the tax year. This election is irrevocable and applies only for the tax year for which it is made. For details on making the election, see **Statement regarding elections** below.

3. Election to forego PTI.—If the corporation wants to forego distributions of PTI, it may elect to do so with the consent of all its affected shareholders (section 1368(e)(3)(B)). Under this election, paragraph 2 under the **General rule** above does not apply to any distribution made during the tax year. This election is irrevocable and applies only for the tax year for which it is made. For details on making the election, see **Statement regarding elections** below.

Statement regarding elections.—To make any of the above elections, the corporation must attach a statement to a timely filed original or amended Form 1120S for the

tax year for which the election is made. In the statement, the corporation must identify the election it is making and must state that each shareholder consents to the election. A corporate officer must sign the statement under penalties of perjury on behalf of the corporation. The statement of election to make a deemed dividend must include the amount of the deemed dividend distributed to each shareholder.

Example

The following example shows how the Schedule M-2 accounts are adjusted for items of income (loss), deductions, and distributions reported on Form 1120S.

Items per return are:

1. Page 1, line 21 income—$219,000

2. Schedule K, line 2 loss—($3,000)

3. Schedule K, line 4a income—$4,000

4. Schedule K, line 4b income—$16,000

5. Schedule K, line 7 deduction—$24,000

6. Schedule K, line 8 deduction— $3,000

7. Schedule K, line 13 jobs credit—$6,000

8. Schedule K, line 17 tax-exempt interest—$5,000

9. Schedule K, line 19 nondeductible expenses—$6,000 (reduction in salaries and wages for jobs credit), and

10. Schedule K, line 20 distributions—$65,000.

Based on return items 1 through 10 and starting balances of zero, the columns for the AAA and the other adjustments account are completed as shown in the Schedule M-2 Worksheet below.

Note: *For the AAA account, the worksheet line 3—$20,000 amount is the total of the Schedule K, lines 4a and 4b incomes of $4,000 and $16,000. The worksheet line 5—$36,000 amount is the total of the Schedule K, line 2 loss of ($3,000), line 7 deduction of $24,000, line 8 deduction of $3,000, and the line 19 nondeductible expenses of $6,000. For the other adjustments account, the worksheet line 3 amount is the Schedule K, line 17, tax-exempt interest income of $5,000. Other worksheet amounts are self-explanatory.*

Schedule M-2   **Worksheet**

		(a) Accumulated adjustments account	(b) Other adjustments account	(c) Shareholders' undistributed taxable income previously taxed
1	Balance at beginning of tax year . . .	-0-	-0-	
2	Ordinary income from page 1, line 21 .	219,000		
3	Other additions	20,000	5,000	
4	Loss from page 1, line 21	( )		
5	Other reductions	(36,000)	( )	
6	Combine lines 1 through 5	203,000	5,000	
7	Distributions other than dividend distributions	65,000	-0-	
8	Balance at end of tax year. Subtract line 7 from line 6	138,000	5,000	

Codes for Principal Business Activity

These codes for the Principal Business Activity are designed to classify enterprises by the type of activity in which they are engaged to facilitate the administration of the Internal Revenue Code. Though similar in format and structure to the Standard Industrial Classification (SIC) codes, they should not be used as SIC codes.

Using the list below, enter on page 1, under B, the code number for the specific industry group from which the largest percentage of total receipts is derived. Total receipts means the total of: gross receipts on line 1a, page 1; all other income on lines 4 and 5, page 1; all income on lines 2, 19, and 20a of Form 8825; and income (receipts only) on lines 3a and 4a through 4f of Schedule K.

On page 2, Schedule B, line 2, state the principal business activity and principal product or service that account for the largest percentage of total receipts. For example, if the principal business activity is "Grain mill products," the principal product or service may be "Cereal preparations."

If, as its principal business activity, the corporation: (1) purchases raw materials, (2) subcontracts out for labor to make a finished product from the raw materials, and (3) retains title to the goods, the corporation is considered to be a manufacturer and must enter one of the codes (2010–3998) under "Manufacturing."

Agriculture, Forestry, and Fishing

Code
0400 Agricultural production.
0600 Agricultural services (except veterinarians), forestry, fishing, hunting, and trapping.

Mining

Metal mining:
1010 Iron ores.
1070 Copper, lead and zinc, gold and silver ores.
1098 Other metal mining.
1150 Coal mining.

Oil and gas extraction:
1330 Crude petroleum, natural gas, and natural gas liquids.
1380 Oil and gas field services.

Nonmetallic minerals, except fuels:
1430 Dimension, crushed and broken stone; sand and gravel.
1498 Other nonmetallic minerals, except fuels.

Construction

General building contractors and operative builders:
1510 General building contractors.
1531 Operative builders.

1600 Heavy construction contractors.

Special trade contractors:
1711 Plumbing, heating, and air conditioning.
1731 Electrical work.
1798 Other special trade contractors.

Manufacturing

Food and kindred products:
2010 Meat products.
2020 Dairy products.
2030 Preserved fruits and vegetables.
2040 Grain mill products.
2050 Bakery products.
2060 Sugar and confectionery products.
2081 Malt liquors and malt.
2088 Alcoholic beverages, except malt liquors and malt.
2089 Bottled soft drinks, and flavorings.
2096 Other food and kindred products.

2100 Tobacco manufacturers.

Textile mill products:
2228 Weaving mills and textile finishing.
2250 Knitting mills.
2298 Other textile mill products.

Apparel and other textile products:
2315 Men's and boys' clothing.
2345 Women's and children's clothing.
2388 Other apparel and accessories.
2390 Miscellaneous fabricated textile products.

Lumber and wood products:
2415 Logging, sawmills, and planing mills.
2430 Millwork, plywood, and related products.
2498 Other wood products, including wood buildings and mobile homes.

2500 Furniture and fixtures.

Paper and allied products:
2625 Pulp, paper, and board mills.
2699 Other paper products.

Printing and publishing:
2710 Newspapers.
2720 Periodicals.
2735 Books, greeting cards, and miscellaneous publishing.
2799 Commercial and other printing, and printing trade services.

Code
Chemicals and allied products:
2815 Industrial chemicals, plastics materials and synthetics.
2830 Drugs.
2840 Soap, cleaners, and toilet goods.
2850 Paints and allied products.
2898 Agricultural and other chemical products.

Petroleum refining and related industries (including those integrated with extraction):
2910 Petroleum refining (including integrated).
2998 Other petroleum and coal products.

Rubber and misc. plastics products:
3050 Rubber products; plastics footwear, hose, and belting.
3070 Misc. plastics products.

Leather and leather products:
3140 Footwear, except rubber.
3198 Other leather and leather products.

Stone, clay, and glass products:
3225 Glass products.
3240 Cement, hydraulic.
3270 Concrete, gypsum, and plaster products.
3298 Other nonmetallic mineral products.

Primary metal industries:
3370 Ferrous metal industries; misc. primary metal products.
3380 Nonferrous metal industries.

Fabricated metal products:
3410 Metal cans and shipping containers.
3428 Cutlery, hand tools, and hardware; screw machine products, bolts, and similar products.
3430 Plumbing and heating, except electric and warm air.
3440 Fabricated structural metal products.
3460 Metal forgings and stampings.
3470 Coating, engraving, and allied services.
3480 Ordnance and accessories, except vehicles and guided missiles.
3490 Misc. fabricated metal products.

Machinery, except electrical:
3520 Farm machinery.
3530 Construction and related machinery.
3540 Metalworking machinery.
3550 Special industry machinery.
3560 General industrial machinery.
3570 Office, computing, and accounting machines.
3598 Other machinery except electrical.

Electrical and electronic equipment:
3630 Household appliances.
3665 Radio, television, and communications equipment.
3670 Electronic components and accessories.
3698 Other electrical equipment.

3710 Motor vehicles and equipment.

Transportation equipment, except motor vehicles:
3725 Aircraft, guided missiles and parts.
3730 Ship and boat building and repairing.
3798 Other transportation equipment, except motor vehicles.

Instruments and related products:
3815 Scientific instruments and measuring devices; watches and clocks.
3845 Optical, medical, and ophthalmic goods.
3860 Photographic equipment and supplies.

3998 Other manufacturing products.

Transportation and Public Utilities

Code
Transportation:
4000 Railroad transportation.
4100 Local and interurban passenger transit.
4200 Trucking and warehousing.
4400 Water transportation.
4500 Transportation by air.
4600 Pipe lines, except natural gas.
4700 Miscellaneous transportation services.

Communication:
4825 Telephone, telegraph, and other communication services.
4830 Radio and television broadcasting.

Electric, gas, and sanitary services:
4910 Electric services.
4920 Gas production and distribution.
4930 Combination utility services.
4990 Water supply and other sanitary services.

Wholesale Trade

Durable:
5008 Machinery, equipment, and supplies.
5010 Motor vehicles and automotive equipment.
5020 Furniture and home furnishings.
5030 Lumber and construction materials.
5040 Sporting, recreational, photographic, and hobby goods, toys and supplies.
5050 Metals and minerals, except petroleum and scrap.
5060 Electrical goods.
5070 Hardware, plumbing and heating equipment and supplies.
5098 Other durable goods.

Nondurable:
5110 Paper and paper products.
5129 Drugs, drug proprietaries, and druggists' sundries.
5130 Apparel, piece goods, and notions.
5140 Groceries and related products.
5150 Farm-product raw materials.
5160 Chemicals and allied products.
5170 Petroleum and petroleum products.
5180 Alcoholic beverages.
5190 Misc. nondurable goods.

Retail Trade

Building materials, garden supplies, and mobile home dealers:
5220 Building materials dealers.
5251 Hardware stores.
5265 Garden supplies and mobile home dealers.

5300 General merchandise stores.

Food stores:
5410 Grocery stores.
5490 Other food stores.

Automotive dealers and service stations:
5515 Motor vehicle dealers.
5541 Gasoline service stations.
5598 Other automotive dealers.

5600 Apparel and accessory stores.

5700 Furniture and home furnishings stores.

5800 Eating and drinking places.

Misc. retail stores:
5912 Drug stores and proprietary stores.
5921 Liquor stores.
5995 Other retail stores.

Finance, Insurance, and Real Estate

Code
Banking:
6030 Mutual savings banks.
6060 Bank holding companies.
6090 Banks, except mutual savings banks and bank holding companies.

Credit agencies other than banks:
6120 Savings and loan associations.
6140 Personal credit institutions.
6150 Business credit institutions.
6199 Other credit agencies.

Security, commodity brokers and services:
6210 Security brokers, dealers, and flotation companies.
6299 Commodity contracts brokers and dealers; security and commodity exchanges; and allied services.

Insurance:
6355 Life Insurance.
6356 Mutual insurance, except life or marine and certain fire or flood insurance companies.
6359 Other insurance companies.
6411 Insurance agents, brokers, and service.

Real estate:
6511 Real estate operators and lessors of buildings.
6516 Lessors of mining, oil, and similar property.
6518 Lessors of railroad property and other real property.
6530 Condominium management and cooperative housing associations.
6550 Subdividers and developers.
6599 Other real estate.

Holding and other investment companies, except bank holding companies:
6744 Small business investment companies.
6749 Other holding and investment companies, except bank holding companies.

Services

7000 Hotels and other lodging places.
7200 Personal services.

Business services:
7310 Advertising.
7389 Business services, except advertising.

Auto repair; miscellaneous repair services:
7500 Auto repair and services.
7600 Misc. repair services.

Amusement and recreation services:
7812 Motion picture production, distribution, and services.
7830 Motion picture theaters.
7900 Amusement and recreation services, except motion pictures.

Other services:
8015 Offices of physicians, including osteopathic physicians.
8021 Offices of dentists.
8040 Offices of other health practitioners.
8050 Nursing and personal care facilities.
8060 Hospitals.
8071 Medical laboratories.
8099 Other medical services.
8111 Legal services.
8200 Educational services.
8300 Social services.
8600 Membership organizations.
8911 Architectural and engineering services.
8930 Accounting, auditing, and bookkeeping.
8980 Miscellaneous services (including veterinarians).

 Printed on recycled paper

Form **1120S**	**U.S. Income Tax Return for an S Corporation**	OMB No. 1545-0130

Department of the Treasury
Internal Revenue Service

▶ Do not file this form unless the corporation has timely filed Form 2553 to elect to be an S corporation.
▶ See separate instructions.

19 95

For calendar year 1995, or tax year beginning _____ , 1995, and ending _____ , 19 ___

A Date of election as an S corporation	Use IRS label. Other- wise, please print or type.	Name **StratoTech, Inc.**	**C** Employer identification number
12-1-93			**10 : 4487965**
B Business code no. (see Specific Instructions)		Number, street, and room or suite no. (If a P.O. box, see page 9 of the instructions.) **482 Winston Street**	**D** Date incorporated **3-1-75**
5008		City or town, state, and ZIP code **Metro City OH 43705**	**E** Total assets (see Specific Instructions) $ **771,334**

F Check applicable boxes: (1) ☑ Initial return (2) ☐ Final return (3) ☐ Change in address (4) ☐ Amended return
G Check this box if this S corporation is subject to the consolidated audit procedures of sections 6241 through 6245 (see instructions before checking this box) . ▶ ☐
H Enter number of shareholders in the corporation at end of the tax year . . . . ▶ **6**

Caution: *Include only trade or business income and expenses on lines 1a through 21. See the instructions for more information.*

Income

1a Gross receipts or sales **1,545,700** **b** Less returns and allowances **21,000** **c** Bal ▶		**1c**	**1,524,700**
2 Cost of goods sold (Schedule A, line 8)		**2**	**954,700**
3 Gross profit. Subtract line 2 from line 1c		**3**	**570,000**
4 Net gain (loss) from Form 4797, Part II, line 20 *(attach Form 4797)*		**4**	
5 Other income (loss) *(attach schedule)* . . . . ▶		**5**	
6 **Total income (loss).** Combine lines 3 through 5 . . . . . . ▶		**6**	**570,000**

Deductions (see page 10 of the instructions for limitations)

7 Compensation of officers		**7**	**170,000**
8 Salaries and wages (less employment credits)		**8**	**138,000**
9 Repairs and maintenance.		**9**	**800**
10 Bad debts		**10**	**1,600**
11 Rents		**11**	**9,200**
12 Taxes and licenses.		**12**	**15,000**
13 Interest		**13**	**14,200**
14a Depreciation *(if required, attach Form 4562)* . . .	**14a** **15,200**		
b Depreciation claimed on Schedule A and elsewhere on return .	**14b**		
c Subtract line 14b from line 14a		**14c**	**15,200**
15 Depletion **(Do not deduct oil and gas depletion.)** . . .		**15**	
16 Advertising		**16**	**8,700**
17 Pension, profit-sharing, etc., plans		**17**	
18 Employee benefit programs		**18**	
19 Other deductions *(attach schedule)* . . . . ▶		**19**	**78,300**
20 **Total deductions.** Add the amounts shown in the far right column for lines 7 through 19 ▶		**20**	**451,000**
21 Ordinary income (loss) from trade or business activities. Subtract line 20 from line 6		**21**	**119,000**

Tax and Payments

22 **Tax: a** Excess net passive income tax *(attach schedule)*. . .	**22a**		
b Tax from Schedule D (Form 1120S)	**22b**		
c Add lines 22a and 22b (see page 13 of the instructions for additional taxes)		**22c**	
23 **Payments: a** 1995 estimated tax payments and amount applied from 1994 return	**23a**		
b Tax deposited with Form 7004	**23b**		
c Credit for Federal tax paid on fuels *(attach Form 4136)* . . .	**23c**		
d Add lines 23a through 23c		**23d**	
24 Estimated tax penalty. Check if Form 2220 is attached . . . . ▶ ☐		**24**	
25 **Tax due.** If the total of lines 22c and 24 is larger than line 23d, enter amount owed. See page 3 of the instructions for depositary method of payment . . . . . . ▶		**25**	
26 **Overpayment.** If line 23d is larger than the total of lines 22c and 24, enter amount overpaid ▶		**26**	
27 Enter amount of line 26 you want: **Credited to 1996 estimated tax** ▶ _____	**Refunded** ▶	**27**	

Please Sign Here

Under penalties of perjury, I declare that I have examined this return, including accompanying schedules and statements, and to the best of my knowledge and belief, it is true, correct, and complete. Declaration of preparer (other than taxpayer) is based on all information of which preparer has any knowledge.

▶ *John H. Green* | **3-10-XX** | ▶ *President*
Signature of officer   Date   Title

Paid Preparer's Use Only	Preparer's signature ▶		Date	Check if self-employed ▶ ☐	Preparer's social security number
	Firm's name (or yours if self-employed) and address ▶			EIN ▶	
				ZIP code ▶	

For Paperwork Reduction Act Notice, see page 1 of separate instructions.   Cat. No. 11510H   Form **1120S** (1995)

Form 1120S (1995)   Page **2**

Schedule A   Cost of Goods Sold (see page 14 of the instructions)

1	Inventory at beginning of year	1	*126,000*
2	Purchases	2	*1,127,100*
3	Cost of labor	3	
4	Additional section 263A costs *(attach schedule)*	4	
5	Other costs *(attach schedule)*	5	
6	**Total.** Add lines 1 through 5	6	*1,253,100*
7	Inventory at end of year	7	*298,400*
8	**Cost of goods sold.** Subtract line 7 from line 6. Enter here and on page 1, line 2	8	*954,700*

9a Check all methods used for valuing closing inventory:
  (i) ☐ Cost as described in Regulations section 1.471-3
  (ii) ☑ Lower of cost or market as described in Regulations section 1.471-4
  (iii) ☐ Other (specify method used and attach explanation) ▶ ....
  b Check if there was a writedown of "subnormal" goods as described in Regulations section 1.471-2(c) . . . . ▶ ☐
  c Check if the LIFO inventory method was adopted this tax year for any goods *(if checked, attach Form 970)*. . . . . ▶ ☐
  d If the LIFO inventory method was used for this tax year, enter percentage (or amounts) of closing
inventory computed under LIFO . . . . | **9d** | |
  e Do the rules of section 263A (for property produced or acquired for resale) apply to the corporation? . . . . ☐ Yes ☑ No
  f Was there any change in determining quantities, cost, or valuations between opening and closing inventory? . . ☐ Yes ☑ No
If "Yes," attach explanation.

Schedule B   Other Information

		Yes	No
1	Check method of accounting: **(a)** ☐ Cash **(b)** ☑ Accrual **(c)** ☐ Other (specify) ▶		
2	Refer to the list on page 24 of the instructions and state the corporation's principal: **(a)** Business activity ▶ *5008 Distributor* **(b)** Product or service ▶ *heavy equipment*		
3	Did the corporation at the end of the tax year own, directly or indirectly, 50% or more of the voting stock of a domestic corporation? (For rules of attribution, see section 267(c).) If "Yes," attach a schedule showing: **(a)** name, address, and employer identification number and **(b)** percentage owned.		✓
4	Was the corporation a member of a controlled group subject to the provisions of section 1561?		✓
5	At any time during calendar year 1995, did the corporation have an interest in or a signature or other authority over a financial account in a foreign country (such as a bank account, securities account, or other financial account)? (See page 14 of the instructions for exceptions and filing requirements for Form TD F 90-22.1.) . . . . If "Yes," enter the name of the foreign country ▶		✓
6	Was the corporation the grantor of, or transferor to, a foreign trust that existed during the current tax year, whether or not the corporation had any beneficial interest in it? If "Yes," the corporation may have to file Forms 3520, 3520-A, or 926		✓
7	Check this box if the corporation has filed or is required to file **Form 8264,** Application for Registration of a Tax Shelter . . . . ▶ ☐		
8	Check this box if the corporation issued publicly offered debt instruments with original issue discount . . ▶ ☐ If so, the corporation may have to file **Form 8281,** Information Return for Publicly Offered Original Issue Discount Instruments.		
9	If the corporation: **(a)** filed its election to be an S corporation after 1986, **(b)** was a C corporation before it elected to be an S corporation **or** the corporation acquired an asset with a basis determined by reference to its basis (or the basis of any other property) in the hands of a C corporation, and **(c)** has net unrealized built-in gain (defined in section 1374(d)(1)) in excess of the net recognized built-in gain from prior years, enter the net unrealized built-in gain reduced by net recognized built-in gain from prior years (see page 14 of the instructions) . . . . . ▶ $ *37,200*		
10	Check this box if the corporation had subchapter C earnings and profits at the close of the tax year (see page 15 of the instructions) . . . . ▶ ☐		

Designation of Tax Matters Person (see page 15 of the instructions)

Enter below the shareholder designated as the tax matters person (TMP) for the tax year of this return:

Name of designated TMP ▶ *John H. Green*   Identifying number of TMP ▶ *458-00-0327*

Address of designated TMP ▶ *4340 Holmes Parkway, Metro City, OH 43704*

Form 1120S (1995)

Page **3**

Schedule K — Shareholders' Shares of Income, Credits, Deductions, etc.

	(a) Pro rata share items		(b) Total amount
Income (Loss)	**1** Ordinary income (loss) from trade or business activities (page 1, line 21)	**1**	119,000
	2 Net income (loss) from rental real estate activities (attach Form 8825)	**2**	
	3a Gross income from other rental activities . . . . . . `3a`		
	b Expenses from other rental activities (attach schedule). `3b`		
	c Net income (loss) from other rental activities. Subtract line 3b from line 3a	**3c**	
	4 Portfolio income (loss):		
	a Interest income	**4a**	4,000
	b Dividend income.	**4b**	16,000
	c Royalty income	**4c**	
	d Net short-term capital gain (loss) (attach Schedule D (Form 1120S))	**4d**	
	e Net long-term capital gain (loss) (attach Schedule D (Form 1120S)).	**4e**	
	f Other portfolio income (loss) (attach schedule)	**4f**	
	5 Net gain (loss) under section 1231 (other than due to casualty or theft) (attach Form 4797)	**5**	
	6 Other income (loss) (attach schedule)	**6**	
Deductions	**7** Charitable contributions (attach schedule).	**7**	24,000
	8 Section 179 expense deduction (attach Form 4562).	**8**	
	9 Deductions related to portfolio income (loss) (itemize)	**9**	
	10 Other deductions (attach schedule)	**10**	
Investment Interest	**11a** Interest expense on investment debts	**11a**	3,000
	b (1) Investment income included on lines 4a, 4b, 4c, and 4f above	**11b(1)**	20,000
	(2) Investment expenses included on line 9 above	**11b(2)**	
Credits	**12a** Credit for alcohol used as a fuel (attach Form 6478)	**12a**	
	b Low-income housing credit:		
	(1) From partnerships to which section 42(j)(5) applies for property placed in service before 1990	**12b(1)**	
	(2) Other than on line 12b(1) for property placed in service before 1990.	**12b(2)**	
	(3) From partnerships to which section 42(j)(5) applies for property placed in service after 1989	**12b(3)**	
	(4) Other than on line 12b(3) for property placed in service after 1989	**12b(4)**	
	c Qualified rehabilitation expenditures related to rental real estate activities (attach Form 3468)	**12c**	
	d Credits (other than credits shown on lines 12b and 12c) related to rental real estate activities	**12d**	
	e Credits related to other rental activities.	**12e**	
	13 Other credits	**13**	6,000
Adjustments and Tax Preference Items	**14a** Depreciation adjustment on property placed in service after 1986	**14a**	
	b Adjusted gain or loss	**14b**	
	c Depletion (other than oil and gas)	**14c**	
	d (1) Gross income from oil, gas, or geothermal properties	**14d(1)**	
	(2) Deductions allocable to oil, gas, or geothermal properties	**14d(2)**	
	e Other adjustments and tax preference items (attach schedule)	**14e**	
Foreign Taxes	**15a** Type of income ▶		
	b Name of foreign country or U.S. possession ▶		
	c Total gross income from sources outside the United States (attach schedule) . . .	**15c**	
	d Total applicable deductions and losses (attach schedule)	**15d**	
	e Total foreign taxes (check one): ▶ ☐ Paid ☐ Accrued	**15e**	
	f Reduction in taxes available for credit (attach schedule)	**15f**	
	g Other foreign tax information (attach schedule)	**15g**	
Other	**16** Section 59(e)(2) expenditures: **a** Type ▶		
	b Amount	**16b**	
	17 Tax-exempt interest income	**17**	5,000
	18 Other tax-exempt income	**18**	
	19 Nondeductible expenses	**19**	16,350
	20 Total property distributions (including cash) other than dividends reported on line 22 below	**20**	65,000
	21 Other items and amounts required to be reported separately to shareholders (attach schedule)		
	22 Total dividend distributions paid from accumulated earnings and profits	**22**	
	23 **Income (loss).** (Required only if Schedule M-1 must be completed.) Combine lines 1 through 6 in column (b). From the result, subtract the sum of lines 7 through 11a, 15e, and 16b	**23**	112,000

Form 1120S (1995) Page **4**

Schedule L — Balance Sheets

Assets	Beginning of tax year (a)	(b)	End of tax year (c)	(d)
1 Cash		14,700		14,514
2a Trade notes and accounts receivable	98,400		33,700	
b Less allowance for bad debts		98,400		33,700
3 Inventories		126,000		298,400
4 U.S. Government obligations				
5 Tax-exempt securities		100,000		100,000
6 Other current assets (attach schedule)		26,300		26,300
7 Loans to shareholders				
8 Mortgage and real estate loans				
9 Other investments (attach schedule)		100,000		100,000
10a Buildings and other depreciable assets	204,700		204,700	
b Less accumulated depreciation	36,000	168,700	45,580	
11a Depletable assets				
b Less accumulated depletion				
12 Land (net of any amortization)		20,000		20,000
13a Intangible assets (amortizable only)				
b Less accumulated amortization				
14 Other assets (attach schedule)		14,800		19,300
15 Total assets		668,900		771,334
Liabilities and Shareholders' Equity				
16 Accounts payable		28,500		34,834
17 Mortgages, notes, bonds payable in less than 1 year		4,300		4,300
18 Other current liabilities (attach schedule)		6,800		7,400
19 Loans from shareholders				
20 Mortgages, notes, bonds payable in 1 year or more		161,300		215,530
21 Other liabilities (attach schedule)				
22 Capital stock		2,000		2,000
23 Paid-in or capital surplus		198,000		198,000
24 Retained earnings		268,000		309,270
25 Less cost of treasury stock		( )		( )
26 Total liabilities and shareholders' equity		668,900		771,334

Schedule M-1 — Reconciliation of Income (Loss) per Books With Income (Loss) per Return (You are not required to complete this schedule if the total assets on line 15, column (d), of Schedule L are less than $25,000.)

1 Net income (loss) per books	106,270	5 Income recorded on books this year not included on Schedule K, lines 1 through 6 (itemize):		
2 Income included on Schedule K, lines 1 through 6, not recorded on books this year (itemize):		a Tax-exempt interest $ 5,000	5,000	
	0			
3 Expenses recorded on books this year not included on Schedule K, lines 1 through 11a, 15e, and 16b (itemize):		6 Deductions included on Schedule K, lines 1 through 11a, 15e, and 16b, not charged against book income this year (itemize):		
a Depreciation $		a Depreciation $ 5,620		
b Travel and entertainment $ Itemized statement attached	16,350		5,620	
		7 Add lines 5 and 6	10,620	
4 Add lines 1 through 3	122,620	8 Income (loss) (Schedule K, line 23). Line 4 less line 7	112,000	

Schedule M-2 — Analysis of Accumulated Adjustments Account, Other Adjustments Account, and Shareholders' Undistributed Taxable Income Previously Taxed (see page 22 of the instructions)

	(a) Accumulated adjustments account	(b) Other adjustments account	(c) Shareholders' undistributed taxable income previously taxed
1 Balance at beginning of tax year	0	0	
2 Ordinary income from page 1, line 21	119,000		
3 Other additions	20,000	5,000	
4 Loss from page 1, line 21	(0)		
5 Other reductions	(42,500)	(850)	
6 Combine lines 1 through 5	96,500	4,150	
7 Distributions other than dividend distributions	65,000	0	
8 Balance at end of tax year. Subtract line 7 from line 6	31,500	4,150	

1995

Department of the Treasury
Internal Revenue Service

Instructions for Schedule D (Form 1120S)

Capital Gains and Losses and Built-In Gains

Section references are to the Internal Revenue Code unless otherwise noted.

Caution: *At the time these instructions were printed, Congress was considering legislation that would change the tax treatment of capital gains. Get* **Pub. 553,** *Highlights of 1995 Tax Changes, for more information. See* **General Instructions** *on page 1 of the Form 1120S instructions for how to get forms and publications.*

Purpose of Schedule

Schedule D is used by all S corporations to report **(a)** sales or exchanges of capital assets (defined below), **(b)** gains on distributions to shareholders of appreciated capital assets (referred to here as distributions), and **(c)** nonbusiness bad debts.

If the corporation filed its election to be an S corporation before 1987 (or filed its election during 1987 or 1988 and qualifies for the transitional relief from the built-in gains tax described in Part IV on page 2), and had net capital gain (line 15) of more than $25,000, it may be liable for a capital gains tax on the gain in excess of $25,000. The tax is figured in Part III of Schedule D.

Generally, if the corporation **(a)** filed an election to be an S corporation after 1986, **(b)** was a C corporation at the time it made the election, and **(c)** has net recognized built-in gain as defined in section 1374(d)(2), **it is liable** for the built-in gains tax. The tax is figured in Part IV of Schedule D.

Sales, exchanges, and distributions of property other than capital assets, including property used in a trade or business; involuntary conversions (other than from casualties or thefts); and gain from the disposition of an interest in oil, gas, or geothermal property, should be reported on **Form 4797,** Sales of Business Property.

If property is involuntarily converted because of a casualty or theft, use **Form 4684,** Casualties and Thefts.

Parts I and II

Generally, report sales or exchanges (including like-kind exchanges) even if there is no gain or loss. In Part I, report the sale, exchange, or distribution of capital assets held 1 year or less. In Part II, report the sale, exchange, or

distribution of capital assets held more than 1 year. Use the trade dates for the dates of acquisition and sale of stocks and bonds on an exchange or over-the-counter market.

What Are Capital Assets?—Each item of property the corporation held (whether or not connected with its trade or business) is a capital asset **except:**

1. Assets that can be inventoried or property held mainly for sale to customers.

2. Depreciable or real property used in the trade or business.

3. Certain copyrights; literary, musical, or artistic compositions; letters or memorandums; or similar property.

4. Accounts or notes receivable acquired in the ordinary course of trade or business for services rendered or from the sale of property described in **1** above.

5. U.S. Government publications, including the Congressional Record, that the corporation received from the Government, other than by purchase at the normal sales price, or that the corporation got from another taxpayer who had received it in a similar way, if the corporation's basis is determined by reference to the previous owner.

Special Rules for the Treatment of Certain Gains and Losses

Note: *For more information, get* **Pub. 544,** *Sales and Other Dispositions of Assets, and* **Pub. 589,** *Tax Information on S Corporations.*

● **Loss from a sale or exchange between the corporation and a related person.**—Except for distributions in complete liquidation of a corporation, no loss is allowed from the sale or exchange of property between the corporation and certain related persons. See section 267 for details.

● **Loss from a wash sale.**—The corporation cannot deduct a loss from a wash sale of stock or securities (including contracts or options to acquire or sell stock or securities) unless the corporation is a dealer in stock or securities and the loss was sustained in a transaction made in the ordinary course of the corporation's trade or business. A wash sale occurs if the

corporation acquires (by purchase or exchange), or has a contract or option to acquire, substantially identical stock or securities within 30 days before or after the date of the sale or exchange. See section 1091 for more information.

● **Gain on distribution of appreciated property.**—Generally, gain (but not loss) is recognized on a nonliquidating distribution of appreciated property to the extent that the property's fair market value exceeds its adjusted basis. See section 311 for more information.

● **Gain or loss on distribution of property in complete liquidation.**—Generally, gain or loss is recognized by a corporation upon the liquidating distribution of property as if it had sold the property at its fair market value. See section 336 for details and exceptions.

● **Gains and losses on section 1256 contracts and straddles.**—Use **Form 6781,** Gains and Losses From Section 1256 Contracts and Straddles, to report gains and losses from section 1256 contracts and straddles.

● **Gain or loss on certain short-term Federal, state, and municipal obligations.**—Such obligations are treated as capital assets in determining gain or loss. On any gain realized, a portion is treated as ordinary income and the balance is considered as a short-term capital gain. See section 1271.

● **Gain from installment sales.**—If a corporation has a gain this year from the sale of real property or a casual sale of personal property other than inventory and is to receive any payment in a later year, it must use the installment method (unless it elects not to) and file **Form 6252,** Installment Sale Income. Also use Form 6252 if a payment is received this year from a sale made in an earlier year on the installment basis.

The corporation may elect out of the installment method by reporting the full amount of the gain on a timely filed return (including extensions).

The installment method may not be used for sales of stock or securities (or certain other property described in the regulations) traded on an established securities market. See section 453(k).

Cat. No. 64419L

● **Gain or loss on an option to buy or sell property.**—See sections 1032 and 1234 for the rules that apply to a purchaser or grantor of an option.

● **Gain or loss from a short sale of property.**—Report the gain or loss to the extent that the property used to close the short sale is considered a capital asset in the hands of the taxpayer.

● **Loss from securities that are capital assets that become worthless during the year.**—Except for securities held by a bank, treat the loss as a capital loss as of the last day of the tax year. (See section 582 for the rules on the treatment of securities held by a bank.)

● **Nonrecognition of gain on sale of stock to an ESOP.**—See section 1042 for rules under which a taxpayer may elect not to recognize gain from the sale of certain stock to an employee stock ownership plan (ESOP).

● **Disposition of market discount bonds.**—See section 1276 for rules on the disposition of any market discount bonds.

● **Capital gain distributions.**—Report capital gain distributions paid by mutual funds as long-term capital gain on line 7 regardless of how long the corporation owned stock in the fund.

● **Nonbusiness bad debts.**—A nonbusiness bad debt must be treated as a short-term capital loss and can be deducted only in the year the debt becomes totally worthless. For each bad debt, enter the name of the debtor and "schedule attached" in column (a) of line 1 and the amount of the bad debt as a loss in column (f). Also attach a statement of facts to support each bad debt deduction.

● **Like-kind exchanges.**—An exchange of business or investment property for property of a like kind is reported on **Form 8824,** Like-Kind Exchanges.

How To Determine the Cost or Other Basis of the Property

In determining gain or loss, the basis of property will generally be its cost (see section 1012 and related regulations). The exceptions to the general rule are provided in sections contained in subchapters C, K, O, and P of the Code. For example, if the corporation acquired the property by dividend, liquidation of another corporation, transfer from a shareholder, reorganization, bequest, contribution or gift, tax-free exchange, involuntary conversion, certain asset acquisitions, or wash sale of stock, see sections 301 (or 1059), 334, 362 (or 358), 1014, 1015, 1031, 1033, 1060, and 1091, respectively. Attach an explanation if you use a basis other than actual cash cost of the property.

If the corporation is allowed a charitable contribution deduction because it sold property to a charitable organization, figure the adjusted basis

for determining gain from the sale by dividing the amount realized by the fair market value and multiplying that result by the adjusted basis.

See section 852(f) for the treatment of certain load charges incurred in acquiring stock in a mutual fund with a reinvestment right.

Increase the cost or other basis by any expense of sale, such as broker's fees, commissions, state and local transfer taxes, and option premiums, before making an entry in column (e), unless the net sales price was reported in column (d).

Part III—Capital Gains Tax

If the net long-term capital gain is more than the net short-term capital loss, there is a net capital gain. If this gain exceeds $25,000, **and** the corporation elected to be an S corporation before 1987 (or filed its election during 1987 or 1988 and qualifies for the transitional relief from the built-in gains tax described in Part IV below), the corporation may be liable for income tax on the gain.

Determine if the corporation is liable for the tax by answering the following questions. If answers to questions A, B, and C are "Yes," the tax applies and Part III of Schedule D must be completed. Otherwise, the corporation is not liable for the tax.

If net capital gain is more than $25,000, and the corporation is not liable for the tax, attach the Part III instructions to Schedule D with questions A, B, and C answered to show why the tax does not apply.

A. Is net capital gain (line 15, Schedule D) more than $25,000, and more than 50% of taxable income (see the instructions for line 19, Schedule D)? . . . ☐ Yes ☐ No

B. Is taxable income (see the instructions for line 19, Schedule D) more than $25,000? . . . . . ☐ Yes ☐ No

C. Does any long-term capital gain (line 14, Schedule D) represent gain from substituted basis property (defined below)? . . . ☐ Yes ☐ No

For purposes of the capital gains tax, **substituted basis property** is property that:

1. Was acquired by the S corporation during the period that began 36 months before the first day of the tax year and ended on the last day of the tax year, and

2. Has a basis determined by reference to the basis of any property in the hands of another corporation, if the other corporation was **not** an S corporation throughout the period that began the later of:

a. 36 months before the first day of the tax year, or

b. The time the other corporation came into existence,

and ended on the date the other corporation transferred the property used to determine the basis of the property acquired by the S corporation.

Line 15.—If the corporation is liable for the tax on excess net passive income (line 22a, page 1, Form 1120S) or the built-in gains tax (see Part IV below), and capital gain or loss was included in the computation of either tax, figure the amount to enter on line 15 as follows:

Step 1—Refigure lines 1 through 3, 7 through 9, and 13 of Schedule D by:

1. Excluding the portion of any recognized built-in capital gain or loss that does not qualify for transitional relief, and

2. Reducing any capital gain taken into account in determining passive investment income (line 2 of the worksheet for line 22a, page 1 of Form 1120S) by the portion of excess net passive income attributable to such gain. The attributable portion is figured by multiplying excess net passive income by a fraction, the numerator of which is the capital gain (less any expenses attributable to such gain), and the denominator of which is net passive income.

Step 2—Refigure lines 4, 10, 14, and 15 of Schedule D using the amounts determined in step 1.

Line 19.—Figure taxable income by completing lines 1 through 28 of **Form 1120,** U.S. Corporation Income Tax Return. Enter the amount from line 28 of Form 1120 on line 19 of Schedule D. Attach to Schedule D the Form 1120 computation or other worksheet used to figure taxable income.

Line 20.—Figure the tax under section 11 on the taxable income shown on line 19 as if the corporation were not an S corporation. You may use Schedule J of Form 1120 to figure the tax. Attach your tax computation to Schedule D.

Line 21.—Figure the excess of the net long-term capital gain over the net short-term capital loss from substituted basis property. Reduce this amount by any excess net passive income attributable to this gain (see the instructions for line 15). Attach to Schedule D your computation of the line 21 amount. Substituted basis property is defined below question C on this page.

Part IV—Built-In Gains Tax

Section 1374 provides for a tax on built-in gains that applies to certain corporations that made the election to be an S corporation after 1986. This tax does not apply to any corporation that has been an S corporation for each of its tax years, unless the corporation acquired an asset with a basis determined by reference to its basis (or the basis of any other property) in the hands of a C corporation.

Transitional Relief From Built-In Gains Tax.—Section 633(d)(8) of the Tax Reform Act of 1986 provides special transitional relief from the built-in gains tax for qualified corporations that elected to be S corporations during 1987 or 1988. A qualified corporation is any corporation, the stock of which:

1. Was more than 50% owned (by value) by a qualified group (defined below) on August 1, 1986, and at all times thereafter before the corporation is completely liquidated, and

2. Had a fair market value of less than $10 million on both the date the corporation made a valid S election and on August 1, 1986. However, if the fair market value of the stock on either date was between $5 million and $10 million, the corporation is given only partial relief from the built-in gains tax. The portion of the built-in gain **not** eligible for relief is a fraction, the numerator of which is the amount by which the fair market value of the corporation on the date it made a valid S election (or on August 1, 1986, if higher) exceeds $5 million and the denominator of which is $5 million.

A qualified group is a group of 10 or fewer qualified persons. A qualified person is:

1. An individual,

2. An estate, or

3. A trust described in section 1361(c)(2)(A)(ii) or (iii).

For any corporation that elected to be an S corporation after March 30, 1988, the qualified group must have owned (or be treated as having owned) more than 50% (by value) of the corporation's stock at all times during the 5-year period ending on the date of adoption of a plan of complete liquidation.

Transitional relief **does not** apply to:

1. Ordinary gains or losses (determined without regard to section 1239),

2. Gains or losses from the disposition of capital assets held for 6 months or less, and

3. Gains from the disposition of any asset acquired by the corporation with a substituted basis, if a principal purpose for acquiring the asset was to secure transitional relief from the built-in gains tax.

Line 24.—Enter the amount that would be the taxable income of the corporation for the tax year if only recognized built-in gains (including any carryover of gain under section 1374(d)(2)(B)) and recognized built-in losses were taken into account.

Section 1374(d)(3) defines a **recognized built-in gain** as any gain recognized during the recognition period (the 10-year period beginning on the first day of the first tax year for which the corporation is an S corporation, or beginning the date the asset was acquired by the S corporation, for an asset with a basis determined by reference to its basis (or the basis of any other property) in the hands of a C corporation) on the sale or distribution (disposition) of any asset, except to the extent the corporation establishes that—

1. The asset was not held by the corporation as of the beginning of the first tax year the corporation was an S corporation (except this does not apply to an asset acquired by the S corporation with a basis determined by reference to its basis (or the basis of any other property) in the hands of a C corporation), or

2. The gain exceeds the excess of the fair market value of the asset as of the start of the first tax year (or as of the date the asset was acquired by the S corporation, for an asset with a basis determined by reference to its basis (or the basis of any other property) in the hands of a C corporation) over the adjusted basis of the asset at that time.

Section 1374(d)(4) defines a **recognized built-in loss** as any loss recognized during the recognition period (stated above) on the disposition of any asset to the extent the corporation establishes that—

1. The asset was held by the corporation as of the beginning of the 1st tax year the corporation was an S corporation (except that this does not apply to an asset acquired by the S corporation with a basis determined by reference to its basis (or the basis of any other property) in the hands of a C corporation), and

2. The loss does not exceed the excess of the adjusted basis of the asset as of the beginning of the first tax year (or as of the date the asset was acquired by the S corporation, for an asset with a basis determined by reference to its basis (or the basis of any other property) in the hands of a C corporation), over the fair market value of the asset as of that time.

A qualified corporation must show on an attachment to Schedule D its total net recognized built-in gain and also list separately the gain or loss that is from **(a)** capital assets held 6 months or less, and **(b)** assets for which the disposition results in ordinary income or loss. A nonqualified corporation must show on an attachment its total net recognized built-in gain and list separately any capital gain or loss and ordinary gain or loss.

Line 25.—Figure taxable income by completing lines 1 through 28 of Form 1120. Enter the amount from line 28 of Form 1120 on line 25. Attach to Schedule D the Form 1120 computation or other worksheet used to figure taxable income.

Line 26.—If for any tax year the amount on line 24 exceeds the taxable income on line 25, the excess is treated as a recognized built-in gain in the succeeding tax year. This carryover provision applies only in the case of an S corporation that made its election to be an S corporation after March 30, 1988. See section 1374(d)(2)(B).

Line 27.—Enter the section 1374(b)(2) deduction. Generally, this is any net operating loss carryforward or capital loss carryforward (to the extent of net capital gain included in recognized built-in gain for the tax year) arising in tax years for which the corporation was a C corporation. See section 1374(b)(2) for details.

SCHEDULE D
(Form 1120S)

Department of the Treasury
Internal Revenue Service

Capital Gains and Losses and Built-In Gains

▶ Attach to Form 1120S.

▶ See separate instructions.

OMB No. 1545-0130

1995

Name

Employer identification number

Part I — Short-Term Capital Gains and Losses—Assets Held One Year or Less

(a) Kind of property and description (Example, 100 shares of "Z" Co.)	(b) Date acquired (mo., day, yr.)	(c) Date sold (mo., day, yr.)	(d) Sales price	(e) Cost or other basis (see instructions)	(f) Gain or (loss) ((d) less (e))
1					

2	Short-term capital gain from installment sales from Form 6252, line 26 or 37	2
3	Short-term capital gain or (loss) from like-kind exchanges from Form 8824	3
4	Combine lines 1 through 3 and enter here	4
5	Tax on short-term capital gain included on line 31 below	5
6	**Net short-term capital gain or (loss).** Subtract line 5 from line 4. Enter here and on Form 1120S, Schedule K, line 4d or line 6	6

Part II — Long-Term Capital Gains and Losses—Assets Held More Than One Year

7					

8	Long-term capital gain from installment sales from Form 6252, line 26 or 37	8
9	Long-term capital gain or (loss) from like-kind exchanges from Form 8824	9
10	Combine lines 7 through 9 and enter here	10
11	Tax on long-term capital gain included on lines 23 and 31 below	11
12	**Net long-term capital gain or (loss).** Subtract line 11 from line 10. Enter here and on Form 1120S, Schedule K, line 4e or line 6	12

Part III — Capital Gains Tax (See instructions **before** completing this part.)

13	Enter section 1231 gain from Form 4797, line 10	13
14	Net long-term capital gain or (loss). Combine lines 10 and 13	14
	Note: *If the corporation is liable for the excess net passive income tax (Form 1120S, page 1, line 22a) or the built-in gains tax (Part IV below), see the line 15 instructions before completing line 15.*	
15	Net capital gain. Enter excess of net long-term capital gain (line 14) over net short-term capital loss (line 4) .	15
16	Statutory minimum	16	$25,000
17	Subtract line 16 from line 15	17
18	Enter 34% of line 17	18
19	Taxable income (see instructions and attach computation schedule)	19
20	Enter tax on line 19 amount (see instructions and attach computation schedule)	20
21	Net capital gain from substituted basis property (see instructions and attach computation schedule) . . .	21
22	Enter 35% of line 21	22
23	**Tax.** Enter the smallest of line 18, 20, or 22 here and on Form 1120S, page 1, line 22b	23

Part IV — Built-In Gains Tax (See instructions **before** completing this part.)

24	Excess of recognized built-in gains over recognized built-in losses (see instructions and attach computation schedule)	24
25	Taxable income (see instructions and attach computation schedule)	25
26	Net recognized built-in gain. Enter the smallest of line 24, line 25, or line 9 of Schedule B (see instructions)	26
27	Section 1374(b)(2) deduction	27
28	Subtract line 27 from line 26. If zero or less, enter -0- here and on line 31	28
29	Enter 35% of line 28	29
30	Business credit and minimum tax credit carryforwards under section 1374(b)(3) from C corporation years	30
31	**Tax.** Subtract line 30 from line 29 (if zero or less, enter -0-). Enter here and on Form 1120S, page 1, line 22b	31

For Paperwork Reduction Act Notice, see page 1 of Instructions for Form 1120S.   Cat. No. 11516V   **Schedule D (Form 1120S) 1995**

 Printed on recycled paper

1995

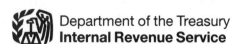

Department of the Treasury
Internal Revenue Service

Shareholder's Instructions for Schedule K-1 (Form 1120S)

Shareholder's Share of Income, Credits, Deductions, etc.

(For Shareholder's Use Only)

Section references are to the Internal Revenue Code unless otherwise noted.

General Instructions

Purpose of Schedule K-1

The corporation uses Schedule K-1 (Form 1120S) to report your pro rata share of the corporation's income (reduced by any tax the corporation paid on the income), credits, deductions, etc. **Please keep it for your records. Do not file it with your tax return.** The corporation has filed a copy with the IRS.

Although the corporation may have to pay a capital gains tax (or built-in gains tax) and an excess net passive income tax, you, the shareholder, are liable for income tax on your share of the corporation's income, whether or not distributed, and you must include your share on your tax return if a return is required. **Your distributive share of S corporation income is not self-employment income and it is not subject to self-employment tax.**

You should use these instructions to help you report the items shown on Schedule K-1 on your tax return.

Where *(attach schedule)* appears next to a line on Schedule K-1, it means the information for these lines (if applicable) will be shown in the "Supplemental Information" space below line 23 of Schedule K-1. If additional space was needed, the corporation will have attached a statement to Schedule K-1 to show the information for the line item.

The notation "(see Instructions for Schedule K-1)" in items A and C at the top of Schedule K-1 is directed to the corporation. You, as a shareholder, should disregard these notations.

Schedule K-1 does not show the amount of actual **dividend** distributions the corporation made to you. The corporation must report to you such amounts totaling $10 or more for the calendar year on **Form 1099-DIV,** Dividends and Distributions. You report actual dividend distributions on Form 1040, line 9.

Basis of Your Stock

You are responsible for maintaining records to show the computation of the basis of your stock in the corporation. Schedule K-1 provides information to help you make the computation at the end of each corporate tax year. The basis of your stock (generally, its cost) is adjusted as follows and, except as noted, in the order listed. These rules generally apply for tax years of the S corporation beginning after 1993. For prior tax years, basis must be determined in a reasonable manner. Return positions consistent with these rules are reasonable. In addition, basis may be adjusted under other provisions of the Internal Revenue Code.

1. Basis is increased by **(a)** all income (including tax-exempt income) reported on Schedule K-1 and **(b)** the excess of the deduction for depletion (other than oil and gas depletion) over the basis of the property subject to depletion.

Note: *You must report the taxable income on your return (if you are required to file a return) for it to increase your basis.*

2. Basis is decreased by **(a)** nondeductible expenses and **(b)** the depletion deduction for any oil and gas property held by the corporation, but only to the extent your pro rata share of the property's adjusted basis exceeds that deduction.

3. Basis is decreased by all deductible losses and deductions reported on Schedule K-1.

4. Basis is decreased by property distributions (including cash) made by the corporation (excluding dividend distributions reported on Form 1099-DIV and distributions in excess of basis) reported on Schedule K-1, line 20.

You may elect to decrease your basis under **3** above prior to decreasing your basis under **2** above. If you make this election, any amount described under **2** that exceeds the basis of your stock and debt owed to you by the corporation is treated as an amount described under **2** for the following tax year. To make the election, attach a statement to your timely-filed original or amended return that states you agree to the carryover rule of Regulations section 1.1367-1(f) and the name of the S corporation to which the rule applies. Once made, the election applies to the year for which it is made and all future tax years for that S corporation, unless the IRS agrees to revoke your election.

The basis of each share of stock is increased or decreased (but not below zero) based on its pro rata share of the above adjustments. If the total decreases in basis attributable to a share exceed that share's basis, the excess reduces (but not below zero) the remaining bases of all other shares of stock in proportion to the remaining basis of each of those shares.

Inconsistent Treatment of Items

Generally, you must report subchapter S items shown on your Schedule K-1 (and any attached schedules) the same way that the corporation treated the items on its return. This rule does not apply if your corporation is within the small S corporation exception and does not elect to have the tax treatment of subchapter S items determined at the corporate level.

If the treatment on your original or amended return is inconsistent with the corporation's treatment, or if the corporation has not filed a return, you must file **Form 8082,** Notice of Inconsistent Treatment or Amended Return (Administrative Adjustment Request (AAR)), with your original or amended return to identify and explain any inconsistency (or to note that a corporate return has not been filed).

If you are required to file Form 8082 but fail to do so, you may be subject to the accuracy-related penalty. This penalty is in addition to any tax that results from making your amount or treatment of the item consistent with that shown on the corporation's return. Any deficiency that results from making the amounts consistent may be assessed immediately.

Errors

If you believe the corporation has made an error on your Schedule K-1, notify the corporation and ask for a corrected Schedule K-1. Do not change any items

Cat. No. 11521O

on your copy. Be sure that the corporation sends a copy of the corrected Schedule K-1 to the IRS. If your corporation does not meet the small S corporation exception, and you are unable to reach agreement with the corporation regarding the inconsistency, you must file Form 8082.

International Boycotts

Every corporation that had operations in, or related to, a boycotting country, company, or national of a country, must file **Form 5713,** International Boycott Report.

If the corporation cooperated with an international boycott, it must give you a copy of its Form 5713. You must file your own Form 5713 to report the activities of the corporation and any other boycott operations that you may have. You may lose certain tax benefits if the corporation participated in, or cooperated with, an international boycott. See Form 5713 and the instructions for more information.

Elections

Generally, the corporation decides how to figure taxable income from its operations. For example, it chooses the accounting method and depreciation methods it will use.

However, certain elections are made by you separately on your income tax return and not by the corporation. These elections are made under—

● Section 59(e) (deduction of certain qualified expenditures ratably over the period of time specified in that section— see the instructions for lines 16a and 16b);

● Section 617 (deduction and recapture of certain mining exploration expenditures); and

● Section 901 (foreign tax credit).

Additional Information

For more information on the treatment of S corporation income, credits, deductions, etc., get **Pub. 589,** Tax Information on S Corporations; **Pub. 535,** Business Expenses; **Pub. 550,** Investment Income and Expenses; and **Pub. 925,** Passive Activity and At-Risk Rules.

These and other publications referenced throughout these instructions may be obtained at most IRS offices. To order publications and forms, call 1-800-TAX-FORM (1-800-829-3676).

Limitations on Losses, Deductions, and Credits

Aggregate Losses and Deductions Limited to Basis of Stock and Debt

Generally, the deduction for your share of aggregate losses and deductions reported on Schedule K-1 is limited to the basis of your stock and debt owed to you by the corporation. The basis of your stock is figured at year end. See **Basis of Your Stock** on page 1. The basis of loans to the corporation is the balance the corporation now owes you, less any reduction for losses in a prior year. See the instructions for line 21. Any loss not allowed for the tax year because of this limitation is available for indefinite carryover, limited to the basis of your stock and debt, in each subsequent tax year. See section 1366(d) for details.

At-Risk Limitations

Generally, if you have:

1. A loss or other deduction from any activity carried on by the corporation as a trade or business or for the production of income, and

2. Amounts in the activity for which you are not at risk,

you will have to complete **Form 6198,** At-Risk Limitations, to figure your allowable loss.

The at-risk rules generally limit the amount of loss (including loss on the disposition of assets) and other deductions (such as the section 179 expense deduction) that you can claim to the amount you could actually lose in the activity. However, if you acquired your stock before 1987, the at-risk rules do not apply to losses from an activity of holding real property placed in service before 1987 by the corporation. The activity of holding mineral property does not qualify for this exception.

Generally, you are not at risk for amounts such as the following:

● The basis of your stock in the corporation or basis of your loans to the corporation if the cash or other property used to purchase the stock or make the loans was from a source **(a)** covered by nonrecourse indebtedness (except for certain qualified nonrecourse financing, as defined in section 465(b)(6)); **(b)** protected against loss by a guarantee, stop-loss agreement, or other similar arrangement; or **(c)** that is covered by indebtedness from a person who has an interest in the activity or from a related person to a person (except you) having such an interest, other than a creditor.

● Any cash or property contributed to a corporate activity, or your interest in the corporate activity, that is **(a)** covered by nonrecourse indebtedness (except for certain qualified nonrecourse financing,

as defined in section 465(b)(6)); **(b)** protected against loss by a guarantee, stop-loss agreement, or other similar arrangement; or **(c)** that is covered by indebtedness from a person who has an interest in such activity or from a related person to a person (except you) having such an interest, other than a creditor.

Any loss from a section 465 activity not allowed for this tax year will be treated as a deduction allocable to the activity in the next tax year.

To help you complete Form 6198, the corporation should specify on an attachment to Schedule K-1 your share of the total pre-1976 losses from a section 465(c)(1) activity (i.e., films or video tapes, and leasing section 1245, farm, or oil and gas property) for which there existed a corresponding amount of nonrecourse liability at the end of the year in which the losses occurred. Also, you should get a separate statement of income, expenses, etc., for each activity from the corporation.

Passive Activity Limitations

Section 469 provides rules that limit the deduction of certain losses and credits. The rules apply to shareholders who—

● Are individuals, estates, or trusts, and

● Have a passive activity loss or credit for the year.

Generally, passive activities **include:**

1. Trade or business activities in which you did not materially participate, and

2. Activities that meet the definition of rental activities under Temporary Regulations section 1.469-1T(e)(3) and Regulations section 1.469-1(e)(3).

Passive activities **do not** include:

1. Trade or business activities in which you materially participated.

2. Rental real estate activities in which you materially participated if you were a "real estate professional" for the tax year. You were a real estate professional only if you met both of the following conditions:

a. More than half of the personal services you performed in trades or businesses were performed in real property trades or businesses in which you materially participated, and

b. You performed more than 750 hours of services in real property trades or businesses in which you materially participated.

For purposes of this rule, each interest in rental real estate is a separate activity, unless you elect to treat all interests in rental real estate as one activity.

If you are married filing jointly, either you or your spouse must separately meet both of the above conditions, without taking into account services performed by the other spouse.

A real property trade or business is any real property development, redevelopment, construction, reconstruction, acquisition, conversion, rental, operation, management, leasing, or brokerage trade or business. Services you performed as an employee are not treated as performed in a real property trade or business unless you owned more than 5% of the stock (or more than 5% of the capital or profits interest) in the employer.

3. The rental of a dwelling unit any shareholder used for personal purposes during the year for more than the greater of 14 days or 10% of the number of days that the residence was rented at fair rental value.

4. Activities of trading personal property for the account of owners of interests in the activities.

The corporation will identify separately each activity that may be passive to you. If the corporation had more than one activity, it will report information in the line 23 Supplemental Information space, or attach a statement if more space is needed, that **(a)** identifies each activity (trade or business activity, rental real estate activity, rental activity other than rental real estate, etc.); **(b)** specifies the income (loss), deductions, and credits from each activity; and **(c)** provides other details you may need to determine if an activity loss or credit is subject to the passive activity limitations.

If you determine that you have a passive activity loss or credit, get **Form 8582,** Passive Activity Loss Limitations, to figure your allowable passive losses, and **Form 8582-CR,** Passive Activity Credit Limitations, to figure your allowable passive credit. See the instructions for these forms for more information.

Material participation.—You must determine if you materially participated **(a)** in each trade or business activity held through the corporation and **(b),** if you were a real estate professional (defined on page 2), in each rental real estate activity held through the corporation. All determinations of material participation are made with respect to your participation during the corporation's tax year.

Material participation standards for shareholders who are individuals are listed below. Special rules apply to certain retired or disabled farmers and to the surviving spouses of farmers. See the Instructions for Form 8582 for details.

Individuals.—If you are an individual, you are considered to materially participate in a trade or business activity only if one or more of the following apply:

1. You participated in the activity for more than 500 hours during the tax year.

2. Your participation in the activity for the tax year constituted substantially all of the participation in the activity of all individuals (including individuals who are not owners of interests in the activity).

3. You participated in the activity for more than 100 hours during the tax year, and your participation in the activity for the tax year was not less than the participation in the activity of any other individual (including individuals who were not owners of interests in the activity) for the tax year.

4. The activity was a significant participation activity for the tax year, and your aggregate participation in all significant participation activities (including those outside the corporation) during the tax year exceeded 500 hours. A significant participation activity is any trade or business activity in which you participated for more than 100 hours during the year and in which you did not materially participate under any of the material participation tests (other than this test **4**).

5. You materially participated in the activity for any 5 tax years (whether or not consecutive) during the 10 tax years that immediately precede the tax year.

6. The activity was a personal service activity and you materially participated in the activity for any 3 tax years (whether or not consecutive) preceding the tax year. An activity is a personal service activity if it involves the performance of personal services in the fields of health, law, engineering, architecture, accounting, actuarial science, performing arts, consulting, or any other trade or business, in which capital is not a material income-producing factor.

7. Based on all of the facts and circumstances, you participated in the activity on a regular, continuous, and substantial basis during the tax year.

Work counted toward material participation.—Generally, any work that you or your spouse does in connection with an activity held through an S corporation (in which you own stock at the time the work is done) is counted toward material participation. However, work in connection with an activity is not counted toward material participation if either of the following applies:

1. The work is not the sort of work that owners of the activity would usually do and one of the principal purposes of the work that you or your spouse does is to avoid the passive loss or credit limitations.

2. You do the work in your capacity as an investor and you are not directly involved in the day-to-day operations of the activity. Examples of work done as an investor that would not count toward material participation include:

a. Studying and reviewing financial statements or reports on operations of the activity;

b. Preparing or compiling summaries or analyses of the finances or operations of the activity; and

c. Monitoring the finances or operations of the activity in a nonmanagerial capacity.

Effect of determination.—If you determine that you materially participated in **(a)** a trade or business activity of the corporation, or **(b)** if you were a real estate professional (defined on page 2), in a rental real estate activity of the corporation, report the income (loss), deductions, and credits from that activity as indicated in either column (c) of Schedule K-1 or the instructions for your tax return.

If you determine that you **did not** materially participate in a trade or business activity of the corporation, or you have income (loss), deductions, or credits from a rental activity of the corporation (other than a rental real estate activity in which you materially participated, if you were a real estate professional), the amounts from that activity are passive. Report passive income (losses), deductions, and credits as follows:

1. If you have an overall gain (the excess of income over deductions and losses, including any prior year unallowed loss) from a passive activity, report the income, deductions, and losses from the activity as indicated on Schedule K-1 or in these instructions.

2. If you have an overall loss (the excess of deductions and losses, including any prior year unallowed loss, over income) or credits from a passive activity, you must report the income, deductions, losses, and credits from **all** passive activities following the Instructions for Form 8582 or Form 8582-CR, to see if your deductions, losses, and credits are limited under the passive activity rules.

Active participation in a rental real estate activity.—If you actively participated in a rental real estate activity, you may be able to deduct up to $25,000 of the loss from the activity from nonpassive income. This special allowance is an exception to the general rule disallowing losses in excess of income from passive activities. The special allowance is not available if you were married, file a separate return for the year, and did not live apart from your spouse at all times during the year.

Only individuals and qualifying estates can actively participate in a rental real estate activity. Estates (other than qualifying estates) and trusts cannot actively participate.

You are not considered to actively participate in a rental real estate activity if, at any time during the tax year, your interest (including your spouse's interest) in the activity was less than 10% (by value) of all interests in the activity.

Active participation is a less stringent requirement than material participation. You may be treated as actively

Page 3

participating if you participated, for example, in making management decisions or arranging for others to provide services (such as repairs) in a significant and bona fide sense.

Management decisions that can count as active participation include approving new tenants, deciding on rental terms, approving capital or repair expenditures, and other similar decisions.

An estate is a qualifying estate if the decedent would have satisfied the active participation requirement for the activity for the tax year the decedent died. A qualifying estate is treated as actively participating for tax years ending less than 2 years after the date of the decedent's death.

The maximum special allowance that single individuals and married individuals filing a joint return can qualify for is $25,000. The maximum is $12,500 for married individuals who file separate returns and who lived apart at all times during the year. The maximum special allowance for which an estate can qualify is $25,000 reduced by the special allowance for which the surviving spouse qualifies.

If your modified adjusted gross income (defined below) is $100,000 or less ($50,000 or less if married filing separately), your loss is deductible up to the amount of the maximum special allowance referred to in the preceding paragraph. If your modified adjusted gross income is more than $100,000 (more than $50,000 if married filing separately), the special allowance is limited to 50% of the difference between $150,000 ($75,000 if married filing separately) and your modified adjusted gross income. When modified adjusted gross income is $150,000 or more ($75,000 or more if married filing separately), there is no special allowance.

Modified adjusted gross income is your adjusted gross income figured without taking into account any passive activity loss, any rental real estate loss allowed under section 469(c)(7) to real estate professionals (as defined on page 2), any taxable social security or equivalent railroad retirement benefits, any deductible contributions to an IRA or certain other qualified retirement plans under section 219, the deduction allowed under section 164(f) for one-half of self-employment taxes, or the exclusion from income of interest from Series EE U.S. Savings Bonds used to pay higher education expenses.

Special rules for certain other activities.—If you have net income (loss), deductions, or credits from any activity to which special rules apply, the corporation will identify the activity and all amounts relating to it on Schedule K-1 or on an attachment.

If you have net income subject to recharacterization under Temporary Regulations section 1.469-2T(f) and Regulations section 1.469-2(f), report such amounts according to the Instructions for Form 8582.

If you have net income (loss), deductions, or credits from either of the following activities, treat such amounts as nonpassive and report them as instructed in column (c) of Schedule K-1 or in these instructions:

1. The rental of a dwelling unit any shareholder used for personal purposes during the year for more than the greater of 14 days or 10% of the number of days that the residence was rented at fair rental value.

2. Trading personal property for the account of owners of interests in the activity.

Specific Instructions

Item C

If the corporation is a registration-required tax shelter or has invested in a registration-required tax shelter, it should have completed Item C. If you claim or report any income, loss, deduction, or credit from a tax shelter, you are required to attach **Form 8271,** Investor Reporting of Tax Shelter Registration Number, to your tax return. If the corporation has invested in a tax shelter, it is required to give you a copy of its Form 8271 with your Schedule K-1. Use the information on this Form 8271 to complete your Form 8271.

If the corporation itself is a registration-required tax shelter, use the information on Schedule K-1 (name of corporation, corporation identifying number, and tax shelter registration number) to complete your Form 8271.

Lines 1 Through 23

The amounts on lines 1 through 23 show your pro rata share of ordinary income, loss, deductions, credits, and other information from all corporate activities. These amounts do not take into account limitations on losses, credits, or other items that may have to be adjusted because of:

1. The adjusted basis of your stock and debt in the corporation,

2. The at-risk limitations,

3. The passive activity limitations, or

4. Any other limitations that must be taken into account at the shareholder level in figuring taxable income (e.g., the section 179 expense limitation).

The limitations of **1, 2,** and **3** are discussed above, and the limitations for **4** are discussed throughout these instructions and in other referenced forms and instructions.

If you are an individual, and your pro rata share items are not affected by any of the limitations, report the amounts shown in column (b) of Schedule K-1 as indicated in column (c). If any of the limitations apply, adjust the column (b) amounts for the limitations before you enter the amounts on your return. When applicable, the passive activity limitations on losses are applied after the limitations on losses for a shareholder's basis in stock and debt and the shareholder's at-risk amount.

Note: *The line number references in column (c) are to forms in use for tax years beginning in 1995. If you are a calendar year shareholder in a fiscal year 1995–96 corporation, enter these amounts on the corresponding lines of the tax form in use for 1996.*

Caution: *If you have losses, deductions, credits, etc., from a prior year that were not deductible or usable because of certain limitations, such as the basis rules or the at-risk limitations, take them into account in determining your income, loss, etc., for this year. However, except for passive activity losses and credits, do not combine the prior-year amounts with any amounts shown on this Schedule K-1 to get a net figure to report on your return. Instead, report the amounts on your return on a year-by-year basis.*

Income (Loss)

Line 1—Ordinary Income (Loss) From Trade or Business Activities

The amount reported on line 1 is your share of the ordinary income (loss) from trade or business activities of the corporation. Generally, where you report this amount on Form 1040 depends on whether the amount is from an activity that is a passive activity to you. If you are an individual shareholder, find your situation below and report your line 1 income (loss) as instructed after applying the basis and at-risk limitations on losses:

1. Report line 1 income (loss) from trade or business activities in which you materially participated on Schedule E (Form 1040), Part II, column (i) or (k).

2. Report line 1 income (loss) from trade or business activities in which you did not materially participate, as follows:

a. If income is reported on line 1, report the income on Schedule E, Part II, column (h).

b. If a loss is reported on line 1, follow the Instructions for Form 8582 to determine how much of the loss can be reported on Schedule E, Part II, column (g).

Line 2—Net Income (Loss) From Rental Real Estate Activities

Generally, the income (loss) reported on line 2 is a passive activity amount for all shareholders. However, the income (loss) on line 2 is not from a passive activity if you were a real estate professional (defined on page 2) and you materially participated in the activity.

If you are filing a 1995 Form 1040, use the following instructions to determine where to enter a line 2 amount:

1. If you have a loss from a passive activity on line 2 and you meet **all** of the following conditions, enter the loss on Schedule E (Form 1040), Part II, column (g):

a. You actively participated in the corporate rental real estate activities. (See **Active participation in a rental real estate activity** on page 3.)

b. Rental real estate activities with active participation were your only passive activities.

c. You have no prior year unallowed losses from these activities.

d. Your total loss from the rental real estate activities was not more than $25,000 (not more than $12,500 if married filing separately and you lived apart from your spouse all year).

e. If you are a married person filing separately, you lived apart from your spouse all year.

f. You have no current or prior year unallowed credits from a passive activity.

g. Your modified adjusted gross income was not more than $100,000 (not more than $50,000 if married filing separately and you lived apart from your spouse all year).

2. If you have a loss from a passive activity on line 2 and you **do not** meet all of the conditions in **1** above, follow the Instructions for Form 8582 to determine how much of the loss can be reported on Schedule E (Form 1040), Part II, column (g).

3. If you were a real estate professional and you materially participated in the activity, report line 2 income (loss) on Schedule E, Part II, column (i) or (k).

4. If you have income from a passive activity on line 2, enter the income on Schedule E, Part II, column (h).

Line 3—Net Income (Loss) From Other Rental Activities

The amount on line 3 is a passive activity amount for all shareholders. Report the income or loss as follows:

1. If line 3 is a loss, report the loss following the Instructions for Form 8582.

2. If income is reported on line 3, report the income on Schedule E (Form 1040), Part II, column (h).

Line 4—Portfolio Income (Loss)

Portfolio income or loss is not subject to the passive activity limitations. Portfolio income includes income not derived in the ordinary course of a trade or business from interest, dividends,

annuities, or royalties, and gain or loss on the sale of property that produces these types of income or is held for investment.

Column (c) of Schedule K-1 tells shareholders where to report this income on Form 1040 and related schedules. Line 4f of Schedule K-1 is used to report income other than that reported on lines 4a through 4e. The type and the amount of income reported on line 4f will be listed in the line 23 Supplemental Information space of Schedule K-1.

If the corporation held a residual interest in a real estate mortgage investment conduit (REMIC), it will report on line 4f your share of REMIC taxable income or (net loss) that you report on Schedule E (Form 1040), Part IV, column (d). It will also report your share of any "excess inclusion" that you report on Schedule E, Part IV, column (c), and your share of section 212 expenses that you report on Schedule E, Part IV, column (e). If you itemize your deductions on Schedule A (Form 1040), you may also deduct these section 212 expenses as a miscellaneous itemized deduction subject to the 2% limit on Schedule A, line 22.

Line 5—Net Gain (Loss) Under Section 1231 (Other Than Due to Casualty or Theft)

Section 1231 gain or loss is reported on line 5. The corporation will identify in the line 23 Supplemental Information space the activity to which the section 1231 gain (loss) relates.

If the amount on line 5 is from a rental activity, the section 1231 gain (loss) is generally a passive activity amount. Likewise, if the amount relates to a trade or business activity and you did not materially participate in the activity, the section 1231 gain (loss) is a passive activity amount.

However, an amount on line 6 from a rental real estate activity is not from a passive activity if you were a real estate professional (defined on page 2) and you materially participated in the activity.

● If the amount is **not** from a passive activity, report it on line 2, column (g) or (h), whichever is applicable, of **Form 4797,** Sales of Business Property. You do not have to complete the information called for in columns (b) through (f), Form 4797. Write "From Schedule K-1 (Form 1120S)" across these columns.

● If gain from a passive activity is reported on line 5, report the gain on line 2, column (h) of Form 4797.

● If a loss from a passive activity is reported on line 5, see **Passive loss limitations** in the Instructions for Form 4797. You will need to report the loss following the Instructions for Form 8582 to determine how much of the loss is allowed on Form 4797.

Line 6—Other Income (Loss)

Amounts on this line are other items of income, gain, or loss not included on lines 1 through 5. The corporation should give you a description and the amount of your share for each of these items.

Report loss items that are passive activity amounts to you following the Instructions for Form 8582.

Report income or gain items that are passive activity amounts to you as instructed below.

The instructions below tell you where to report line 6 items if such items are **not** passive activity amounts.

Line 6 items include the following:

● Income from recoveries of tax benefit items. A tax benefit item is an amount you deducted in a prior tax year that reduced your income tax. Report this amount on Form 1040, line 21, to the extent it reduced your tax.

● Gambling gains and losses.

1. If the corporation was not engaged in the trade or business of gambling:

a. Report gambling winnings on Form 1040, line 21.

b. Deduct gambling losses to the extent of winnings on Schedule A, line 27.

2. If the corporation was engaged in the trade or business of gambling:

a. Report gambling winnings in Part II of Schedule E.

b. Deduct gambling losses to the extent of winnings in Part II of Schedule E.

● Net gain (loss) from involuntary conversions due to casualty or theft. The corporation will give you a schedule that shows the amounts to be reported on **Form 4684,** Casualties and Thefts, line 34, columns (b)(i), (b)(ii), and (c).

● Net short-term capital gain or loss and net long-term capital gain or loss from Schedule D (Form 1120S) that is **not** portfolio income (e.g., gain or loss from the disposition of nondepreciable personal property used in a trade or business activity of the corporation). Report a net short-term capital gain or loss on Schedule D (Form 1040), line 5, column (f) or (g), and a net long-term capital gain or loss on Schedule D (Form 1040), line 13, column (f) or (g).

● Any net gain or loss from section 1256 contracts. Report this amount on line 1 of **Form 6781,** Gains and Losses From Section 1256 Contracts and Straddles.

Deductions

Line 7—Charitable Contributions

The corporation will give you a schedule that shows the amount of contributions subject to the 50%, 30%, and 20% limitations. For more details, see the Form 1040 instructions.

Page 5

If property other than cash is contributed, and the claimed deduction for one item or group of similar items of property exceeds $5,000, the corporation is required to give you a copy of **Form 8283,** Noncash Charitable Contributions, and you must attach it to your tax return. Do not deduct the amount shown on Form 8283. It is the corporation's contribution. You should deduct the amount shown on line 7, Schedule K-1.

If the corporation provides you with information that the contribution was property other than cash and does not give you a Form 8283, see the Instructions for Form 8283 for filing requirements. A Form 8283 does not have to be filed unless the total claimed deduction of all contributed items of property exceeds $500.

Charitable contribution deductions are not taken into account in figuring your passive activity loss for the year. Do not enter them on Form 8582.

Line 8—Section 179 Expense Deduction

Use this amount, along with the total cost of section 179 property placed in service during the year from other sources, to complete Part I of **Form 4562,** Depreciation and Amortization. Part I of Form 4562 is used to figure your allowable section 179 expense deduction from all sources. Report the amount on line 12 of Form 4562 allocable to a passive activity from the corporation following the Instructions for Form 8582. If the amount is not a passive activity deduction, report it on Schedule E (Form 1040), Part II, column (j).

Line 9—Deductions Related to Portfolio Income (Loss)

Amounts on line 9 are deductions that are clearly and directly allocable to portfolio income reported on lines 4a through 4f (other than investment interest expense and section 212 expenses from a REMIC). Generally, you should enter line 9 amounts on Schedule A (Form 1040), line 22. See the instructions for Schedule A, lines 22 and 27, for more information.

These deductions are not taken into account in figuring your passive activity loss for the year. Do not enter them on Form 8582.

Line 10—Other Deductions

Amounts on this line are other deductions not included on lines 7, 8, 9, 15e, and 16a, such as:

● Itemized deductions that Form 1040 filers enter on Schedule A (Form 1040).

Note: *If there was a gain (loss) from a casualty or theft to property **not** used in a trade or business or for income-producing purposes, you will be notified*

Page 6

by the corporation. You will have to complete your own Form 4684.

● Any penalty on early withdrawal of savings.

● Soil and water conservation expenditures. See section 175 for limitations on the amount you are allowed to deduct.

● Expenditures for the removal of architectural and transportation barriers to the elderly and disabled that the corporation elected to treat as a current expense. The deductions are limited by section 190(c) to $15,000 per year from all sources.

● Interest expense allocated to debt-financed distributions. The manner in which you report such interest expense depends on your use of the distributed debt proceeds. See Notice 89-35, 1989-1 C.B. 675, for details.

If the corporation has more than one corporate activity (line 1, 2, or 3 of Schedule K-1), it will identify the activity to which the expenses relate.

The corporation should also give you a description and your share of each of the expense items. Associate any passive activity deduction included on line 10 with the line 1, 2, or 3 activity to which it relates and report the deduction following the Instructions for Form 8582 (or only on Schedule E (Form 1040), if applicable).

Investment Interest

If the corporation paid or accrued interest on debts properly allocable to investment property, the amount of interest you are allowed to deduct may be limited.

For more information on the special provisions that apply to investment interest expense, get **Form 4952,** Investment Interest Expense Deduction, and **Pub. 550,** Investment Income and Expenses.

Line 11a—Interest Expense on Investment Debts

Enter this amount on Form 4952, line 1, along with investment interest expense from Schedule K-1, line 10, if any, and from other sources to determine how much of your total investment interest is deductible.

Lines 11b(1) and (2)—Investment Income and Investment Expenses

Use the amounts on these lines to determine the amounts to enter in Part II of Form 4952.

Caution: *The amounts shown on lines 11b(1) and 11b(2) include only investment income and expenses reported on lines 4a, 4b, 4c, 4f, and 9 of this Schedule K-1. If applicable, the corporation will have listed in the line 23 Supplemental Information space any other items of investment income and*

expenses reported elsewhere on this Schedule K-1. Be sure to take these amounts into account, along with the amounts on lines 11b(1) and 11b(2) and your investment income and expenses from other sources, when figuring the amounts to enter in Part II of Form 4952.

Credits

Caution: *If you have credits that are passive activity credits to you, you must complete Form 8582-CR in addition to the credit forms named below. See the Instructions for Form 8582-CR for more information.*

Also, if you are entitled to claim more than one general business credit (i.e., investment credit, jobs credit, credit for alcohol used as fuel, research credit, low-income housing credit, enhanced oil recovery credit, disabled access credit, renewable electricity production credit, Indian employment credit, credit for employer social security and Medicare taxes paid on certain employee tips, and credit for contributions to selected community development corporations), you must complete Form 3800, General Business Credit, in addition to the credit forms named below. If you have more than one credit, see the instructions for Form 3800 for more information.

Line 12a—Credit for Alcohol Used as Fuel

Your share of the corporation's credit for alcohol used as fuel from all trade or business activities is reported on line 12a. Enter this credit on **Form 6478,** Credit for Alcohol Used as Fuel, to determine your allowed credit for the year.

Line 12b—Low-Income Housing Credit

Your share of the corporation's low-income housing credit is shown on lines 12b(1) through (4). Your allowable credit is entered on **Form 8586,** Low-Income Housing Credit, to determine your allowed credit for the year.

If the corporation invested in a partnership to which the provisions of section 42(j)(5) apply, it will report separately on lines 12b(1) and 12b(3) your share of the credit it received from the partnership.

Your share of all other low-income housing credits of the corporation is reported on lines 12b(2) and 12b(4). You must keep a separate record of the amount of low-income housing credit from these lines so that you will be able to correctly compute any recapture of the credit that may result from the disposition of all or part of your stock in the corporation. For more information, see the instructions for **Form 8611,**

Recapture of Low-Income Housing Credit.

Line 12c—Qualified Rehabilitation Expenditures Related to Rental Real Estate Activities

The corporation should identify your share of rehabilitation expenditures from each rental real estate activity. Enter the expenditures on the appropriate line of **Form 3468,** Investment Credit, to figure your allowable credit.

Line 12d—Credits (Other Than Credits Shown on Lines 12b and 12c) Related to Rental Real Estate Activities

The corporation will identify the type of credit and any other information you need to compute credits from rental real estate activities (other than the low-income housing credit and qualified rehabilitation expenditures).

Line 12e—Credits Related to Other Rental Activities

If applicable, your share of any credit from other rental activities will be reported on line 12e. Income or loss from these activities is reported on line 3 of Schedule K-1. If more than one credit is involved, the credits will be listed separately, each credit identified as a line 12e credit, and the activity to which the credit relates will be identified. This information will be shown on the line 23 Supplemental Information space. The credit may be limited by the passive activity limitations.

Line 13—Other Credits

If applicable, your pro rata share of any other credit (other than on lines 12a through 12e) will be shown on line 13. If more than one credit is reported, the credits will be shown and identified in the line 23 Supplemental Information space. Expenditures qualifying for the **(a)** rehabilitation credit from other than rental real estate activities, **(b)** energy credit, or **(c)** reforestation credit will be reported to you on line 23.

Line 13 credits include the following:

• Nonconventional source fuel credit. Enter this credit on a schedule you prepare yourself to determine the allowed credit to take on your tax return. See section 29 for rules on how to figure the credit.

• Unused investment credit from cooperatives. Enter this credit on Form 3468 to figure your allowable investment credit.

• Credit for backup withholding on dividends, interest income, and other types of income. Include the amount the corporation reports to you in the total that you enter on line 55, page 2, Form 1040. Be sure to check the box on line 55 and write "From Schedule K-1."

• Credit for increasing research activities (Form 6765).

• Jobs credit (Form 5884).

• Disabled access credit (Form 8826).

• Enhanced oil recovery credit (Form 8830).

• Qualified electric vehicle credit (Form 8834).

• Renewable electricity production credit (Form 8835).

• Empowerment zone employment credit (Form 8844).

• Indian employment credit (Form 8845).

• Credit for employer social security and Medicare taxes paid on certain employee tips (Form 8846).

• Credit for contributions to selected community development corporations (Form 8847).

Adjustments and Tax Preference Items

Use the information reported on lines 14a through 14e (as well as adjustments and tax preference items from other sources) to prepare your **Form 6251,** Alternative Minimum Tax—Individuals, or Schedule I of **Form 1041,** U.S. Income Tax Return for Estates and Trusts.

Lines 14d(1) and 14d(2)—Gross Income From, and Deductions Allocable to, Oil, Gas, and Geothermal Properties

The amounts reported on these lines include only the gross income from, and deductions allocable to, oil, gas, and geothermal properties included on line 1 of Schedule K-1. The corporation should have reported separately any income from or deductions allocable to such properties that are included on lines 2 through 10. This separate information is reported in the line 23 Supplemental Information space. Use the amounts reported on lines 14d(1) and 14d(2) and any amounts reported separately to help you determine the net amount to enter on line 14f of Form 6251.

Line 14e—Other Adjustments and Tax Preference Items

Enter the line 14e adjustments and tax preference items shown in the line 23 Supplemental Information space, with other items from other sources, on the applicable lines of Form 6251.

Foreign Taxes

Use the information on lines 15a through 15g, and attached schedules, to figure your foreign tax credit. For more information, get **Form 1116,** Foreign Tax Credit (Individual, Estate, Trust, or Nonresident Alien Individual), and its instructions.

Other

Lines 16a and 16b—Section 59(e)(2) Expenditures

The corporation will show on line 16a the type of qualified expenditures to which an election under section 59(e) may apply. It will identify the amount of the expenditures on line 16b. If there is more than one type of expenditure, the amount of each type will be listed on an attachment.

Generally, section 59(e) allows each shareholder to elect to deduct certain expenses ratably over the number of years in the applicable period rather than deduct the full amount in the current year. Under the election, you may deduct circulation expenditures ratably over a 3-year period. Research and experimental expenditures and mining exploration and development costs qualify for a writeoff period of 10 years. Intangible drilling and development costs may be deducted over a 60-month period, beginning with the month in which such costs were paid or incurred.

If you make this election, these items are not treated as adjustments or tax preference items for purposes of the alternative minimum tax. Make the election on Form 4562.

Because each shareholder decides whether to make the election under section 59(e), the corporation cannot provide you with the amount of the adjustment or tax preference item related to the expenses listed on line 16a. You must decide both how to claim the expenses on your return and how to compute the resulting adjustment or tax preference item.

Line 17—Tax-Exempt Interest Income

You must report on your return, as an item of information, your share of the tax-exempt interest received or accrued by the corporation during the year. Individual shareholders should include this amount on Form 1040, line 8b. Generally, you must increase the basis of your stock in the corporation by this amount.

Line 18—Other Tax-Exempt Income

Generally, you must increase the basis of your stock in the corporation by the amount shown on line 18, but do not include it in income on your tax return.

Line 19—Nondeductible Expenses

The nondeductible expenses paid or incurred by the corporation are not deductible on your tax return. Generally, you must decrease the basis of your stock in the corporation by this amount.

Page 7

Line 20

Reduce the basis of your stock in the corporation by the distributions on line 20. If these distributions exceed the basis of your stock, the excess is treated as gain from the sale or exchange of property and is reported on Schedule D (Form 1040).

Line 21

If the line 21 payments are made on indebtedness with a reduced basis, the repayments result in income to you to the extent the repayments are more than the adjusted basis of the loan. See Regulations section 1.1367-2 for information on reduction in basis of a loan and restoration in basis of a loan with a reduced basis. See Rev. Rul. 64-162, 1964-1 (Part 1) C.B. 304 and Rev. Rul. 68-537, 1968-2 C.B. 372, for other information.

Lines 22a and 22b—Recapture of Low-Income Housing Credit

The corporation will report separately on line 22a your share of any recapture of a low-income housing credit from its investment in partnerships to which the provisions of section 42(j)(5) apply. All other recapture of low-income housing credits will be reported on line 22b. You must keep a separate record of recapture from line 22a and 22b so that you will be able to correctly figure any credit recapture that may result from the disposition of all or part of your corporate stock. Use the line 22a and 22b amounts to compute the low-income housing credit recapture on Form 8611. See the instructions for Form 8611 and section 42(j) for additional information.

Supplemental Information

Line 23

If applicable, the corporation should have listed in line 23, Supplemental Information, or on an attached statement to Schedule K-1, your distributive share of the following:

1. Taxes paid on undistributed capital gains by a regulated investment company. (Form 1040 filers, enter your share of these taxes on line 60 of Form 1040, check the box for Form 2439, and add the words "Form 1120S." Also reduce the basis of your stock in the corporation by this tax.)

2. Gross income from the property, share of production for the tax year, etc., needed to figure your depletion deduction for oil and gas wells. The corporation should also allocate to you a proportionate share of the adjusted basis of each corporate oil or gas property. See Pub. 535 for how to figure your depletion deduction. Also, reduce the basis of your stock in the corporation by the amount of this deduction to the extent the deduction does not exceed your share of the adjusted basis of the property.

3. Recapture of the section 179 expense deduction. If the recapture was caused by a disposition of the property, include the amount on Form 4797, line 18. The recapture amount is limited to the amount you deducted in earlier years.

4. Recapture of certain mining exploration expenditures (section 617).

5. Any information or statements you need to comply with section 6111 (registration of tax shelters) or 6662(d)(2)(B)(ii) (regarding adequate disclosure of items that may cause an understatement of income tax).

6. Gross farming and fishing income. If you are an individual shareholder, enter this income, as an item of information, on Schedule E (Form 1040), Part V, line 41. Do not report this income elsewhere on Form 1040.

For a shareholder that is an estate or trust, report this income to the beneficiaries, as an item of information, on Schedule K-1 (Form 1041). Do not report it elsewhere on Form 1041.

7. Any information you need to figure the interest due under section 453(l)(3). If the corporation elected to report the dispositions of certain timeshares and residential lots on the installment method, your tax liability must be increased by the interest on tax attributable to your pro rata share of the installment payments received by the corporation during its tax year. If applicable, use the information provided by the corporation to figure your interest. Include the interest on Form 1040, line 54. Also write "453(l)(3)" and the amount of the interest on the dotted line to the left of line 54.

8. Any information you need to compute the interest due under section 453A(c) with respect to certain installment sales of property. If you are an individual, report the interest on Form 1040, line 54. Write "453A(c)" and the amount of the interest on the dotted line to the left of line 54. See the instructions for **Form 6252,** Installment Sale Income, for more information. Also see section 453A(c) for details on making the computation.

9. Capitalization of interest under section 263A(f). To the extent certain production or construction expenditures of the corporation are made from proceeds associated with debt you incur as an owner-shareholder, you must capitalize the interest on this debt. If applicable, use the information on expenditures the corporation gives to you to determine the amount of interest you must capitalize. See Regulations sections 1.263A-8 through 1.263A-15 for more information.

10. Any information you need to compute the interest due or to be refunded under the look-back method of section 460(b)(2) on certain long-term contracts. Use **Form 8697,** Interest Computation Under the Look-Back Method for Completed Long-Term Contracts, to report any such interest.

11. Your share of expenditures qualifying for the **(a)** rehabilitation credit from other than rental real estate activities, **(b)** energy credit, or **(c)** reforestation credit. Enter the expenditures on the appropriate line of Form 3468 to figure your allowable credit.

12. Investment credit properties subject to recapture. Any information you need to figure your recapture tax on **Form 4255,** Recapture of Investment Credit. See the Form 3468 on which you took the original credit for other information you need to complete Form 4255.

You may also need Form 4255 if you disposed of more than one-third of your stock in the corporation.

13. Preproductive period farm expenses. You may elect to deduct these expenses currently or capitalize them under section 263A. See Pub. 225, Farmer's Tax Guide, and Temporary Regulations section 1.263A-4T(c) for more information.

14. Any information you need to figure recapture of the qualified electric vehicle credit. See Pub. 535 for details, including how to figure the recapture.

15. Any information you need to figure your recapture of the Indian employment credit. Generally, if the corporation terminated a qualified employee less than 1 year after the date of initial employment, any Indian employment credit allowed for a prior tax year by reason of wages paid or incurred to that employee must be recaptured. For details, see section 45A(d).

16. Any other information you may need to file with your individual tax return that is not shown elsewhere on Schedule K-1.

SCHEDULE K-1 (Form 1120S)	Shareholder's Share of Income, Credits, Deductions, etc.	OMB No. 1545-0130

Department of the Treasury Internal Revenue Service

▶ See separate instructions.

For calendar year 1995 or tax year
beginning , 1995, and ending , 19

1995

Shareholder's identifying number ▶	Corporation's identifying number ▶
Shareholder's name, address, and ZIP code	Corporation's name, address, and ZIP code
John H. Green 4340 Holmes Parkway Metro City, OH 43704	Strato Tech, Inc. 482 Winston Street Metro City, OH 43705

A Shareholder's percentage of stock ownership for tax year (see Instructions for Schedule K-1) . . . . . . ▶ **45** %

B Internal Revenue Service Center where corporation filed its return ▶ _Cincinnati, OH_

C Tax shelter registration number (see Instructions for Schedule K-1) . . . . ▶

D Check applicable boxes: **(1)** ☐ Final K-1 **(2)** ☐ Amended K-1

	(a) Pro rata share items		**(b)** Amount	**(c)** Form 1040 filers enter the amount in column (b) on:
Income (Loss)	**1** Ordinary income (loss) from trade or business activities . . .	**1**	53,550	See pages 4 and 5 of the Shareholder's Instructions for Schedule K-1 (Form 1120S).
	2 Net income (loss) from rental real estate activities	**2**		
	3 Net income (loss) from other rental activities	**3**		
	4 Portfolio income (loss):			
	a Interest	**4a**	1,800	Sch. B, Part I, line 1
	b Dividends	**4b**	7,200	Sch. B, Part II, line 5
	c Royalties	**4c**		Sch. E, Part I, line 4
	d Net short-term capital gain (loss).	**4d**		Sch. D, line 5, col. (f) or (g)
	e Net long-term capital gain (loss)	**4e**		Sch. D, line 13, col. (f) or (g)
	f Other portfolio income (loss) *(attach schedule)*	**4f**		(Enter on applicable line of your return.)
	5 Net gain (loss) under section 1231 (other than due to casualty or theft)	**5**		See Shareholder's Instructions for Schedule K-1 (Form 1120S).
	6 Other income (loss) *(attach schedule)*	**6**		(Enter on applicable line of your return.)
Deductions	**7** Charitable contributions *(attach schedule)*	**7**	10,800	Sch. A, line 15 or 16
	8 Section 179 expense deduction	**8**		See page 6 of the Shareholder's Instructions for Schedule K-1 (Form 1120S).
	9 Deductions related to portfolio income (loss) *(attach schedule)* .	**9**		
	10 Other deductions *(attach schedule)*	**10**		
Investment Interest	**11a** Interest expense on investment debts	**11a**	1,350	Form 4952, line 1
	b (1) Investment income included on lines 4a, 4b, 4c, and 4f above	**b(1)**	9,000	See Shareholder's Instructions for Schedule K-1 (Form 1120S).
	(2) Investment expenses included on line 9 above	**b(2)**		
Credits	**12a** Credit for alcohol used as fuel	**12a**		Form 6478, line 10
	b Low-income housing credit:			
	(1) From section 42(j)(5) partnerships for property placed in service before 1990.	**b(1)**		Form 8586, line 5
	(2) Other than on line 12b(1) for property placed in service before 1990	**b(2)**		
	(3) From section 42(j)(5) partnerships for property placed in service after 1989	**b(3)**		
	(4) Other than on line 12b(3) for property placed in service after 1989	**b(4)**		
	c Qualified rehabilitation expenditures related to rental real estate activities	**12c**		See page 7 of the Shareholder's Instructions for Schedule K-1 (Form 1120S).
	d Credits (other than credits shown on lines 12b and 12c) related to rental real estate activities	**12d**		
	e Credits related to other rental activities.	**12e**		
	13 Other credits	**13**	2,700	
Adjustments and Tax Preference Items	**14a** Depreciation adjustment on property placed in service after 1986	**14a**		See page 7 of the Shareholder's Instructions for Schedule K-1 (Form 1120S) and Instructions for Form 6251
	b Adjusted gain or loss	**14b**		
	c Depletion (other than oil and gas)	**14c**		
	d (1) Gross income from oil, gas, or geothermal properties . .	**d(1)**		
	(2) Deductions allocable to oil, gas, or geothermal properties	**d(2)**		
	e Other adjustments and tax preference items *(attach schedule)*	**14e**		

For Paperwork Reduction Act Notice, see page 1 of Instructions for Form 1120S. Cat. No. 11520D **Schedule K-1 (Form 1120S) 1995**

Schedule K-1 (Form 1120S) (1995) | Page **2**

	(a) Pro rata share items		(b) Amount	(c) Form 1040 filers enter the amount in column (b) on:
Foreign Taxes	**15a** Type of income ▶			Form 1116, Check boxes
	b Name of foreign country or U.S. possession ▶			
	c Total gross income from sources outside the United States *(attach schedule)*	**15c**		Form 1116, Part I
	d Total applicable deductions and losses *(attach schedule)* . . .	**15d**		
	e Total foreign taxes (check one): ▶ ☐ Paid ☐ Accrued . .	**15e**		Form 1116, Part II
	f Reduction in taxes available for credit *(attach schedule)* . . .	**15f**		Form 1116, Part III
	g Other foreign tax information *(attach schedule)*	**15g**		See Instructions for Form 1116
Other	**16** Section 59(e)(2) expenditures: **a** Type ▶			See Shareholder's Instructions for Schedule K-1 (Form 1120S).
	b Amount	**16b**		
	17 Tax-exempt interest income	**17**	*2,250*	Form 1040, line 8b
	18 Other tax-exempt income	**18**		
	19 Nondeductible expenses	**19**	*7,358*	See page 7 of the Shareholder's Instructions for Schedule K-1 (Form 1120S).
	20 Property distributions (including cash) other than dividend distributions reported to you on Form 1099-DIV	**20**	*29,250*	
	21 Amount of loan repayments for "Loans From Shareholders" .	**21**		
	22 Recapture of low-income housing credit:			
	a From section 42(j)(5) partnerships	**22a**		Form 8611, line 8
	b Other than on line 22a	**22b**		

23 Supplemental information required to be reported separately to each shareholder *(attach additional schedules if more space is needed)*:

....

....

....

....

....

....

....

....

....

....

....

....

....

....

....

....

....

Printed on recycled paper

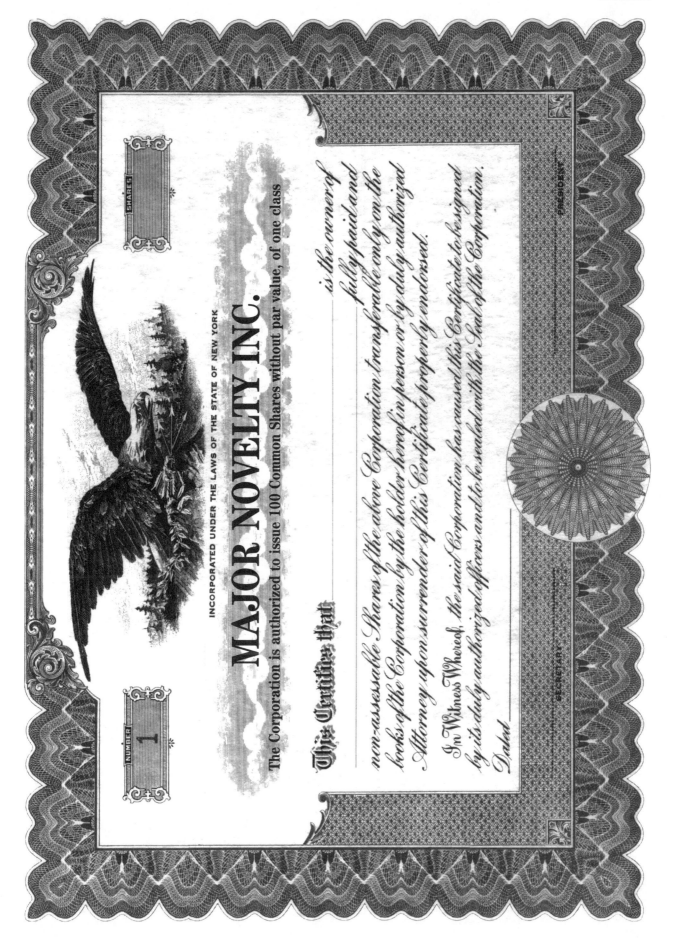

INCORPORATED UNDER THE LAWS OF THE STATE OF NEW YORK

MAJOR NOVELTY INC.

The Corporation is authorized to issue 100 Common Shares without par value, of one class

NUMBER
1

SHARES

This Certifies that

is the owner of

fully paid and non-assessable Shares of the above Corporation transferable only on the books of the Corporation by the holder hereof in person or by duly authorized Attorney upon surrender of this Certificate properly endorsed.

In Witness Whereof, the said Corporation has caused this Certificate to be signed by its duly authorized officers and to be sealed with the Seal of the Corporation.

Dated

SECRETARY

PRESIDENT

THE X CORPORATION EXHIBIT: STOCK LEDGER

NAME OF STOCKHOLDER	ADDRESS OF STOCKHOLDER	DATE BECAME OWNER	CERTIFICATES ISSUED		FROM WHOM SHARES WERE TRANSFERRED (If Original Issue Enter As Such)
			CERTIF. NOS.	NO. OF SHARES	
Arlo Anders	100 Division St. Anytown, IL 60930	2/10/96	1	100	
Susan Boyle	300 W. Main St. Orange, MD 20904	2/10/96	2	100	
Carla Babson	488 Winston St. Metro City, OH 43705	2/11/96	3	200	

AMOUNT PAID THEREON	DATE OF TRANSFER OF SHARES	TO WHOM SHARES ARE TRANSFERRED	CERTIFICATES SURRENDERED		NUMBER OF SHARES HELD (BALANCE)	VALUE OF STOCK TRANSFER TAX STAMP AFFIXED
			CERTIF. NOS.	NO. OF SHARES		
$10,000						$100
$10,000						$100
$20,000						$200

Blank Legal Forms

T he five legal forms in this appendix have been left blank and can be removed for your use. The first four forms have been reprinted with permission from: *Corporate Practice Handbook,* published by New York State Bar Association, One Elk Street, Albany, New York 12207.

FORM 1

CERTIFICATE OF INCORPORATION
OF
[CORPORATION]
UNDER SECTION _____ OF THE
BUSINESS CORPORATION LAW

I, [NAME OF INCORPORATOR], being of the age of eighteen years or over, for the purpose of forming a corporation pursuant to Section _____ of the Business Corporation Law of _____ , do hereby certify:

1. The name of the corporation is [NAME OF CORPORATION].

2. The purposes for which it is formed are:

To purchase, receive, take by grant, gift, devise, bequest or otherwise, lease or otherwise acquire, own, hold, improve, employ, use and otherwise deal in and with real or personal property, or any interest therein, wherever situated; and

To have and to exercise all rights and powers that are now or may hereafter be granted to a corporation by law.

The foregoing shall be construed as objects, purposes and powers, and the enumeration thereof shall not be held to limit or restrict in any manner the powers now or hereafter conferred on this corporation by the laws of the State of _____ . The objects and powers specified herein shall, except as otherwise expressed, be in no way limited or restricted by reference to or inference from the terms of any other clause or paragraph of these articles. The objects, purposes, and powers specified in each of the clauses or paragraphs of this Certificate of Incorporation shall be regarded as independent objects, purposes, or powers.

3. The office of the corporation is to be located in the City of _____ , County of _____ , State of _____ .

4. The aggregate number of shares of stock which the corporation shall have the authority to issue is _____ (_____) shares of Common Stock, each of which shall have a par value of _____ Dollars ($ _____) per share.

5. The Secretary of State is designated as the agent of the corporation upon whom process against the corporation may be served. The post office address to which the Secretary of State shall mail a copy of any process against the corporation served upon him is: _____
_____ .

6. The name and address of the registered agent which is to be the agent of the corporation upon whom process against it may be served are:
_____
_____ .

IN WITNESS WHEREOF, I have made and signed this certificate this _____ day of _____ , 19_____ , and I affirm the statements contained herein as true under penalties of perjury.

_____
[Name and Home or Business Address of Incorporator]

FORM OF NOTARIZATION

STATE OF _____)

                       : ss.:

COUNTY OF _____)

    On this _____ day of _____ , 19 _____ , before me personally came [NAME OF INCORPORATOR], to me personally known, who, being by me duly sworn, did depose and say that (s)he resides at [HOME ADDRESS OF INCORPORATOR]; that (s)he is the individual who executed the within instrument; and that (s)he signed [his] [her] name thereto.

                                    _____

                                           Notary Public

FORM 2

SAMPLE BY-LAWS

ARTICLE I

OFFICES

Section 1. The office of the Corporation shall be located in the City of
_____ , in the County of _____ , in the State of _____ .

Section 2. The Corporation may also have offices at such other places both
within and without the State of _____ as the board of directors may
from time to time determine or the business of the Corporation may require.

ARTICLE II

ANNUAL MEETINGS OF SHAREHOLDERS

Section 1. All meetings of shareholders for the election of directors shall be
held in such City, County and State and at such time and place as may be fixed
from time to time by the board of directors and set forth in the notice of such
meeting.

Section 2. Annual meetings of shareholders shall be held on the third
Friday in _____ of each year if not a legal holiday, and if a legal holiday, then
on the next business day following at which they shall elect by a plurality vote
a board of directors, and transact such other business as may properly be
brought before the meeting.

Section 3. Written or printed notice of the annual meeting stating the place,
date and hour of the meeting shall be delivered not less than ten nor more than
fifty days before the date of the meeting, either personally or by mail, by or at
the direction of the president, the secretary, or the officer or persons calling
the meeting, to each shareholder of record entitled to vote at such meeting.

ARTICLE III

SPECIAL MEETINGS OF SHAREHOLDERS

Section 1. Special meetings of shareholders may be held at such time and place within or without the State of _____ as shall be stated in the notice of the meeting or in a duly executed waiver of notice thereof.

Section 2. Special meetings of shareholders, for any purpose or purposes, unless otherwise prescribed by statute or by the certificate of incorporation, may be called by the president, the board of directors, or the holders of not less than a majority of all the shares entitled to vote at the meeting.

Section 3. Written or printed notice of a special meeting stating the place, date and hour of the meeting and the purpose or purposes for which the meeting is called shall be delivered not less than ten nor more than fifty days before the date of the meeting, either personally or by mail, by, or at the direction of, the president, the board or, if the special meeting is called by holders of not less than a majority of all the shares entitled to vote at the special meeting, the secretary, to each shareholder of record entitled to vote at such meeting. The notice should also indicate that it is being issued by, or at the direction of, the person calling the meeting.

Section 4. The business transacted at any special meeting of shareholders shall be limited to the purposes stated in the notice.

ARTICLE IV

QUORUM AND VOTING OF STOCK

Section 1. The holders of a majority of the shares of stock issued and outstanding and entitled to vote, represented in person or by proxy, shall constitute a quorum at all meetings of the shareholders for the transaction of business except as otherwise provided by statute or by the certificate of incorporation. If, however, such quorum shall not be present or represented by proxy shall have power to adjourn the meeting from time to time, without notice other than announcement at the meeting, until a quorum shall be present or represented. At such adjourned meeting at which a quorum shall be present or represented, any business may be transacted which might have been transacted at the meeting as originally notified.

Section 2. If a quorum is present, the affirmative vote of a majority of the shares of stock represented at the meeting shall be the act of the shareholders, unless the vote of a greater or lesser number of shares of stock is required by law or the certificate of incorporation.

Section 3. Each outstanding share of stock having voting power shall be entitled to one vote on each matter submitted to vote at a meeting of shareholders. A shareholder may vote either in person or by proxy executed in writing by the shareholder or by his duly authorized attorney-in-fact.

Section 4. The board of directors in advance of any shareholders' meeting may appoint one or more inspectors to act at the meeting or any adjournment thereof. If inspectors are not so appointed, the person presiding at a shareholders' meeting may, and, on the request of any shareholder entitled to vote thereat, shall, appoint one or more inspectors. In case any person appointed as inspector fails to appear or act, the vacancy may be filled by the board in advance of the meeting or at the meeting by the person presiding thereat. Each inspector, before entering upon the discharge of his duties, shall take and sign an oath faithfully to execute the duties of inspector at such meeting with strict impartiality and according to the best of his ability.

Section 5. Whenever shareholders are required or permitted to take any action by vote, such action may be taken without a meeting on written consent, setting forth the action so taken, signed by the holders of all outstanding shares entitled to vote thereon.

ARTICLE V

DIRECTORS

Section 1. The number of directors shall be _____ (_____), which number may be increased or decreased by amendment of these by-laws. Each director shall be at least eighteen years of age. The directors need not be residents of the State of _____ nor shareholders of the Corporation. The directors, other than the first board of directors, shall be elected at the annual meeting of the shareholders, except as hereinafter provided, and each director elected shall serve until the next succeeding annual meeting or until his successor shall have been elected and qualified. The first board of directors shall hold office until the first meeting of shareholders.

Section 2. Any or all of the directors may be removed, with or without cause, at any time by the vote of the shareholders at a special meeting called for that purpose.

Any director may be removed for cause by the action of the directors at a special meeting called for that purpose.

Section 3. Unless otherwise provided in the certificate of incorporation, newly created directorships resulting from an increase in the board of directors and all vacancies occurring in the board of directors, including vacancies caused by removal without cause, may be filled by the affirmative vote of a majority of the board of directors; however, if the number of directors then in office is less than a quorum, then such newly created directorships and vacancies may be filled by a vote of a majority of the directors then in office. A director elected to fill a vacancy shall hold office until the next meeting of shareholders at which election of directors is the regular order of business, and until his successor shall have been elected and qualified. A director elected to fill a newly created directorship shall serve until the next succeeding annual meeting of shareholders and until his successor shall have been elected and qualified.

Section 4. The business affairs of the Corporation shall be managed by its board of directors, which may exercise all such powers of the Corporation and do all such lawful acts and things as are not by statute or by the certificate of incorporation or by these by-laws directed or required to be exercised or done by the shareholders.

Section 5. The directors may keep the books of the Corporation, except such as are required by law to be kept within the State of, at such place or places as they may from time to time determine.

Section 6. The board of directors, by the affirmative vote of a majority of the directors then in office, and irrespective of any personal interest of any of its members, shall have authority to establish reasonable compensation of all directors for services to the Corporation as directors, officers or otherwise.

ARTICLE VI

MEETINGS OF THE BOARD OF DIRECTORS

Section 1. Meetings of the board of directors, regular or special, may be held either within or without the State of _____ .

Section 2. The first meeting of each newly elected board of directors shall be held at such time and place as shall be fixed by the vote of the shareholders at the annual meeting and no notice of such meeting shall be necessary to the newly elected directors in order legally to constitute the meeting, provided a quorum shall be present, or it may convene at such place and time as shall be fixed by the consent in writing of all the directors.

Section 3. Regular meetings of the board of directors may be held upon such notice, or without notice, and at such time and at such place as shall from time to time be determined by the board of directors.

Section 4. Special meetings of the board of directors may be called by the chairman of the board of directors or by the president or by any two directors at any time. Notice of any special meeting shall be mailed to each director addressed to him at his residence or usual place of business at least two days before the day on which the meeting is to be held, or if sent to him at such place by telegraph or cable, or delivered personally or by telephone, not later than the day before the day on which the meeting is to be held.

Section 5. Notice of a meeting need not be given to any director who submits a signed waiver of notice whether before or after the meeting, or who attends the meeting without protesting, prior thereto or at its commencement, the lack of notice. Neither the business to be transacted at, nor the purpose of, any regular or special meeting of the board of directors need be specified in the notice or waiver of notice of such meeting.

Section 6. A majority of the directors shall constitute a quorum for the transaction of business unless a greater or lesser number is required by law or by the certificate of incorporation. The vote of a majority of the directors present at any meeting at which a quorum is present shall be the act of the board of directors, unless the vote of a greater number is required by law or by the certificate of incorporation. If a quorum shall not be present at any meeting of directors, the directors present may adjourn the meeting from time to time, without notice other than announcement at the meeting, until a quorum shall be present.

Section 7. Unless the certificate of incorporation provides otherwise, any action required or permitted to be taken at a meeting of the directors or a committee thereof may be taken without a meeting if a consent in writing to the adoption of a resolution authorizing the action so taken shall be signed by all of the directors entitled to vote with respect to the subject matter thereof.

Section 8. Unless otherwise restricted by the certificate of incorporation or these by-laws, members of the board of directors, or any committee designated by the board of directors, may participate in a meeting of the board of directors, or any committee, by means of conference telephone or similar communications equipment by means of which all persons participating in the meeting can hear each other, and such participation in a meeting shall constitute presence in person at the meeting.

ARTICLE VII

EXECUTIVE COMMITTEE

Section 1. The board of directors, by resolution adopted by a majority of the entire board, may designate, from among its members, an executive committee and other committees, each consisting of three or more directors, and each of which, to the extent provided in the resolution, shall have all the authority of the board, except as otherwise required by law. Vacancies in the membership of the committee shall be filled by the board of directors at a regular or special meeting of the board of directors.

Section 2. Any member of a committee may resign at any time. Such resignation shall be made in writing and shall take effect at the time specified therein, or, if no time be specified, at the time of its receipt by the president or secretary. The acceptance of a resignation shall not be necessary to make it effective unless so specified therein.

Section 3. A majority of the members of a committee shall constitute a quorum. The act of a majority of the members of a committee present at any meeting at which a quorum is present shall be the act of such committee. The members of a committee shall act only as a committee, and the individual members thereof shall have no powers as such.

Section 4. Each committee shall keep a record of its acts and proceedings, and shall report the same to the board of directors when and as required by the board of directors.

Section 5. A committee may hold its meetings at the principal office of the Corporation, or at any other place which a majority of the committee may at any time agree upon. Each committee may make such rules as it may deem expedient for the regulation and carrying on of its meetings and proceedings. Unless otherwise ordered by the executive committee, any notice of a meeting of such committee may be given by the secretary or by the chairman of the committee and shall be sufficiently given if mailed to each member at his residence or usual place of business at least two days before the day on which the meeting is to be held or if sent to him at such place by telegraph or cable, or delivered personally or by telephone, not later than 24 hours prior to the time at which the meeting is to be held.

Section 6. The members of any committee shall be entitled to such compensation as may be allowed them by resolution of the board of directors.

ARTICLE VIII

NOTICES

Section 1. Whenever, by law or by the provisions of the certificate of incorporation or of these by-laws, notice is required to be given to any director or shareholder, it shall not be construed to mean personal notice, but such notice may be given in writing, by mail, addressed to such director or shareholder, at his address as it appears on the records of the Corporation, with postage thereon prepaid, and such notice shall be deemed to be given at the time when the same shall be deposited in the United States mail. Notice to directors may also be given by telegram.

Section 2. Whenever any notice of a meeting is required to be given by law or by the provisions of the certificate of incorporation or these by-laws, a waiver thereof in writing signed by the person or persons entitled to such notice, whether before or after the time stated therein, shall be deemed equivalent to the giving of such notice.

ARTICLE IX

OFFICERS

Section 1. The officers of the Corporation shall be chosen by the board of directors and shall be a president, a vice president, a secretary and a treasurer, and such other officers, as may be appointed in accordance with the provisions of Section 3 of this Article IX. The board of directors in its discretion may also elect a chairman of the board of directors. The board of directors may also choose one or more additional vice presidents, and one or more assistant secretaries and assistant treasurers.

Section 2. The board of directors at its first meeting after each annual meeting of shareholders shall choose a president, a vice president, a secretary and a treasurer, none of whom need be a member of the board.

Any two or more offices may be held by the same person, except the offices of president and secretary. When all the issued and outstanding stock of the Corporation is owned by one person, such person may hold all or any combination of offices.

Section 3. The board of directors may appoint such other officers and agents as it shall deem necessary who shall hold their offices for such terms and shall exercise such powers and perform such duties as shall be determined from time to time by the board of directors.

Section 4. The salaries of all officers and agents of the Corporation shall be fixed by the board of directors.

Section 5. The officers of the Corporation shall hold office until their successors are chosen and qualify. Any officer elected or appointed by the board of directors may be removed at any time by the affirmative vote of a majority of the board of directors. Any vacancy occurring in any office of the Corporation shall be filled by the board of directors.

CHAIRMAN OF THE BOARD OF DIRECTORS

Section 6. The chairman of the board of directors shall be a director and shall preside at all meetings of the board of directors at which he shall be present and shall have such power and perform such duties as may from time to time be assigned to him by the board of directors.

THE PRESIDENT

Section 7. The president shall be the chief executive officer of the Corporation, shall preside at all meetings of the shareholders and, in the absence of the chairman of the board of directors, shall have general and active management of the business of the Corporation and shall see that all orders and resolutions of the board of directors are carried into effect.

He shall have the power to call special meetings of the stockholders or of the board of directors or of the executive committee at any time.

Section 8. He shall execute bonds, mortgages and other contracts requiring a seal under the seal of the Corporation, except where required or permitted by law to be otherwise signed and executed and except where the signing and execution thereof shall be expressly delegated by the board of directors to some other officer or agent of the Corporation.

THE VICE PRESIDENTS

Section 9. The vice president or, if there shall be more than one, the vice presidents in the order determined by the board of directors shall, in the absence or disability of the president, perform the duties and exercise the powers of the president and shall perform such other duties and have such other powers as the board of directors may from time to time prescribe.

THE SECRETARY AND ASSISTANT SECRETARIES

Section 10. The secretary shall attend all meetings of the board of directors and all meetings of the shareholders and record all the proceedings of the meetings of the Corporation and of the board of directors in a book to be kept for that purpose and shall perform like duties for the standing committees when required. He shall give, or cause to be given, notice of all meetings of the shareholders and special meetings of the board of directors, and shall perform such other duties as may be prescribed by the board of directors or the president, under whose supervision he shall be. He shall have custody of the corporate seal of the Corporation, if any, and he shall have authority to affix the same to any instrument requiring it and, when so affixed, it may be attested by his signature. The board of directors may give general authority to any other officer to affix the seal of the Corporation and to attest the affixing by his signature.

Section 11. The assistant secretary or, if there be more than one, the assistant secretaries in the order determined by the board of directors shall, in the absence or disability of the secretary, perform the duties and exercise the powers of the secretary and shall perform such other duties and have such other powers as the board of directors may from time to time prescribe.

THE TREASURER AND ASSISTANT TREASURERS

Section 12. The treasurer shall have the custody of the corporate funds and securities and shall keep full and accurate accounts of receipts and disbursements in books belonging to the Corporation and shall deposit all moneys and other valuable effects in the name and to the credit of the Corporation in such depositories as may be designated by the board of directors.

Section 13. He shall disburse the funds of the Corporation as may be ordered by the board of directors, taking proper vouchers for such disbursements, and shall render to the president and the board of directors at its regular meetings, or when the board of directors so requires, an account of all his transactions as treasurer and of the financial condition of the Corporation.

Section 14. If required by the board of directors, he shall give the Corporation a bond in such sum and with such surety or sureties as shall be satisfactory to the board of directors for the faithful performance of the duties of his office and for the restoration to the Corporation, in case of his death, resignation, retirement or removal from office, of all books, papers, vouchers, money and other property of whatever kind in his possession or under his control belonging to the Corporation.

Section 15. The assistant treasurer or, if there shall be more than one, the assistant treasurers in the order determined by the board of directors shall, in the absence or disability of the treasurer, perform the duties and exercise the powers of the treasurer and shall perform such other duties and have such other powers as the board of directors may from time to time prescribe.

ARTICLE X

CERTIFICATES FOR SHARES

Section 1. The shares of the Corporation shall be represented by certificates signed by the chairman or the president or a vice president and the sec-

retary or an assistant secretary or the treasurer or an assistant treasurer of the Corporation and may be sealed with the seal of the Corporation or a facsimile thereof.

When the Corporation is authorized to issue more than one class of shares, there shall be set forth upon the face or back of the certificate, or the certificate shall have a statement, that the Corporation will furnish to any shareholder upon request and without charge, a full statement of the designation, relative rights, preferences and limitations of the shares of each class of stock which the Corporation is authorized to issue.

Section 2. The signatures of the officers of the Corporation upon a certificate may be facsimiles if the certificate is countersigned by a transfer agent or registered by a registrar other than the Corporation itself or an employee of the Corporation. In case any officer who has signed or whose facsimile signature has been placed upon a certificate shall have ceased to be such officer before such certificate is issued, it may be issued by the Corporation with the same effect as if he were such officer at the date of issue.

LOST CERTIFICATES

Section 3. The board of directors may direct a new certificate to be issued in place of any certificate theretofore issued by the Corporation alleged to have been lost or destroyed. When authorizing such issue of a new certificate, the board of directors, in its discretion and as a condition precedent to the issuance thereof, may prescribe such terms and conditions as it deems expedient, and may require such indemnities as it deems adequate, to protect the Corporation from any claim that may be made against it with respect to any such certificate alleged to have been lost or destroyed.

TRANSFER OF SHARES

Section 4. Upon surrender to the Corporation or the transfer agent of the Corporation of a certificate representing shares duly endorsed or accompanied by proper evidence of succession, assignment or authority to transfer, a new certificate shall be issued to the person entitled thereto, and the old certificate cancelled and the transaction recorded upon the books of the Corporation.

The board of directors may make other and further rules and regulations concerning the transfer and registration of certificates for stock and may

appoint a transfer agent or registrar or both and may require all certificates of stock to bear the signature of either or both.

FIXING RECORD DATE

Section 5. For the purpose of determining shareholders entitled to notice of or to vote at any meeting of shareholders or any adjournment thereof, or to express consent to or dissent from any proposal without a meeting, or for the purpose of determining shareholders entitled to receive payment of any dividend or the allotment of any rights, or for the purpose of any other action, the board of directors may fix, in advance, a date as the record date for any such determination of shareholders. Such date shall not be more than fifty nor less than ten days before the date of any meeting nor more than fifty days prior to any other action. When a determination of shareholders of record entitled to notice of or to vote at any meeting of shareholders has been made as provided in this section, such determination shall apply to any adjournment thereof, unless the board fixes a new record date for the adjourned meeting.

REGISTERED SHAREHOLDERS

Section 6. The Corporation shall be entitled to recognize the exclusive right of a person registered on its books as the owner of shares to receive dividends, and to vote as such owner, and to hold liable for calls and assessments a person registered on its books as the owner of shares, and shall not be bound to recognize any equitable or other claim to or interest in such share or shares on the part of any other person, whether or not it shall have express or other notice thereof, except as otherwise provided by the laws of the State of New York.

LIST OF SHAREHOLDERS

Section 7. A list of shareholders as of the record date, certified by the corporate officer responsible for its preparation or by a transfer agent, shall be produced at any meeting upon the request thereat or prior thereto of any shareholder. If the right to vote at any meeting is challenged, the inspectors of election, or person presiding thereat, shall require such list of shareholders to be produced as evidence of the right of the persons challenged to vote at such meeting and all persons who appear from such list to be shareholders entitled to vote thereat may vote at such meeting.

ARTICLE Xl

GENERAL PROVISIONS DIVIDENDS

Section 1. Subject to the provisions of the certificate of incorporation relating thereto, if any, and to the laws of the State of New York, dividends may be declared by the board of directors at any regular or special meeting. Dividends may be paid in cash, in shares of the capital stock or in the Corporation's bonds or its property, including the shares or bonds of other corporations, subject to the laws of the State of New York and to the provisions of the certificate of incorporation.

Section 2. Before payment of any dividend, there may be set aside out of any funds of the Corporation available for dividends such sum or sums as the directors from time to time, in their absolute discretion, think proper as a reserve fund to meet contingencies, or for equalizing dividends, or for repairing or maintaining any property of the Corporation, or for such other purpose as the directors shall think conducive to the interest of the Corporation, and the directors may modify or abolish any such reserve in the manner in which it was created.

CHECKS

Section 3. All checks or demands for money and notes of the Corporation shall be signed by such officer or officers or such other person or persons as the board of directors may from time to time designate.

FISCAL YEAR

Section 4. The fiscal year of the Corporation shall be fixed by resolution of the board of directors.

ARTICLE XII

AMENDMENTS

Section 1. These by-laws may be amended or repealed or new by-laws may be adopted at any regular or special meeting of shareholders at which a quorum is present or represented, by the vote of the holders of shares entitled to vote in the election of any directors, provided notice of the proposed alter-

ation, amendment or repeal be contained in the notice of such meeting. These by-laws may also be amended or repealed or new by-laws may be adopted by the affirmative vote of a majority of the board of directors at any regular or special meeting of the board. If any by-law regulating an impending election of directors is adopted, amended or repealed by the board, there shall be set forth in the notice of the next meeting of shareholders for the election of directors the by-law so adopted, amended or repealed, together with a precise statement of the changes made. By-laws adopted by the board of directors may be amended or repealed by the shareholder.

FORM 3

MINUTES OF ORGANIZATION MEETING OF BOARD OF DIRECTORS OF [CORPORATION]

The first meeting of the board of directors of [NAME OF CORPORATION] was called and held at _____ , _____ on the _____ day of_____, 19 _____ at _____ .

PRESENT:

There were present:

[NAMES OF DIRECTORS]

being all the directors.

_____was chosen temporary chairman and _____ was chosen temporary secretary of the meeting.

The secretary presented and read a waiver of notice of the meeting, signed by all the directors, which was ordered filed with the minutes of the meeting.

The minutes of the incorporator were read and approved.

The chairman stated that the first business to come before the meeting was the election of officers.

The following persons were thereupon nominated to the offices set forth opposite their respective names, to serve until the next annual meeting and until their successors are chosen and shall qualify:

President _____

Secretary _____

All the directors present having voted, the chairman announced that the aforesaid persons had been unanimously elected as said officers respectively.

The president and the secretary thereupon entered upon the discharge of the duties of their respective offices.

Upon motion, duly made, seconded and carried, it was

RESOLVED, that the form of stock certificate presented and read be and it is hereby approved and adopted, and the secretary is instructed to insert a specimen thereof in the minute book.

Upon motion, duly made, seconded and carried, it was

RESOLVED, that the seal, an impression of which is hereto affixed, be and it is hereby adopted as the corporate seal of the corporation.

The secretary was authorized and directed to procure the proper corporate books.

Upon motion, duly made, seconded and carried, it was

RESOLVED, that the president be and he hereby is authorized to open a bank account on behalf of this corporation in a bank selected by the president.

RESOLVED, that until otherwise ordered said bank be and it hereby is authorized to make payments from the funds on deposit with it upon and according to the check of this corporation, signed by its president.

Upon motion, duly made, seconded and carried, it was

RESOLVED, that an office of the corporation be established and maintained at _____ , in the City of _____ , in the County of _____ , in the State of _____ , and that meetings of the board of directors from time to time may be held either at such office in the City of or elsewhere, as the board of directors shall from time to time order.

Upon motion, duly made, seconded and carried, it was

RESOLVED, that the president and secretary be and they each are authorized to execute and file, or cause to be filed, with the New York State Tax Commission a certificate pursuant to Section 275-a of the New York Tax Law.

The president stated that the corporation had received a subscription to _____ shares of the common stock of this corporation having a par value of _____ Dollars ($ _____) per share.

The president stated further that the subscriber had tendered to the corporation the sum of _____ Dollars ($ _____) in full payment at par for the common stock subscribed.

Upon motion, duly made, seconded and carried, the president and the secretary were authorized to issue to the said subscriber or its nominee certificates representing fully paid and nonassessable common stock of this corporation to the amount of the subscription.

Upon motion, duly made, seconded and carried, it was

RESOLVED, that for the purpose of authorizing the corporation to do business in any state, territory or dependency of the United States or any foreign country in which it is necessary or expedient for this corporation to transact business, the officers of this corporation are hereby authorized to appoint and substitute all necessary agents or attorneys for service of process, to designate and change the location of all necessary statutory offices and, under the corporate seal, to make and file all necessary certificates, reports, powers of attorney and other instruments as may be required by the laws of such state, territory, dependency or country to authorize the corporation to transact business therein, and whenever it is expedient for the corporation to cease doing business therein and withdraw therefrom, to revoke any appointment of agent or attorney for service of process and to file such certificates, reports, revocation of appointment or surrender of authority as may be necessary to terminate the authority of the corporation to do business in any such state, territory, dependency or country.

Upon motion, duly made, seconded and carried, it was

RESOLVED, that the fiscal year of the corporation shall begin the first day of _____ in each year.

Upon motion, duly made, seconded and carried, it was

RESOLVED, that the treasurer be and he hereby is authorized to pay all fees and expenses incident to and necessary for the organization of the corporation.

Upon motion, duly made, seconded and carried, the meeting thereupon adjourned.

_____
[Name of Secretary elected at meeting]

FORM 4

SHAREHOLDERS AGREEMENT

This SHAREHOLDERS AGREEMENT, dated _____ , 19 _____ , is entered into by and among _____ ("Shareholder A"), _____ ("Shareholder B") and _____ ("Shareholder C") (each individually a "Shareholder" and collectively the "Shareholders"), who are all of the shareholders of _____ , a _____ corporation (the "Corporation"). The Shareholders agree as follows:

1. Share Ownership. Each Shareholder owns _____ shares of the Common Stock, $ _____ par value per share, of the Corporation, representing 33 1/3 percent of the total issued and outstanding shares of the Corporation (the "Shares").

2. Legended Certificates. Each certificate representing Shares currently owned by a Shareholder shall be stamped or otherwise imprinted with a legend in substantially the following form:

THE SHARES OF [CORPORATION] REPRESENTED BY THIS CERTIFICATE ARE SUBJECT TO THE TERMS AND, RESTRICTIONS SET FORTH IN A SHAREHOLDERS AGREEMENT, DATED AS OF _____ , 19 _____ , AMONG [SHAREHOLDER A], [SHAREHOLDER B] AND [SHAREHOLDER C]. THESE SHARES MAY NOT BE SOLD OR OTHERWISE TRANSFERRED EXCEPT AS SET FORTH IN SAID AGREEMENT.

3. Subsidiaries. Except as provided in Section 5, the Corporation owns and will own all of the outstanding stock of two other corporations: _____ , a _____ corporation ("Subsidiary A"), and _____ , a _____ corporation ("Subsidiary B"); (Subsidiary A and Subsidiary B each individually a "Subsidiary" and collectively the "Subsidiaries").

4. Issuance and Sale of Shares of the Corporation. Additional Shares of the Corporation, any other equity security of the Corporation or any security convertible into or exchangeable for any equity security of the Corporation

may be issued only with the unanimous written consent of all three Share-holders. During the period beginning on the date hereof and ending _____ years after the date hereof, no Shareholder may sell, give or otherwise transfer in any way whatsoever any Shares of the Corporation or Subsidiaries without the express written consent of the other Shareholders, which consent may be withheld for any reason. At any time after the expiration of such _____ -year period, any proposed transfer by a Shareholder (the transferring Shareholder") may only be made upon written notice to the other Shareholders of the terms of the proposed transfer, including the number of Shares proposed to be transferred, the consideration for such Shares, the method and timing of the transfer and the identity of the proposed transferee, which notice shall include a written copy of the proposed offer from the prospective transferee. Such notice shall constitute an irrevocable offer by the Transferring Shareholder to sell all, but not less than all, of the Shares specified in the notice to the other Shareholders on a pro rata basis and on the same terms as are contained in such notice. In the event that one of the other Shareholders chooses not to accept the Transferring Shareholder's offer, the remaining Shareholder must elect to purchase all or none of the Shares being offered by the Transferring Shareholder. The other Shareholders shall have sixty (60) days from the date notice is given to accept or reject such offer. The acceptance or rejection by the other Shareholders of such irrevocable offer shall not constitute the exclusive remedy of such other Shareholders in the event that the Transferring Shareholder shall convey Shares contrary to the terms and provisions of this Section 4.

5. Distribution of Equity Ownership in Subsidiaries. Any sale or distribution of equity interests in either Subsidiary shall require the unanimous written consent of the Shareholders.

6. Shareholder Entitlements. The Shareholders shall enjoy equal rights and shall be entitled to equal compensation, including perquisites, under this Agreement. Any interference or attempt to interfere by two Shareholders with the rights of a third Shareholder under this Agreement, including but not limited to failing to elect a Shareholder as director of the Corporation and the Subsidiaries and failing to grant a Shareholder compensation (including salary, benefits and perquisites) equal to that received by the other two Shareholders, shall constitute the firing (the "Firing") of that third Shareholder (the "Fired Shareholder") and shall entitle him to sell his Shares back to the Company in the following manner: the Fired Shareholder shall give notice to the Corporation of his intention to sell

his Shares to the Corporation pursuant to this Section 6, which notice shall specifically set forth the events and/or acts which constitute the Firing. The Corporation shall cause to be conducted an audit of the Corporation within a reasonable time following the date of such notice (the "Notice Date"). Such audit shall determine the Fired Shareholder's Net Income (as defined in Section 7 hereof) as of the Notice Date. Within two weeks of completion of the audit the Fired Shareholder shall sell to the Corporation, and the Corporation shall buy, the Fired Shareholder's Shares for a purchase price equal to [_____] times the Fired Shareholder's Net Income. The purchase price shall be paid in the following manner: _____ percent of the purchase price shall be paid on the date the Fired Shareholder tenders his Shares (the "Tender Date") and _____ percent of the purchase price shall be paid on each succeeding one-year anniversary of the Tender Date until the purchase price is fully paid. In the event that, as of the Notice Date, the Corporation's assets include real property or any interest in real property, and so long as the Corporation, in its sole discretion, shall continue to hold such real property or such interest in real property, the Fired Shareholder shall be entitled to (a) one-third of the net income, if any, generated by such real property or interest in real property; and (b) upon sale, if any, of any such real property or interest in real property, one-third of the net income, if any, from such sale.

7. Shareholder Net Income. Under this Agreement, a Shareholder's Net Income shall equal an amount, the numerator of which shall be the aggregate average yearly income of the Subsidiaries based upon the eight fiscal quarters preceding a Notice Date (as that term is defined in Sections 6 and 16) or, in the case of the death of a Shareholder, the date of the death, less all expenses of the Subsidiaries other than salaries, benefits and perquisites of the Shareholders, and the denominator of which shall be three. Any calculation of Shareholder Net Income pursuant to this Agreement shall be according to generally accepted accounting principles.

8. Voluntary Departure of a Shareholder. Any Shareholder who wishes to terminate his employment with the Corporation shall give the Corporation notice of his intention to sell his Shares, and the Corporation shall purchase such Shareholder's Shares in accordance with the provisions of Section 16 hereof.

9. Death or Disability of a Shareholder.

(a) Death: Within a reasonable time after the death of a Shareholder, the Corporation shall cause to be conducted an audit of the Corporation, which

audit shall determine the deceased Shareholder's Net Income. Within two weeks of completion of such audit, the deceased Shareholder's estate shall sell, and the Corporation shall purchase, the deceased Shareholder's Shares. The purchase price shall be _____ times the Shareholder's Net Income as determined by the audit, and shall be paid to the Shareholder's estate in the following manner: the Corporation shall pay to the estate at the time of such purchase one-third of the deceased Shareholder's Net Income. Of the remaining amount, one-half shall be paid to the estate one calendar year after the completion of the audit and the other one-half shall be paid to the estate two calendar years after the completion of the audit. In the event that, as of the date of the Shareholder's death, the Corporation's assets include real property or any interest in real property, and so long as the Corporation, in its sole discretion, shall continue to hold such real property or such interest in real property, the deceased Shareholder's estate shall be entitled to (a) one-third of the net income, if any, generated by such real property or interest in real property; and (b) upon sale, if any, of any such real property or interest in real property, one-third of the net income, if any, from such sale.

(b) Disablement: Upon the permanent disablement of a Shareholder such that his ability to contribute significantly to the Corporation and/or Subsidiaries is substantially impaired, or if a Shareholder is temporarily disabled and it is expected that he will remain disabled as described above for more than _____ years, he shall resign from the Corporation, and he shall sell to the Corporation, and the Corporation shall purchase, his Shares in the manner provided in Section 16. If a Shareholder is temporarily disabled and it is expected that he will remain disabled as described above for more than _____ months, but less than _____ years, for the period of his disablement his salary shall be reduced to one-half of that received by the other Shareholders but his benefits and perquisites shall not be reduced in relation to those received by the other Shareholders. Upon a Shareholder's death, permanent disablement or temporary disablement which is expected to continue for more than three years, in addition to the above, said Shareholder or his estate shall receive a sum of $ _____ per annum from the Corporation for each of _____ consecutive years immediately following his disablement or death. Payments will be made in equal bimonthly installments.

10. Key Man Insurance. Within fifteen (15) days after the execution of this Agreement, the Corporation shall obtain a life and disability insurance policy on each of Shareholder A, Shareholder B and Shareholder C, each in the

face amount of $ _____ , and shall maintain the same until such time as Shareholder A, Shareholder B or Shareholder C, as the case may be, shall have ceased to own any Shares of the Corporation. The Shareholders may, from time to time, cause the amounts of such policies to be increased in equal amounts. Upon the death or disability of any Shareholder, the proceeds from his life and disability insurance policy shall be the property of the Corporation and shall not be included as an asset of the Corporation for purposes of the audit described in Sections 6, 9 and 16.

11. Board of Directors of the Corporation. The Corporation shall be governed by a Board of Directors, which shall consist of Shareholder A, Shareholder B and Shareholder C, as long as each continues to be a Shareholder. In the event that a director ceases to be a Shareholder, the Board of Directors shall consist of the remaining Shareholders.

12. Control of Subsidiaries. Each Subsidiary will be controlled by a Board of Directors comprised of all three Shareholders and any other persons whom the Shareholders shall unanimously elect. The Board of Directors of each Subsidiary will select a chief executive officer or officers for that Subsidiary who will be responsible to the Board of Directors of that Subsidiary for its operations. The corporate objectives, policies and strategies of each Subsidiary will be determined by its Board of Directors and be carried out by its chief executive officer.

13. Other Activities. No Shareholder may undertake or otherwise engage in any of the business activities in which the Corporation or Subsidiaries are normally involved or plan to be involved in any manner that is separate and apart from the activities of the Corporation and Subsidiaries without the express permission of all the other Shareholders. However, business undertaken prior to the signing of this Agreement may be completed by any Shareholder so involved in a manner separate and apart from the Corporation and Subsidiaries' activities.

14. Allocation of Time to the Corporation and Subsidiaries. Every Shareholder shall devote his full time, attention and energies to the business of the Corporation and Subsidiaries and shall not, so long as he remains a Shareholder, be engaged in any other business activity, whether or not such business activity is pursued for gain, profit or other pecuniary advantage, except as otherwise permitted in Sections 13 and 15. Any Shareholder who vio-

lates this provision and continues to so act after written notice from the other Shareholders may have his salary withheld and, in the event of such withholding, shall forfeit said salary from the time of such written notice until he ceases to so act. If such behavior continues for more than _____ months from said written notice, the other Shareholders by unanimous decision may require him to sell his Shares to the Corporation in the manner provided in Section 16, less $ _____ , which sum he shall forfeit.

15. Other Permitted Activities. In the application of the provisions contained in Section 14 hereof, activities which will strengthen the credentials of the Shareholder, and thereby the Corporation and Subsidiaries, will be treated more liberally. However, even in such circumstances, at least a majority of the Shareholder's business time must be devoted to the business of the Corporation and Subsidiaries. The type of activities to be treated more liberally would include, but are not limited to, a membership on a Board of Trustees or Board of Directors or a comparable position with a charitable, corporate, governmental, religious or similar entity.

16. Purchase of a Shareholder's Shares by the Corporation. If the Corporation purchases the Shares of any Shareholder pursuant to Section 8, 9(b) or 14 hereof or for any reason except the death or Firing of a Shareholder, payment for such Shares shall be made in the following manner: the Corporation shall give written notice to a Shareholder (the "Selling Shareholder") of its intention to purchase such Shareholder's Shares pursuant to this Agreement. The Corporation shall cause to be conducted an audit of the Corporation within a reasonable time following the date of such notice (the "Notice Date"). Such audit shall determine the Selling Shareholder's Net Income as of the Notice Date. The Selling Shareholder shall sell to the Corporation, and the Corporation shall buy, his Shares within two weeks after completion of the audit.

In the case of a permanently or temporarily disabled Shareholder, the purchase price shall be _____ times the Shareholder's Net Income, one-third of which shall be paid on the date the Selling Shareholder tenders his Shares to the Corporation pursuant to this Section 16 (the "Tender Date"), one-third of which shall be paid to the Shareholder one calendar year after the Tender Date and the final one-third of which shall be paid to the Selling Shareholder two calendar years after the Tender Date.

In all other cases the purchase price shall be the Shareholder's Net Income, one-fifth of which shall be paid on the Tender Date and one-fifth of which shall be paid on each succeeding anniversary of the Tender Date, until the purchase price is fully paid.

In the event that, as of the Notice Date, the Corporation's assets include real property or any interest in real property, and so long as the Corporation, in its sole discretion, shall continue to hold such real property or such interest in real property, the Selling Shareholder shall be entitled to (a) one-third of the net income, if any, generated by such real property or interest in real property; and (b) upon sale, if any, of such real property or interest in real property, one-third of the net income, if any, from such sale.

17. Solicitation Not Permitted. So long as a Shareholder continues to own Shares, he shall not (a) offer employment to any person who is an employee or prospective employee of the Corporation or Subsidiaries (other than on behalf of the Corporation or a Subsidiary); or (b) solicit any securities brokerage or investment advisory business (other than for the Corporation or a Subsidiary) from any client or customer of the Corporation or Subsidiaries. In the event that any Shareholder (the "Departing Shareholder") ceases to be a Shareholder, then the Departing Shareholder agrees that, for a period of _____ months from the date he sells his Shares, he will not, directly or indirectly, as a sole proprietor, member of a partnership or stockholder, investor, officer or director of a corporation or as an employee, agent, associate or consultant of any person, firm or corporation other than the Corporation or its Subsidiaries, (y) offer employment to any person who is an employee or prospective employee of the Corporation or Subsidiaries upon the date of the sale of his Shares or who was an employee at any time during the one-year period preceding such event; or (z) solicit business of the type engaged in by the Corporation or the Subsidiaries (other than for the Corporation or Subsidiaries) from any person who is a client or prospective client of the Corporation or Subsidiaries upon the date of the sale of his Shares or who has been a client of the Corporation or Subsidiaries at any time during the one-year period preceding such sale.

18. Liquidated Damages and Injunctive Relief. Inasmuch as any damages arising from the breach of Section 17 hereof would be difficult to determine, any Shareholder or Departing Shareholder who violates Section 17 agrees to be liable in the following manner:

(a) Any Shareholder or Departing Shareholder who violates Section 17(a) or 17(y), as the case may be, shall be liable in an amount equal to _____ times the yearly salary or salaries of the employee or employees who were subject to the solicitation which resulted in the violation of Section 17(a) or 17(y). In the event that an employee is a prospective employee, the amount of damages shall be _____ times the yearly salary for the position for which the prospective employee was being considered.

(b) Any Shareholder or Departing Shareholder who violates Section 17(b) or 17(z), as the case may be, shall be liable in an amount equal to _____ times the average fees paid or due and owing to the Corporation or the Subsidiaries by the customer annually over the two years preceding the violation of Section 17(b) or 17(z). In the event that a solicited customer has been a customer for less than two years, damages shall be in an amount equal to _____ times the total amount of fees the solicited customer would have paid had he remained a customer for two years, based upon the average size of the customer's advisory account (if the customer was an investment advisory client) during the period he was a customer and/or based upon the customer's average monthly brokerage fees (if the customer was a brokerage client) during the period he was a customer. In the event that the solicitation is of a prospective customer, damages shall be in an amount equal to $ _____ .

19. Attorneys' Fees. In the event of any breach by any Shareholder or Departing Shareholder of the provisions of Section 17 hereof which leads to a settlement or an injunction, an award of damages or other judgment against the Shareholder or Departing Shareholder, the Shareholder or Departing Shareholder hereby agrees to pay all costs and expenses of every kind, including reasonable attorneys' fees, incurred by the remaining Shareholders and the Corporation or Subsidiaries in connection with obtaining such settlement or injunction, award of damages or other judgment.

20. Arbitration. Any and all disputes, controversies and claims arising out of or relating to this Agreement, or with respect to the construction of this Agreement, or concerning the respective rights or obligations hereunder of the parties hereto and their respective permitted successors and assigns shall be determined by arbitration in _____ , State of _____ , in accordance with and pursuant to the then existing rules of the American Arbitration Association. The arbitration award shall be final and binding upon the parties and judgment thereon may be entered in any court of the State of _____

and federal courts in said state, the jurisdiction of which courts is hereby consented to by the parties for such purposes. The service of any notice, process, motion or other document in connection with an arbitration award hereunder may be effectuated either by personal service upon a party or by certified or registered mail.

21. Survival of Agreement. Any Shareholder who, for any reason, ceases to own Shares shall thereafter have no voting or other rights regarding the operation and control of the Corporation and the Subsidiaries or regarding decisions to be made by the Shareholders pursuant to this Agreement, but shall otherwise continue to be bound by the terms of this Agreement.

22. Entire Agreement. This document sets forth the entire Agreement between the parties. There are no verbal or other written agreements that are part of this Agreement.

23. Termination. This Agreement may be terminated by the unanimous written consent of all the Shareholders owning Shares on the date of termination. This Agreement may be terminated by the written consent of two Shareholders but in such event, for a period of _____ months following the termination, the two Shareholders who consented to the termination (the "Consenting Shareholders") shall not, together, as members of the same partnership, as stockholders, investors, officers or directors of the same corporation or as employees, agents, associates or consultants of or to the same person or company, engage in business of the type engaged in by the Corporation or the Subsidiaries.

24. Successors and Assigns. This Agreement shall be binding on any and all successors and assigns of the Shareholders.

25. Retention of Attorney. Each of the parties signing below certifies that he has thoroughly read and fully understands all the provisions herein and that he has shown this contract to an attorney who has represented him and acted as his advisor in the signing of this Agreement.

26. Governing Law. This Agreement shall be governed by and construed in accordance with the laws of the State of _____ .

We, the undersigned, hereby agree to all the provisions of this Agreement this _____ day of _____ , 19 _____ .

_____

[Shareholder A]

_____

[Shareholder B]

_____

[Shareholder C]

FORM 5

FORM OF VOTING AGREEMENT

AGREEMENT entered into as of this _____ day of _____ , 19 _____, by and among _____ ("Shareholder A") and _____ ("Shareholder B") (individually referred to as the "Shareholder" and collectively as the "Shareholders").

Each Shareholder owns the number of shares of issued and outstanding voting common stock of _____ , a _____ corporation (the "Corporation").

The Shareholders desire to maintain the continuity and stability of the policy and management of the Corporation; and believe it to be in their best interests and the best interests of the Corporation that the shares of the Shareholders now owned or hereafter acquired (the "Shares") be voted in accordance with the terms and conditions.

The Shareholders hereby agreed as follows:

A. Voting

1. The Shareholders hereby agree to pool the voting of their Shares, and to vote or consent with respect to all of their Shares as a block or unit in all votes, in person or by proxy at any and all meetings of the shareholders.

(a) *Vote for Directors.*

(i) *Election.* So long as the board of directors of the Corporation shall consist of _____ directors, the Shares shall be voted for _____ persons nominated by Shareholder A and _____ persons nominated by Shareholder B. Votes for the remaining director position shall be cast for such nominee as the Shareholders are able to agree upon from time to time. If the Shareholders fail to agree upon a nominee, then the nominee shall be _____ or _____ .

(ii) *Replacement.* If any director so elected should die, resign, be removed or become incapacitated or otherwise refuse to act in his or her capacity as

director, the Shareholder who nominated such director shall be entitled to nominate a person as a replacement director.

(b) *Vote on Other Issues.* In the event of a vote of the shareholders involving authorization of any amendment to the Corporation's Certificate of Incorporation or Bylaws; merger, consolidation or binding share exchange; sale or other disposition of all or substantially all of the assets of the Corporation; bankruptcy; dissolution; or any other matter submitted to a vote of the shareholders, the Shareholders agree to pool their Shares and to vote them as a block or unit.

B. Arbitration. If the Shareholders are unable to agree on any matter subject to a vote of the Shareholders, the dispute and the manner of voting the Shares shall be submitted to an independent third party arbitrator in accordance with the rules of the American Arbitration Association.

C. Proxy. In order to facilitate the resolution of any dispute referred to in Section B of this Agreement the Shareholders may grant to such other person as may be designated by the arbitrator chosen by the methods set forth in Section B of this Agreement, an irrevocable proxy to vote the Shares in his or her sole discretion. This irrevocable proxy shall take effect only upon the occurrence of a dispute regarding the manner of voting the Shares.

D. Provisions to Survive Death or Incapacity of any Shareholder. In the event of the death, incapacity or incompetency of any Shareholder, the provisions of this Agreement will be binding on the estate, committee or personal representative of such Shareholder and such estate.

E. Transfer of Shares. Shares may be transferred only in accordance with the terms and conditions of the Shareholders Agreement.

F. Termination of Shareholder Status. A Shareholder shall no longer be treated as a Shareholder hereunder when he ceases to own any Shares.

G. Endorsement of Share Certificates. Certificates for Shares of the Corporation subject to this Agreement shall be endorsed in accordance with the terms stipulated on the back of each certificate.

H. Termination. This Agreement shall terminate upon the happening of the earliest of any of the following events:

1 . Reduction in the number of Shareholders to one;

2. The written agreement of all of the Shareholders;

3. The expiration of the term of this Agreement or the failure of some or all of the remaining Shareholders to agree to renew this Agreement;

4. The merger or consolidation of the Corporation with another entity or a binding share exchange between the Corporation and another entity, if the Corporation is not the surviving corporation.

I. Term. This Agreement shall become effective upon the date of this Agreement and shall continue in effect for a period of_____ years from this date.

J. Renewal. This Agreement may be renewed for successive yearly periods. Written consent to such renewal must be given prior to the expiration of this Agreement.

K. Amendment. This Agreement may be amended only by the written agreement of all of the parties to this Agreement, or their lawful heirs and legal representatives or successors.

L. Benefit. This Agreement shall be for the benefit of and binding on the parties to this Agreement, or their lawful heirs and legal representatives or successors.

M. Governing Law. This Agreement shall be governed and construed in accordance with the laws of the State of _____ .

IN WITNESS WHEREOF, the Shareholders have executed this Agreement as of the date and year first written above.

Number of Shares   *Shareholders*

_____   _____

_____   _____

APPENDIX 5 Stock Certificates

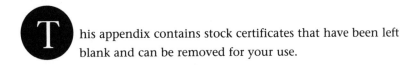 his appendix contains stock certificates that have been left blank and can be removed for your use.

For Value Received, _____ *hereby sell, assign and transfer*

PLEASE INSERT SOCIAL SECURITY OR OTHER
IDENTIFYING NUMBER OF ASSIGNEE

unto _____

_____ *Shares*

represented by the within Certificate, and do hereby irrevocably constitute and appoint

_____ *Attorney to transfer the said Shares on the books of the within named Corporation with full power of substitution in the premises.*

Dated _____ *19* _____

In the presence of

_____   _____

NUMBER
1

SHARES

INCORPORATED UNDER THE LAWS OF THE STATE OF NEW YORK

The Corporation is authorized to issue 100 Common Shares without par value, of one class

This Certifies that

is the owner of

fully paid and

non-assessable Shares of the above Corporation transferable only on the books of the Corporation by the holder hereof in person or by duly authorized Attorney upon surrender of this Certificate properly endorsed.

In Witness Whereof, the said Corporation has caused this Certificate to be signed by its duly authorized officers and to be sealed with the Seal of the Corporation.

Dated

PRESIDENT

SECRETARY

NOTICE. THE SIGNATURE OF THIS ASSIGNMENT MUST CORRESPOND WITH THE NAME AS WRITTEN UPON THE FACE OF THE CERTIFICATE, IN EVERY PARTICULAR, WITHOUT ALTERATION OR ENLARGEMENT OR ANY CHANGE WHATEVER.

For Value Received, _____ *hereby sell, assign and transfer*

PLEASE INSERT SOCIAL SECURITY OR OTHER
IDENTIFYING NUMBER OF ASSIGNEE

unto _____

_____ *Shares*

represented by the within Certificate, and do hereby irrevocably

constitute and appoint

_____ *Attorney to*

transfer the said Shares on the books of the within named Corporation

with full power of substitution in the premises.

Dated _____ *19* _____

In the presence of

_____   _____

NOTICE. THE SIGNATURE OF THIS ASSIGNMENT MUST CORRESPOND WITH THE NAME AS WRITTEN UPON THE FACE OF THE CERTIFICATE, IN EVERY PARTICULAR, WITHOUT ALTERATION OR ENLARGEMENT OR ANY CHANGE WHATEVER.

For Value Received, _____ *hereby sell, assign and transfer*

PLEASE INSERT SOCIAL SECURITY OR OTHER
IDENTIFYING NUMBER OF ASSIGNEE

unto _____

_____ *Shares*

represented by the within Certificate, and do hereby irrevocably constitute and appoint

_____ *Attorney to transfer the said Shares on the books of the within named Corporation with full power of substitution in the premises.*

Dated _____ *19* _____

In the presence of

_____   _____

For Value Received, _____ *hereby sell, assign and transfer*

PLEASE INSERT SOCIAL SECURITY OR OTHER
IDENTIFYING NUMBER OF ASSIGNEE

unto _____

_____ *Shares*

represented by the within Certificate, and do hereby irrevocably

constitute and appoint

_____ *Attorney to*

transfer the said Shares on the books of the within named Corporation

with full power of substitution in the premises.

Dated _____ *19* _____

In the presence of

_____   _____

SHARES

NUMBER
1

INCORPORATED UNDER THE LAWS OF THE STATE OF NEW YORK

The Corporation is authorized to issue 100 Common Shares without par value, of one class

This Certifies that

is the owner of

fully paid and

non-assessable Shares of the above Corporation transferable only on the
books of the Corporation by the holder hereof in person or by duly authorized
Attorney upon surrender of this Certificate properly endorsed.

In Witness Whereof, the said Corporation has caused this Certificate to be signed
by its duly authorized officers and to be sealed with the Seal of the Corporation.

Dated

SECRETARY   PRESIDENT

For Value Received, _____ *hereby sell, assign and transfer*

PLEASE INSERT SOCIAL SECURITY OR OTHER
IDENTIFYING NUMBER OF ASSIGNEE

unto _____

_____ *Shares*

represented by the within Certificate, and do hereby irrevocably

constitute and appoint

_____ *Attorney to*

transfer the said Shares on the books of the within named Corporation

with full power of substitution in the premises.

Dated _____ *19* _____

In the presence of

_____   _____

NUMBER
1

SHARES

INCORPORATED UNDER THE LAWS OF THE STATE OF NEW YORK

The Corporation is authorized to issue 100 Common Shares without par value, of one class

This Certifies that

_____ is the owner of

_____ fully paid and

non-assessable Shares of the above Corporation transferable only on the books of the Corporation by the holder hereof in person or by duly authorized Attorney upon surrender of this Certificate properly endorsed.

In Witness Whereof, the said Corporation has caused this Certificate to be signed by its duly authorized officers and to be sealed with the Seal of the Corporation.

Dated _____

_____ SECRETARY

_____ PRESIDENT

For Value Received, _____ *hereby sell, assign and transfer*

PLEASE INSERT SOCIAL SECURITY OR OTHER
IDENTIFYING NUMBER OF ASSIGNEE

unto _____

_____ *Shares*

represented by the within Certificate, and do hereby irrevocably

constitute and appoint

_____ *Attorney to*

transfer the said Shares on the books of the within named Corporation

with full power of substitution in the premises.

Dated _____ *19* _____

In the presence of

_____   _____

NUMBER
1

SHARES

INCORPORATED UNDER THE LAWS OF THE STATE OF NEW YORK

The Corporation is authorized to issue 100 Common Shares without par value, of one class

This Certifies that

_____ is the owner of

_____ fully paid and

non-assessable Shares of the above Corporation transferable only on the
books of the Corporation by the holder hereof in person or by duly authorized
Attorney upon surrender of this Certificate properly endorsed.

In Witness Whereof, the said Corporation has caused this Certificate to be signed
by its duly authorized officers and to be sealed with the Seal of the Corporation.

Dated _____

_____
SECRETARY

_____
PRESIDENT

For Value Received, _____ *hereby sell, assign and transfer*

PLEASE INSERT SOCIAL SECURITY OR OTHER
IDENTIFYING NUMBER OF ASSIGNEE

unto _____

_____ *Shares*

represented by the within Certificate, and do hereby irrevocably constitute and appoint

_____ *Attorney to transfer the said Shares on the books of the within named Corporation with full power of substitution in the premises.*

Dated _____ *19* ____

In the presence of

_____   _____

INDEX